Sailing Against The Wind

Toni Larson

Sailing Against The Wind © Copyright 2021 Toni Larson

For more information, email larson_toni@hotmail.com

Dedication

for Roger Larson
(In Memorium 1930--1995)

and for my wonderful children
Ron Larson
Janice Wilson
Thomas Larson

CHAPTER 1: IT STARTED WITH ANCHOVIES

Roger was clearly annoyed that fall afternoon, when he strolled into the kitchen, sat down at the table, and announced, "I have just spent five hundred dollars with that doctor while he tested everything about me from how fast I can run, to how much earwax I can produce in a week. Now, the only thing concrete he can tell me is that I have an allergy to anchovies!"

It was a surprise merely to have him home in the afternoon and, putting aside the mending I'd been working on, I gave him my full attention. "Anchovies? How many have you eaten lately?"

"I think I had an anchovy pizza a few months ago. Those little critters must be potent."

I didn't buy it. The doctor surely found more wrong than anchovies. "What else did he say?" Pouring us a cup of coffee, then sitting down across from him, I studied his face carefully. For weeks he'd been threatening to see the doctor, but he'd never been very definite as to why. It was clear he was using the allergy as a smoke screen, and I suspected he was trying to tell me more. However, I was totally unprepared for his eventual revelation.

"It's what most doctors say? Get some rest! Go fishing! If they can't cure you then they blame overwork, stress, or an allergy to something."

"Okay, Roger, what do you think?" The creased forehead and slumped shoulders told me he was tired, but I'd known that for months.

"The doctor said the allergy is minor in comparison to the stress and he's right." Roger's voice was unusually low as he went on, "I guess I started to realize it when I had a few dizzy spells. At first I thought it was just a lack of sleep."

When he paused, I feared he would stop, so I pushed a little. "What else? You're still hiding something from me."

"One day I found myself trying to eat something, and I couldn't swallow. My throat would just tighten up." His finger traced a circle around the rim of the cup, and he stared at it with absent concentration. "Other things happened, a burning sensation in my stomach, headaches, even morning sickness." He looked up at me and grinned.

His silly smile didn't cover his concern. He was the classic workaholic with one exception, he no longer enjoyed his work. Obviously, his body didn't either.

"Roger, I don't think I would have diagnosed an allergy to anchovies, but I sure could have predicted the overwork and stress. Why don't you hire a manager for the restaurant and let us get away?"

"Because we can't afford a manager. The restaurant is a challenge as it is. Without constant supervision it could quickly get out of control." With that, he jumped up and checked his watch. It was 4:00 p.m. "I'd better get back. Dinner hour is about to begin, and we are short a waitress." As he hurried toward the door he turned and dropped the bomb: "I'm chucking it, Toni. I'm selling the business." When I caught my breath and opened my mouth to speak, he raised a hand to stop me. "It's decided! I'm calling Mr. Clausen in the morning."

This was something we really needed to talk about, but I didn't get my chance. Our three kids came barreling up the steps, slammed open the screen door, and arrived in a flood of chatter. Noticing their dad, they gave him a quick "Hello," then "Goodbye," and didn't even ask what he was doing home at that hour. They were too busy demanding food.

The sound of the car as it started, revved hard, and sped away down the street told me I'd have the rest of the evening to think on it. Turning from the door I doled out cookies to the kids and thought about Roger's parting remark. Had he meant it? Would he really sell the business? And did I want him to? I wasn't sure. But how bad was his health? Just the fact that he'd finally shared what was bothering him, told me how worried he was.

Sending the kids out in the backyard to play, I sat down with my coffee and pondered the situation.

Roger and I had met fourteen years earlier at a party in New Orleans. I was a sophomore in college at the time, he was the food comptroller for a large hotel, and our paths would likely never have crossed if my roommate had not invited me to an impromptu gathering one Sunday afternoon. Roger was there as a friend of my roommate. We were introduced, and within ten minutes of conversation, I had discovered that the good-looking, dark-haired young man had been reared in a small town in the Midwest; had worked his way through an ivy-covered college; wore skinny ties and button-down shirts; kept his dark hair trimmed close to his head; and voted conservatively. He also had intense, deep-brown eyes that made my heart skip crazily. Here was the husband I had been looking for: domestic, stable, and responsible. I was in love! He wasn't yet.

It took three months for him to call for the first date and a year and a half for him to propose, but when he finally did, I knew beyond any doubt my life was going to be wonderful.

The honeymoon over, I plunged into the wifely role of housekeeping, opened six charge accounts, and enrolled in the Betty Crocker Cookbook of the Month Club. Roger accepted a job with an oil company in South America! I couldn't have been more stunned if he had revealed himself to be a philanderer.

I attributed the unfortunate flaw in his personality to his Norwegian heritage. Obviously, he was a descendant of Leif Ericson, who hadn't been known as a homebody either. I believed Roger was simply enjoying a last fling, so I accepted the challenge to change him. We lived one year in South America before I convinced him to return home to the States. Then I pleaded we were not going another step until we'd acquired a station wagon, a large house (with a large mortgage), and kids! He relented reluctantly. In five years we had the basics, in ten years we were living in Santa Barbara, California with all the trimmings, but in our twelfth year of marriage, there was more wrong than anchovies.

Finishing my coffee, I started dinner for the kids, and Ron was first on the scene. "What are we eating?"

"Boiled beets in cream sauce," I said as he sat down at the table. Without blinking, our ten-year-old son picked up his fork and looked around expectantly for anything that wasn't moving. He did not care what appeared on his plate, it was the amount that mattered.

Ron was so tall and skinny that my mother insisted he suffered from some fatal, undiagnosed disease, or more likely, I was starving him to death. The fact that he ate forty pounds of food per day and never so much as ran a fever had no bearing on her opinion.

As I put the casserole on the table Tommy and Janice appeared, hunger being the only thing more powerful than their love/hate, play/fight, sibling games. I sent them to wash up and Janice was the first to return to the table.

"What's for dinner?" She asked.

"Ham and cheese casserole," I answered truthfully.

"Yuck! Why can't we have hamburgers?" she complained as she wrinkled her nose.

"Because Betty Crocker and Home Ec. 101 only taught me how to make ham casseroles!" I answered then chided myself for being so short with her.

Tommy arrived with dirty hands and face, and water splotches down the front of his shirt, and I wondered how it was possible that a six-year-old could get wet all over without removing even one speck of dirt. "Go wash again," I ordered in my best drill sergeant voice.

Dinner was the usual. Tommy teased Janice; she picked the ham out of the casserole then gave the rest to Ron; and he quietly ate everything. I dined on cottage cheese and carrot sticks and told myself they were tasty, filling, and would make me thin—and didn't believe a word of it. But food wasn't what I missed. It was Roger's company I most longed for.

How many months had it been since he had sat down to a meal with us? The kids never saw him anymore, and lately, I found myself resenting the fact that their discipline was entirely my responsibility, and I knew the resentment showed. I knew they were typical, middle-class American kids but I would gladly have let Roger take over for a while.

Tommy was the youngest, and looked deceptively like a Norman Rockwell creation: blond, blue eyed, freckle faced, and temporarily toothless.

Only the devilish spark in his eyes gave him away. An incurably mischievous child, he awoke each morning teasing his sister and never stopped the rest of the day. He loved jokes but told them over and over again, and with his two front teeth missing, he lisped, which sometimes helped to make the jokes humorous. Though he was tops in the first grade and made the honor roll regularly, he disrupted every class so completely I often received calls from his distraught teacher begging me to "Do something!"

Though there seemed to be weekly meetings with Tommy's teacher, I met Janice's only at report card times, when I was called to school to discuss her grades. They were terrible—they were always terrible. She couldn't tell time, calculate change from a dollar if she bought a quart of milk, do her times table past two, or remember her address and phone number. To compound her learning problems, she was asthmatic and lost long periods of school due to regular bouts of wheezing, pneumonia, and generally poor health. Oatmeal cookies and multi vitamins hadn't helped her at all. But she drew ethereal pictures with great color and imagination, wrote sensitive Haiku poetry, and knew the words of every song or commercial she'd ever heard. When Roger was around, she was "Daddy's girl" and her quick sunny smile could melt his heart. She had soft brown curls, hazel eyes, a dusting of freckles on her upturned nose, and a timid disposition. Anything new scared her, a new haircut, new math, even food. (especially food) But she loved all dolls, animals, and people. Everyone except Tommy. To her Tommy was GROSS! To Tommy, Janice was a gold mine. She was so completely gullible, he thrived on telling her outrageous lies then giggled in glee when she discovered the truth.

Where Tommy was Janice's cross to bear, Ron was her hero. For her, Ron could do no wrong. And poor Ron certainly needed the hero worship. As I looked across the table at my oldest son, silently shoveling food into his mouth, I felt a twinge of envy. Was there ever a time I could eat with such abandon and not gain five pounds for every one pound I ingested? I knew my weight problems were minor compared to what he endured.

He was tall for his age and, at ten, already showed signs of being a strikingly handsome adult with olive skin, thick black hair and moody, dark brown eyes. But his good looks were temporarily hidden by the fact that his limbs seemed to be held together by stretched-out rubber bands and his feet and hands clearly belonged to someone else.

Whenever Ron attempted to traverse a room, elbows would suddenly dart out to catch lamps, feet would mysteriously entangle in chair legs, and hands would abruptly upset full glasses of milk at thirty paces. Dogs, cats, and small children ran from his approaching steps, adults hid their treasures when he appeared on the scene, but cruelest of all, his classmates laughed. Every sport in school gave him trouble; his awkwardness made him shy. He had begun to stutter and his only solace, in school and out, was his books. He read. He gave up everything for reading including schoolwork. His grades were abysmal, and his teacher was already hinting that he would not pass.

Clearing the dinner table, I thought again of Roger's remark about selling the restaurant. Perhaps, with another kind of business, we could become a family once more. Ron needed his dad now more than ever; Tommy could use a firm hand occasionally on his rear, and Janice would benefit if someone besides Sergeant Mom were to drill her on her math.

While the kids watched TV, I washed dishes and pondered how we'd managed to reach this point. In the mid 1970s we suffered from the commonest of disorders, *The Middle-Class Suburbia Syndrome*. And suddenly Roger was talking about curing it by selling the restaurant.

It was two days later when he broached that subject again. "I saw Mr. Clausen today." he announced casually.

Mr. Clausen was a young man who had appeared at the restaurant a month earlier, told Roger he represented a large restaurant chain, and was interested in purchasing ours. He left his card, but Roger had never called him back until now.

"You did? Is he still interested?" I tried to keep my voice even but wondered why we always seemed to be discussing things after the fact. "Not only is he interested, but he also brought me an offer." Roger reached into his back pocket, pulled out a legal-looking piece of paper, and handed it to me.

With ambivalent feelings, I looked at the document and a dozen questions entered my head. The first to pop out was, "What do we do now?"

"Sign on the dotted line, of course, then take a day off." Roger was obviously pleased with the whole idea-so why wasn't I?

Some people talk about leaving the pressures of city life to live in the country and farm or raise chickens. Others dream of a log cabin on a mountaintop, a thatch-roofed hut on a Mexican beach, retiring to an island in the South Pacific. It is not uncommon; most people seem to have a dream of a different and usually easier life than the one they are struggling with. Roger had often talked of sailing when we retired, and the restaurant was pushing him to slow down.

The Fig Tree Restaurant was a landmark in the city, operated for decades by various owners. We had bought it five years earlier when it was in the throes of bankruptcy and had worked long and hard to bring it back into a paying business. But a restaurant that is open 18 hours per day, serves breakfast, lunch, and dinner, and has 25 to 30 employees is not an easy task.

We were sitting in bed one night not long after Mr. Clausen's offer when Roger remarked offhandedly from his side of the bed, "Now's our chance."

"To do what?" I looked up from the book I'd been reading.

"To go sailing," he answered in the same casual tone. He'd been working over a pile of business papers all evening and they were strewn all around him.

I was puzzled at first, then realization hit. "You mean LIVE on a boat? All of us? You can't be serious! How big would this boat be?"

"Forty feet should do it," he spoke with confidence and his brown eyes sparkled with enthusiasm.

Of course, he had to be dreaming, but I decided I'd make certain. "Forty feet sounds fine if you like togetherness." As an afterthought, and to be sure he caught my meaning, I asked, "Are you prepared for twenty-four hours a day of Tommy and Janice bickering?"

"Not really." He hesitated for only a minute before adding, "Maybe they can learn to get along."

The man obviously did not know his children. Watching him closely, I asked, "Have you thought about their schooling?"

"At the rate they are going they will be lucky to graduate from the sixth grade." It was the first thing he'd said that I could agree with.

"Okay, I'll play this game." I propped my head with one arm so I could keep an eye on him as we talked. "How much money do you expect to make from the sale? Somehow I wasn't expecting us to be able to retire."

"We wouldn't have enough money to retire, but there should be enough to buy a used boat if we shop carefully." And he held out one of the sheets of paper. I looked at it but all I saw were rows of figures.

"Then what would we live on? It wouldn't hurt me if we gave up eating, but I think Ron would balk at that idea."

"Well, we can't take the entire amount of the sale in one lump sum. Taxes would get too big a bite." He showed me a second sheet, but I ignored it. Didn't he know this was a game? He went on, "If we spread the payments out over a few years, five for example, we should have enough income to live on. We could also eat a lot of fish."

"You're allergic to anchovies," I reminded him. I didn't like the sound of this at all.

"The ocean produces more than just anchovies," he came back. "For example, how about lobster?"

I knew it, he was looking for my weak spot. "But we don't know how to sail." I had him there.

"Remember me telling you, when I was in the Navy, I did a lot of sailboat racing? They were small boats, but surely the principle is the same."

I frowned. "Somehow, I doubt that it is that simple."

"Then we can learn. Besides, you worry too much." he teased.

"And if I don't worry, who will?" I sat up and crossed my arms. This was serious. "What if we get seasick?"

"There are pills."

"Janice has asthma."

"We'll talk to the doctor."

"I don't swim."

"It's about time you learned."

"Where would we go?"

"Around the world maybe."

"Aha! I detect a note of doubt. What about storms, and sharks, and falling overboard?"

Roger stopped a moment, then smiled confidently and dismissed all catastrophes with, "We'll manage." I think he believed it, too.

We had the children and far too many responsibilities. There would be too much to learn. Maybe someday but not now. I had been yearning for more of his company but living on a sailboat wasn't exactly what I had in mind.

He collected all the papers into a neat stack beside the bed and as he reached to turn out the light, he said, "Fish aren't fattening."

I blurted out, "When can we leave?"

It was the first week in February when Roger signed on the dotted line. It was an absolute fact; the restaurant was sold. But we had three months before he could completely walk away from the business. To me, there were so many obvious reasons why the idea was impossible that I just stopped mentioning them. I would play his game and sooner or later he would find out for himself the idea was impossible. Surely his conservative nature would prevail. I had forgotten about South America.

We began taking a few afternoons off to visit the marinas along the California coast. It was a pleasant diversion, and the kids enjoyed the unaccustomed time with Dad. Roger looked at, and priced, thousands of sailboats and learned very little, except that boats were a lot more expensive than he had originally believed. But his spirits remained undaunted.

After one exhausting day of sales pitches by over-eager boat brokers, I groaned, "Why do all sailboats look alike to me? What is a 'yawl' and is it better or worse than a 'ketch,' whatever that is?" We were sitting on the wharf, pondering the myriad of boats before us in the marina.

Roger laughed. "I know what you mean. I'm really getting bored with salesmen who have to impress us with their whole nautical vocabulary. What we need to do is talk to a real sailor."

Glancing down the dock I noted all the weekend mariners milling about and asked, "How do you know a real one when you see him?"

As if on cue, a portly gentleman strolled by, a white Admiral's cap on his head, and a miniature poodle under one arm. He nodded politely then stepped aboard a shiny new and obviously expensive powerboat, put the dog down on the indoor-outdoor green carpet, and slid open the glass door. A moment later he was sitting in a monogrammed deck chair, sipping a martini.

"I see what you mean about real sailors," Roger whispered. "I tell you what, you stop the first guy you see that has a tattoo on his arm and walks funny and ask him if he prefers a ketch or a yawl."

I couldn't help but giggle, "That sounds like a sure way to get arrested for soliciting. There must be an easier way."

So, we began to read. Roger bought all the sailing magazines from the newsstands and I found myself looking through the books in the library. My immediate reaction was that the books available were either about horrendous catastrophes or worded in the same language spoken by yacht brokers. Did a novice ever just get on a boat and sail happily into the sunset? If he had, he sure hadn't written a book. Or maybe it wasn't possible.

That was it! We could be the first to get in *The Guinness Book of World Records*. The first family to sail around the world and encounter no disasters. Was I becoming as looney as Roger? Deep down I could picture only the worst catastrophes: being bitten by a shark, performing an appendectomy at sea, sailing through a hurricane. But there was no reason to worry, nothing would come of this wild dreaming.

One Saturday in late February, Roger talked me into enrolling in a sailing class. Then he lined up a babysitter and went down to pay the sailing fee. I gave in. Besides, what could it hurt? And it might be fun.

The instructor turned out to be a patient man named Pete, who answered all my questions in one-syllable words and spent eleven of the twelve sessions sailing me around inside the harbor. Our craft were small thirteen-to-eighteen-foot open boats, with (Thank God!) only one mast and one sail.

During the last lesson, Pete and I ventured into the open ocean and I was terrified, but by the time my hour was up, something had changed. The experience was, at once, exciting, exhilarating, and wonderfully quiet. And some of the mystery surrounding a wind-driven vessel disappeared. I could see, though the wind was uncontrollable, the boat was-with the right amount of skill.

How would the kids do as sailors? Roger had talked to them about living on a sailboat, and their reactions had been only slightly more enthusiastic than my own. On a scale of one to ten, they thought the idea was better than going camping at Pismo Beach, but not as good as getting a new puppy. So, Roger convinced them that they needed to try it, and we took them down to the harbor and turned them over to Patient Pete for the afternoon. Pete had been so good for me, I was sure the kids would be in good hands, but it wasn't the kids I should have worried about.

Wearing his Captain's hat and smoking his favorite pipe, Pete helped the three excited youngsters onto the deck of the boat and told them where to sit. Roger and I assisted by untying the lines, then we watched as the tiny boat glided out into the harbor. As was normal for them, the kids immediately began shifting places, arguing with each other, and I could hear them asking questions in rapid succession, "Can I steer? What's this? How fast are we going? Will it tip over?"

"We should have warned him," I told Roger as they disappeared around the end of the dock.

"Oh, he can handle the kids," Roger reassured me. "Don't worry so much."

An hour later they came back into view, Janice wearing Pete's hat; Tommy standing in the bow; and Ron both steering and shouting at Tommy, "Sit down! I can't see anything!"

As they neared the dock, Pete seemed torn between retrieving the tiller from Ron and grabbing Tommy, who was obviously poised to jump off first. Too late, Pete lunged for Tommy, who deftly avoided his hand by bolting quickly and safely from the boat to the dock. In the effort, Pete lost his pipe overboard. The boat hit the dock with a nasty scrape, but Pete didn't seem to notice. He was gazing intently into the water at the rapidly disappearing pipe.

"Wow! That was neat!" Ron announced while tripping over his feet as he climbed onto the dock.

"Yeah, can we do that again next week?" begged both Janice and Tommy.

The look on Pete's face told us not to bother asking.

We learned two things from that experience. The three kids were not afraid of sailing and they would be great fun to live with on a sailboat. (Sarcasm intended!) I hoped Roger was paying attention.

Then we met Deak Albert.

"There's a boat for sale up the coast," Roger said as he put aside the classifieds from the Sunday newspaper. "It's only thirty-five feet long but the ad sounds interesting. Let's take an afternoon this week and go look at it."

"We need to start talking about another business instead of a boat," I tried to reason with him. "This whole idea has gotten out of hand. You are closing out the real world and filling it with fantasies instead. Why can't we talk about a little daysailer, one we could trailer around and practice on. That would really make much more sense."

"The ad says it's equipped for cruising." Roger's eyes were focused into outer space.

"You aren't even listening to me!" I moaned in frustration.

"Sure I am. All I want to do is look at it. Besides the drive along the coast is always nice."

Just for the ride, I agreed to go. With instructions to the kids to go to the neighbors after school, we left for the afternoon. The two-hour trip was beautiful as expected and we had no trouble locating the boat: a white, wooden-hull sloop resting on a giant cradle in a grassy field on the outskirts of the seacoast town. The freshly painted wood and the polished brass gleamed in the sun.

Without even boarding it, Roger could see the boat was too small for five people, but I was not sorry we'd taken the time to look. It was the first handmade boat I'd seen, and for once, it wasn't a carbon copy of a thousand others.

"Hi, I'm Deak Albert," said a slight, gray-haired man who stepped out of his car and approached with his hand extended. "Are you the Larsons?"

We introduced ourselves then said we were sorry we'd bothered him since it looked like the boat was not large enough for our family.

"Yep, she would be a mite crowded with five on board all the time." He nodded. "I built her myself, you know. Just me and my wife. We were going to retire on her and sail 'til we died. Dreamed all our lives of doing that. Sailing." He looked up at the boat and there was pride in his face. "It took us five years. We worked on her every night, weekends, days off, vacations. She's built real sound."

"It doesn't even look like it's been in the water," Roger noted.

"Just once. We put her in at Morro Bay for a trial run. She did great."

I thought it strange how sailors always spoke of their boats as She.

Mr. Albert went on, "No one could have built her better. She'll take anything that ocean wants to throw at her." And he lovingly rubbed his hand along the keel.

"I don't mean to pry, Mr. Albert," I said, "but why do you want to sell the boat now?"

"Some things just don't work out, I guess." His voice stopped, he looked away from us, and was quiet for a moment before answering simply, "My wife got sick."

The sadness in his voice told it all.

"Oh, I'm sorry." I was ashamed that I couldn't think of anything more to say.

He glanced up at the boat one more time then turned and smiled broadly. "Building her was most of the fun anyway." He wasn't fooling me, but I wondered if he had been able to convince himself.

Quickly we thanked him, shook hands, and wished him well as we got into our car and drove away.

Roger and I were silent, lost in our own thoughts as we headed back toward Santa Barbara. The road twisted and turned, hugging the edge of an ocean unusually calm for a winter day.

So, what did I want us to do anyway? Buy another restaurant? That answer was easy: not even if we were starving! Roger deserved a less-demanding job for a while, and we all needed something that would give us more time together and structure as a family. Would living on a sailboat be fair to the kids? Or good for them? Who could say? One thing for sure, and it was hard to admit, but the status quo wasn't exactly turning them into well-adjusted geniuses. My dream of the perfect family was slightly jaded, but was that a reason to let my dream go? And for how long? To what extreme?

I thought of Mr. Deak Albert and his wife. Would I always find reasons why we couldn't do anything as reckless as sailing? If I waited long enough, we might find ourselves like Mr. Albert's wife, with some problem that was insurmountable. Roger's health might be the beginning of that problem, and if his stress came from the effort he'd made to be the ideal husband and to fit into my mold, didn't he deserve a chance now?

Looking out at the horizon, I saw the distinctly drawn line separating the soft blue-white sky from the cold steel-gray water. The sky was a curtain that dropped to the sea and I couldn't picture anything beyond. It didn't exist. But the world wasn't flat. Columbus had proven that. And if there had been a Mrs. Columbus, would that voyage ever have happened?

"What are you thinking?" Roger interrupted my thoughts.

When I glanced at him, I saw by his smile, he was reading my mind. "I think Mr. Albert just changed our lives," I answered.

Organization is my obsession. It always has been and probably always will be. When I'm not organizing me, I go to work on the family who much to my chagrin either ignore me, or like Roger, are merely amused at my efforts.

Out of frustration I have been known to organize the kids' underwear drawers, alphabetize the bookcase, arrange my sewing threads by colors (using the color wheel, of course), and once, spent an afternoon rearranging the Monopoly money by denomination and in ascending order!

Suddenly I had an outlet for my obsession. If we were going sailing, then naturally I had to get us organized. I began with swimming. It was my number one fear, so I enrolled Janice and me in classes at the 'Y.' I tried to get Roger to take the Power Squadron's Navigation course but he couldn't fit it into his schedule so I did the next best thing and signed up Ron and myself thinking between the two of us we might learn something. We learned a lot more than I expected and enjoyed it too. For the first time in months, Ron sat through classes with obvious interest, and the big plus was that we began to understand the strange language of "nauticalese."

Roger found time to take a night course in SCUBA and became a certified diver, then followed that with a celestial navigation course at the local college.

I made lists. The most important to me was the "We Can't Live Without" list. At the top I put, #1 sufficient living area for five people, #2 double bed for Roger and me, #3 wall-to-wall carpeting, #4 shower, #5 good-sized kitchen with large refrigerator and freezer, #6 hot and cold running water, and #7 lots of storage. There were other items of lesser importance (like food) but I did not intend to give up the luxuries of home.

The library helped with my second list, "Survival Equipment." I was sure that any disaster could be avoided with a little foresight and planning. Searching out every book for the cause of each catastrophe, I decided what piece of equipment could have prevented it and added that to the list. I was determined that we were going to have only smooth sailing.

On 3x5 cards I copied everything I could find on preserving foods, cleaning and preparing unusual creatures (squid, conch, turtles): salting, smoking, drying, and curing meats and vegetables; making soap; keeping down mildew; making butter, cheese, bread; and cooking under adverse conditions. (Until then, I thought adverse conditions meant rain on a camping trip.) And when I read somewhere that the airtight plastic food containers that burp, or hiccup, or whatever were perfect for keeping food on a boat, that was all it took—I bought a small fortune's worth.

We were ready. Now all we needed was a boat.

Roger continued to look but found none large enough that we could afford. It was the final month before the restaurant changed hands and six weeks away from the end of the school year, when he announced, "I think I'll fly to Florida."

What now? I wondered. "That's nice," I said. "When did we become members of the Jet Set?"

"I'm serious. I've talked to several brokers who have lived on both coasts. They tell me prices for sailboats are a lot less in Florida than they are in California, not to mention dock fees."

"Roger, what is the matter with you? We can't do that!"

"Why not?"

"Because, if we go to Florida, we'll have to sell the house!" I began.

"But you knew that would happen anyway. We can't afford both a house and a boat."

Were we on the same wavelength? I certainly had my doubts. "Somehow I pictured us moving onto the boat gradually after we learned to sail it. I didn't expect to make the change all at once and not all the way to Florida!" Looking around at our renovated fifty-year-old home I realized I had never thought about selling it at all. I simply didn't want to. "Couldn't we rent it out?"

He gave me a disgusted look. "I can think of a lot of reasons why not, starting with the fact that a boat is going to cost a great deal more than originally planned and we'll need the equity from the house, as well as the restaurant, to manage."

"But selling the house hurts to even think about it."

"Toni, you have to decide if you want to live on a boat or in a house, but we can't do both."

"Okay, how much time do I have to make up my mind?" I asked as he started out the door for the car.

"Before I catch my plane in the morning," he grinned, and the door closed behind him.

It wouldn't have mattered what I decided—there was no stopping him. He was determined and nothing was going to change his mind. And while my doubts and fears kept getting in the way, Roger seemed to have none. He also had no more stress symptoms, but mine were only beginning.

He was gone a week, and when he returned, his first announcement was, "We have our boat!"

So, there it was. We were actually going sailing! And, to my surprise, I was excited. We were sitting in the living room amidst his luggage, and he had barely finished kissing me hello when I started in. "Tell me about the boat. What does it look like? How big? How soon?"

He took some Polaroid pictures out of his pocket and showed me a beautiful forty-foot ketch. "It is five years old and has everything you wanted. The carpet is brown and gold, the bed in the forward cabin is almost king-sized, and there is a shower, refrigerator, and freezer. It is also equipped for cruising, which makes me happy. So, all we do now is wait."

"How soon will we know?" I asked as I looked through the pictures.

"The broker promised a report in the mail within two weeks. I left a sizeable down payment, which he will return if the survey doesn't meet with our approval. Otherwise, the sale will go through as soon as we get to Florida." He sounded so positive, but I was stunned by the enormity of what was happening.

"Oh my God!" I wailed.

"What's the matter?"

"We're running out of time! I've got to get organized!"

Suddenly there really was too much to do. The lists grew. Everything we owned had to be put on a list: things to sell, things to store, things to give away, things to throw away, things to ship ahead to Florida, and things to take on the trip across the country. The accumulation of things was staggering, and I was daily more aware of how attached I was to them.

The biggest thing of all was the house, my beautiful house we'd so painstakingly restored and lived in for five years. We put it on the market and sold it within three days to a young artist and his wife, who fell in love with it at first sight. Their apparent delight made it somewhat easier for me to let the house go, but the day we completed the sale, I was shocked at my emotions. The depression was so severe I might have been at the funeral of a close friend, instead of at a house sale. I vowed, then and there, never to allow another material possession gain that much importance with me. After all, feelings that strong should be reserved for people, not things.

The kids had the same problem. It took a lot of tears to convince them that they wouldn't need 40,000 Lincoln Logs; there was no room on a boat for three bicycles; all the dolls would just get wet and be ruined; and the stuffed animals were nice but where would the rest of us sleep? They stared at me in open-mouthed shock when I broke the news. We were not taking the TV. "Mom! What will we do if we don't have TV?" They wailed in unison.

"Read! Talk! Think!" was my reply.

"Huh?" By the looks on their faces I could tell they didn't know the meaning of the words. A light flashed in Janice's eyes. "How do we go to school if we are out sailing around?" she asked.

"Well, you won't be going to a regular school...." I started.

"No school! Mom says no school!" The whole idea was suddenly appealing.

"Hey, wait a minute! I didn't finish, that's not what I meant!"

"No school! No school!" they chanted. They weren't going to hear anything else.

We told our parents and friends, who thought we were crazy. And maybe we were but it was too late to back out.

The sale of the restaurant was completed the week the phone call came from the broker in Florida. "There's nothing wrong with the boat except some minor hull work," he explained. "According to the broker it won't take more than three hundred dollars to repair a few scratches in the fiberglass. Otherwise, the boat is quite sound."

Roger gave his approval, and the broker promised that a copy of the survey would be sent to us immediately. Then he assured us again, "The boat is as sound as a dollar!"

We were elated but we should have checked the newspaper that day, the dollar was falling faster than it had in years. With complete innocence we believed the broker, the boat was ours, all we needed to do was get to Florida and sign the papers.

Both of our cars were traded in on a van to use for the trip. We gave the dog and the cat to family friends, and spent a miserable weekend throwing a garage sale. As the kids cried over every toy sold, more than one person left with a guilty conscience for having made a purchase.

We stored baby pictures, prized possessions, and memorabilia with my mother, and that left me with two lists: things to put in the van for traveling and things to ship ahead to Florida.

Roger helped out by building wooden crates for shipping. When finished, the crates were huge and once packed, there were five of them. He was stunned at the number and at the shipping costs. As he loaded the last crate into the van to take to the Express Office he complained, "Toni, this boat is forty feet not eighty feet. All this stuff will not fit."

"Oh yes it will, just wait and see. Besides, I only packed the bare necessities."

It was done. We loaded the van, climbed in, and backed out of the driveway for the last time. But as I looked out the window at that beautiful old house, tears welled up in my eyes. "Oh my God!" I cried. "What have we done?"

Everything fell into place so remarkably well before leaving Santa Barbara that we were a little surprised when disasters began to happen. We had scheduled two weeks to make the trip across the country, camping as often as possible along the way, but the trip took more than three due a van breakdown and a recurrence of Janice's asthma. As her breathing progressively worsened, my guilt feelings over what we were doing to all three of them grew, and by the time we checked into the Holiday Inn in Miami, late on the afternoon of the 4th of July, we were utterly exhausted.

Unpacking the van, we transported mountains of dirty clothes, three grubby kids, and ourselves into the motel room. I sent Janice to shower first; her wheezing had slowed some, but dark circles accented her hazel eyes and she looked so pale I wanted her in bed as soon as possible.

The boys showered next and were like frisky puppies just waking from a nap as the hot water revived them. Putting Janice to bed with a large dose of medication, I tried my best to quiet the boys while Roger talked to the broker on the phone.

"We will come by in the morning and pick up the keys to the boat and a copy of the survey," he was saying. I noticed him frown before adding, "No, we never received a copy." He paused then said, "You're right, sometimes the mail is slow."

When he hung up, I asked, "What's wrong?" and felt a twinge of an approaching headache. I hoped it was only because I was tired.

"I'm not sure." Roger answered. "But I think I'll call the surveyor." He reached for the phone book while I went to look for aspirin.

Even though it was late, he found Mr. Peterson at home and I listened to a lot of indecipherable, "uh huhs" before he hung up and said, "I think we have a serious problem. Mr. Peterson will stop by the motel tomorrow morning with a copy of the report, but I already know what's in it and it's not good." I raised a hand to quiet him and he understood my concern. Hoping not to upset the kids, we agreed not to discuss it any further until we saw Mr. Peterson, but we spent a miserable night worrying. That was only the beginning.

The surveyor was a friendly young man, suntanned to the color of a new penny and dressed casually in cords and a pullover terry top. He met us in the restaurant and over coffee, we listened to him explain what he'd found.

"The boat was just returning from a six-month cruise in the Bahamas when you hired me to survey it," he began.

"I knew that," Roger interrupted. "But tell us what you found and let's see what we can do about it."

Mr. Peterson selected his words carefully and it was evident he was worried for us. "Somewhere the boat must have run aground or hit some coral. Anyway, there is a three-foot-long gash in the hull. But when I was aboard her, I checked the bilge very carefully for any water and didn't find any. The construction of the hull is such that water probably had not started to seep into the bilge. You see, the boat is made of plywood with a skin of fiberglass over the wood; it is an excellent method of construction until the fiberglass is punctured then it becomes one of the costliest to repair. Seawater seeps between the glass and the plywood, and will, if it hasn't already, begin to find its way into the bilge. But it is the rot caused by the seawater on the unprotected plywood that will eventually undermine the strength of the hull."

"This sounds a lot worse than the 'scratch' the broker mentioned on the phone," Roger said, then smiled ruefully. "The broker assured us that it would take only three hundred dollars to repair the hull. What do you think?"

We were not at all surprised when Mr. Peterson shook his head slowly. "If you haul the boat out of the water and buy enough resin to fill the gash, it might not cost more than three hundred dollars, but that would be like curing skin cancer with a Band-Aid. Take a look at the survey there. I show the steps I recommended to repair the damage and you'll be lucky if it costs no more than ten times the three hundred. Twenty times would be more realistic and even then I'm not sure I would vouch for the strength of the hull. A lot depends on how long she's been in the water with that damage."

We were stunned. I hadn't even seen the boat yet and already we were talking about repairs—possibly six thousand dollars' worth!

Roger looked at the date shown on the top of the survey in his hand and abruptly asked, "How soon after this was dated did you mail me a copy?"

"I didn't mail it from the office, Mr. Larson. Your broker called me and asked if he could pick it up. He said you were waiting to get a copy and he would take care of it personally. From that, I assumed he was working in your behalf and that you were still in Miami and waiting for me to finish with it. I did a rush job and the broker even came to the office and picked it up on the date shown. I'm truly sorry to learn you never saw it. There is no doubt in my mind now, I should have mailed a copy as well."

We asked him what he would recommend we do next.

"If it were me, I would forget this boat and find another. If you have any trouble canceling the deal, then let me know. I'll do all I can, I can't help but feel some of your problem was caused by my neglect when I did not mail the report myself."

We paid the check, said we would call him if we had any more questions, then went back to the room to think about the situation before Roger met with the broker.

"Do you think the surveyor is telling the truth?" I started. "Is it possible he and the broker are pulling a fast one on us?"

"I guess it's possible," said Roger, "but it would be pretty coincidental. I chose the surveyor myself and did not even tell the broker about him until after I had made the arrangements. My instincts tell me we can trust Mr. Peterson. It's the broker that I wonder about." He then picked up the phone and placed a call to my mother in California. She was collecting our mail and Roger asked, immediately, if there was anything from the broker that had arrived after we left.

"No, nothing from Florida at all," she answered.

We assured her we were fine and after hanging up, Roger took the van keys and started for the door. Opening it, he turned and said, "No matter how bad the mail might get, if something does not arrive in a month's time it is a sure bet it was never mailed. I'm going to see the broker now. I'll be back in an hour."

I'd never seen him so angry before.

The motel room was a disaster. It did no good to sit and worry so I corralled the boys and, between the three of us, we tidied the room as best we could. Janice sat in bed, propped against a pile of pillows, looking listless but better than the night before. She was also enjoying the queenly treatment. We'd brought her breakfast in bed and now we cleared away the dishes.

When some order was restored to the room, Ron curled up in a corner with a book while Janice and Tommy alternately watched a comedy show and played cards. Tommy had ceased his teasing for a while, either in deference to his sister's asthma, or because he sensed our worry.

I read the paper, then washed my hair and did my nails, all the time trying not to think about the boat. When Roger returned, he looked angrier than when he'd left. He suggested we go have lunch and he would tell me what had happened. The kids joined us as we walked to the restaurant and they slid into the booth behind ours with my instructions to behave themselves and not to order the steak.

"Well, tell me about it," I asked as the waitress left with our order.

"I got the keys first and took another look at the boat," he sighed. "I checked out the bilge and the surveyor was right, there was water there. Not much, but I found signs that it had recently been higher. I would guess that the bilge pump had been turned on either last night or this morning."

"What did the broker say?"

"He dismissed the bilge water as 'nothing serious.' I told him that the survey report was still not in Santa Barbara, and of course, his excuse was that the Post Office was responsible. He insisted that he'd mailed it."

I looked at the sandwiches the waitress put on our table but didn't feel hungry. "Did you tell him what Mr. Peterson said about the needed repairs and the cost?"

"Yes. He said the figure was too high. He even agreed there was damage to the hull but refused to admit it was as extensive or as costly as that shown in the report. I told him his interpretation didn't matter. If we had known what the survey said from the beginning we wouldn't have agreed to the boat. We went round and round and finally I said I wanted to cancel the whole deal."

"Well, I don't see what else we can do," I agreed. "We were too innocent in this and now we've learned a lesson. We'll just have to look some more." I noticed the concern in his eyes and knew immediately it wasn't that simple.

"The broker claims we can't get the down payment back. He says it's too late."

"Too late!" I looked around the restaurant and realized my voice must have carried all the way to the other side. In a lower tone, I hissed, "He's lying!"

Roger shook his head. "No, he's not. According to the papers I signed with the original offer, we had thirty days from our approval of the survey to close the deal or lose the deposit. According to the broker, we approved the survey over the phone thirty-two days ago."

"But he didn't tell us what was in the survey! He misinterpreted everything it said. We never even saw the survey until yesterday!"

"I agree with what you say," Roger fiddled with his water glass. "In a very simple way I think we've been had."

"What do we do now?"

"As I see it, we have two choices. We can continue with the deal and take the boat as is, repair it, and hope it doesn't cost any more than Mr. Peterson indicated. And also hope that we have a strong boat when we are through. Or we can go see a lawyer."

"There is no choice!" I blurted out, my temper flaring to the surface. "I want to expose that broker for the cheat he really is!" And for the second time, I noticed I had drawn stares from the other customers in the restaurant.

Roger smiled. "Somehow I expected you to say that."

At that moment we were actually confident.

We found a marine lawyer and described what had happened. The man assured us we had an excellent case and would have no trouble getting our money back through the courts. He promised to file suit, to schedule our case on the docket as soon as possible, and to subpoena the surveyor as our witness.

We spent a week looking for a place to stay. The motel room was overcrowded; the kids were unbelievably restless, even though they swam in the pool from dawn to dusk; and Roger and I were alarmed at the amount of money disappearing from our bank account.

We took a small apartment in one of the classic 1940s pink stucco motels in Hollywood Beach, moved in, and sat back to wait for the date of our lawsuit.

Our lawyer was true to his word and the case came up within the month.

When we arrived at the courthouse, the lawyer met us at the door.

"Where's Mr. Peterson?" Roger looked around the hallway. "Has he arrived yet?"

"He won't be here today." The lawyer glanced at his feet. "He's out of town and won't be back until next week."

"But he can't be!" Roger sounded alarmed. "He was subpoenaed, wasn't he?" I couldn't believe it either. Most of our case rested on the surveyor's testimony.

"Well," the lawyer avoided Roger's eyes. "Yes, he was but the subpoena arrived after he left."

"Left? So why wasn't this postponed until he returned? We don't have much of a case without his testimony."

"It was too late." The lawyer was beginning to perspire. Roger's voice came in measured tones and I had the distinct feeling he was going to explode. "When did you serve him?"

"Yesterday," the lawyer said as he fidgeted with his tie. "I'm sorry, Mr. Larson. I simply forgot to get it out sooner."

Roger was boiling with rage, but at that moment, the judge appeared and probably saved the lawyer from bodily harm.

The case went as expected under the circumstances. Without the surveyor, the issue was reduced to our word against the broker's. The broker claimed he'd mailed us the survey, as well as reading a copy of it to us over the phone. And we approved it.

We claimed he gave us 'his interpretation' of the survey and it was grossly understated. And if we'd never heard or read the real survey, how could we approve it? The verdict was obvious before the case was even finished. We lost.

As we left the courthouse and climbed into the car, the lawyer approached. "I want to say I'm sorry." He stopped for a minute and adjusted his tie. "Just forget about my fee," he mumbled.

Roger looked up at him and with icy calm, said, "I already have."

CHAPTER 2: HALCYON MEAN PEACEFUL

We loved combing Hollywood Beach. I enjoyed the scenery and the surprisingly warm water of the ocean as the breaking waves washed the sand off my feet. The beach was within a block of the apartment and we walked there daily. The kids discovered sandcastles and had contests to see who could build the biggest or the fanciest and if Janice looked like she was winning, Tommy found cause to nonchalantly stroll over and 'accidentally' fall on hers. Then she would beat him up. With her asthma gone, she was back to defending herself.

While the kids played, Roger and I spent a lot of time mulling over the situation. *How much had we lost*, I wondered? Enough to say we might have to shelve the whole idea and find something else to do. We were eating our money away at a horrifying rate.

I knew it was hard to live within the scheduled note payments, but all was not bad. Mr. Clausen was making his payments monthly and on time.

I raised an eyebrow. Maybe Roger didn't feel beaten, but I sure did, and I started to say so when he interrupted me. "What if we lower our sights a little. The boat could be older, maybe one we could fix up."

"Oh Roger, what is the matter with you? It was all a mistake! We've sold our business, our home, uprooted our kids, and moved all the way across the country for a boat that had a hole in the bottom! Now we have no home, no job, no boat and are running through our money!" I took a deep breath and quieted down a little but didn't stop arguing. "I have to admit you did not drag me here against my will. Sailing was not something I would have selected on my own, but I did get excited about the idea, too. It just didn't happen—and now we have to forget it."

We walked a few steps further down the beach and I could tell he was thinking over what I had said. Then he stopped, put a hand on my shoulder, and by the expression on his face I knew I was not through arguing my case.

"Okay," he said. "I'll begin to hunt for a job tomorrow. But I would like to keep looking at boats for a few more weeks just until school starts. If we don't find something by then, we'll forget the whole thing. Agreed?"

"Okay," I said, but, behind my back, I had my fingers crossed.

Collecting the kids, we got back to the apartment and, when we opened the door, the phone was ringing. I answered it to find Mr. Peterson on the line.

"I just returned to town and learned about the subpoena from my wife. The hotel gave me your phone number, and I called to apologize for not being available at the trial."

I told him the outcome and he sounded sympathetic. "I can't tell you how sorry I am that things worked out this way. If you are still looking for a boat, I'll keep an eye out. I see so many every day and if any of them look promising, I'll give you a call."

I thanked him, hung up, and hoped it was over. Roger just had to face it. We'd made a very costly mistake, but now it was time to get out of the slump and find something productive. And true to his word, Roger began job hunting, but he didn't stop checking the boat section in the paper every morning.

It was a week after his first phone call when Mr. Peterson appeared at the apartment door and, knowing full well I would be sorry, I let him in.

"The boat is not what you were looking for originally, but I think you might be interested," and he proceeded to tell us about a boat he had seen that day on the west coast of the Florida peninsula.

"How is it different?" I was wary.

"Well, it's a lot older than you wanted. It's a one-of-a-kind that was built in the 1950s. That makes it about twenty-five years old. But it has been very well cared for through the years."

"One of the classics?" Roger was eager to hear more.

"Well, you might say that. Except that the hull is not wood, it's steel."

"Steel!" I balked as visions of a tugboat entered my head. "I don't think we are interested."

"Wait a minute, Toni. Let's hear what Mr. Peterson thinks."

"Well, it's forty feet long and sleeps six people. It was also built for very heavy sailing. I wouldn't worry about the safety factor."

"Does it have carpeting?" I asked. "Or a shower? Hot water? Air conditioning? A double bed in the forward cabin? How about a forward cabin?" I watched Mr. Peterson's head shake with each question and with each shake, I was decidedly less interested.

"It does have a forward cabin," he said. "But the beds are bunks. It really wasn't built for comfort like the newer sailboats are."

"Well, thank you for thinking of us but we'll pass on this one."

"I'd like to see it." Roger grabbed a pen and paper. "Just give me the man's name and we'll drive to Fort Meyers tomorrow."

I directed one of my dirtier looks at Roger but kept my mouth shut.

The following day we took the drive and Roger was thrilled with what he saw. "Look at that paneling and it's not plywood either! She was built to last. No wonder she's in such good shape!"

I started to say something then stopped. What had I heard? Roger had called the boat "she."

"Hey, we have to go." I tried again. I was getting nervous. "You're wasting our time. We can't afford *HER."*

"You are probably right," he said as he pulled his head out of the engine room. "But we won't know if we don't make an offer."

That afternoon, Roger made the offer, most of what we had left in the bank. To my surprise the offer was accepted. Roger and the kids were elated. I wasn't sure.

Ron on aft deck of the S/V Halcyon

We remained in Fort Meyers a few more days while Roger arranged to have the boat hauled and surveyed. This time he stayed with the surveyor through the whole process and came away satisfied that it/she was not only sound but, according to the expert, "Built like a battleship."

"Well, I like her name," I said. "*Halcyon*, I think it's Greek. Anyway, it means 'Peaceful' and maybe that is a good omen. I could sure use some peace for a while."

A week after all the papers were signed, Captain Smith, the seller, brought the boat around the peninsula and up to Miami where we took possession of our new home. We hung onto Captain Smith as long as possible, asking him every imaginable question, but there was nothing more he could do for us. We took him to the bus station, and he boarded the bus for the return trip to Fort Meyers. We were suddenly aware that we were now responsible for the care and nurturing of a forty-foot sailboat and we knew almost nothing about her!

Back at the marina, we climbed timidly aboard *Halcyon*. The kids seemed not to worry at all. They scampered about, chattering wildly over their new toy while Ron showed off what he knew of the various pieces of equipment. I was glad he'd been included in the navigation course with me; it gave him a little extra head start and he was clearly enjoying the role of the expert. "That's called a 'pinnacle'..." I heard him say and looked to see him pointing at the 'binnacle'.

As Roger and I descended the companionway steps, I wondered if it was too late to back out. Looking around the cabin, I felt a twinge of claustrophobia. There was good headroom and that helped but the floor space was minimal.

"There is more room on *Halcyon* than on most of the boats we've looked at," Roger tried to ease my worries. "You'll get adjusted to the close quarters, just wait and see."

I wondered if he was right. I was determined to try.

Roger removed a door under the companionway that led to the engine room and the sixty-horsepower diesel engine and crawled happily inside. While he examined the motor, I gazed around the cabin. The first impact was of wood—a warm, rich, mahogany wood on walls, floor, ceiling, and cabinets, and all solid. On my mental list of assets, I put one hash mark.

To the left, or port side, of the companionway stood a three by four-foot cabinet that was apparently used for the chart table, but lifting the top, I discovered a cavernous icebox. Reaching in, I could barely touch the bottom. *So much for the refrigerator freezer,* I sighed. Does the Iceman still cometh? Above the chart table/ icebox combination was an old long-range AM radio and an icepick.

To the right, or starboard side, of the companionway was a raingear and tool locker. Undoubtedly, the locker was meant to hold greasy motor parts, but the sturdy shelves would be perfect for a food pantry and I vowed to clean it out right away.

The main cabin was different in its layout from others we'd seen. Comfort and beauty were not important, utility was.

The walkway leading forward was overall three feet wide, but a slender divider ran the full length and cut the floor space in half. The divider was constructed with two large-hinged leaves on either side that, when opened, became a table that completely covered the floor. Settees pulled out from the walls to provide seating, or extra bunks when the table was folded. Apparently, eating, sleeping, and walking would have to be done in shifts.

The backrests for the settee bunks were drawers and lockers. Atop the lockers were two more bunks, one on each side and though situated high up, they had sufficient headroom for sitting in bed and reading. The cabin was ventilated through the companionway and six opening portholes, three on each side.

The galley was on the port side beyond the main cabin and built into a cabinet was a dollhouse-sized sink, equipped with one hand pump. Pulling on the handle, I cringed at the cold water that dribbled out. Scratch hot and cold running water.

Beside the sink sat a three-burner alcohol stove with an oven and broiler underneath. Upon examining it I decided it was not much more complicated than our camp stove. It was mounted, stationary, into the cabinetry, but above it hung something I'd never seen before: a small one-burner, kerosene, gimballed stove. Because of the intricate double-hinging system, I discovered the burner would tilt freely in any direction, and I forced myself not to imagine the conditions under which I might have to use it.

On the starboard side opposite the galley was the bathroom. *Head! Head!* I told myself. We had to start speaking "nauticalese" or the whole world would know how dumb we were. I opened the door to the head and stepped in.

It was about the size of half an airplane restroom and with the door closed there was no way to do much more than exhale. Inhaling as well as changing clothes, would be tricky. The only fixtures were another itsy-bitsy hand sink (cold water again) and a toilet, operated with valves that had to be opened and closed with each flushing. The toilet sat on a high platform and I lowered the lid and sat down.

With the porthole open I could gaze out over the marina. The view was nice. A small motorboat came zipping alongside and when the driver passed the port, he looked directly at me and said, "Hello."

I gave a start and a nervous giggle as I wondered if he could tell where I was sitting.

Located beyond the galley and the head was the forward cabin, and there I found two more bunks that formed a V in the forepeak of the boat. Under the bunks were more drawers and small lockers. I rapped my shin as I tried to close the door, and in order to make room, I climbed into one of the bunks.

It was a rude shock when I felt the hard bed. Not the inner spring mattress of our king- sized bed back home but a two or three-inch foam mat on a wooden frame.

Sitting on the bunk, I looked through a porthole at eye level and realized the opening was situated in the perfect spot like the toilet. I had only to turn my head to see out. With a large hatch overhead and four portholes, the ventilation in the cabin was more than ample. But putting my face close to the porthole, I looked down, and gasped. The water was less than three feet below my nose! While in the cabin I had experienced the illusion of being well above waterline when, in fact, the cabin floor was three feet below waterline. This was going to take some getting used to.

Walking back through the cabin, I had to agree with Roger, the boat was well built. Brass kerosene lamps hung over each bunk, in the galley, and in the head. The boat was equipped with a set of 12V battery-operated lights and another of 110V shore-powered lights to be plugged in at dockside. On one wall hung a barometer, a thermometer, and a ship's clock that chimed the watch change, all brass. The drawer and locker fixtures were also brass. A fathometer that read to one hundred feet was mounted next to the companionway.

Halcyon looked seaworthy all right. There wasn't a piece of plastic anywhere. And even though the quarters were close, air flowed freely through the cabin.

She was so steady, even with the kids on deck running back and forth between boat and dock, *Halcyon* hardly moved. I sensed she could take a lot of rough seas. At least I hoped so. Reaching out, I ran my hand along the fine wood rail of a bunk, looked around the cabin, and said, "I think I like you." The thought startled me. Instead of bemoaning the lack of luxury and space, here I was, admiring the style of another era when boats were built with care and were meant to survive; when sailors were rugged individuals who were daring, self-sufficient, and brave. Gone was the suburban housewife, and in her place was Mrs. Horatio Hornblower, with adventures to experience and worlds to explore.

When Roger crawled out of the engine room, I was ready for him. "All right, Sailor, let's get moved in!"

Janice and I did the cleaning while Roger and the boys made the five trips necessary to transport our wooden crates from the Express Office to the boat. The boxes were much too large to fit through the companionway, so we lined them up on the dock and unpacked them there.

The kids carried everything down the stairs while I put things away, but before long, stuff was returning to the dock to land in a great heap. I had run out of room!

"Everyone has to reduce their books by half," I ordered. "And all comic books must go."

The kids groused as they climbed back up the companionway with comic books, toys, clothes, my hair curlers and makeup, Roger's electric shaver, all dress-up clothes (except for one suit each), and high-heeled shoes. From then on halters, shorts, and swimsuits were going to be our new wardrobe.

Dangling one of my bras and giving me a mischievous glance, Roger said, "Maybe the sacrifices won't be so bad after all." Then he scooped up a pile of my underthings and headed for the ladder, humming as he went.

As he disappeared onto the deck, I realized he was already looking more relaxed. No longer were there frown lines in his forehead; and the conservative shirts, ties and wing-tip shoes had been replaced by sport shirts or no shirt at all, shorts, and tennis shoes. Most remarkable of all, ever since I had first known him, he had worn his thick brown hair so short I never knew it was naturally curly. Now, it was longer, down to his ears, and a solid mass of dark, unruly curls.

I liked the new Roger but wondered a little about the change. Why, for the first time in years, did he have to seem so content?

Returning to my work I was dismayed to discover that my great purchase of those wonderful, burping, plastic, food containers was a hopeless waste of money. Most did not fit onto the shelves and those that did, took too much room for the amount they held. The containers followed all the other items back into the crates on the dock. "Well, that's it," I announced as the last item disappeared into a drawer. It all fit."

"Except for what is on the dock," Roger reminded me.

"Well, I expected to have to do some weeding out. How much is up there?"

"Four crates full," he answered.

"Four crates! That's impossible! Are you sure?"

"Yep," he grinned. "Four crates full of the bare necessities of life."

I dashed up on deck, only to realize he was right. As we transported the four crates to the Salvation Army, I was thankful he didn't remind me of what it had cost us to ship them to Florida.

Halcyon was not peaceful. We had to learn to live in a gyrating house with drawers, doors, and a table that, alone or in concert, leaped out and caught us in the shins every time we tried to navigate the three-foot-wide walkway.

In our cozy little home lived five people of explosive personalities and directly opposing schedules of eating, sleeping, and dressing. Our days became a constant turmoil. I felt if we could get four in bed and one on the floor, we would have had it made. But, alas, we tended to have the opposite at all times. And that was at dockside! What would it be like at sea?

For four months we made an earnest effort to learn to sail and often begged anyone that seemed to know anything about the sport to go along with us for a few hours and give us pointers. Later we would use what we'd learned to practice on our own.

During relatively calm days we spent time doing nothing more than raising and lowering sails. Since a ketch-rigged boat has two masts, the combination of sails, usable at any given time and under various conditions, is mind-boggling to a novice. We had six different sails to choose from and I couldn't even remember their names much less when to use them, how to rig them, raise them, lower them, trim them, or furl them. They also had a life of their own and the minute the wind caught one, it became a fight to the death like trying to hang a wet bedsheet on a clothesline in a hurricane.

During one practice session Roger grew annoyed with my ineptness. "Take the wheel!" he ordered. "I'll raise the sail!" The tone of voice he had begun using with the kids and me was unnerving. "Turn the bow into the wind! I'll never get the sail up!" he hollered.

"Which way is the wind?" I asked while spinning the wheel.

"Not that way!" he roared.

Unexpectantly, the wind filled the sail (which was already halfway up the mast); Roger grabbed the bottom and found himself momentarily converted into something akin to a tail on a kite. His feet actually left the deck, but he missed being slung overboard only because I'd thought to reverse the wheel. The bow of the boat swung back, the sail ruffled, and Roger regained his footing. But the bow continued to move and once again the sail filled with air from the opposite side. And this time it hit Roger full across the face!

He came at me like a man bent on homicide. "Can't you see the wind?" He bellowed.

"No. What color is it?" I spoke innocently while gazing around at the sky.

"Ron! Bring me some string!" Roger ordered. The kids were all wisely hiding in the cabin.

"Roger, will you quit ordering us around." I found my backbone. "This isn't a naval warship you know!"

"Well, it is a sailboat and sailboats use wind to run! You are going to have to learn to find the wind if we are ever going to get anywhere!"

Ron crept up on deck and handed his dad a ball of my bright orange knitting yarn. Roger snatched it and began tying two-foot lengths all over the rigging.

"Now, when those streamers are flying straight back, you know you are pointed at the wind," he said. "Learn to watch them when we raise and lower sails!"

Those streamers stayed with us from that day on and, before long, I began to "find the wind."

More of a challenge than raising sails was learning how to dock a forty-foot boat without losing our cool and shouting profanities at each other loudly enough to amuse the entire marina. No one had ever warned us that a muttered oath could carry five miles over open water and the sound of a running motor.

Mercifully we never hit another boat. but we seemed to hit everything else as we approached our dock slip too fast. *Halcyon* had an achingly slow reverse action and "Dammits," "Oh Hells," and "Oh my Gods" filled the air as we bounced off one piling then the other. We usually came to a stop because at least two of us were slung between boat and dock, toes gripping the boat rail, arms hugging the dock pilings.

With "docking" and "raising sails" under our belts we concluded it was time to take a little trip. One day, Roger struck up a friendship with a native Floridian who claimed he had spent the better part of his youth fishing with his father on the bay.

"I know these waters better than my backyard," he bragged.

On one lovely Sunday afternoon we thought he would be a good one to take us out and show us some of the better fishing spots. While motoring around the shallower, south end of Key Biscayne, Roger noted by our charts that we were nearing dangerously low water.

"Don't worry about it," our new friend assured us. "The water here is at least six feet deep."

He was wrong by a foot. The feeling in the pit of my stomach when we hit that sandbar was a lot like the time I backed our car, full speed, in reverse, into a telephone pole! (Sudden lack of motion sickness is what it's called.) First there was a THUMP! Then the boat seemed to rise up into the air! In a split-second *Halcyon* was absolutely still, and leaning awkwardly to one side.

Our charts told us the tide was returning and would peak in about four hours, so we waited for our chance. Roger put on his bathing suit and jumped over the side to survey the bottom. Since *Halcyon* took five and a half feet of water to float her, it was a shock to watch six-foot Roger walk around the boat with his head and shoulders well out of the water.

He looked for and found a deeper channel a few yards to one side of the boat and as the tide started back, we began the process of "kedging" or pulling a grounded boat with its own anchor. It was a trick I'd learned from one of those disaster books and I felt so smug. All that reading and learning were going to pay off.

Roger and our friendly guide brought the dinghy alongside and put the largest anchor in it, then they rowed as far out into the deeper water as the line would allow and dropped the anchor. As it settled into the sand the rest of us proceeded to pull on the line, trying to force the boat toward the anchor. *Halcyon* wouldn't budge.

The situation was serious. The sun was sinking, and we had not planned to spend the night on the bay. But with only two high tides per twenty-four hours, we had to succeed within the next three or wait until the following day.

We took turns playing tug of war with the anchor. At one point Roger put up the mainsail and tried to lean the boat sideways enough to float her. He had no wind and no luck. During the final hour before high tide all six of us pulled on the line non-stop.

Tommy was leaning over the handrail with the flashlight and playing it over the water when he burst out, "*Halcyon*'s moving!"

We cheered, breathed a collective sigh of relief, pulled in the anchor, revved the motor, pointed the boat toward deeper water—and fifteen seconds later we hit another sand bar!

I didn't have to find the tide table. I already knew we were in trouble. It was 10 p.m. and high tide. The water was not going to get any deeper.

We worked an additional hour anyway, trying to kedge *Halcyon* off for the second time, but she was well stuck in the sand. The tide receded quickly, the boat rolled sideways, and we found it hard to walk on deck.

In desperation, Roger wrapped the anchor line around the mast then carried the anchor way out on the opposite side of the tilt and dropped it. Our new fear was that *Halcyon* would lay completely over on her side and, when the tide started back in, she might fill up with water through the hatches and vents before she floated. (The possibility of such an event happening was unlikely, but at the time we didn't know that.) I wasn't sure an anchor line could keep sixteen thousand pounds of steel boat sitting upright but none of us could think of anything else to try.

Roger went below and placed a distress call to the Coast Guard over the radio. "This is the *Halcyon*, (documentation number), aground two miles south of Key Biscayne, (chart coordinates). We are in danger of taking on water. Does anyone read me? Over."

There was no response.

In times of distress, I always feel it necessary to either cry, or feed everyone. Sometimes I do both. This was one of those times. I started cooking dinner. The macaroni kept rolling out of the pot, everything I put on the counter slowly slid onto the floor, and tears streamed down my face. Were these the "adverse conditions" I'd read about back in Santa Barbara?

The kids crawled into a bunk with the Monopoly game, while our passenger paced the floor and mumbled something about "shifting sands."

"This is the *Halcyon*," Roger repeated into the radio. His voice grew more insistent. "DO YOU READ ME? OVER."

Crackle. "This is the Coast Guard, we read you *Halcyon*. More crackle of static then, "Please state the names of your Captain, crew, and passengers, over."

Cheers went up for the second time that night.

"This is the *Halcyon*. We are aground two miles south of Key Biscayne and need a tow."

Roger gave the exact location then asked, "Do you read me? Over." Snap, crackle, "This is ... Guard, *Halcyon*,...crew... (more crackles), repeat we do not read. POP!

The radio went dead! We just stared at it. What now? The lessons were coming fast, and Murphy's Law was one of them. For some unknown reason I recalled an item on my "Survivor's List:" a good working radio!

We tried a few more times but nothing. The radio was dead.

Our passenger was apologetic, the kids were scared, I was near panic, then Roger did the unforgivable. He reverted back to his old, cool, unruffled self and calmly went to bed!

"We can't do anything until daylight or high tide so we may as well go to sleep for a while," he logically explained.

I felt the least he could do was pace the floor and look worried.

The remainder of us gave up and sought the most comfortable spots to lie down. But no one got any sleep. Every time someone dozed off, they rolled out of bed and woke the rest of us.

Extreme low tide came about 4 a.m. By then we were all staring at the ceiling and listening to the water slap at the side of the hull, mere inches below the portholes on the low side.

Once, Roger went up on deck and measured the depth with a boat hook. It was two and a half feet deep! *Halcyon* must have looked most undignified with her fat belly exposed.

The anchor line was drawn as taut as a violin string in a valiant attempt to keep *Halcyon* upright. We knew that if the line snapped it would whip around like a striking snake. It could have wiped that deck clean and severely hurt anyone in its way. We opted to stay below as much as possible.

Ron found the searchlight and started flashing the SOS signal from the porthole. No one responded but it might have been because he couldn't remember which came first the dots or the dashes. It was more important that he thought he was helping, and he was. Considering this was the first crisis our family had ever faced as a unit; it was reassuring to see how hard each child tried to do their part.

Another hour passed and the sun's first light revealed a fishing boat passing about a mile away.

We rallied everyone and started using all the signals we could think of. Ron blew through the ship's horn, Janice rang a bell, Roger fired two flares in rapid succession, and the rest of us waved our arms and made as much racket as we could. The boat came closer, then turned, grew smaller, and finally disappeared on the horizon. We had probably scared the poor guy to death. Through it all, I was convinced the Coast Guard had not read our position; otherwise, they would have been there. Somehow, we were going to have to attract a passing boat if we expected to get help.

About 10 a.m. a second boat approached from the west. Roger fired the last flare, we gathered all the noisemakers we could find, and I took some old rags and soaked them in fuel. I was going to stop that boat if I had to set *Halcyon* on fire to do it! Putting the rags in my frying pan, I threw a match on them.

We must have resembled the 4th of July when the Coast Guard boat pulled alongside horns blowing, bells ringing, shouts, cheers, and a burning skillet.

An officer boarded us, told me to put out the fire, then informed us he had heard our position over the radio the night before.

"Where have you been?" I wailed. Roger gave me a look that translated to, "Shut up!"

The officer explained, "We didn't see any point in coming after you until high tide we couldn't have moved you before then anyway." All the same I sure would have slept better if I'd known they heard us.

The officer connected a towline to our bow, and at exact high tide, their engines revved, and *Halcyon* slid off the sandbar.

We were in Miami by mid-afternoon where we gladly said goodbye to our passenger. He was equally happy to see the end of us.

Our lessons were not as costly as they might have been. Obviously, we were going to have to do our own navigating and not trust someone else's memory over our own better sense. Other people's knowledge might be helpful, but after all it was our boat and our lives.

In addition, we vowed never to sail in shallow waters at high tide and we began to look for a nice fat timber to carry on deck to help hold us up the next time we ran aground. Somehow we knew there would be a next time. (If we'd known then, how many times, we would have forgotten the timber and equipped *Halcyon*'s keel with wheels.)

When the monthly check arrived, I grudgingly forgot about the curtains I wanted for the portholes and the new bedspreads I'd planned on for the bunks. We had the radio repaired instead.

It was September and time to do something about schoolwork. I explored the possibility of enrolling the kids in the public system, but Roger vetoed the idea immediately. He didn't want to restrict our sailing time to weekends only when there would be too many boats on the bay for us to collide with. He also thought it unwise to start the kids in classes only to take them out again in a few months; he definitely had plans to sail beyond Biscayne Bay soon.

We learned of a correspondence school on the East Coast that offered fully accredited courses for elementary grades, and the brochure assured us the courses were designed to be taught by semi-literate parents. So, I postponed the new curtains, the new bedspreads, and carpeting for the floor, put us on a no-frills budget, and purchased grades two through eight.

At first the kids were disappointed that their vacation was over but changed their minds when the cases of books arrived. It was like Christmas! Schoolbooks, workbooks, art books, storybooks, poetry books, tablets of paper, pencils, crayons, lots of colored construction paper, and scissors. The kids were enthusiastic for a full twenty-four hours.

More and more we were settling in. When Roger wasn't playing the role of Captain Bligh, he was relaxed and eager to spend time with his children and his new mistress. And *Halcyon* was a demanding mistress indeed. Whatever she desired, Roger was eagerly willing to provide.

There were minor changes for everyone. Ron's awkwardness continued to plague him, but his stuttering ceased the very moment he began discussing motors or navigation with his dad. It gave me pleasure to watch them work together but I often wished Ron would feel so self-assured when it came time for a spelling lesson.

Day and night Tommy and Janice harassed each other. Ron ignored them; Roger never heard them; I separated them. To me it all seemed a mixed bag of blessings, but did I expect more? And had my personality altered? Not much. I continued doggedly to organize everyone: I established study hours, planned menus, and even began a project of inventorying all the cabinets in hopes I could find something without first emptying most of the lockers into the middle of the floor.

One morning, when Roger was off at the marine store, I took the liberty to clean out the tool locker by the companionway. I was preparing to convert it into a pantry when Roger caught me. "Thanks for cleaning that out," he said. "But why bother?"

"Well, I thought we might use it for a food pantry, then I can keep all the food in one place." The idea seemed reasonable to me. At that point food was stowed under every bunk, in cupboards, in the bilge, and even in the head. Once it took me four days to find all the ingredients for a pot of soup and I was still looking for the onions. I had a sneaky feeling they would make themselves known to me before much longer.

"And what am I supposed to do with the spare parts?" Roger asked.

"Can't you keep them in the engine compartment?"

"No!"

"Why not?"

"No room."

"How about someplace else?"

"Okay, everywhere you take out food I will put in parts."

I thought about greasy engine parts under the bunks, in cupboards, in the bilge, and in the head and meekly gave him back the tool locker.

The more sailing time we logged the less fear I had of rolling over, sinking, or being run over by a bigger boat. Of course, we were only sailing in a protected bay with winds not higher than fifteen mph, but I tried not to think about that.

To my dismay, the boys had no fear at all. Under sail, they seemed always to be riding on the bowsprit, climbing up the ratlines, hanging over the stern to watch the propeller, and generally giving me gray hair and a foul temper. Roger kept saying, "Don't worry so much, Toni."

All the same, I insisted the kids wear ski belts whenever they were on deck, and as an added protection, man-overboard drills were initiated as a routine practice when we ventured into open water.

Roger would introduce each drill with no previous warning by blowing the horn and shouting, "(Name) is Overboard!" At the same time, he threw the life ring and a plastic milk jug into the water. The person named was presumed to be in the water; and that person sat and did nothing until the drill was over.

The objective was to retrieve the jug and the life ring as soon as possible. At the sound of the horn the remaining four stopped whatever they were doing, reported instantly to assigned stations, turned the bow into the wind, released the sails, noted the compass course, started the engine, got a life jacket for everyone, brought the boat around, retraced the course by the compass, found the boat hook, made sure we didn't run over the victim and if lucky, rescued him or her.

Any onlooker who happened by must have been aghast as the first two dozen practice sessions produced confusion, commotion, and loud (often rude) language. But we were proud on the day we rescued the milk jug in under four minutes. At last we were prepared for the wide-open ocean.

We have mail at the apartment in Hollywood Beach," Roger mentioned one morning. "We need to go pick it up."

"We can drive over this afternoon," I suggested.

"How about going in the morning by boat."

"You mean go out into the ocean? The ATLANTIC Ocean?"

"Of course, why not? We could make it to Fort Lauderdale by nightfall then take the Intercoastal Waterway back to the apartment. Come on, aren't you game?"

No, I thought. "Sure," I said. "We can do it."

"Yeah!" the kids agreed. "No schoolwork!"

It was beautiful. The day dawned warm and sunny, and the wind was light. We had no trouble whatsoever reaching Fort Lauderdale, where we tied up at the docks for the night.

The next morning we had an early breakfast and, since there were no sails to rig, I stayed below to put away the food and wash dishes. Roger and the kids untied the dock lines, and we began the motor ride along the Waterway to Hollywood Beach.

Eager to experience the trip, I hurried with the dishes. So many times before, we had sat on the banks of the canals and rivers and watched the beautiful boats wander by. Now it was our turn, and I didn't want to miss a minute. While I worked, a powerboat came zooming up to our stern, then roared on by, but I did not see the giant wake it created on the narrow canal. Seconds after the boat passed, Ron yelled, "Hang on!"

I grabbed for some of the dishes on the counter, and reached them in time, but too late I noticed the butter sitting on the table. Because it was a very warm September morning, the butter was not firm. As a matter of fact, it was nearly liquid and when it hit the floor it splattered from stem to stern!

It took only a few moments for *Halcyon* to stop her lurching and I looked under the sink to discover all I had for cleaning up the mess was a bottle of ammonia. It would have to do. Grabbing the bottle, I stooped down on my knees and began wiping up the floor.

The ammonia fumes mingled with the smell of warm butter, and for the first time, I detected the oily smell of diesel from the engine. Looking up from the floor I tried to focus on the cabin, but it was rolling around me, and suddenly, a funny, lightheaded, and very warm feeling rushed over me.

"Oh my God! I'm going to be sick!" I moaned. I made it to the head just in time. That was a mistake, too. In that close undulating cabin, new odors accosted me even less welcome or pleasant than the ones I'd left behind. For the next hour, I caught a glimpse of that lovely canal every time I lifted my head out of the head and hung it out the porthole.

Once my traitorous stomach settled down, the rest of the day went well. But I'd learned one lesson: I was not impervious to seasickness and I'd best stay on deck as much as possible.

Seasickness is Fate's way of getting revenge. From the start we didn't know who would or who wouldn't. None of us ever had. Roger proved the strongest. He could stick his head in the engine room, the air blue with exhaust fumes and the boat rolling from side to side, then return to the galley and fix himself a bologna sandwich.

We expected Janice to get seasick, after all she had a long history of illness anyway. But the day we moved aboard *Halcyon* she stopped wheezing, sneezing, coughing, or throwing up. She just stopped! As though she could no longer depend on her crazy parents to protect her from germs. They were too busy protecting her from naval disasters. And if she wasn't going to have asthma then why bother with being seasick? Besides, it was so messy.

Ron bloomed the minute the boat left the dock. *Halcyon* was the only thing he found more interesting than a book and, underway, he would steer, help Roger chart a course, trim sails, fiddle with the radio, and once, he even talked to us! Sailing was too much fun to ruin by being sick.

Then there was Tommy. The little darling who thrived on telling Janice her spaghetti was worms, hot dogs were mooshed up pig's innards, and one time he even spit on her ice cream so she wouldn't eat it. He obliged, of course. The little angel that drove us mad with his elephant jokes, sick jokes, and knock-knock jokes. The little sweetheart that believed bodily functions were fit topics of conversation for mixed company. The child that made us all seasick on land, got his!

The ride from Fort Lauderdale back to Miami was a bit rougher. When Tommy began to pale, no one noticed; but when his incessant chatter ceased, we all stared at him in amazement and held our collective breath. There he sat quietly on the deck, as his skin changed shades from fish white to pea green. When he lunged for the handrail, I grabbed his shirttail and anchored him while he lost his lunch over the side.

Looking at his upturned rear, Roger callously remarked, "Tommy, always remember to go to the downwind side of the boat—otherwise you will discover something worse than being seasick."

Tommy sat back and looked at his Dad with glazed over eyes, then stood on shaky legs and without a word made his way to the cabin, and his bunk. All of us should have been ashamed of our lack of sympathy at his discomfort, but we were too busy enjoying the sudden peace on board the *Halcyon*. And from out of the heavens came a resounding voice, proclaiming, "GOT CHA!"

In November we left the marina and traveled five miles away to stay in a small boatyard on the Miami River. The journey was as much as we dared since we still felt unprepared for ocean travel, the motor needed minor repairs, we wanted to sell the van, and money was a problem. Our monthly income was barely stretching and hardly a day passed that we didn't swear at a shifty broker and a shiftless lawyer. That lost deposit was a blow we would feel for a very long time.

We were pleased to find a night watchman's job at the boatyard, and even though the job paid nothing, there were no slip fees if we kept intruders out of the yard after hours. That freed approximately seventy-five dollars per month, which I was determined to use for new bedspreads. *Halcyon* yearned for a little color and so did I.

The Miami River was another world. Though very narrow, it was amazingly deep, and daily, foreign ships journeyed up and down, passing less than twenty feet from our stern. Our greatest pleasure was to take schoolwork to the deck and watch the steel gray giants glide past us as we read *The Iliad, Robinson Crusoe*, and *Lorna Doone*.

Directly across from the boatyard was a park, and the view at sundown was captivating. As the traffic slowed, the soft green shade trees were able to cast their leafy reflections into the bayou-smooth water and only an occasional small boat skimmed by to disturb the pictures on the glassy surface. Over it all, the iridescence of oil might have been offensive except for the lovely pastel colors created by its pollution.

Before long, fishermen, shrimpers, tug operators, and pleasure boaters were as familiar to us as any neighbor. The river was our neighborhood, and our backyard was the dock. The kids played there daily making friends with the animals they found, and there were many.

Ron caught a bucket of tadpoles and kept them on the stern of the boat until they all mysteriously disappeared. It was a lesson in nature when, not long afterward we found tiny frogs croaking from every corner of the boat.

Tommy discovered fishing. Using a spool of line and a hook, which he baited with anything he could con out of me, he caught fish by the dozens, then learned about water pollution when I explained why I wouldn't cook them. But he continued to fish anyway and either examined the specimen and released it or tossed it out to a passing seagull or pelican.

The first manatees to visit us were awesome. Never had we seen sea creatures so huge or so ugly. We spied them often, feeding around the boats, and learned they were mammals, vegetarians, gentle, and nearly extinct. It was obvious why they were a threatened species when we saw one with a nasty gash the length of its back, made by the motor from one of the many boats on the river. The manatees were just too slow to avoid being hit.

Janice thought these pets were nearly as repulsive as Tommy, but her own personal nemesis lived under the shower. The bath house was a crudely enclosed shed located at the end of the dock; it extended out over the water for quick and effective drainage, and the only thing appealing about it was the piped in hot water. Standing inside took courage as the room was dark, musty, and small. If we showered during the day, sunlight crept in through all of the cracks. So did a little blue crab. The crab resided beneath the floorboards and chose to make his presence known only after the occupant was stark naked and had shampoo in her hair and eyes. At that very moment the crab would come creeping up through a hole and run straight across said occupant's toes.

That was all it took for Janice to give up showering altogether. However, after two weeks of spit baths in the head, we were ready to feed Janice to the manatees. One day I discovered that, with a bit of food, the crab could be pacified for the duration of one very quick shower, and I passed this information on to Janice. She tested the theory and began to shower again, but never without an apple or a peanut butter sandwich.

My personal pet cost us our free dock space. He was the biggest wharf rat in Miami, lived happily in the boatyard, and liked to casually explore all the unoccupied boats around. To overcome my revulsion whenever I saw him skittering along the planks, I named him Henry. But it didn't help, and I prayed he would not deem it necessary to call on the *Halcyon*. My prayers weren't heard.

One very warm and humid night Roger and the kids went to sleep early. Propped up in my bunk I was enjoying the night breezes through the porthole as I read a particularly engrossing mystery. I was well into guessing whether the hero would survive, when the tiniest of movements drew my attention. Slowly I turned my head and looked directly into Henry's beady little black eyes. That rat was less than six inches from my left shoulder, poised on the sill of the porthole, and ready to jump right into the middle of my stomach! When his whiskers twitched, I screamed, leaped to the floor, and threw my book, narrowly missing his furry little skull. He was gone in a flash, but I couldn't stop screaming.

I slammed the ports—all sixteen of them—in rapid succession, and never once did I let up on the screams. "Get off this boat! Scat! Go!" Roger and the kids sat up in their bunks and silently watched me running, screaming, and slamming ports. In thirty seconds I had the boat shut up tighter than a drum, but still couldn't stop the shudders sweeping over me. For lack of any more ports, I grabbed the broom and began to beat on the roof of the cabin with the handle until I was certain there were no more tiny feet running around on the deck.

"Can we open the ports now?" Roger asked with amusement.

"Not on your life! That rat might come back. Do you realize that if I hadn't been awake, or screamed when I did, a rat would be loose in this cabin right now?"

"We are going to smother in this heat." He was unconcerned.

"Well, I am not going to open this boat again after dark until we have screens on the hatches. I simply will not live with a rat!"

It took two days to get screens made and, in the meantime, the boat stayed closed. We died from the heat, but worse than that, with the ports closed we did not hear any noise on the docks. A thief came into the yard one night and stole a boat, a very expensive boat, and it was tied less than thirty feet from our own!

The owner of the boatyard was not pleased with us and let us know by charging us dock fees from that moment on. Every time I saw Henry after that I thought of someone's lost boat and the bedspreads we couldn't afford. If I could have caught that rat, I believe I would have overcome my fear of him long enough to strangle him, bare-handed!

Christmas was coming and so was my mother. Excitement reigned. Because of the rat, because of the luxuries we were doing without, because of the cramped living quarters, and because my husband seemed to be thrilled to death with the whole thing, I had an overwhelming need to see my mother, have her pat me on the head, and tell me everything would be all right.

Christmas was certainly going to be unusual this year. Where would we put a tree? How would I cook a turkey? What would presents be? And where would we store another thing? We were still eliminating the unnecessary items I'd been so sure we needed, and Roger kept replacing them, daily, with such treasures as bilge pump parts, engine parts, tool parts, and books about parts.

As I worked on the gift list, I wondered if there was any way we could eke out money for carpeting. It would certainly cheer up the dark wood interior of the boat. Then dismissing the idea as being out of reach, I thought about the kids. Wouldn't they be thrilled to open their very own personal survival kits, complete with C rations, salt tablets, and suturing equipment? Not quite the same as bicycles, I bet.

Roger and I talked over the gift problem and he eliminated all luxury items from my list in lieu of snorkel gear for everyone. I had to admit it made more sense, and though dull, it was affordable.

But we did hit on a great idea for the kids. We would take them to a large shopping mall, give them five dollars each and a list of the people they had to buy gifts for. What a great way for them to use imagination and teamwork—or so I thought.

As we sat over root beer floats in Woolworth's, Roger and I gave them the preliminary pep talk. "You each have Mom, Dad, and Grandma on your lists. If you work together, you can combine the gifts and have more money to spend on each. Then any two of you can join up and buy the gift for the third." They listened to our ideas only long enough to slurp up their sodas, then they were off in a dead run—in three different directions!

Janice returned first, in exactly four minutes and twelve seconds. In her hand were five of the tiniest brown paper bags I'd ever seen; tucked in her cheek was a wad of bubble gum the size of a baseball.

"Did you get all the gifts on your list?" Roger prodded her.

"Yep."

"Did you spend all your money?" He tried again.

"Glmph." she replied as she blew a bubble, and that was all the information she was willing to divulge.

Twenty minutes later, Tommy returned, carrying one extra-large brown bag, and he looked thoroughly proud of himself.

"Did you get everyone on your list?" Roger asked,

"No, just Grandma, and she's going to love it too."

"How about the other four gifts? Do you want to go get those now?" I wondered.

"Okay, but I need more money." he beamed.

Roger frowned a little. "Tommy, how much do you need? How much do you have left?"

"Twelve cents," was Tommy's reply.

"Twelve cents!" I said. "That's all? You spent all your money on one gift? What did you buy?"

He reached into the bag and pulled out a large, bright blue, stuffed pig wearing a top hat and carrying a cane. "That's for Grandma?" we both asked in unison. "Yep. And his name is Piggy. I bet she'll be sooo happy," he predicted.

Roger and I exchanged glances and we each knew what the other was thinking. Somewhere back in Santa Barbara was a much loved and much—missed teddy bear. Tommy's message was loud and clear.

Two hours later we were still frantically searching for Ron. We kept fanning out asking clerks, store managers, security guards, and customers if they had seen him. We were on the verge of calling the police when he reappeared, approaching the mall from a block away

"Where have you been?" Roger asked sternly.

"Down the street," Ron answered.

"Why did you leave the mall?"

"Because they didn't have anything I liked." I guess that made sense to him. He seemed utterly amazed that we were worried.

On Christmas Eve I cooked a turkey in the pressure cooker, then we found a tiny, bedraggled, near needleless tree which we set up on the afterdeck of the boat, (there simply was no room below.) The kids spent all afternoon decorating it with popcorn, ribbons, aluminum foil and love. They wrapped their gifts and put them under the tree and miraculously *Halcyon* looked very Christmassy indeed.

Roger met Mother at the airport at 11 p.m. that night and when they returned, we were all sitting on the deck waiting. It is a credit to my mother that she found nothing unusual about opening presents at midnight, on the stern of a boat, in a dirty boatyard, at the edge of the river.

For us all it was a thoroughly delightful evening. Snorkel gear was passed around, then we opened our gifts to find we each had received one pencil eraser from Janice. If my calculations were right, she had $3.80 worth of gum in her mouth. Ron gave Tommy and Janice a card game, me a new pair of thongs, and Roger a white Captain's hat purchased from that store down the street.

Grandma really was sooo happy to receive Piggy, and afterwards we all oohed and ahhed, kissed and hugged, and laughed a lot. The experiment was a definite success.

At 2 a.m. the kids and Roger went to bed; Mother and I stayed on deck until the break of dawn. In the early—morning hours, I unloaded all my new-found frustrations onto her shoulders. To my surprise she was amused. As I thought about it, the humor of our existence crept into my head, and I began to laugh with her. For a little while life really was all right.

To Mother, our world was utterly enchanting, and she spent her days exploring the surroundings with the kids. They eagerly introduced her to all their pets, and she unconditionally met and accepted them.

Every evening after the others were in bed, Mother would join me and together we would enjoy the serenity of the river from the deck and talk until the wee hours. The New Year arrived with us sitting, our feet propped on the stern rail and sharing a bottle of wine.

L-to-R: Ron, Tom, Janice, Toni, & Grandma Vivian

The water lay like a mirror, reflecting lights from all around us, and there was an unreal orange glow from the mercury vapor lights in the park across the way. At midnight, firecrackers exploded, continued sporadically for an hour, and then stopped altogether. The night grew eerily still and softly warm.

A movement in the park caught our attention. I glanced across the river to see an enormous green dragon gliding slowly through the trees. I looked at Mother, she looked at me, and we both looked at our wine glasses. We'd had some to drink, but not that much! Behind the two-story dragon, a group of daisies emerged followed by a thirty-foot caterpillar riding silently on top of a very large mushroom. Next came a rocket, some towering palm trees, and then a bevy of butterflies.

After the first shock, we came to the conclusion that we were getting a preview of the Orange Bowl Parade. Anything else would have made us subjects for a psychiatrist's couch.

We watched for two hours as the whole procession drove quietly along the river front, looking even more make believe because of the orange glow and the reflection in the water. And as the last strange vision disappeared into the night Mother smiled at me and said, "Toni, few people have such a wonderful magical backyard. Enjoy it, it may not last forever."

I promised to try, but thought to myself, *It would be a lot easier with more money, and a slightly more sympathetic husband.*

On New Year's Day, Mother took the kids downtown to see the parade, and reported back that it was not as impressive as the one from the night before. "I guess magic cannot be planned," she said, and I knew what she was trying to tell me.

While packing her suitcase to return to California, she discovered a very distressing fact. Piggy simply would not fit into the luggage. She tried as hard as seemed necessary but couldn't find room for that stuffed pig. Finally, turning to Tommy, who had been standing attentively at her side, she asked, "Could you keep Piggy for me until I visit next time?"

"Oh yes!" He beamed from ear to ear, then grabbed the pig and squeezed it tightly. "I'll take good care of him for you."

Someone had received exactly what he wanted for Christmas.

CHAPTER 3: HAPPINESS IS PEANUT BUTTER AND A WHISTLE

When Roger found a buyer for the van, I was convinced the money from the sale could be used for some worthy cause such as curtains for the port holes, carpeting, or a new hairdo for me. However, no amount of begging, pleading, or demanding could soften old Scrooge's heart. He bought a dinghy with a motor, and it cost every cent of the money from the van. But I forgot my disappointment when a week after New Year's Day, we tied the new dinghy to the stern of the *Halcyon* and left the Miami River for good.

Cruising south for two days we felt wonderfully free and a tiny bit scared, but the wind and water were calm, and we experienced only two minor mishaps of hitting bottom when we ventured too close to shore. Obviously, our instinctual urge to "see land" was more powerful than the common sense that told us *Halcyon* was a sailboat, not a car.

Still the navigational skills of our crew proved adequate, at least we knew where we were all the time and we pointed with pride to identifiable Keys, towers, buildings, and bridges as we traveled.

Two days from Miami, thirty miles into the Keys and southwest of the peninsula, we crossed under a drawbridge and headed for a tiny marina called Tollgate, on Lower Matecumbe Key.

The Key was narrow. It barely accommodated the marina on the Gulf side, a marine store on the Atlantic side, and the highway between the two. As *Halcyon* approached the dock, I thought it a good opportunity to explain to Janice the phenomena of having both bodies of water in such close proximity.

"You see, the Atlantic Ocean is the water we sailed on from Miami," I said. "When we crossed under the bridge, we entered the Gulf of Mexico."

She wasn't impressed. Gazing over the side of the boat, she remarked, "The water all looks the same color to me." I remembered that she had been equally unimpressed with the changing of the states when we drove across the country.

All around us were dozens of boats of assorted sizes and shapes; some were tied up at the long wooden dock, and a few smaller power boats were near the ramp, waiting to launch. People milled about: fishermen, sailors, and one shaggy-haired boy sitting near the fuel pumps with a fishing line in the water. A lazy pelican perched atop an end piling blissfully asleep until our kids jumped onto the dock, rattled his roost, and sent him looking for more peaceful surroundings.

We felt warmly welcomed by the sailors who willingly caught our lines, snubbed them down, and asked us the customary questions.

"Where are you from?"

"Miami."

"Where are you headed?"

"Haven't decided yet."

"How was the trip?"

"Not bad."

I had to smile at the nonchalance with which Roger answered the last question as though we'd been cruising for years.

We really didn't know where we were going. Key West perhaps, but anywhere that the water was clean enough to swim in and the dock fees were reasonable. We spent time chatting with the sailors, then filled our fuel and water tanks, and donned snorkel gear for an afternoon of lazy fun. Serious decisions could come later.

The boys were in the water first—they were always first. They never seemed to get their fill of the fascinating life under the surface and were well on the way to becoming expert divers as they plunged to the bottom to capture some unsuspecting shell or starfish to bring up for our inspection. And it was their fantasy to imagine the underwater creature returning home to tell his family about being captured by aliens from another world.

Janice took longer getting into the water. First, she had to put on her mask and snorkel, then she added a ski belt and a life jacket, and for insurance, she looped one arm through the life ring. Only then did she ease herself down into the water. With one hand grasping the boarding ladder and the other holding the life ring, she took a deep breath and lowered her face to the surface. Three seconds later her head jerked up, and as she yanked the snorkel out of her mouth to get a breath (none of us had been able to convince her she could breathe through the apparatus), she shouted, "Mom! Dad! Look down here!" Finally, she'd found something that impressed her.

Roger and I were the last in and felt as thrilled as the kids to enter such an accessible, entrancing environment. We floated around the hulls of the other sailboats, moved in and out of the pilings, explored a few old tires and an oil drum, and marveled at the dozens of varieties of brightly colored fish.

For a while a barracuda followed us at arm's length and just behind my right shoulder. Whenever I turned, the fish stopped as still as a piece of driftwood, then started again the moment I did. After a bit he went away, and I breathed easier.

At one point Roger put his hand out to get my attention. Treading water in front of us was an apparition; a perfect, miniature seahorse, and other than in photographs, I'd never seen one before. I never truly believed they existed. Unicorns, dragons, mermaids, and seahorses had all been products of the imagination until that moment.

The captivating little horse was unafraid, only curious to see such funny fish in his neighborhood. Carefully Roger extended his hand, the seahorse wrapped his tail around a little finger and hitched a free ride as we swam. If a mermaid were to come by at that moment, I would merely have smiled and waved. We had found our magic world.

The decision was made. Tollgate would be our home for a while. The other residents of the dock were friendly, the atmosphere was relaxed, the water in the harbor was clean enough for swimming and clear enough for snorkeling, the dock fees were one third the rates of Miami, and the marina manager said we could work occasionally in his restaurant/bar/boat supply store to help defray the costs of food, rent, and fuel.

Though I had never thought of our life in California as being affluent, in comparison to our money situation on the boat, it certainly must have been. Out of necessity, we agreed to work whenever the manager needed us.

Ron got the first job cleaning up around the store and restaurant and his adjustment to the world of the employed was phenomenal.

An excerpt from his diary told all:
January 15—Today I got a job at the restaurant. January 16—Today I went to work. January 17—Today I went to work. January 18—Today I went to work. January 19—Today I went to work.
January 20—Today I went to work and got paid $15.10. January 21—Today I quit my job!
Well, money wasn't everything.

Our days stayed busy and surprisingly full. If ever I expected boredom would be a problem, it was before we moved on board the boat. Schooling became a ritual and we set regular hours that stuck. I took two hours with each child to give him or her the lesson for the day, and that child would then take the assignment to a corner of the boat to work on it. And even though it was often a struggle, the kids accepted school as their fate in life.

Our favorite spot was the bowsprit, which we designated the "private place" and anyone sitting there was not to be bothered. It was a perfect haven for studying as well as sulking or daydreaming, and each of us found time to do our share.

When lessons were completed we worked on the boat or in the restaurant, fished, snorkeled, or played around the marina.

If Tommy wasn't around, Janice spent her leisure time drawing pictures or writing poetry. She also showed a bent for organization by taping signs all over the boat to help us remember the various names of the head, galley, sole, main, mizzen, boom, and binnacle. But when she wrote "port" and "starboard" on the backs of her hands, I knew for certain she was a chip off the old block.

Otherwise, she played board games with Tommy in an endless quest to beat him just once. The rest of us suspected he cheated.

It was a special event when the boys found an old inner tube and a broken umbrella in a garbage pile behind the marine store.

Ron, Tom, and inner tube

They devoted hours to patching the holes in both, and when they found a paddle with a broken handle, the combination of umbrella, inner tube, and oar became one of the swiftest sailing vessels in the Keys.

It also taught them the science of wind propulsion. One would perch on the tube while holding the umbrella aloft to catch the wind, and the other sat on the opposite side and used the paddle as a rudder to steer. Just to keep from capsizing the inner tube took great agility and Ron's coordination began to improve markedly. The two boys became very proficient at sailing.

Then Janice, spurred on by her jealousy of the boys' fun, deserted her artwork, plunged into the water, and learned how to swim.

For a while I sensed what the cruising life was all about. The months in Miami had not been the adventure I'd hoped for and I had stayed ready to pack at the first clue from Roger that he was willing to quit. But I began to perceive that the miniscule living space on the *Halcyon* might be bearable if we could have such a beautiful swimming pool at our backdoor, and the calm, uncluttered lifestyle of Tollgate around us.

Still, it was hard for me to adjust. All the room on the boat combined did not equal the space of even one of the bedrooms in our house in Santa

Barbara, and daily I regretted the loss of privacy, modesty, secrets, and personal possessions. To at least supply privacy from the outside world, I began a new project: crocheting granny squares to cover the portholes. Why I had clung to my skeins and balls of multicolored yarns probably related to my yearnings for hearth and home, but the crocheting kept my hands busy during lesson time, and every few days, I hung a new granny square, the first in the head, and felt immeasurably better as the colors brightened *Halcyon*'s dark interior.

However, of all the adjustments we were making in our lives, of all the pleasures we were learning to do without, sex was not one we were ready to give up. Nevertheless, three kids were effectively putting a crimp in our love life. It was the dinghy that solved that problem.

As much as I begrudged the purchase of that little boat, I soon found I cherished it more than any other luxury we might have bought. Ron had learned to row it like a pro, and one day we thought to capitalize on his new skill.

Feeling much like devious teenagers, Roger and I took *Halcyon* out for a few hours and found a secluded anchorage near a sandy beach. We then put the kids in the dinghy with peanut butter sandwiches, a whistle, and instructions to row to the beach and build sandcastles. They were told, if they got into trouble or wanted to return to the boat, all they had to do was blow the whistle and we would come up on deck and watch them row back. For a short time, we were alone. Our immediate discovery was that the length of time the kids were willing to play happily on the beach was directly related to the amount of food I packed for them, and it wasn't long before I was measuring time by peanut butter sandwiches.

Making love became a production requiring a great deal of planning. The elements necessary to succeed began with two desires that would outlast a week-long rainstorm. At the first sign of clear weather, work and school schedules were coordinated, a suitable location selected and charted, fuel tanks filled, sandwiches packed, whistle tracked down, an hour-long trek to the anchorage, and the kids coaxed into the right frame of mind.

Even then it didn't always work out. On one such effort at romance, Roger made the mistake of putting the kids into the dinghy while they were fighting. Before they had reached the beach they were turned around and headed back to the boat, Tommy with a black eye, Janice crying, and Ron trying to make both sit still before the dinghy capsized.

But, when everything and everyone cooperated, it was worth it. And like anything else that is rare, scarcity made it more valuable.

Our living expenses were less in the Keys, but money continued to be a problem. *Halcyon* was the main reason. There was always something she needed, and she had an insatiable appetite for nuts, bolts, screws, hoses, and pumps. She was also a virtual alcoholic when it came to paint and seemed to drink it by the gallon.

No matter how hard we tried, our monthly income barely stretched. To provide more funds Roger announced it was time to feed ourselves from the sea. Besides, it was lobster season and we wanted to get our share. All we needed to do was to find out how.

A local fisherman told us about "netting" lobsters. "It takes a lot of practice," he explained. "But, if you have the right equipment and don't give up, you'll soon get the hang of it."

He told us to purchase a bully net made especially for the sport. It was an apparatus designed with an unusually long handle, and the net end bent at a right angle to the pole. The trick was to hold the handle straight up and down and the net directly over the lobster and at precisely the right moment, shove the net down over the prey. If lucky, a large, spiny, delicacy of the deep would back up into the net and entangle itself enough to be lifted out of the water.

We quickly discovered why there are still lobsters in Florida. They are so fast they usually vanish as soon as they are sighted. In addition, lobster feed after dark and 'netting' is done only at night by dinghy or rowboat and in very shallow flat areas of open water. We also learned that, to see below the surface, there must be NO tide, and NO wind, to disturb the surface. We tried anyway.

Using directions from the fisherman, Roger fixed a platform on the bow of our dinghy to hold the kerosene lantern, and with it we hoped we would have plenty of light to spot the elusive creatures.

On our initial first time out, we took the kids, and the five of us made enough racket to give all the lobster in the Florida Keys migraines. Regardless of the noise we saw many, chased a dozen or more, and caught none. We had a good time anyway.

Deciding to get serious, we chose a particularly peaceful night, left the kids asleep aboard *Halcyon,* and set out on our own in the dinghy. We did not venture far but stayed within sound of the boat. I selected the best job right away: standing in the bow and sighting while Roger rowed slowly through the shallow water. His part was boring and because it was, I made every excuse possible to get him to do it.

As we moved silently along, dozens of sea creatures appeared before my eyes, and even though I'd had trouble spotting lobster (due in part to the thick growth of conch grass) I had no difficulty at all picking out the puffer fish, sea cucumbers, moray eels, stingrays, and barracudas that swam momentarily into the ring of lantern light. Of course, Roger couldn't see a thing since the light did not reach to the back of the dinghy.

I found the sea life fascinating and once I gasped loudly as a three-foot-long nurse shark glided by, just inches below our hull, totally unperturbed by our presence.

"How about rowing for a while?" Roger asked then tried, for the third or fourth time, to switch places.

"You know I am no good at rowing—we'll never get a lobster if I do." My front-row seat was worth fighting for.

"Maybe so, but at least I'd get to see something besides your backside," he complained.

"There was a time when you enjoyed looking at my...." Then I saw it a lobster to the left of the bow. "Over there!" I shouted. "Hurry! Now faster. Okay, back-paddle easy...."

Roger moved us into position, then I leaned out over the side of the dinghy and pushed down hard on the net and knew immediately the lobster was snared! At that same moment I realized I was suspended out over the water like a hammock, slung between net pole and boat.

"Roger! Paddle! I can't hold on!" In slow motion, the boat slid backward, gravity took over, and I made a perfect belly flop into three feet of water. Being all too aware of the sea monsters I had seen just moments earlier I scrambled, back into the boat, and when I looked up at Roger through my dripping-wet hair he was wearing the faintest of amused smiles.

"You dumped me on purpose!"

Composing his face, he denied he'd done it, but he had, and if he was trying to teach me a lesson, he succeeded. The next time we went out for lobster, I played fair and rowed, and before long we were getting our share.

A scrawny, three-colored cat wandered onto our dock, and for days afterward, the kids and I waged war over it. Each morning I woke to find the cat asleep in one of their bunks, and I would put it off the boat, only to have the kids feed it and coax it back when I wasn't looking.

"It" became a "she", then "she" became "Sea Coral", and as everyone knew she would, Sea Coral became a member of the family. I reasoned, three-colored cats were supposed to be lucky, and a little luck couldn't hurt.

A steel boat may be sturdy, but it also rusts, and as February approached, Roger made the decision to paint the deck. Where once *Halcyon* had been white, she was now mottled with ugly orange rust streaks and I could no longer deny, that she was looking more like a river tug every day.

Before painting came chipping, then scraping, sanding, priming, and finally painting. For weeks, the racket on deck was enough to set my teeth on edge. Add three super-active kids and a cat that regularly brought us presents of lizards, field mice, and other people's discarded fish, and I began to contemplate pulling the plug. To add to the misery, once painting was underway footprints began to appear in the cabin, pastel sheets became multicolored, our clothes grew indistinguishable from the paint rags, and Ron developed an uncanny knack for kicking over fifty-dollar cans of paint the minute the lids were removed. And it was at the peak of the "Paint Festival" that a streamlined motor yacht chose to cruise into our modest little harbor.

Roger and I had just readied the afterdeck for its final coat of paint after two weeks of back-breaking preparations and we were sitting on the dock resting when the elegant new arrival came purring up to the dock. A sixty-five-foot-long yacht is something to behold, all glistening white, with its flags sharply snapping in the breeze. The boat tied up directly ahead of us and I sat for a long time just admiring the sheer elegance of it and wondering what it was like to cruise in such luxury, or to have so much room.

Late in the day I headed for the showers hoping the new soap I'd borrowed from a fellow sailor would get the anti-corrosive paint out from under my chipped and peeling fingernails. I had almost resigned myself to red, white, and blue hair (anti-corrosive paint, deck paint, and hull paint, in that order), but my hands resembled crab claws and my legs were suntanned in a Salvadore Dali design as one layer of paint peeled, and another was applied in artistic, asymmetrical profusion.

When I passed the yacht, out stepped a very well-groomed lady in a sparkling clean and ironed, crisp white linen dress. (Dress! Did women still wear such apparel?) She looked my way just as the left half of my last pair of matching flip-flops flopped. Picking up the shoe, I muttered, "Good afternoon," and as I continued to the shower, I chided myself for feeling so unlovely, so sailorish.

Returning with a towel around my damp hair and an armload of paint-smeared clothes, I noticed the lady and her male companion; they were sitting together, having dinner at a table on the afterdeck. A real table that did not fold into a bed or a bench or cover a john or do anything but just behave like a table with four legs and a top that you put stuff on. And on that table was a tablecloth! Silverware! Fresh flowers! And the dishes were not only not plastic, but they all matched!

As I climbed aboard the *Halcyon* Roger yelled, "Is there any place else to keep the garbage bucket except at the foot of the toilet? I have to practically stand in the thing and the smell of old garbage in this tiny room doesn't do much for my stomach either!"

I glanced once more at that sleek white giant docked ahead of us (*I bet they have a room just to keep the garbage pail*), then descended the companionway to explain why the head was the only place we could keep ours without knocking it over.

We awoke at 8 am to an 85-degree temperature. Roger and I sent the kids into the water so we could apply the final coat of paint. By 10 am the temperature was topping 90 degrees, and the kids were fighting over the inner tube. And though we could ignore them, the cat was another matter. When she walked through a newly painted spot for the third time, I locked her below, only to be bombarded by her mournful yowls. Clenching my teeth, I kept on painting.

At 11:00 am the temperature reached a sweltering 95 degrees and the kids began begging for lunch. As I put my brush away and opened the hatch, Sea Coral went flying between my legs and across the wet painted deck.

"Dammit, Toni! Watch the cat!" Roger roared.

I opened my mouth to say something sweet and wifely just as our new neighbors strolled by in matching linen walking shorts, designer shirts, and sun visors. "How are you?" they called.

"Fine," Roger answered. I hoped my smile looked sincere.

After lunch Roger returned to the painting and the kids went outside again. I put away the food and dishes, then stepped into the head to wash the sweat off my face and to comb my hair. With the first pass of the comb, the teeth snagged on a glob of paint. Working at it a few minutes I thought I could comb out some of the wretched stuff that matted my long thick mane, but the harder I tried, the more it hurt. And the more it hurt, the more I perspired. The shoebox-sized head felt as though it was shrinking even smaller, and the smell of warm garbage was overwhelming. When the comb stuck fast in the tangle, I yanked and succeeded only in entangling it more.

Completely exasperated, I whirled around, headed for the sewing kit, and snatched up my scissors. Back in the head I grabbed the trapped comb and the handful of paint-snarled hair, and with one clean whack, I took care of both the hair and the comb. I looked at the evidence of my tantrum clutched in my hand, then back at the mirror on the wall. So I wanted a new hairdo? Okay, I was going to get one! I had no plan; I took no care to be neat or stylish. I just grabbed a hank and WHACKED!

As I worked feverishly, Roger's voice came to me from outside, "Toni, the cat! Grab the cat!"

With my hand poised in mid-air, I turned around and saw a little green lizard go scooting by the door, followed closely by Sea Coral and behind her a perfect pattern of white paw prints. It was the last straw.

While the cat and the lizard raced back and forth through the cabin, I calmly finished the haircut, reached for my beach bag, tossed in a few belongings, picked up my sun hat, stepped over the cat and the lizard, and marched up the companionway.

As I appeared on deck, Roger asked again, "Did you catch the cat...." His mouth fell open. "What happened to your hair?"

"It's my new hairdo!" I started calmly enough but my voice rose shakily out of control the more the words rolled out. "Roger, I can't take any more of this! Why can't you grab the cat! And the kids! And your precious *Halcyon* and sail to the moon for all I care! But you can go without me! I'm LEAVING!"

With that, I stomped off the boat and down the dock past the dozen other boats, with their occupants standing around watching us, past the kids in the water fighting over the inner tube, past the expensive white yacht where the immaculately neat couple were enjoying their very civilized mid-afternoon tea.

I walked with determination, all the way to the end of the dock, then stopped. Where was I going? Home? If I even knew where home was, I didn't have the money to get there. Tears ran down my cheeks, and I wondered what had come over me.

A young couple came out of the restaurant and headed in my direction; quickly I turned to my left and walked toward a grove of palm trees at the edge of the marina. Throwing myself under the first one I came to, I proceeded to cry into my knees. I'd had enough! This life was just too primitive! I ran my fingers through my hair. The hair that once had been perfectly groomed, the hair that I considered to be my best feature, was now only two inches long and sticking out in a mass of cowlicks all over my head.

I glared out over the steamy hot marina at that motor yacht, so pristinely clean and cool. And right behind it sat *Halcyon*, two days of wet bathing suits hanging from the handrail, paint cans and brushes tossed carelessly about the deck. The contrast simply made me angrier and more frustrated. Snatching up my beach bag, I rummaged around until I found a pen and my journal. If Roger wasn't going to provide any sympathy, then perhaps my journal would. I wrote until the anger subsided, then put the pen down, leaned back against the tree, and dozed.

When I opened my eyes the sun was sinking into the Gulf, and *Halcyon*'s masts were two great black crosses against the brilliant orange sky. From somewhere, the thrum of a banjo came to me as someone played a wistful version of "Laura's Theme." I looked to see a group of our neighbors gathered on the dock near *Halcyon*. I recognized the banjo player's wife; she was handing a plate of something to the kids, and I knew it would be a batch of her delicious homemade bread. I could almost taste it.

Tommy was there, fishing with a handline, and Janice and Ron were kneeling on the dock next to someone named Don, who, every evening, told the most exciting ghost stories.

A young couple emerged from an old wooden yawl, strolled toward the gathering, greeted the others, then sat down and joined in the chorus of a popular sea chanty. Someone laughed. Roger appeared from the *Halcyon* carrying the coffeepot, and he poured coffee around. Tommy squealed and showed the group a six-inch fish hanging from the end of his line.

I glanced over at the couple on the yacht and saw they were still sitting on the afterdeck, watching the people on the dock. Someone called an invitation for them to join in, but they declined, and when the group began to sing a boisterous rendition of "Mary Ann," the couple stood up from their deck chairs. For a moment I thought they were going to change their minds, but they turned instead, went inside their boat, and closed the door. As the final rays of the sunset entered their double glass sliding doors, I saw that crispy-clean lady pull down the shades to block it out.

A mosquito buzzed my ear and I shook it off. Obviously, I was not going to spend the night under the palm tree. Besides, I was hungry and a cup of coffee and some of that homemade bread would certainly taste good. Packing my gear into the beach bag, I stretched my cramped legs and returned to the dock.

Mercifully, no one mentioned a thing about my new haircut or my absurd behavior, and then I knew that, at least for a while, I was home.

The motor yacht left the following morning, and I didn't even go up to watch. I was too busy brushing my hair. The new style was a great deal cooler and even a little stylish.

During the three winter months we stayed at Tollgate, many boats came and went. Some were completing ocean crossings, others were just beginning, and many more were on long weekends from Miami or other Florida cities. Except for the huge white yacht that sat smugly in our midst for a few days, all visitors were friendly and eager to share experiences and stories. We never learned the many travelers last names, nor they, ours. No one bothered to ask another what he did (or had done) for a living—it wasn't important. Neither was social status, amount of material wealth, religion, political party, race, sex, or how many different knots one could name. How many one could tie was something else.

People were remembered for their sense of humor, imagination, and self-sufficiency. It also helped if they knew all the verses to "Island in the Sun," could make a gourmet meal from grits or peanut butter or could catch anything edible from the sea.

When we arrived at Tollgate that first week in January, the *Imagine*, a thirty-two-foot sloop from Michigan, was already there. We tied up across the dock from her and promptly met the crew Hobie, Emogene, and their cat C.K. (short for Captain Kidd). C.K. was an enormous tiger striped tom that made his bed on any boat that looked cool or convenient. He also scratched any one with the effrontery to attempt to evict him. Perhaps the clumsiest cat alive, he managed somehow to fall into the water as often as three times per day and we began to wonder if the poor thing needed glasses. More than likely, he did it for the quick dip since his yowling invariably brought everyone to his rescue.

A long-handled fish net always lay on the dock, specifically for scooping C.K. out of the drink. After rescue, he would spend the remainder of the day basking in the sun and licking himself dry. With all the help C.K. received, he never found it necessary to learn how to swim.

Hobie and Emogene were in their mid-forties. Their children were grown, and when the youngest left home for good, the couple sold their home and struck out for Florida.

Hobie

Emogene was a friendly, sandy-haired blond, who possessed a fantastic library of paperback books (an automatic asset in the cruising world) and made the best homemade bread in the Keys. We learned she was also a registered nurse on the day a hermit crab sunk its claw into Ron's little finger. After Roger pried the claw loose with a pair of pliers, Emogene devoted a good part of the morning bandaging Ron, using much the same attention she would have given to an open-heart surgery patient. She topped the operation off with a cup of hot chocolate, and Ron was forever smitten.

Emogene's husband, Hobie, was the "Dock Psychiatrist", owing to his great philosophy on life. "Do as little as possible in the way of real work and then, only under extreme duress."

One day, Hobie found a piece of driftwood on the beach that was the perfect beginning for a shelf. He laid it on the dock, and everyone tripped over it for three days.

The fourth day Hobie emptied all the cupboards looking for his tools, and while he was sawing the driftwood to the right size, Tommy joined him to watch. An hour later Emogene discovered Hobie's tools and miscellaneous gear from the cupboards scattered all about the boat, and Hobie gone! He and Tommy had retired to the beach with fishing poles and there they stayed the entire afternoon, practicing how to fly cast.

Bright and early the morning of the fifth day Hobie went to work again, and to Emogene's dismay, he insisted on sanding the shelf on board their boat. (He claimed the sun was too hot to work on the dock.) After fifteen minutes it was time for a break, so he picked up his banjo to check out the tuning. An hour later the strings were adjusted just right and not wanting to waste a fine tuning, Hobie used the rest of the day to serenade the other residents of the dock.

On the sixth day he hung the shelf. It was perfect! But, before he tackled the disagreeable task of cleaning up his mess, he asked Tommy to go with him for a spin in the dinghy. Hours later we could still hear the dinghy motor as Hobie taught Tommy how to stop, go, steer, race, go in circles, and make figure eights. And once we caught sight of Tommy, who was steering happily around the marina while Hobie lounged in the bow, dozing contentedly under his straw hat. To seven-year-old Tommy, Hobie was the best friend anyone could have. Emogene had other thoughts as she cleaned up Hobie's mess.

On the seventh day Hobie rested.

When Hobie wasn't busy building shelves, playing the banjo, fishing, or teaching Tommy the skills of wasting time, he was snorkeling with Roger. And through those winter months, Emogene and I became the best of friends as we compared notes on which husband was the most impossible.

GoldenGirl, a thirty-two-foot sloop from New York, was usually anchored away from the dock to save money. Her crew were four boys, aged sixteen to twenty-four, named Dave, Bobby, Henry, and Al. Dave's father had loaned his son the boat for one year as a graduation present, and Dave took the gift and three friends to Florida.

The boys encountered trouble on their way south, but they survived it all with the use of grit and determination, all except for one minor mishap. They were hit by a bathtub!

It happened early one Sunday morning while they were anchored in Chesapeake Bay. Everyone was soundly asleep when a loud crash sent them rushing onto the deck. Looking over the side of their vessel they discovered a very agitated boater, sitting aft in a bathtub! The tub was equipped with an outboard motor on the stern and the bow of the odd vehicle was rammed neatly into the side of the *GoldenGirl.* The boater explained indignantly that a regatta was underway, bathtub races were a part of the event, and the *GoldenGirl* was anchored in the middle of the course.

Daddy wasn't too happy when he received the phone call from Dave asking for money. He was also somewhat disbelieving of the story, but he paid for the repairs anyway.

Once in the Keys, the boys took turns working to feed themselves. One of them waited tables in a local restaurant while the other three fished. They survived on lobster, fish, peanut butter, and pancakes that were big and light enough to pass for cake.

Beach Party with Golden Girl crew

Everyone in the marina enjoyed the *GoldenGirl* crew, mainly because of their determination, but best of all, they opened a world of imagination to our kids. Dave and Al taught Ron how to make kites from pelican and gull feathers; Henry taught Janice how to create jewelry from shells and driftwood. And Bobby's talent was making games from anything— seeds, egg cartons, stones, and shells, while Tommy absorbed it all.

The oldest resident of the dock was Max, and he was the solitary crew member on the *Minnie*, a classic, Chinese-built, teak and fiberglass, twenty-eight-foot sloop. Max was also from Michigan, had traveled south with the *Imagine* was divorced, fiftyish, and his children were grown and had families of their own. Max looked like a true salty sailor, with leather tanned skin, gray-flecked hair, and a full bushy beard. The only things missing were a gold earring, a parrot on his shoulder, and experience. He was as green at sailing as the rest of us. But no one would have guessed because he kept the *Minnie* so nautically ship-shape. Where Hobie worked as little as possible, Max worked all the time. His boat was the perfect example of well-oiled teak,

Sailing Against the Wind – Toni Larson   55

polished brass, and tender loving care. And somewhere aboard that boat, neatly tucked away in a locker, were a crisp, clean, new pair of jeans, a freshly starched shirt, and the shiniest pair of black patent leather shoes seen anywhere outside of church. Max had one love above all else, dancing. And he never missed a chance to bring out those duds at the first sound of an electric guitar.

The only boat in the marina older than our own was the *LuckyLou* a forty-year-old, forty-foot long, wooden yawl with a boomkin (whatever that is). Frank and Kathy were the crew; young, athletic, friendly, and a real pleasure to have around. They could also catch fish when no one else had a bite, which gave them high status in a world of green cruisers. In addition, Frank could tie more knots than anyone else and Kathy could carry a tune during the sing-alongs. Some people have all the talent.

There was a third boat from Michigan. A thirty-two-foot sloop called the *Talisman* that had traveled the coast with the *Minnie* and the *Imagine.* The crew were Don and Madeline, an improbably matched couple in their late thirties who loved to war with each other for the sheer pleasure of making up.

The first we saw of them they were riding their dinghy around the marina with Madeline rowing and Don singing *"Paddling Madeline Home"* which, we soon discovered was their favorite activity after fighting and making up.

Don was the least likely sailor of anyone we'd ever met. And though he swore like a sailor with complete abandon and great imagination, he would swim only in swimming pools (the result of reading *Jaws,* he said), got seasick even at dockside, hated the taste of fish, was scared of the dark (but told wonderfully spooky ghost stories), and believed all sailboats were designed as instruments of torture.

Don's primary goal in life was to devise a plan of survival when the *Talisman* sank, and he was absolutely convinced she would sink, he just didn't know when. At one of the many dock parties, we were all sitting, watching the sunset, when Don relayed his latest plan. In all seriousness he said he was going to take a line and weave it throughout the boat, tying everything to it that he wanted to save—his wallet, his favorite fishing hat, a bottle of scotch, a jar of peanut butter, and a life jacket. And as the *Talisman* sank slowly beneath the surface of the ocean, he would grab the end of the line and jump. For a while he tried to think of a way to add a loaf of bread, but finally gave up. There seemed to be no way to keep it from getting soggy.

Madeline ignored most of Don's nonsense. She was a good-natured, sunny-faced blond who seemed to always be game for anything. Being the best sport on the dock also made her the perfect target, as she was regularly thrown off the end of the pier. She always came up laughing. The kids loved her, and no wonder: besides being forever happy, she also made wonderful coconut cream pies.

During those evening parties, we talked endlessly of cruising together. We had so much in common. Our ages, for example, ranged from six to fifty. Our sailing abilities were fair to non-existent. Our desires to sail around the world were universal; our chances of doing so were barely to not at all. We were all living on meager allotments, money from home, life savings, or sheer imagination. And the trait we shared most of all: we were scared to death to get out there and "go it alone." So, we banded together and formed "The Fleet" unanimously elected Don as the Admiral, chose the Bahamas as our first destination, and the end of March as our sail date.

Once the decision to cruise the Bahamas was made, there seemed to be no end to the preparations. Deck painting was no sooner finished before an engine checkup turned *Halcyon* into a mess of black grease for days. But the anticipation of cruising kept my temper on an even keel.

It was the last week in February when a "blue norther" came through the Keys and left behind it a phenomenon that happens occasionally after a strong north wind. The water along the Atlantic shore went out—way out. The beach was pushed toward the ocean and exposed for all the world to see were a vast array of tide pools and conch grass riddled with shells.

Since shells were the only souvenirs, we could afford to collect, we wanted to take advantage of the extreme low tide to look for treasures. And even though we received admonitions from the local inhabitants to watch out for the returning tides, I packed a picnic, Roger rounded up the kids, and we walked across the highway to find a likely spot.

The kids were thrilled to find, at their doorstep, mile upon mile of wet, pliable sand, and they not only planned to build sandcastles, they wanted to erect cities of them. Roger and I left them busily digging moats around Camelot as we waded out into the tide pools. We had prepared ourselves well with tennis shoes to protect our feet, long-sleeved shirts to shield our backs from the sun, and masks for peeking into the deeper waters. And in addition, Roger held a mesh bag, and I had a bucket for the "keepers."

We explored for an hour in the clear warm water that was no more than a few inches deep and were entranced to see all the strange creatures living amidst the conch grass. Everywhere we discovered whelks and tulip shells, the ocean's jewels, their beautiful patterns so perfect they could only have been painted by a God with unlimited artistic talents.

When I held one up to show Roger, he seemed not to notice; he was looking towards shore. "What's the matter?" I asked, then alarmed, checked to see if the kids were still where we'd left them. Apparently, they were. I could see three tiny dots bent over in the sand. It was then I realized we had not only lost track of time, but of distance as well.

Sailing Against the Wind – Toni Larson　　　57

"I think we had better start back," Roger said. "The tide is coming in fast."

And indeed it was. I felt a touch of fear when I noticed the force of the water rushing past my legs; it was rising higher every second.

We were wading in, with only a hundred yards to go, when we came across a long trench that ran parallel to the shore. Somehow when we'd walked out earlier, we must have circled around it, but now it was too late to do that again. If we waited much longer the water would be too deep.

Well, I know how to float, I thought. After all, I had been snorkeling around the marina for weeks. The trench was only twenty feet across, and with my snorkel and mask on, I was sure I could manage it. But I cursed the fact that the swimming lessons back in Santa Barbara had done little for me except to teach me how not to sink.

Roger, carrying the mesh bag full of coral and shells, set off immediately and had no problem at all. I fixed snorkel and mask in place; held tightly to my hat and glasses in one hand and the bucket in the other and started after him. Midway across, I raised my head to get my bearings and accidently filled the snorkel with water. As soon as I breathed in, I experienced panic, but pushed it aside as I tried to blow the water out of the tube. The tube wouldn't clear! When I inhaled, seawater filled my mouth and throat. Instantly, my heart was pumping, and my legs thrashed ineffectively to keep my head up. But the more I fought, the more the water poured into the tube!

A cramp hit my leg and the pain was terrifying. Yanking the snorkel out of my mouth I let out a scream and went under. Gallons of water gushed into my lungs. Roger appeared from somewhere under me and I felt him push but, as my head cleared the surface, I screamed again and swallowed more water.

"My God, Toni, relax!" he yelled. "Don't fight me! Please don't fight me!"

But I did anyway. I couldn't reason at all. I just beat at him and could think of nothing but getting air, precious air. Through a blur of water, I caught a glimpse of his face and saw he was afraid! I'd never seen him afraid before and then I knew beyond any doubt that I was drowning.

The world misted over and a peaceful, "this is how it will end" feeling came over me. I relaxed. From some faraway place I could feel him prodding and pushing at me, then against my ear, his voice said, "You can stand up now." But he had to hold me under the arms and force me to do it.

When I touched bottom my legs shook with such violence they collapsed, and I fell to my knees in a spasm of coughing. Roger pulled me up again and supported me until my lungs cleared and my legs gained strength enough to walk. And through it all, I could feel him shaking too.

We waded the last few yards to shore, and as we reached dry sand Roger noticed that he had dropped his mesh bag. At that reminder we looked down at my hands and saw I still carried the sunglasses, hat, and bucket of shells! Combined with being fully dressed and wearing tennis shoes, it was no wonder I didn't float. We laughed but there was a touch of hysteria to the laughter and both of us knew full well how close disaster had come.

I was relieved to learn the kids hadn't seen or heard a thing. After admiring their sandcastles, we walked back to the marina and once on board the *Halcyon*, I fell into my bunk and slept soundly for ten hours. I awoke to find every muscle in my body aching, and a black terror kept creeping in from odd corners of my mind. Brushing the feeling away, I looked around to see it was dark and the kids were asleep. With some effort, I ascended the ladder and found Roger sitting on the deck staring out at the water.

I walked over, sat down beside him, and tried to tell him how I felt. "You saved my life and I know that. If you hadn't been there, if you had given up .... I guess all I can say is, Thank you."

He looked at me a long time, then slowly a grin spread across his face and he said, "Isn't there an old Chinese proverb that says, When someone saves your life you are forever that person's slave?"

His teasing must have been what I needed because the tension suddenly disappeared from my body. I returned his light remark by saying, "Are you sure 'slave' is the word? And 'forever' isn't right either. I'm sure the debt is cancelled if the favor is ever returned."

Putting his arms around me, he laughed softly. "Okay, maybe it's not forever, but only until you save me from some great calamity. And it must be a big one, I won't settle for less."

Neither of us believed it at the time, but I would eventually get a chance to do just that.

CHAPTER 4: THE HORNBLOWERS LIVE!

A small cay in the Exuma chain of the Bahama Islands.

The islands that make up the Bahamas begin forty miles east of Florida and wander in a southeasterly direction for more than five hundred miles, almost to the coast of Haiti. Altogether there are over twenty-five hundred small cays and rock outcroppings, but only seven hundred can be called islands, and only ten percent of those are inhabited.

The islands or cays are laid out in groupings or chains and they stretch along large areas of shallow water called banks. The banks average twenty feet deep or less and are feeding and spawning grounds for vast varieties of marine life. In most areas the cays protect the Banks from the prevailing southeast winds and the ferocity of the open Atlantic Ocean. In cruising from island to island, it seemed logical that we could sail on the Atlantic side of the chains on the calmer days and choose the more protected waters of the banks on rougher weather days.

However, there were several problems to sailing the Bahamas. Newspapers had begun to publish reports of smugglers and hijackings in the Caribbean and the stories sounded frightening. But we felt that if we stayed together, we had less to fear from the bad guys. It was the natural elements that worried us more. For example, the wind direction always blew from the southeast. As the islands were situated southeast of Florida, we were sure to have a head-on wind for at least half of the trip, and that meant lots of fuel or lots of tacking back and forth.

Another concern was our charts. They showed a number of lights or beacons, but the great abundance of channel markers and hazard buoys found in our U.S. waters seemed to be totally lacking in the Bahamas. Navigation was obviously going to be done by sight, dead reckoning, instrument, and common sense if we were going to stay off the reefs and shoals.

And the Bahamas are very dry, with a severe shortage of fresh water. Rain or desalinization (the process of converting sea water to fresh) seemed to be the only source of supply for the natives. It looked like cooking, bathing, and doing laundry were going to be challenges for a while.

It was the last week in March and while the Fleet waited in the Keys, we took *Halcyon* to Miami for four days of provisioning. Our stay at Tollgate had given us the opportunity to save a little money and for the first time in many months I felt rich. But while I was busy making lists of the goodies I wanted to buy (carpeting being at the top), Roger went out and bought a Honda 70 motorbike.

Feeling completely disappointed, I watched as Roger and Ron loaded the bike onto the deck, covered it with plastic, and tied it down.

"Did we really need a motorbike?" I swallowed the lump and mentally tore the shopping lists to shreds.

"Just look at it as a car," Roger suggested, and began to carry more engine parts and pieces on board the boat.

"That's what you said about the dinghy."

"The dinghy's for reaching land, the motorbike is for shopping."

"Shopping for what? We just spent all our money on the bike!"

"Well, what do you want to buy? What else do we need?" His sincerity was even more annoying than his words.

"How about carpeting or anything that isn't greasy, smelly, and doesn't leak or need painting?" He gave me a look that told me he had no idea what I was talking about.

With our provisioning completed, we rendezvoused with the Fleet at Pumpkin Key. It was our jumping-off place to Bimini, which was less than ten hours away from the Keys by sail if we managed to maintain our course. Upon our arrival at the anchorage, Max had a surprise for us: a very cute gal had signed onto the *Minnie* as crew and Max was sporting a very bright twinkle in his eyes. He was obviously pleased with his good fortune.

Since no one among us was too sure of our prowess at maintaining an accurate course, we wanted to allow for sufficient daylight in case of navigation error. When we left Pumpkin Key, our plans were to arrive at Bimini Harbor by morning.

No member of our group had ever sailed more than ten miles offshore, and suddenly all were headed out into the notorious Gulf Stream in the dead of night! But no one was more afraid than Admiral Don. Roger and Hobie sensed his fear and stayed in radio contact with him, coaxing and encouraging him along, and when it looked as though Don might turn back, Hobie positioned the *Imagine* ahead of the *Talisman* and Roger trailed close behind to prevent his escape. The next day we learned it hadn't been necessary. Don's fear of the dark was so strong he'd decided it was safer to follow the lights of the other boats than to retreat.

The voyage determined how seaworthy we all were. Not very! All three kids developed seasickness, Ron and Janice for the first time. Tommy just stayed in his bunk and moaned.

I was nauseated as well, but soon forgot about throwing up. It took too much energy to pick up things that leapt off shelves and out of cupboards, to clean up the messes, to relieve Roger at the wheel, and to reassure the kids that we were fine even though I had my doubts.

Roger didn't get seasick at all. Not even woozy. He spent the entire crossing playing his role of Captain to the hilt: dashing between sail adjustments, navigation plotting, and compass readings. If he was as frightened as we were of the pitch-black night and the monster waves, he managed to hide it admirably.

The passage was not so bad. It was the fear of not knowing what *Halcyon* could do that had me in a turmoil. And in the black of night, the waves appeared to be much more ominous than they probably were.

Eventually the kids slept, but Roger didn't, and I couldn't, and by morning we were exhausted. The shout of "land ahoy" at 9 a.m. was as exciting as anything from those B movies I'd seen as a kid. What an accomplishment to find that our navigation had led us right to Bimini. We'd done it! It was the first real step; the U.S. was behind us! We had sailed to another country—who cared that it was only forty miles from Miami? We felt as proud as Armstrong when he stepped on the moon.

After waiting around the dock for an hour for the customs man to come and clear us into the Islands, Roger and I decided to go looking for him.

We found a door marked "Customs and Immigration" on the second floor of the only building around; the office had a window overlooking the harbor. A portly man in uniform looked up from his desk, yawned a greeting, nonchalantly stamped our passports, turned to the window and glanced out at the boat, stamped a few more papers, handed everything back, and returned to his work. As casual as that we were officially in the Bahamas.

All of the Fleet arrived within thirty minutes of one another. Don actually kissed the ground when he stepped off his boat.

Max seemed disgruntled. It was later that we heard the reason why. His new crew member had taken it upon herself to rearrange his cupboards while he steered. (The Tidy Housewife Syndrome—it's instinctive). During the crossing Max went looking for a particularly important chart and found dried onion soup instead. Later when he complained to me, he was understandably upset. And to help, I optimistically assured him that "a little bit of Paradise" would smooth things out. He didn't look convinced.

Oh, the water! What a delight! The Florida Keys had been surrounded by relatively clean water and seemed wonderful after three months in Biscayne Bay and on the Miami River. But the waters of the Bahamas far surpassed the Keys! We were in awe of the clarity and spectacular colors. To be able to stand on deck during slack tide and watch fish swim in and out of coral in twenty-five feet of water; to see the ocean teeming with tropical fish in rainbow colors so intense they glowed was, as Janice quipped, "Better than TV!"

Tommy discovered he could get the fish to swarm to the boat by the thousands if he sprinkled food off the stern. The fish liked grits best, and I had to quickly put a limit on the quantity of food I was willing to see tossed in the drink. After all, we had not provisioned for the whole ocean.

Snorkeling was instantly the favorite activity for most of the Fleet. We moved *Halcyon* from the dock to the anchorage, then everyone jumped in. Almost everyone. I put on my gear, descended the ladder, stuck the snorkel in my mouth, and stretched out to float. No sooner did my face touch the water then I was hyperventilating. The world closed in around me and that black feeling popped up from some dark region of my mind. It was exactly as though I were drowning again. In a flash, I was back on the deck and shaking with cold.

"Are you joining us?" Roger called.

"I think I'll follow you in the dinghy," I answered. "Someone might get tired and need a rest." Using the glass-bottomed bucket I viewed the underworld, but it wasn't the same. For a while it would have to do.

Another surprise were the Bahamians. How nice to have such a completely island-like people living so close to the U.S. Everyone we met on our stroll smiled and greeted us with a sing-song, "Hello, Mon."

We walked through the village, bought a loaf of the famous Bahama bread, and tore off pieces, sharing and eating as we went. We saw humble little cottages, but no poverty. We watched a weathered old fisherman stooping under a sea grape tree, cleaning his impressive catch. Fishing and tourism were the only industries of Bimini and obviously the natives did well enough.

We came upon a small pastel green house, supported on cement blocks a foot or more above the sandy yard. Encircling the house were flowerbeds bordered in bright pink conch shells that were far more colorful than the straggly, nondescript plants struggling for life in the sandy soil. Realizing the house was a store, we went inside to find a clothing shop in the front room and a miniscule, four-table restaurant in the rear. We chose a table, sat, and ordered conch fritters, our first of many. They were different and delicious, with an abalone taste. Ron and Tommy ate with relish; Janice declined.

As tired as everyone was, that night when the sounds of music reached the Fleet at anchor in the harbor, everyone had to go ashore and find the source.

When Max appeared in his "dancing duds" but without his crew member, I asked about her. "She doesn't like to dance!" he said with a scowl.

No one uttered a word, but we all wondered the same thing: how long would this relationship last?

The dance was held in an undersized thatched-roof pavilion. The entire population of the island was there as well as all the fleet and most of the other boaters. The lack of adequate floor space created intimacy, and the music was perfect for the surroundings—a tinge of calypso and a lot of soul. Roger and I danced to the great amusement of our children, who had never witnessed their parents acting so silly before.

Janice glowed when Roger asked her to dance; Ron and Tommy turned me down with looks that said, "You'll have to fight me first!"

The young men of the *GoldenGirl* discovered the golden-skinned girls, and Max had no trouble finding willing partners as he was easily the best dancer on the floor.

It was well past midnight when we rowed back to our boats with strains of "St James Infirmary Blues" floating out from the pavilion to follow us to bed. Bimini was indeed Paradise.

But not for everyone. When Roger, the kids, and I went ashore shopping the following afternoon, we met Max's crewmember for the last time. She was sitting sullenly on her suitcase at the end of the dock waiting for a ride to the Bimini airport. Her face showed a great deal of consternation while her fingers drummed away on her knee.

We stopped and chatted for a moment, then I wished her a safe trip home. As we walked away, I felt sorry for her. How was she to know that the main requirement for crewing with Max was not sailing, but dancing?

The experience brought about a change in Max. His dancing shoes went back into the locker and from then on, he expended all energies oiling his teak deck.

Our island-hopping began in earnest. Gun Cay provided the first glimpse of a deserted island and a shipwreck. We explored both thoroughly.

The government provided a huge cistern on the cay for the sole purpose of storing rainwater for the sailors and fishermen, and it was our first indication of the value of fresh water in the Bahamas. We filled our portable water jugs, then hiked over to explore the wreck on the beach. When I saw the great hull lying there, I felt queasy. The boat had been as long as the *Halcyon*; a wooden sloop with once-beautiful teak decks. The four-foot square, jagged hole gave testimony to the reason for the tragedy. I was reminded that none of us were stronger or smarter than the sea and one wrong move could easily put us up on the beach, or worse.

As I walked around the wreck, my toe touched something in the sand and I picked up a child's doll, one arm and one leg missing. Wondering about it and the unknown child, I shivered, then turned and looked at our three kids romping in the sand. Were we being foolish?

Roger and I began a practice that day that we continued for the rest of our travels. We salvaged at least one thing, a screw, a bolt, a piece of wood, from every wreck we found and used it on our boat.

Tom at the wheel

That night we anchored off the posh resort of Cat Cay and when we pulled to their dock to fuel, we found for the first time that sail-boaters were not very welcome.

It seemed there was a distinction between the two types of boats that navigated the Islands. One type was the very expensive, gas-consuming, high-speed power boat with air conditioning, wet bar, and piped-in music. Sailors referred to them as 'Motor Odors'.

The other type were the sailboats that used little gas, poked along at five or six miles an hour, had right of way over just about everybody, and were usually anchored out rather than tied to a dock. The Power Boaters called them "Stick Boats" or "Rag Pickers."

In other words, Motor Odors had money, and Rag Pickers didn't.

When we pulled to the Cat Cay dock to fuel, the people were not welcoming. Since their private development catered to the large motor cruisers from Florida, they seemed to resent our presence even to buy fuel.

To me it seemed sad, but soon we learned that in the Bahamas, Cat Cay was the exception. Elsewhere snobs are in the minority and we Rag Pickers were welcomed almost everywhere.

We left Cat Cay at daybreak, headed across the banks for the Berry Islands, and were out of sight of land for two days. With the banks being relatively shallow, we dropped anchor for the night in twenty feet of water in the middle of nowhere. We felt strange, exposed and very alone, with nothing on the horizon. Even though the night was dark, and the wind and waves pounded at our hull, we slept well. After all, if the anchor broke loose, we could drift until morning and still not hit anything.

Using the radio at dawn, Roger called each of the other boats to see how they had fared. All were accounted for and none the worse for wear. The *GoldenGirl* crew were the most chipper and eager to continue on, but Admiral Don growled at us and said he hadn't slept at all.

In early afternoon we crossed the north tip of the "Tongue of the Ocean," so called because the ocean cuts into the banks and creates a particularly deep area that is surrounded on three sides by the shallower waters of the banks. We watched as the depth went from twenty feet to over six thousand and the color change was spectacular. A light aquamarine marked the shallows, and the deep water turned a dark blue purple.

We stayed in Chub Cay several days longer than planned while everyone recuperated from what we suspected was seasickness. Most of the Fleet seemed to be affected—feeling tired, achy, and out of sorts. Some of us were even sure we were losing weight, but we rested, relaxed, and forgot about it. After all whatever it was would pass.

The conch (pronounced "conk"), is the beautiful, large, pink ocean shell known as the "hamburger of the Bahamas." The snail inside the shell can be eaten in at least thirty different ways and before our trip was over, we would have tried at least twenty-nine.

Our protected anchorage turned out to be a breeding ground for the prolific seafood and before I could find my recipe cards on cooking conch, the Fleet had gathered nearly a hundred of them. When I found the recipe, I was dismayed to see it start, "Take one pound of ground conch meat..."

The meat had to be removed from the shell, peeled, then cleaned. We soon learned there was a skill involved; unfortunately, the skill eluded us. It took three hours and sixteen people working diligently, on the beach, and on the stern of the *Halcyon*, before we were through.

The kids and I raised buckets of water to the deck and rinsed off the remarkably slimy mess created by the cleaning, then the Fleet all scrambled into their dinghies and headed for shore.

It was our first beach party. With sixteen people in our group, every get-together was a party, and well worth repeating, time and again. The custom grew to bring a dish, something to eat out of, something to eat with, something to drink from, and a drink to share.

Using a portable kerosene stove, we made conch fritters. Each boat donated its own secret sauce for dipping, and we feasted. Janice whined for hamburgers, and Admiral Don agreed with her that McDonald's was better than conch any day. But the rest willingly ate their share. Hobie played his banjo, we sang, told ghost stories, and Frank passed a cleaned-out ex bleach bottle filled with rum, Tang, and Kool-Aid.

The day after the party a sticky substance appeared on the deck and defied removal. I used every cleanser I could find and still it worsened. Sand from the beach stuck to it and the deck felt like #30 sandpaper. It took a lot of scrubbing before it dawned on us that the goo was coming from the conch that were cleaned on the deck. They gave off a juice that put Elmer's glue to shame. A new edict was issued from the First Mate: "All conch will henceforth be cleaned on shore!"

Chub Cay was the southernmost of one of the chains known as the Berry Islands. To take advantage of the winds, the Fleet voted and elected to do one northerly run and spend a few days at Alder Cay, midway up the same chain.

With the wind on our stern quarter the sailing experience went as smoothly as flying. Tommy turned green and went to bed but the rest of us lounged on deck, and as each of the five hours passed, we relaxed a little more and allowed *Halcyon* to take over. She moved so smoothly, and we knew how much she was enjoying the sail when she began to hum in a high soprano from her rigging.

Our charts led us into a channel between two low, sparsely covered cays, Little Harbor on the north and Alder on the south. Alder had a small, protected cove and we inched our way in. With me on the bowsprit and Ron in the ratlines, both of us pointed out the sandbars and coral heads to Roger at the wheel. As we dropped anchor a few dozen yards from the *Lucky Lou*, I looked around. The *Minnie* and the *Imagine* were coming in behind us, and the others in the Fleet had anchored ahead of us. Otherwise, no other boat was there. We had the cove all to ourselves.

The anchorage was only a third of a mile across at its widest point. White beaches and sea grape trees ringed the emerald green, still water and, as the last boat shut down its motor, a total stillness floated out over us. We had entered a world that I did not believe existed. A world of no cars, nor motors, crowds, phones, or horns. A world of no noise. It was so peaceful we stayed a week.

Conch were everywhere. We ate them fresh (either fried or raw); dried and used them later for bait; or put holes in the shells, ran a string through the holes and hung them over the side of the boat, to walk around

The Fleet at anchor somewhere in the Exumas

on the bottom until needed. We went fishing every day in the dinghy but caught nothing. Then, in despair, we began leaving a line out at night, and twice woke up to find a nice red snapper on the hook.

Kathy from the *Lucky Lou* discovered that the green succulent plants growing along the shore were a nice substitute for celery in tuna salad, and the red fruit that grew on cactus was delicious mixed with honey and lime juice and eaten on pancakes. We all felt like Robinson Crusoes and each of us took great pleasure in discovering something new to share with the others. It was no small surprise when Janice began to enjoy the new foods, too.

On our third afternoon at Alder Cay, we motored over to meet the one inhabitant on Little Harbor Cay, Arthur Smith. A fisherman, he caught and dried fish and conch, and once a month took them into Nassau to the market. A very quiet, sincerely friendly man, he showed us how to salt and dry fish, how to clean conch (correctly), and even invited us to move into one of the long-deserted houses on the island. It was tempting and he was such a serenely happy man, I felt sure his lifestyle was one I could adapt to. It was a surprising discovery to me how appealing solitude could be.

Sailing Against the Wind – Toni Larson 68

On the fourth day, a storm set in, but it didn't matter. The waters of our cove were too protected to notice, and it only gave us an excuse to stay longer. I had an ample supply of peanut butter on hand and when the calmer afternoon winds allowed, the kids were more than happy to leave Roger and I on the boat and go ashore to explore on their own.

Schoolwork filled many hours. The boys struggled with spelling and Janice her multiplication tables, but everyone improved when I thought to reward them with raisins for each correct answer. They played a form of Scrabble that Tommy created. At least he was imaginative. After making up a word (complete with definition), he would then convince Janice that the word existed. Janice's vocabulary increased by leaps and bounds with words like sturkz, frimich, and glert. Ron avoided the games and either swam or read.

Max oiled his teak from dawn to dusk; Don worried about sharks, sinking, smugglers, hurricanes, and what would he eat when the canned stew ran out. Madeline, Emogene, Kathy, and I swapped books and recipes over coffee, very much like any neighborhood back in suburbia.

Frank, Roger, Hobie and the crew of the *GoldenGirl* got together, designed, then made a half dozen Hawaiian slings. They were crude spears, propelled from slingshots made of wood and strips of rubber. And with the slings the Fleet began to spear fish. The first few were small but we cooked them anyway, and before long the hunters were bringing in large groupers, grunts, porgies, and redfish. And even though we were eating well, we were still strangely losing weight.

Evenings melted away into a continuous string of beach parties or gatherings on the *Halcyon* deck, and the revelry received a boost from the bleach bottle. Each boat brought its own to the affair and a competition arose to guess the contents. Competition demanded a palate as sensitive as any wine tasters in the vineyards of France. As rum and orange juice diminished, vodka and lime juice, or grapefruit Tang were substituted. When those ran out, a bottle of wine, or some powdered fruit drink would turn the concoction pink. Once Roger added a can of pineapple juice to ours, but the powdered grape juice made the concoction less than appetizing. Happily, no one suffered from hangovers since alcohol was scarcer than drink mixes and water. Besides, Hobie kept reminding us we needed the fruit juice to prevent scurvy. It must have worked—not one case of scurvy was reported by anyone.

As the Fleet pulled anchor and headed south for Nassau, I looked back at the two tiny cays that had been our home for a week. There was no doubt any longer, cruising was fun.

We tried to sail into the wind for three hours, tacking back and forth and cutting the angle as closely as possible. Then Roger took a fix, examined the charts, and raged in total exasperation, "We are losing ground!"

The sails came down, the motor went on, and for the rest of the day we listened to the dull roar from *Halcyon*'s depths as we motored our way south. I could tell by her groans she didn't like the intrusion of noise and vibration any more than I did.

Nassau was the most populated town in the Bahamas, but still it maintained a relaxed island atmosphere throughout the bustling town. The architecture incorporated the French, Spanish, and Victorian English of its heritage; the streets were clean; the people were friendly and uncommonly happy.

After anchoring off the Sheraton Colonial Hotel with the whole marketplace and downtown as our landscape, some of the Bahamian children from the beaches ventured out to the boat and used our anchor line to rest for a while. Our three kids willingly showed them the boat, visited with them, and seemingly experienced no language or cultural barrier. As a matter of fact, Janice discovered she had a natural ear, and before long she was imitating the accent perfectly.

Sightseeing and shopping were our diversions. We had a lot of restocking to do, and to our dismay, we found food, as well as everything else, to be expensive even in the open-air market. But fruit remained a bargain and we bought all we could carry, including a stalk of bananas that we hung from the end of the mizzen boom.

The severe shortage of water, as well as having a limited supply on board, tested our ingenuity. Learning to cook with sea water whenever possible had been a challenge, now we did all our bathing off the side of the boat and even had to eliminate our fresh-water rinses. The kids dove in each morning and swam several laps around *Halcyon*, then climbed back on deck so I could pour shampoo over them. They scrubbed hair, ears, etc., then dove in and rinsed. But, if we toweled completely dry, there was no salt residue, and our hair and skin grew soft and silky.

My fear of the water led to some decidedly interesting baths. For a while I sat on deck and soaped, then hauled up buckets of water to rinse. But shampoo always filled my eyes at the very moment the bucket ran dry. Next, I tried plugging the cockpit drain, then spent an exhausting length of time hauling up enough water to fill the 4 X 4 X 2-foot space. That worked well at night when I had darkness to shield me and allow me a "bath in the buff." But then it was too dark to shave my legs. And hauling up water was work!

Necessity being the mother of invention, I took the horseshoe life ring and tied four long strings at intervals around it. On the end of the strings, I tied a bottle of shampoo, a bar of soap, a washcloth, and my razor. Then, when everyone jumped in for their daily baths, I buckled on the life ring and, with paraphernalia dangling about my legs, joined them. Roger and the kids laughed at my contraption, but when I needed something, I simply pulled on the appropriate string.

Laundry was something else. Clothes washed in salt water never dry, so we learned to catch rainwater. As clouds formed we would: collect all pots, pans, and buckets; put up the awning to trap the water; clean out the dinghy; put on swimsuits; collect shampoo, soap, and towels; then wait for a downpour. When the first drops fell, we would soap up good, then dash about the deck collecting water, replenishing our tanks, and as we worked, the rain would wash the soap off—sometimes. As often as not, the rain stopped before the soap was gone.

Laundry day on Halcyon

Once the tanks were full, we saved water for the laundry by filling the dinghy, cockpit, portable ice chests, and anything else we could find, and by then, we were blue from the cold, eyes red from the soap, and all dead tired. As soon as the weather cleared, we started the wash. It took a quarter of a box of soap and an equal amount of bleach to turn the dinghy into a washing machine. Roger (with all the dirty clothes) would climb into the dinghy and stomp back and forth over the laundry, doing a fair imitation of the little winemaker. He also did a lot of grumbling, which led me to believe his fantasy of "The Great Sea Captain" did not include doing laundry.

Once clean, Roger would pass each piece of laundry back to the kids and me to be rinsed in the ice chest, wrung out, then hung in the rigging. After a good rain, we could literally cover the boat with flapping sheets, towels, and underwear.

One such time, after we had all the laundry hung to dry gently in the breeze, I took a book up on deck to rest for a while. First people came out of the hotel and snapped pictures. Then little boats circled us and took pictures. And finally, one of the great cruise ships from Miami arrived in the harbor, complete with one thousand eager tourists all hanging over the sides of the ship with their movie cameras ready to get that keepsake picture of the exotic port of Nassau. But they totally ignored the quaint town, colorful fishing boats, and spectacular beaches lined with coconut trees. Where were their cameras pointed? At our laundry!

We spent three weeks in Nassau when we'd originally planned only three days. First the *GoldenGirl* had motor trouble, which took time to repair. Others in the Fleet were waiting for mail to be forwarded and the Bahama Post Office was as casual as everything else on the island. But we were determined to stay together as long as possible, so we all waited. And partied, swam, went sightseeing, fished, studied schoolwork, and relaxed some more.

The *GoldenGirl* crew gave a chili dinner for Roger and me on our thirteenth wedding anniversary, and the Fleet joined us later on the *Halcyon* for cake, popcorn, and rum.

As we gorged on the high-calorie junk food, Hobie commented that, no matter how much he put away in a day, and it was considerable, he seemed to be losing weight.

We polled the group and found that, except for the kids, all of us had lost pounds.

Roger said, "I can't keep my cut-offs up without a belt, anymore."

"I'm sure we have some strange parasite and we're all wasting away, and we just don't know it," Admiral Don worried. "One of these mornings I'm going to wake up and be gone!

No one took Don seriously, but we discussed the situation further, comparing notes. With our initial two weeks in the islands most of us had suffered from aching muscles, but the aches soon sub- sided and then disappeared completely. At the same time, we'd suffered some stomach upsets that seemed to vanish as soon as we had our first swim, or breath of fresh morning air. Seasickness? Maybe, but why the aching?

The next impulse was to blame the water, but we discounted that. Rainwater had been our only supply and we were all purifying our tanks with an assortment of methods. Food? But Don wouldn't eat conch or anything else that did not come from a can. Some of us did not drink rum. The kids were not sharing the bleach bottle cocktails and they were eating essentially the same as the rest, but not one of them showed any of the same symptoms.

What were we doing that was different? Swimming had increased for some but not others. Hiking and beachcombing? But we all had been active at Tollgate. Except for Hobie. Then it hit us. We were anchoring. Every night! A boat tied to a dock is relatively stationary, especially after dark when other boats ceased moving around and making wakes. But a boat at anchor moves constantly, shifting with the tides, currents, wind, and every movement on board. Usually, the motion is so slight as to be unnoticeable but, at other times, in ocean-exposed areas, pillows had even been necessary to keep us from rolling around in our sleep. We were actually exercising twenty-four hours a day!

I thought back to the years of wonder diets, then looked at my new figure. What a perfectly painless way to lose middle-aged spread, secretary's seat, beer bellies, and housewife's pudgies.

"What a wonderful anniversary present!" I said. "Pass the cake!"

After everyone had gone, Roger and I took our mattresses up on deck and made a bed under the stars. For a rare moment the water was calm, and the other boats appeared to be suspended in mid-air, their shadows floating across the sand below. Not even a ripple disturbed the view of the bottom, ten feet beneath our keel.

The lights from the town and the moonlight were enough to see by; somewhere on the beach a band played the island rhythms that are surprisingly listenable considering the crudeness of the instruments— whistles, bamboo sticks, and plastic milk jugs full of dried beans.

"All anniversaries should be like this," I sighed.

"I agree," said Roger. "Now I'd like to explore that new figure of yours more closely. Do you suppose the kids would like to row ashore and build some sandcastles?" He put his arm around me.

"In the middle of the night?"

"Well, it was a thought," he said.

CHAPTER 5: LAGNIAPPE MEANS "SOMETHING EXTRA"

We struck out at dawn for a day's run to the Exuma chain of islands. Once more we were motoring into a head-on wind, and more and more, I detested the sound of that engine. A boat under sail was a most peaceful, relaxing way to travel. A sailboat under motor was like riding a drunk horse. The motion was unnatural and upsetting and the smell of the engine kept both Tommy and me on the verge of seasickness the whole way.

Roger, Ron, and Janice manned the wheel, and to my delight, they all proved they could hold a compass course better than I could. I was especially grateful for their skills as I curled up across from Tommy, and together we slept our way to the Exumas.

Allen and Leaf Cays, situated side by side, form a perfect harbor. Allen is completely uninhabited, but Leaf Cay is well populated...with iguanas. For years the great lizards had been a source of food to the islanders but, by the time we arrived, they were on the verge of extinction. Leaf was the only cay left in the Bahamas with any of the prehistoric creatures and the government had declared them a protected species. They were tame enough that, when we picnicked, they came close to accept our offerings of oranges and popcorn. The kids were fascinated, and I never remembered them sitting so quietly before, as they waited patiently for one of the iguanas to approach an outstretched hand. (It would be two years later, and miles away, that we would meet a sailor who had been to the Exumas. We listened to him brag of catching some of those lizards and cooking them just to see how they tasted. "Awful," the man said. "I threw most of the meat away!" The world may be full of such insensitive, uncaring people, but if there is a future for any of us, they need to become more extinct than the lizards.)

When we motored into the cove we were met by a fierce, outgoing tide. Ron and I dropped the anchors, one from the bow, the other from the stern. Then we pulled both lines through one chock in the bow. Clearly one of us failed to secure the forward anchor, and while we were below eating dinner the line began to slip. The sudden shift in the boat alerted us, but by the time we reached the bow, there was barely enough line left to make a loop around the stanchion post.

In the process of "losing line" the boat turned sideways, and the keel snagged on the rear anchor line. Suddenly, and dangerously, we found ourselves suspended sideways to the tide. The force against the hull was immense. The anchor lines hummed with the force of the rushing water, and *Halcyon* quivered nervously. We couldn't move her at all; if we started the

Sailing Against the Wind – Toni Larson   74

engine, we would surely snarl the propeller. Our only chance was to wait until morning when the tide slackened, then re-anchor.

For the night, however, we would have to take turns sitting up and watching to make sure that one of the anchors did not give or break loose under the pressure and put us up on the rocks.

Anchor watch came for me at 3 a.m. The tide had slowed to a faint ripple and the weather was perfectly calm. My turn was going to be a cinch.

I took a book, a cup of coffee, and the searchlight then went up on deck to relieve Roger and wait for the sun to come up. After he went to bed, I had the quiet night all to myself.

With no moon, the stars were cold and gave little light in a harbor wrapped in black velvet. At eye level, I could barely discern the rail of our boat, and I postponed turning on the deck light for a while; I wanted to savor the aloneness. The gentle swishing noise the waves made on the beach came to me clearly from the port side, just a few dozen yards away. The occasional splash of a flying fish hitting the water rang like a shot in the still night.

I turned on the deck light mounted over the Captain's seat and sat down to read. In moments a strange, new sound reached me and I glanced in the direction of the other boats in the Fleet. There were no lights. I peeked at my watch and noticed it was 3:30 a.m. too early for anyone to be awake.

But the noise hadn't come from there anyway; it had come from the starboard side near the entrance to the cove. I listened closely then heard it again. There were voices singing! I could almost make out the words to the song. By the volume there had to be more than two or three people, and as the sound grew closer, I was sure they were singing a hymn.

Turning on the spotlight, I scanned the harbor entrance but saw nothing, and with the sudden glare of my light, the singing stopped completely. I switched off the light, sat down, and felt somewhat silly and also a bit uneasy. It had to be my imagination. Shrugging it off, I started to read again when I heard something else like the sound of the waves on the beach, but not quite the same. This time I switched off the deck light, walked to the handrail, stared hard into the darkness, and listened. There it was again, and I knew that it was the sound of oars dipping in the water; rhythmic and steady and getting closer and louder.

I dove for the searchlight and held it ready, but my hand was shaking, and my heart was pounding. I waited, peering intently into the dark, but it was useless. My eyes wouldn't adjust. And even though I couldn't see, I could hear the noise of the rowing of the boat, or whatever. And it was close; if I wanted to see it, all I had to do was push the switch on the light. But I couldn't. For some reason I didn't want to!

The light hit the deck with a crash, and I was down the companionway in an instant, shaking Roger awake. Reluctantly he came up on deck and listened, nothing. He played the spotlight all around the cove,

Sailing Against the Wind – Toni Larson   75

nothing. We talked about the possibility that the sound had been fishermen. But if there were fishermen out there, where were they now, and where did they come from in a rowboat, miles from any inhabited island? Roger was skeptical and it annoyed me, but I couldn't blame him as there simply was nothing there.

That was my only ghost. I'd never experienced one before, and never did again, but I was utterly convinced that I had that night. So, who needed to fear smugglers and hijackers if there were hymn singing spirits floating about?

About 6 a.m. we re-anchored the boat and got some sleep. When we woke the second time, the kids made me tell them about "my ghost," again and again. At least they believed me.

Roger and Ron found many chances to use the newly made spears for fishing and we enjoyed a fresh supply of protein each morning. Breakfast became "grunts and grits"; lunch was often conch fritters or chowder; dinner was sometimes lobster or dried, salted fish. Like the natives I collected sea salt along the coral beaches to use for drying our surplus. By cutting slits in the sides of the fish, packing them with salt, then hanging them in the ratlines to dry, they would keep for months. To cook the fish, I soaked one overnight, then drained the water, boiled it, and drained it again. By then the meat flaked easily off the bone. After mixing the meat with eggs, chopped onions, and celery, then rolling the mixture in breadcrumbs, we had codfish-like cakes. Deep fried and served with lemon, we could eat them almost daily. They were that good!

I started making fish stew that I kept in a pressure cooker on the stove—for two months! I re-boiled it each day (sometimes twice daily) to keep it from spoiling. Every time we had an overabundance of fish or conch, I added it to the stew. It was delicious and different—Campbell would have been envious.

By then we had gone a month without refrigeration and had lost very little food. I was surprised at how well I could adapt to no modern conveniences and was more than a little proud of my successes.

Most certainly I missed the frozen, canned, prepackaged, precooked luxuries of that "other world" and at times I even craved something cold, anything cold—water, tea, beer, or lemonade. There were nights I dreamed about ice cubes. My game was believing I could always go back to civilization, but for now, I would pretend I was a pioneer woman feeding my pioneer family.

On the way to Saddle Cay the Fleet trolled for dolphin, each using his or her own favorite feather for a lure. The kids were relieved to learn that the Atlantic dolphin, (or Dorado) was not a porpoise but a fish and in no way resembled Flipper. We all soon discovered it was a sportfish worth catching. One weighing twenty-five to thirty pounds was a terrific fighter and could take up to thirty minutes to bring aboard the boat. Janice received the thrill of her life when she caught the first. We raised the fleet on the radio to brag, then learned that between the six boats we had seven dolphin— two hundred pounds of fish!

Sea Coral gets the first Bite

It was an exceptional beach party that night. Before dinner Janice rowed over to join Madeline on the *Talisman* where the two of them cooked up coconut pies, and officially became the Fleet's Gourmet Pastry Chefs. Madeline also whipped up a teriyaki sauce for sharing, and Hobie prepared his famous curry. It was a smorgasbord not to be missed.

After dinner Admiral Don passed his jug around, and we each described the landing of our fish and talked about the ones that got away. In addition to our fish, we bragged about our cat Sea Coral. She was also beginning to learn the thrill of the catch. At the moment a dolphin struck the line, the reel let out a loud buzzing which brought Sea Coral running from wherever on the boat she had been catnapping. She dashed to the side of the boat and looked over into the water. Of course, the fish was a thousand yards behind the boat, but she stayed there at the side, looking straight down. The moment she spotted the flashing blue and green fish, her ears perked up, her tail twitched, and her eyes never strayed from the approaching feast. We very nearly kicked her overboard in the excitement of landing the monster, but she held her footing and was rewarded with the first bite from its tail.

Norman's Cay was a private development owned by some absentee Americans. At the time of our arrival, we found dozens of unsold lots, a fancy clubhouse and marina, and a few islanders who cared for the property.

When we fueled up at the marina, I discovered another way to do laundry. After asking the dockmaster if we could use the shower, I divided the dirty laundry into five piles, wrapped them in towels, and gave each of us a bundle. In the showers we spread the clothes out on the floor, sprinkled them with soap, and stomped while we bathed. By the time we were clean, the clothes were too. But we did look peculiar as we walked back down the dock, laden with dripping-wet bundles.

Janice's eleventh birthday was celebrated with a cake baked by Madeline and a barbecued dolphin dinner prepared by Frank and Kathy. I gave her a pocket-sized rag doll I'd been sewing for weeks while she was swimming, visiting the other boats, or sleeping, and she was utterly surprised that I had been able to make it without her seeing me.

The *GoldenGirl* guys made her a shell necklace and a card that read, "To someone who is fast becoming the prettiest shell on the beach instead of the toughest conch in the harbor." And Tommy let her win five games of Monopoly in a row!

It was a happy day for us but the next one was mournfully sad. We had to say our
"farewells" to the *GoldenGirl*. We had known the boys since January and the boats from Michigan had teamed up with them the November before, but now they were returning to New York to go back to school or to work. Their engine had given them so much trouble, they felt it would be wise not to venture any further south.

The bon voyage party began at noon. We toasted them, each other, their trip home, our trip to wherever, our friendship, the Fleet, and the fact that the Fleet had been a family.

Hobie brought out his banjo for the occasion and we sang sailing chanties. The more we toasted, and the more we sang, the more tearful the farewell became. Madeline cried, Emogene presented them with some of her bread, but the unhappiest of all was Admiral Don, who was naturally the most emotional of the Fleet. Don gave them all his fatherly advice and, as the *GoldenGirl* sailed out of the harbor, he called them on the radio every five minutes for an hour begging them to turn around and come back. For a while I thought Don would leave with them, but he was not ready to re-cross the Gulf Stream, yet.

Norman Cay's water supply was brackish, and we hadn't taken on fresh in days. The islanders informed us that neighboring Shroud Cay had some fresh water natural wells, so we told the Fleet we'd meet them at a spot beyond Shroud and took off alone.

Tommy and Janice were fidgety and cranky all morning. Schoolwork was reduced to a miserable chore and, by the time we were underway, everyone was in a foul mood. Then Roger hit on the perfect solution for bored children.

We slowed the boat to a crawl and pulled the dinghy alongside. The kids, wearing sunhats and carrying a police whistle, climbed into the dinghy and we let the towline out its full length of one hundred feet. I sat and watched them while Roger steered the boat slowly toward Shroud Cay and for the next hour there was complete quiet aboard the *Halcyon*. Judging by the animated way the kids were laughing and talking, they enjoyed it too.

After anchoring for the night, we set out the following morning to find the wells on the deserted island. Hiking inland on a footpath through sea grape and thatch palm trees, we came upon sizeable coral formations pockmarked with several deep holes—all filled with trapped rainwater. The water was crystal clear, ice cold and we couldn't have been happier if we had found gold.

We filled our tanks by carrying the water in jugs to the dinghy then rowing to the boat. With so much free water, it seemed a waste not to take advantage of it and wash the linens and towels that hadn't been done since Nassau. We set up an assembly line on the beach complete with dinghy full of soapsuds and a plumber's friend to agitate the clothes. There was no shade, the day turned out to be
the hottest of the year, and after two hours on Shroud Cay of hauling water and washing clothes, we were utterly spent. Back on the boat we hung the clean clothes in the rigging and the kids swam around the boat while Roger and I lay down in our bunks, trying to cool off.

From his side, Roger said wearily, "For once a swim doesn't sound good enough. I'd rather have a bath. An ice cold, freshwater bath."

I leaped out of my bunk, grabbed him by the arm and shouted, "Well, what are you waiting for?"

We left the kids playing happily in the sand while we hiked once more, back to the wells. Stripping off all our clothes, we proceeded to pour buckets of ice-cold water over each other's heads, then we squealed and giggled, and scared all the birds and curly tailed lizards with our commotion.

The Fleet met us in the north harbor of Warderick Wells, and all went ashore for a day of exploring. The cay was riddled with caves, blowholes, interesting coral formations, and the waves surging through the blowholes were probably why the island was said to be haunted. Ron suggested that my ghosts may have come from there.

It was a fun day as we wore out our tennis shoes on the sharp coral, and I could see we should have brought a dozen pairs apiece. Roger found a giant fish net snared in the coral, and he and Hobie thought it perfect for making hammocks. They cut the net in half, and each took one piece. Roger spent the better part of the afternoon making sure his hammock was symmetrical, securely tied, and pleasing to look at. Hobie cut out a big chunk, tied a knot at each end, strung it between two palm trees, then stretched out in it sipping rum and grapefruit juice while he watched Roger work on his.

I couldn't help but remember the day we had all sailed into Bimini Harbor. The crew on the *Halcyon* had spent an hour before docking, scrubbing the deck, putting away gear, tying the sails, and generally making the boat ship shape. But when Hobie and Emogene pulled in alongside, their sails were strewn all over the deck, and jugs, jackets, lines, laundry, cat, and crew were comfortably spread about as well. After noticing how carefully we had cleaned up, Hobie remarked, "I never bother with all that 'ship shape' stuff. Whenever anyone comes along, I simply tell him, 'Phew, you should've seen the storm we just came through!'

Hobie knew what cruising was about before he ever bought the boat. But I also noticed that Emogene was developing a very deep frown line in her forehead.

The men went spearing and came back with a dozen fish, mostly groupers and grunts. Also, they had one lobster that weighed over ten pounds and was as long as Tommy from tentacles to tail.

The Fleet ate lobster dinner on the *Halcyon,* complete with three kinds of homemade bread. Everyone had begun baking their own by then. Emogene started us by making a fried bread that was so good the entire Fleet found cause to hang around the *Imagine* during baking time. It was even good enough to pull Max away from his teak oil.

We each had a favorite bread baking technique. I baked mine in a heavy pot set atop a tin coffee can that had been cut in half, then placed over the burner of the stove. As provisions disappeared, the breads became more interesting: wheat germ, oatmeal, cornmeal, honey, eggless, salt water, and potato breads. The kids took turns kneading, everyone helped eat it, and soon, the smells of baking yeast dough were emanating from every boat in the Fleet.

Even though we were still feasting, we were also fast running out of things like flour, oil, sugar, and GRITS! And what was a breakfast without grits? We would have to make Georgetown soon, or fish would be our only food.

We anchored in a treacherously rough spot known as Conch Cut, and the surge from the open ocean curled around the miniature island and kept us rocking awake all night.

Emogene & CK

Groggily I climbed out of bed the next morning to shouts from the kids that Sea Coral was finally having her kittens. It had been common knowledge that she was pregnant, but the mystery remained as to the father. I was sure C.K. was responsible and had a bet with Hobie, who was just as sure that C.K. was a virgin. We were both about to find out the truth.

Turning on the radio, we informed the fleet of the big event and it wasn't long before everyone was sitting in our cabin to watch. At 11 a.m. a male kitten appeared, and there was no mistaking who the father was. We named the tiger-striped kitten, Hobie Cat, brought out the jug to toast its arrival, and Hobie paid up.

Sailing Against the Wind – Toni Larson

As the drama of the birth of kittens picked up, so did the surge in the anchorage. All twelve of us sitting in such tight quarters, as well as the birth itself, and possibly the combination of flavors in the jug going around the cabin, soon took its toll on Admiral Don. First, he turned an unattractive shade of green, then before the arrival of another kitten, he bolted for fresh air on the deck.

There were four kittens, two males and two females. Hobie Cat was the largest; then Chick Charney, who was named after a mischievous Bahamian elf that the islanders blamed for everything that went wrong (sort of the Island Murphy), Seaweed was third; and Periwinkle last.

We officially declared the day a holiday with no school and no traveling. The kids were content to just lie on the floor next to Sea Coral's box and watch the kittens while the rest of the Fleet took their dinghies and went exploring the cay.

Late in the afternoon it rained, and the surge of waves worsened. The boats commenced rocking and, when the wind switched around, it left our sterns aimed dangerously at the rocky shore. Roger went up on deck to let out more anchor line, hoping to ease the bucking of the boat. When we swung around on the longer line, we unexpectedly crossed the *Talisman's* line and drug their anchor loose. Don saw it happen and tried to start his engine but managed to only coil his line in the propeller. The *Talisman* began drifting back into the *Minnie.*

We could see Don pacing back and forth on the deck and once heard him shout at Madeline, "Bring up the life vests, Maddie! This motherless excuse for a sea vessel is finally going to the bottom!"

Roger and Max acted quickly, diving into the water and heading for the *Talisman.* Between them they unsnarled the anchor lines and reset the *Talisman's* anchor.

Amid the excitement, *Imagine's* dinghy broke loose and started bouncing out to sea. Through the blinding rain, Janice spotted it and called the *Imagine* on the radio. Hobie, moving faster than I'd ever seen him, pulled anchor and tore off after the runaway little boat.

Twenty minutes later the *Imagine* returned with dinghy in tow, and that night everyone maintained watches to make sure the anchors did not slip again. By morning the storm was gone. Hobie gave Janice a big hug and a cardboard medal and we all agreed it was frightening how one miscalculation could set off a whole series of mishaps.

We motored all the way to Staniel Cay, and as soon as we prepared to anchor, a second catastrophe hit. With Roger at the wheel and me standing on the bow waiting to drop the anchor, he slowed the motor, put it into reverse and we heard a horrendous wrenching noise. Back into forward, but no forward! I threw the anchor; the boat was moving too fast, and we had to get it stopped before we hit something. Grabbing for the end of the line I did one wrap around the stanchion post and hung on for dear life. The boat drug the line through my hands anyway, and I was holding nothing more than the bitter end when *Halcyon* whipped her bow around like a bulldogged calf. Fearing something would snap, I held my breath, but everything held.

As I snubbed off the line, Roger shut down the motor and checked. There was water in the transmission fluid! He reported that it looked serious, then went ashore in the dinghy to find out if the little community had a mechanic. When he returned, I asked, "Any luck?"

"There is a diesel mechanic that lives here but he is in Nassau for the next three days. We'll just have to wait for him to get back."

"What do you think is the problem?"

"I hate to say this, but I think we just lost our transmission."

"That sounds expensive," I moaned. Wasn't everything expensive that went on a boat? And especially on *Halcyon*.

"To put a new transmission on her here is certain to cost a thousand dollars or more."

"A THOUSAND DOLLARS! No way!" My mind couldn't even fathom it. "Roger, we don't have it unless we don't eat, use any fuel, get sick, or break anything else." This was one time *Halcyon* wasn't going to get all our money.

"We can sail her home," Roger said, and his voice certainly sounded depressed.

"Then what?"

"We could go to work, seriously work, both of us, or we could sell her." Then he turned and went up on deck to sit by himself.

I walked forward, climbed into my bunk, and looked out at the water. I could see three or four little islands off in the distance. A fisherman came by in a small Bahamian sloop. I heard him call a friendly welcome to Roger and the kids on the deck.

Roger was not the only one to experience depression. Just as I was feeling more secure about the boat, her capabilities, and being more at home in her cramped quarters, she had to go and do this! Here we were miles from a home port, and with little money, but somehow it was more than that. I simply did not want the trip to end. Not yet, not like this! I was finally beginning to understand the true meaning of *Halcyon's* name.

Staniel Cay was a tiny island with one community of approximately seventy-five Bahamians, plus two English families (one was the mechanic). The town had two stores, two bars, two restaurants, and one church.

We visited one of the churches on Sunday and discovered more about the Islanders in an hour than in possibly all the other weeks we'd been in the islands.

The parishioners appeared to be very fundamental and devout in their religion, stern with their children, and Victorian in their lifestyle. And with only three in the choir that day, Janice was accurate when she said, "Those three people sound like twenty!"

Ron, Janice, Tom & Toni dressed for church

An unsmiling, elderly man sat in the front row, swinging a switch, and when any of the children failed to behave, he turned and waved it menacingly at them. Everyone was expected to sing, and his piercing eyes kept close watch to make sure we all did our share. Halfway through a hymn, the man rose, walked down the aisle, and flicked one young lad on the head with the switch. There was no doubt, he meant business. After that, we all sang—even Ron and Roger. And Tommy sat still!

At the end of a stirring "Hellfire and Brimstone" service, the entire congregation stood, and single file walked over to our seats to shake our hands, even the youngest child. They knew who we were and about our motor trouble. Then each one wished us well as they walked away.

As worried as we were about the boat, the support we received from the Fleet made it easier. In so many ways we were learning the value of being together with others like ourselves instead of cruising for the first time on our own. During our depressing wait for the mechanic, each Fleet member made a daily visit to the *Halcyon* to cheer us up. And by the time the mechanic returned, we were prepared for the worst.

But he diagnosed the problem, told us we needed a new heat exchanger, and said it would cost one hundred dollars for the part and installation. Undoubtedly, he thought we were crazy when we began laughing and thanking him as though he had just told us we'd won the Irish Sweepstakes.

Then the problem became, how to get a heat exchanger for a sailboat in the Out Islands of the Bahamas? The dock master told us about a friend that was arriving from the States within a week. We radioed the friend and convinced him to bring a heat exchanger with him, then we waited some more.

It was a lazy, warm, morning when Roger talked me into exploring a nearby, underwater cave with him and the kids. The cave was a mile from Staniel Cay, the location where part of the James Bond movie "Thunderball" was filmed. The cave was situated in the hollow center of an inconspicuous coral outcropping, and only partly underwater. From the outside the miniature cay sat by itself, looking like an upside-down bowl floating on the ocean. The inside was completely carved out by the ocean currents, and the only way into it was to dive under a ledge, then surface on the inside. I made the excursion only once. I really didn't relish the thought of swimming under that ledge, but I put on a ski belt and life jacket, and Roger pulled me while Ron pushed. The effort was worth it. When we emerged on the inside, I looked around and gaped in wonder. The cave was a masterpiece of beauty.

There were holes in the rock ceiling that allowed sunlight to filter in and light up the wondrously clear pool of water which teemed with every kind of tropical fish. The effect was that of a theater. Silent except for an occasional drip of water, with shafts of light spilling down to spotlight the ballet of colorful fish gliding back and forth in the pool below. The effect was so complete that even the kids were quiet as they sat in the unreal cathedral setting.

We rested for a long time on the ledge our feet dangling in the water while I wondered, *How old? How long had it been here? How had it been formed?*

Receiving word that the weekly seaplane was due, we dinghied ashore to meet the dock master's friend. Upon arrival we discovered he'd forgotten the part! But he assured us his wife would be joining him the following week and he would ask her to bring it then.

We waited some more. The kids kept up with their schoolwork, and in their free time Tommy and Janice played checkers. Janice was determined to find a game that would give her a fighting chance with him. But every time she got close to winning, he would accidently hit the board and dump all the playing pieces.

Roger and Ron spent more hours together, spearing and swimming. Ron had become the best swimmer of all of us and he should have been, he was willing to practice ten hours a day.

During one spearing expedition, Ron incurred Roger's wrath. When I found Ron in tears and Roger scolding him severely, which was something I seldom saw, I asked, "What has he done?"

"He wanted to use the spear," Roger explained. "And I warned him to be absolutely sure his target was in the open and close enough for complete accuracy. He got too anxious."

"I lost the spear," Ron whispered. He was so contrite I felt truly sorry for him.

"Don't we have more?" I asked Roger.

"But those spears are what feed us, and we only have a few. We can't afford carelessness!"

I turned back to Ron and asked, "How did it get lost?"

"I saw a really big grouper," he said. "But it wouldn't come away from the coral head. I waited and waited, then I thought I could hit it, so I tried."

"He speared the fish but didn't kill it," Roger spoke more calmly. "The grouper carried the spear back under the coral and out of our reach."

Then Roger turned to Ron and said, "I know the spear is not that serious; we still have more, but we can't afford to be careless. More important than that spear, is that fish. We aren't out there for target practice on them, but to get food to eat. I don't ever want you to shoot at anything we can't eat, and if you wound it, go get it!"

With that admonition, Ron became a superb diver, and if ever he wounded one, he tracked it and retrieved it every time. There were no more lost spears or fish.

We were out of money! We'd put aside enough to pay for the heat exchanger and the mechanic, then counted what was left: $8.20 in pennies! We were also out of food, toilet paper (!), razor blades, shampoo, and patience. Taking the pennies (coppers the grocer called them) to a tiny market we purchased toilet paper, some fresh vegetables, and enough grits to get us to Georgetown, if we hurried.

Hunger must not have been a serious problem for us. We caught two five-foot sharks while sitting at anchor, took them ashore to clean, and in the process, attracted a small gathering of onlookers. As we gutted the ugly fish, the adults around us began whispering among themselves; and the children giggled behind their hands. Were sharks edible? Back on the boat we fed some of the meat to Sea Coral. She lived. Then we opted to use the rest of it for bait. Maybe the natives knew something we didn't, and we did not need another problem. But we got one anyway.

It was 9 a.m. and we had just finished breakfast. Still in my nightclothes, I stood at the sink, cleaning up the dishes. The kids played with the kittens on the floor, and Roger sat on a settee, sharpening the spears. With no warning sound of any kind *Halcyon* jolted, then leaned over, way over! Dishes and fishing gear spilled onto the floor, and we all screamed. Something had hit us HARD!

Grabbing the side of the cabinet, I looked out the porthole, and saw nothing except steel, a solid gray mass of it! And we heard a horrendous, loud, wrenching noise.

"We've been hit! We're sinking!" I yelled. (Wondering why I could never hold my head together in a crisis.)

The kids scrambled for the deck, and as Ron reached the top of the companionway, he shouted, "We have been hit BY A SHIP!"

As the vessel passed beyond our stern, it was clear we were not sinking. But we had been struck a mighty blow by the Esso tanker that went from island to island with fuel for the marinas.

Calming down, we examined the damage and noted that it was minimal. The hull had a new dent and quite a few scratches in her paint; the bowsprit was twisted out of shape, but not beyond repair; one turnbuckle was bent; and the anchor line had been dangerously stretched. The thing we were most grateful for was our steel hull. If *Halcyon* had been anything but steel, she would have been destroyed.

At the dock we met the Captain of the tanker and he explained to us that one of his thrusters had failed as he entered the channel to the marina. With that, the tide caught him sideways, pushed him into the anchorage, and ultimately on a collision course with us. The Captain was very upset and promised that Esso would pay for all damages to our boat when we returned to the States.

Were we jinxed? I was getting edgy.

Lo and behold, the wife arrived with our heat exchanger. At last!

Roger and the mechanic worked for a full day installing *Halcyon*'s new part. That meant tools, debris, and grease all over the main cabin. It was too much competition for schoolwork, and I declared another school holiday. Tommy and Ron welcomed the sudden liberty to go diving at the cave with Hobie and Frank; Janice curled up in the forward cabin and played with her doll; I found peace sitting on the deck reading.

Once I looked up from my book to see a flashy, red powerboat come roaring into the harbor and up to the docks. The two occupants went ashore, and an hour later returned, boarded their boat, and motored over to the cave. Sometime later, Hobie delivered the boys to the *Halcyon* and I learned who our new visitors were.

"Joe Namath is here," Hobie said. "And wow! You should see the girl he's with!"

Girl, phooey! It was Joe Namath! The sexiest male on two legs! I'd never been a sports fan, having long ago placed football in the same category as taxes, politics, and body odor to avoid whenever possible. But Joe Namath was something else. I'd thought him so sexy, one time I had allowed Roger to take me to a Jets game, but only once. Soon after that game, Joe retired and so did my interest in the sport. Now, here he was, in this remote corner of the world.

"They are staying with the dockmaster for a few days," Hobie continued. "Wait'll Roger gets a look at that girl!" He winked broadly, waved goodbye, then sped away in his dinghy.

Roger and the mechanic crawled out of the engine room about dusk, and the mechanic left with the promise to return in the morning and finish the job. I took one look at Roger covered with sweat, grease, and engine dust, relayed Hobie's news, and asked, "Can we go into the marina tonight?"

"No way," was his reply. "I'm going for a swim, then to bed. I'm dead tired." If it had been Raquel Welch, he would have gone.

The next day saw the engine finished, and when we started it up, the gears worked beautifully. The red power boat was nowhere in sight.

When the *Imagine* tied to the dock, C.K. went running off after a fluffy gray feline with long silky fur and we waited for hours in hopes he'd return. By nightfall, the Fleet elected to go back out and anchor while Hobie and Emogene stayed at the dock. Maybe the amorous cat would get hungry and come home.

But the next morning there was still no cat, and Emogene was out walking the island and calling his name. We knew she was worried. C.K. was almost as special to her as a child.

The rest of us waited at anchor. I spied the red powerboat tied behind *Imagine*, but Roger wasn't interested in going ashore. He was reading a John D. MacDonald mystery and had just gotten to the good part.

One more day and the Fleet voted again, with the results to go on to Darby Cay and wait for *Imagine* there.

The day was blazing hot as we wound our way out of the narrow channel. I had donned my mini bikini and was feeling pleased with my new figure and spectacular tan until Roger came up on deck and asked me with a silly grin, "Aren't your legs getting a little hairy?"

"Don't you remember? We are out of razor blades!" I answered him coldly, but I looked down and thought to myself that my legs were probably hairier than Joe Namath's.

Roger assigned me to the wheel, then went forward to the bowsprit to watch for coral heads. Within seconds he was shouting back at me to watch where I was going before I ran us aground in the tricky passage. I was trying to concentrate but it was difficult. Ron and Janice were arguing over who was going to ride in the ratlines. Being unable to leave the wheel, I attempted to referee by yelling—in between Roger's verbal blasts at me.

As if that weren't enough racket, Tommy came strolling up from the cabin below, wearing a plastic garbage bag—on his head!

"Are you out of your mind? Take that thing off!" I roared.

Tommy was the only one of us that wasn't yelling when the little red powerboat pulled alongside—with Broadway Joe Namath at the wheel. And next to him was a gorgeous sleek blond (without hairy legs). And there we were, a boatload of bellowing banshees!

Joe took one look and decided not to hang around. Turning the boat out to sea, he called over his shoulder, "Have a nice day," and raced away.

"Wow, did you see that girl?" Roger asked as he watched them go.

"Grrr!" was all I could think of to answer.

The *Imagine* joined us at Darby—minus C.K. Our kittens were fatherless. As for the kittens, three of them were growing rapidly, but the fourth, Periwinkle, was not. Sea Coral had rejected her and the others were so much stronger, they were beating her out for food.

Janice spent hours feeding Periwinkle milk from her fingertips, and I hoped she could keep her alive. Each morning I climbed out of my bunk and held my breath as I went to check on the tiny kitten and only let my breath out when I found her still alive. She was so pathetic and helpless we couldn't help but love her best.

The anchorage at Darby was perfectly still and protected. It was a great hurricane hole, and a perfect breeding spot for mosquitoes. The screens kept them out, but the No-see-ums worked their way through the mesh to give us one of the worst nights we'd had the whole trip. I didn't know Paradise had insects.

It was Roger's birthday and we celebrated with creamed chipped beef, his favorite, but our last jar of beef. Food was running out!

An hour after sailing away from Darby, the weather turned foul and we ran for cover at Rolleville, on the north end of Great Exuma Island, until things calmed down. Georgetown would just have to wait a few more days.

As we approached the Rolleville harbor, the fishing line we always trailed underway began to whine. We brought in a barracuda; rebaited the hook, and within minutes had a second, third, and a fourth. Was there anything else in that ocean except Barracuda or shark? The stories about people getting sick from barracuda kept us from trying them, but we knew the islanders ate them all the time. Here was our chance to negotiate a trade.

We found a rowboat of fishermen who were interested, and they swapped two small groupers weighing about five pounds, for our barracuda weighing more than sixty pounds. As they rowed away we could hear them chuckling, and somehow, I had the feeling we had a lot more to learn about trading.

Rolleville was a lovely community, the largest in the Exumas. The countryside was plush velvet green, but we saw more signs of poverty than we had elsewhere in the islands. Houses were smaller and more open to the elements, and there were deserted cars beside the dusty road all overgrown with vines and weeds. Kids and dogs played everywhere along the beach, raggedy and dirty, but seemingly happy and well fed.

Our three were giddily excited about going ashore and meeting others their own age. Within ten minutes of stepping ashore, Janice received an invitation to one little girl's house and returned to the boat an hour later with four coconuts and two dozen potatoes.

We met Mr. Rolle (everyone on that end of the island is named Rolle), a taxi driver whose brother owned a farm. When we heard that bit of information, we told the taxi driver we were going to Georgetown, and if he happened to be there sometime in the near future and if his brother wanted to sell any fresh vegetables, we would be interested in buying, once we collected our money.

During our two days in Rolleville, Roger and Hobie went spearing and returned with six huge lobsters, one prehistoric crab (not shown in my fish book), and a twenty-five-pound grouper. It was seafood at every meal—and not much else.

We cheered as Georgetown came into view. The boat had hardly stretched out on the anchor line when everyone hit the beach on a dead run for the post office. The twelve of us descended on the poor postmaster with such zeal—and racket—for a moment I thought he was going to bolt and run. But he handed us our precious envelopes and we retired to the front lawn to laugh and cry and share the news.

There was mail for everyone, money from home, and bills, which were a reminder of a real world out there somewhere. Two and a half months was a long time to be completely cut off from family, and for a while Santa Barbara seemed so close and also a million miles away.

There were unusual references in several of the letters that eventually led us to the conclusion that some of the mail had not made it. Well, perhaps it would catch up later. It did—two years later.

Tommy was overjoyed to get a letter from his favorite cousin, Mike. After reading it, he hugged it to his chest, and I saw in his sad blue eyes that he, like the rest of us, was experiencing a touch of homesickness. But we had a treat to lift our spirits: Roger's niece, Jeanie, would be arriving in Nassau to join us—in ten days!

The excitement of the mail over, we cashed a check and went grocery shopping. An old man, sitting in the shade of a poinciana tree, directed us to Georgetown's General and Variety Store.

"It be the biggest in town," he told us.

As we opened the squeaking screen door and entered the cool, dark, musty-smelling interior I knew we were in for another lesson in survival.

"Look at the price of oil!" I exclaimed. "I've seen cheaper French perfume."

"Instead of frying fish maybe we could boil it in rum," Roger suggested as he hefted a bottle and noted the price was less than a third that of the oil.

The sugar, rice, flour, dried beans, and cornmeal were all sold from burlap sacks and all open to the dusty air. We were a long way from those pristine supermarkets back home but after months of living on a boat I hardly gave it a thought.

I checked out the hamburger meat, but it was so expensive I passed it up. After collecting a few more items including toilet paper and razor blades, we left the store. Everything was so expensive, I felt frustrated.

As we continued down the street I griped, "When we get back to the States I want to spend six hours in a supermarket and have an orgy!"

"Well, what else do we need now?" Roger asked in his annoyingly unsympathetic way.

"We still need fresh vegetables. But most of all, I want some meat! Real tough, juicy beef! Medium rare! With mushrooms on top! I want to chew and chew and chew." I was almost drooling.

"And as soon as you get a steak you will want conch, or lobster, or fish. How many people would love to eat lobster—daily?"

"They should have lobster for breakfast and lunch, then lobster spaghetti for dinner—somehow that kills the craving. I haven't even been able to swallow a piece of conch in two weeks, and the smell of frying fish is turning me into a vegetarian."

"Well, if you are going to become a vegetarian then we better try and find a farm somewhere."

We put the meager supplies away, distributed the kids among the Fleet, took *Halcyon* dockside,
and removed the motorbike for a trip inland to the farm country.

Great Exuma Island is pastorally beautiful with clean villages, small houses in pastel colors, and fertile green farmland. We saw only modest farms, each equipped with a kitchen open to the out-of-doors, a rock-lined pit fireplace in the center of the kitchen floor, a primitive cornmeal grinder in the yard, and a garden just outside the door. The yards—and sometimes the kitchens—accommodated goats, chickens, cats, dogs, and children.

The people were primarily Baptist in their religion, and as is customary with their faith, they addressed everyone as "Brother" and "Sister." Lagniappe (something extra that is free) was a common practice of the Exumans and we soon discovered the charm of the tradition the people had adopted from the French.

After traveling five miles we stopped first in front of a small restaurant and Roger went in to ask where we might buy fresh vegetables. Before leaving, he purchased a beer and while restarting the bike, the owner came out of the restaurant and asked if we would like to take some limes from his tree—no charge. We picked a dozen.

The man's directions led us to a house with onions spread on the front porch to dry. We bought one pound from the lady, but she gave us two and a half pounds because "They be small."

She also had a few banana trees in the yard, and we bought one large, just-ripe stalk. This time she picked twenty-five hot peppers and pushed them on us. When I tried to pay for them, she said, "Oh, no Sister, they be Lagniappe!"

She also donated a cardboard box for us to carry our supplies.

Our third stop was a modest pink stucco house on a hill. We spied a very large grandmotherly woman sitting in a straight-backed chair on the porch, her bright flowered dress spread across her knees, and her lap filled with a bowlful of pink pigeon peas that she was shelling. We asked if she would like to sell any.

She nodded, then using extreme care, she measured out two pints of peas into a brown bag and collected money for two pints. Then she picked up the bowl of peas that were left and dumped them all into the bag. There were at least five pints altogether.

Asking us to wait, she disappeared into the house and returned with four large sweet potatoes. "These be good as candy, Sister," she said as she put them into my hands.

She walked down the path with us, picked a dozen limes from her tree and put them in our box. Roger tried to pay her but with no success. She stood smiling and waving to us as we rode down the hill.

And it continued; we stopped at a store and bought one pound of okra. The storekeeper measured out one pound exactly, then promptly put a second pound on top of the first and topped it all with a double handful of peppers. The total cost was for one pound of okra only!

We stopped at a restaurant to buy coffee. "Lagniappe" was two more fresh limes.

Next door to the restaurant we watched a lady grinding fresh corn. She gave us a pound of cornmeal and a pound of grits, then didn't want to take any money at all, but we put our foot down. Enough was enough.

We stopped shopping only because we had no more room to carry anything. And there we were, the two of us, traveling ten miles down a bumpy farm road on a small Honda motorbike, balancing a cardboard box heaped to the top with food, and one large bunch of bananas topped it all. I sat behind Roger, holding the box on my lap, and clasping the bike frame as tightly as possible with my knees. Giggling and gasping with each pothole we hit, I tried to shout to Roger over the roar of the engine.

"What's that you said?" he called back to me.

"I said, this is better than all those modern supermarkets! This is fun!"

The generosity of Bahamians was truly overwhelming.

We would have further experiences with food before we left. Roger, the kids, and I had gone ashore to the hotel to ask if we could gather coconuts from their trees. Not only did they agree but they loaned us a ladder so we could collect fresh ones instead of those on the ground, Roger proceeded to climb coconut trees and toss down the nuts until we had completely loaded up the dinghy.

We were well provisioned, we thought, but as we prepared to row back to the boat, a taxi pulled up and out stepped Mr. Rolle from Rolleville. He had seen his brother the farmer, and now he had a trunk full of fresh produce for us.

We bought all he had, green peppers, onions, bananas, and potatoes, for about ten cents a pound. Putting the vegetables on top of the coconuts in the dinghy, we rowed out to every boat in the Fleet, plus a few others that were anchored about, and shared our excess. It was a pleasant way to spend the day, and who knew, we may have found our next business venture—Paddling Roger's Traveling, Vegetable Stand.

It was time to part ways. The rest of the Fleet chose to stay behind in Georgetown in hopes more mail might arrive, but we had to get to Nassau to meet Jeanie. We weren't sure we'd see the Fleet again and we had been traveling or living together for a very long time. Parting was going to be difficult for all of us, and especially for Janice. She sat on the stern and waved until the harbor, and the four other boats, were merely specks in the distance.

Tom with dinner

CHAPTER 6: THE DOWNHILL RUN

The step was a big one. It was a milestone to get out and go it alone. At last, we were sailing! We'd covered over four hundred miles after leaving the Keys and always we'd seemed to be bucking a headwind. Now we were turned north, and the wind was on our stern. It was downhill all the way! Of course, the wind was only ten mph, and the going was slow, but I didn't care. We'd finally turned off that infernal engine!

Roger had planned for us to lay over at Staniel for some rest, but when he saw the full moon and gentle wind and waves, he chose to sail straight through to Norman's Cay. That was all right with me.

The kids split up the day with one hour at the wheel and two hours off, and they held their course like old salts. Roger and I split the night.

My shift came from 2 a.m. until 7 a.m., while everyone else slept. The only sounds were the waves lapping at the hull, and the wind rustling the sails. The moon was so bright I could have read by it. The closest land was the Exumas ten miles to the west, but I took that on faith since there wasn't a light to be seen and why should there be a beacon when there are navigation aids like the Pointer Star or Orion's Belt?

Sheet lightning flashed on the horizon; a flying fish skipped across the surface. Nature wrapped so closely around me I felt a part of it and it a part of me. *Halcyon* moved in perfect synch with the wind and the water, a slow rise, a swoosh, then a gentle lazy fall. So, who needed Dramamine?

But it didn't last. As we approached Norman's Cay the second afternoon, we spotted a squall rolling in. At first, we thought it would miss us, but when the wind changed, we knew we were in for it.

Hastily, we dropped the sails, started the engine, secured everything on deck, and handed out rain gear. The winds built fast and unfortunately, they were coming from the west, the direction we were headed. The only advantage we had was that Norman's Cay protected us from the wave action. If we'd been more experienced sailors, we would have stayed at sea and rode it out, but we were chicken. We could also see the harbor entrance. If we motored hard, we felt sure *Halcyon* could beat the storm. Besides, the wind in those storms never climbed over thirty mph anyway. (Who said that?)

We were a half mile from the entrance when the full force hit us. The rain came in a solid sheet and we couldn't see. It was like trying to navigate through Niagara Falls. When the bow of the boat swung too far to starboard and a gust of wind caught us hard against the hull, we heeled over as though we were a toy boat in a bathtub. And we didn't even have a sail up!

Revving the engine as high as she'd go, we turned *Halcyon* toward the harbor and, as we plowed through the entrance, Roger estimated we were doing a half knot or less. It was our first storm at sea and I was scared. But *Halcyon* merely trudged ahead, without a shudder or a groan. I had a distinct impression she was laughing at my discomfort.

So was Roger. He was positively exhilarated by the challenge, and watching him at the wheel, I felt a smattering of jealousy. There was no denying he was in love with his Iron Lady.

We dropped anchor as the gray afternoon disappeared into an inky black night, and we went below to listen to the driving rain for two more hours. The next morning, when the Nassau radio reported the winds had exceeded sixty mph, I had to give *Halcyon* the respect she was due. She was quite a boat.

We were proud of the kids. They had followed all orders well and had refrained from fighting during the worst of the passage. And certainly, I was proud of me. Though scared, for once I hadn't panicked.

The weather remained unstable for two days, so we waited at Norman's Cay. I wasn't up to more than one storm per week anyway. Then, just as I was learning to like *Halcyon*, she turned on me again.

An unbelievable odor emerged from her bilge and transformed the close cabin into a torture chamber of smells.

Roger performed exploratory surgery on her automatic pump and diagnosed the problem: she needed a new one. Somehow, I could have guessed that was coming.

We were reduced to clearing the bilge and holding tank with a manual suction pump designed to give hernias to elephants. Roger assigned the job to Ron, then every few minutes, we assured him that his biceps were growing right before our eyes.

Reaching Nassau, we dashed ashore and called Roger's niece in Minnesota to let her know we could meet her on time. It was during that phone call that we learned Roger's brother had been trying to reach us to tell us Roger's mother, Ruth, had died of a heart attack only one day after we'd left Georgetown. It had happened suddenly with no warning, and Roger could not have made it home before she'd died. Somehow, I felt we should have known sooner.

Again, the lonely feeling of being completely out of touch with our family and friends. People that mattered to us, people that were important in our lives seemed as far away as if we were on some distant planet.

And Ruth had been one of those people. She was one of the loveliest women in my life, and I knew how fortunate I was to have had such a gentle and caring mother-in-law. In all the years of my marriage to Roger, Ruth and I had never shared a cross word between us. She never spoke in anger or hate. She was my friend, and I would miss her terribly. We didn't know it then, but we would hear from her again in an unexpected way and in a most unusual place.

My husband's niece, Jeannie, arrived on schedule. It was certainly a treat to have a smiling, bubbly seventeen-year-old on board. She stayed with us all the way back to Miami and proved to be a real trouper, but she had to be. She had arrived after we'd been three months cruising, nursing a broken bilge pump, low on supplies, with four kittens and enough sand on board to build our own island, and everyone tired, crabby, and scaly with sunburn. Her immediate response was "I love it!" Ah, there is no suppressing the spirit of youth.

Jeanie in Nassau

We rented a car to pick her up at the airport, then took advantage of the mobility to tour the island. It was Sunday morning, and we went to the staid, old established church in the center of the town to hear a sermon entitled, "We're all in the Same Boat." I hoped we might learn something, but the minister spoke in such monotones that it was all we could do to stay awake. He hadn't been in the same boat with us. In contrast, while driving around the island that afternoon; we passed a small, modest, white clapboard church and were startled at the music coming from inside. The sounds of drums, horns, and such enthusiastic singing stopped us in our tracks. We simply had to go in.

Though we tried to ease into a pew at the back, a friendly usher caught us and pushed us to the front of the church. We settled into the pew and listened through several more very energetic hymns, and it wasn't long before we were clapping and singing and praising the Lord along with everyone else.

Then the minister stepped up to the podium, looked our way, and asked us to stand. After welcoming us warmly, the entire congregation stood and applauded. We had never been applauded in church before. Janice was so amazed, she leaned over to me and whispered, "What did we do?"

We stayed another hour, and it was with reluctance that we left. We were getting hungry. On the way into town, we stopped at a small, out-of-the-way restaurant and introduced Jeannie to her first raw conch salad and fried turtle burgers. She ate both with exclamations of "How different!" and "Wait until I tell my brothers!"

"We eat this stuff all the time," bragged Ron.

He was right, but then he had never been very discriminating about anything he ate.

The wonder was our other two finicky eaters who were also devouring everything put in front of them—cooked or raw. I smiled and realized we had come a long way from T.V. dinners.

Halcyon was ready to leave Nassau when the *Imagine* pulled into the harbor and we were overjoyed that they had caught up. Hobie explained that when they stopped at Staniel Cay, who should be sitting on the dock, but C.K. the cat. Tired, dirty, a lot thinner, but happy to be back on the *Imagine* again. So, we kissed Hobie, Emogene, and even C.K. And felt warm pleasure in their company and the sense of security in having a companion boat again.

Andros Island is the largest in the Bahamas and boasts the longest living coral reef in the Western Hemisphere. With the reef protecting the entire northeast part of the island, we found good anchorage midway between it and the town, within easy rowing distance of both.

I surprised myself by going out snorkeling with Roger, Jeannie, and the kids. All around us we found a world of breathtaking underwater canyons, in colors more vivid than those seen in any canyon on land. Vast schools of tropical fish wove intricate patterns in and out of immense forests of staghorn coral.

Unfortunately, there are too few ways in our experience that allow us to become a part of nature without disturbing it. It is a world that operates much more efficiently and spectacularly without the invasion of machines, pollution, noise, or man. Sailing a boat through a moonlit night off the Exuma Islands or snorkeling over Andros Reef were very nearly religious experiences for me. I saw, I felt, I touched, I tasted. And when we left, I hoped there was no evidence we'd ever been there. That's the way it should be.

We went ashore on the tenth of July to help the islanders celebrate their newly won Independence from England. The celebration was to take place ten miles inland, so we marched out onto the road, stuck out our thumbs, and in a remarkably short time caught a ride in the back of a pickup truck. As we climbed aboard, we found ourselves sitting amidst drums, horns, cymbals, and guitars. We were riding with the band.

The music was infectious, and everyone danced until midnight. After enjoying the food, the people, the hospitality, and the dancing, we returned the way we had come: in the back of the truck all huddled together for warmth as we sang under the stars. Our bubbly teenage guest was clearly enjoying it all.

By the time we spotted Chub Cay, Roger reached the conclusion that he was an expert sailor. Always before we'd furled the sails a half mile offshore and motored into the harbors to anchor. Not this time! Captain Larson wanted to prove his prowess and sail into Chub Harbor fully rigged!

The anchorage was packed with twenty-five boats or more and my knees turned to water at the thought of it. We would surely hit a boat, I just hoped it wouldn't be more than one.

The Captain handed out duties. He announced he would drop the jib, main, and furl the jib; Ron would furl the main and mizzen; Tommy would drop the mizzen; Janice would man the lines and deliver the sail ties where needed; Jeannie would drop the anchor; and I would man the wheel! (Huh?)

I broke out in a cold sweat and my stomach began to do strange things. Knowing Roger would divorce me on the spot if I upstaged his big scene by throwing up over the side, I took a deep breath and resolved to hold the wheel and my stomach steady no matter what.

Our entrance was spectacular to say the least. All sails full, we glided neatly past two or three boats without hitting them or their anchor lines. I pointed *Halcyon* into the wind and straight for the beach. Roger and Ron released the sails. It was perfect. Right? *Wrong!*

Both the main and jib winches jammed; Roger forgot the order to drop the anchor; and I insisted upon shouting that the beach was getting too close. With only yards to spare, Roger and Ron forced the sails down, Roger remembered the anchor, and *Halcyon* slowly fell back on the anchor line just as though we'd planned it that way. As the boat came to a stop I sat forward and stuck my head between my knees; there was absolutely no blood left in my veins from the waist up.

Hobie, who had anchored earlier in the day and was watching our performance from the *Imagine*, was the first over to congratulate us. He said it was such a spectacular sight he hardly noticed the colorful language coming from our crew.

Captain Larson and the lesser swabbies spent the rest of the evening on the afterdeck basking in the compliments as the crews from the other boats dinghied over to get the Captain's expert advice on tides, currents, weather conditions, sail handling, cruising, etc. I went below, took two aspirin and laid in the bunk until dinner time.

It was our last day in the Bahamas and we took advantage of it by diving over the "Bimini Wall." The Wall is an unexplained mystery like Stonehenge or the statues of Easter Island. It first appears one mile offshore of Bimini in approximately fifteen feet of water, and from there it continues out to a depth of a hundred feet or more. Made of large square stones, to me it resembled a garden wall that had fallen over.

The natives informed us that the composition of the stone did not resemble anything found on the neighboring islands; obviously it was built when the location was dry land. But how long ago was that? We wondered about the people who had left their mark in that part of the ocean. The Lost Civilization of Atlantis?

The next morning we recrossed the Gulf Stream. The *Imagine* stayed in Bimini because of the weather but we were too eager to get back, and as it turned out we had a gentle enough crossing with only an occasional squall.

The kids played checkers most of the trip. Tommy won but Janice continued to try. And in between games, she fed Periwinkle, who, though still small, was definitely a survivor. Jeannie refereed the games, Ron read, Roger and I had cocktails on the deck and enjoyed the uneventful sailing.

Roger observed, "I think Tommy's seasickness is improving."

"You may be right," I said. "It only shows up now when it is his turn to take the wheel."

He thought about that, then asked, "Do you suppose he's conning us like he does Janice?"

At that remark, I could do nothing more than smile.

By late afternoon, the wind died, and a mist settled over the water. As it blurred the horizon we were soon floating in a heavy gray cloud. Dropping the sails, we started the motor, then returned to our cocktails and conversation.'

"When we began this trip," I reminded Roger, "I was most worried about Janice and her asthma. Have you noticed she hasn't even wheezed in all the time we've been on the boat? You would think the dampness would make it worse, but it hasn't."

"Sailing may be therapy for all kinds of problems," Roger answered.

"You may be right. They certainly have adapted well to this life. I think it's even been easier for them than it has been for me,"

I studied Roger for a moment before adding, "Your new image is a change. With that mustache and goatee, you look like a pirate

"You've changed too," he grinned. "I really like that funny haircut. It suits you"

I giggled, then hugged and kissed him, and thought, "Joe Namath, eat your heart out!"

We spotted Miami before dusk, checked our charts, then altered our course slightly and headed for the harbor entrance. At the first crack of dawn we tied up to the docks, three and a half months after leaving Pumpkin Key.

Janice, Toni, Tom, Jeanie, Ron, and Kittens

CHAPTER 7: UP A CRAZY RIVER

The sun had gone down in a blaze, and we were sitting on the deck enjoying the dramatic skyline that surrounds the Miami Marina. Kittens tumbled about in the cockpit under the watchful eye of Sea Coral; the kids were below in their bunks whispering secrets before going to sleep.

We'd been back in Florida a week and it was time for regrouping and discussing what to do next. Jeannie had gone home to Minnesota with great memories that would last a long time. The *Imagine* followed us into Miami by one day, and the *Talisman* and the *Minnie* made a peaceful crossing of the Gulf Stream to appear several days later.

Admiral Don had been quite proud of himself for making the "Great Voyage" without sinking! Within five minutes of his landing, he proclaimed he was starving for an American hamburger after that awful diet of fresh fish and lobster. Then he and Madeline took our kids and ventured off in search of Big Macs and French fries.

When the three boats departed for the Keys, we felt very lonely and out of sorts. We'd hoped for a while to see the *Lucky Lou* come in, but word arrived through a fellow traveler that Frank and Kathy were planning to remain in the Bahamas for another two or three months. They were doing the things we had learned to enjoy so much: sailing, fishing, island-hopping, exploring new anchorages.

So, what were we going to do? Where were we headed? Beyond any doubt Roger was committed to the boat and the new lifestyle, and I had to admit, it could be fun. But, beyond the relaxation, the adventure, the enjoyment of the loosely structured life we'd fallen into, the single most rewarding discovery for me was that our family possessed great ingenuity, stamina, and a very deep instinct for survival. That, I thought, might come in handy someday.

We counted the months we'd been on the boat and it amounted to over eleven. What a shock! Where had the time gone and what had we accomplished? We should have been a third of the way around the world by then, and there we were sitting in Miami—exactly where we'd started. Obviously, there were several things Roger had not considered in his original plans. For example, we were very slow learners. How could we sail around the world when we were still calling the 'head' the bathroom? And furthermore, I was sure half of the last eleven months had been spent doing laundry. Sir Francis Drake may have circumnavigated the globe in three years, but he probably smelled terrible when he got home to England.

Looking at the notebook in my lap, I asked Roger, "Is it absolutely necessary that we get all of the stuff on this list done now? And how do you propose to finance it?" The repair list was endless: leaking water pumps, leaking head, broken bilge pump, a short in the running lights, a galley stove that worked sporadically, and a million spare parts to replace those *Halcyon* had consumed in the Bahamas.

"That's only the 'must do' list," Roger answered. "If we plan to cruise any more, we are going to have to also add a lot of new equipment."

"How about carpeting?" I asked hopefully.

"Carpet?" When I started to reply, he skimmed right past it. "No, I was thinking of another forty-gallon fresh-water tank. We know the sixty we carry is just not adequate for the five of us. We also need a life raft, a radio direction finder for navigating, and a second stove that uses an alternate fuel such as alcohol, and...."

"Wait a minute! If you just want to make lists, that's one thing, but if we really need all of this stuff, then how are we going to pay for it?"

"Well, the first thing we can do is get the bowsprit repaired by Esso, and that won't cost us anything."

"Roger! You still haven't answered my question about the rest of this list. Where do you plan for us to get the money?"

"How about work?"

"As Janice would say—YUCK!"

So, we returned to our old slip in the boatyard on the Miami River and made arrangements to stay a few months. I wasn't thrilled about the location, but agreed it was probably the best place to be for accomplishing all we had to do. We found the Esso offices and made provisions to have the repairs done to the bowsprit. The people there were courteous and apologetic, and lost no time arranging for the work.

Then Roger and I began job hunting. We had one skill that made getting a job with alternating hours easy: waiting tables. As restaurant owners, many times we found ourselves carrying trays and filling in for sick, overworked, or absent employees. True, we'd never done it on a steady basis, but we certainly knew what was expected of a waiter.

Roger looked for a day shift so he could work on the boat in the cooler hours of the evening. I wanted a night shift so I could continue schooling with the kids during the day. Our luck won out and we were hired at the first try, and both restaurants were within two miles of the boatyard. Then we discovered a new problem: transportation.

For Roger, it was easy; he could get back and forth on the motorbike. For me, it was another matter. I simply was not willing to drive the bike by myself. It was often temperamental, and I feared being on the Miami streets at night and having the thing stall out on me.

We sat on the deck pondering the dilemma when I looked out at the dinghy and an idea struck. "Why don't I motor to work? The restaurant is right on the river barely a mile and a half by water. Besides, going by dinghy would be fun."

"You can't mean you'd be willing to navigate that river at ten at night?" Roger sounded surprised. "It seems to me that would be more frightening than the streets."

"I don't think so. There are people living all along it: the fishermen, other cruisers, crews on the ships, plus all the houseboats and apartments. I would never be out of calling range if I wanted help. But, what mugger or rapist is going to dive into that murky water to get to me anyway? No one is that sex crazed."

"But seriously, what if the engine stalls on you?"

"Come on, Roger, I haven't had any trouble starting it or running it before, and even if it quits altogether, I have the oars. I could row the entire distance; it might take me a while, but I think I can handle it if I have to."

"What if it rains?"

"Now you are being silly. If I can bathe, sail, and do laundry in the rain, then surely, I can stand a little shower or two. And if I carry my rain gear, a gas can with extra fuel, my life vest, a flashlight, air horn, and the flare gun, then I'll be prepared for anything, right?"

"Maybe so," he gave in.

And, of course, we weren't prepared for everything.

Our routines began and even though everything should have worked, it was business as usual. The Bahamas were forgotten as the old miseries of cramped quarters and trying to do too much in too small a space, soon frayed our nerves. The kids did not seem interested in lessons and once September arrived, I was sorely tempted to enroll them in school. I stalled, believing it would get easier. I should have known better.

The kittens were no help either. They grew larger and more playful with each passing day, and in a fit of fury I exiled them to the deck. After all, we had to concentrate more on math and less on the frolicking balls of fur. But the deck was too hot, hence into the forward cabin they went. Then closing the door meant losing valuable air. No matter how hard I put my foot down, the kittens seemed always to be under it and as uninvited guests in our classroom.

When the temperatures soared and the humidity made life miserable, my only relief was to climb into the dinghy and revel in the cool, quiet, thirty-minute trip to work.

Each day, as I prepared to leave, Roger would arrive home in a flurry of activity. He began every afternoon by tearing the boat apart in an effort to repair the leaks, or the bilge pump, or to install the new water tank. Following those messes came a myriad of other jobs that entailed grimy engine parts, utter turmoil, dust, dirt, and tons more grease. With the passing days of summer, the boat turned into a living nightmare.

The kids all but stopped doing assignments once I was out of sight of the boat. Contending with the kids was only a minor part of the problem. It was a very untidy Roger who made me want to mutiny. The debris from the boat repairs appeared in every corner and stayed there. Returning from work, I often found odd assortments of tools in my bunk, dirty dishes in the sink, a stove that didn't work, a grease smeared husband, cranky kids, and utter chaos. Where were those wonderful Halcyonic days?

Enough was finally enough. I made a resolution to alleviate one part of our discomfort, and at breakfast I announced, "The kittens have to go!" The kids pleaded their cases, but I stood firm. The kittens would be cats before long and no one would want them if we didn't act quickly. However, I was willing to give in to the kid's pleading on one thing: Periwinkle was still less than half the size of her brothers and sister and I agreed we would keep her a little longer, but not forever. I had to admit she was unbelievably endearing with ears and eyes way too big for her gray furry body, and there was something special about the kitten we'd saved by handfeeding for two months.

"Who'll take the kittens?" Janice had tears in her eyes.

"Well, you three already go to the park for an hour each day. Why don't you make a 'Free Kittens' sign and sit under that tree? If you take them along with you, someone will surely adopt them."
The park was on the opposite side of the river within easy sight of the *Halcyon*.

After lunch they made the sign, then put it and the kittens in a cardboard box and climbed into the dinghy to row across the river. I watched as they sat under the tree and within minutes, people were stopping and talking. Who could resist kids or kittens? Before their hour in the park was up, Hobie Cat, Chick Charney, and Seaweed had new homes. Finally, some small amount of sanity was restored to the *Halcyon*.

The park was a favorite spot for the kids to unwind. Most of the people visiting it were the retired elderly, but I often worried about some of the strange characters I saw wandering around there. The kids had been well warned about the dangers that might befall them and they generally heeded my warnings.

Then, one afternoon, I was watching from the deck while the kids played tag. They seemed safe, at least safe enough that I could go below and dress for work while I still had the boat all to myself. When I reappeared on deck the kids were gone, and I was frantic. I tried calling as loudly as I could, then I went to the air horn, which they'd always responded to before. I could see the entire park across the river from the boat and where my voice didn't carry, I was sure the horn did. And soon, though it seemed interminably long, they came running down the street to climb into the dinghy. When they were back on board the boat I demanded to know where they'd been.

"At Sandy's house," Ron said.

I was furious and gave my usual "Mother speech" about leaving the park, going off with strangers, taking candy, and on and on.

"But you'd like Sandy." Ron tried to soothe my anger. "She likes cats."

Toni, preparing for work.

"Ron, you don't understand! I don't know Sandy or where she lives!"

"We know her," Janice explained. "We see her all the time and she lives over there." She pointed at an apartment building on the edge of the park.

"And she buys us ice cream," grinned Tommy. "Lots!"

Roger appeared and it was time for me to leave for work. I told him about the incident and he warned the kids, that if they ever left it again, the park would no longer be their playground. They agreed to do as they were told, and I hoped that was the end of it.

When we first stayed on the river it had frightened me. Some of the areas in that part of town were dangerous: warehouse districts, slums, old and abandoned fish canneries and factories.
But there were many other sections less threatening such as boisterous colorful Little Havana, the boatyards and marinas full of people just like us, the modern high rise apartments for the very rich, and the little park that was a haven of solitude for the elderly. In the months we spent there, the river became more familiar, and slowly my fears subsided until I truly looked forward to the adventure of traveling the river to work each day.

The fishermen often greeted me with "Ahoy" and once they knew me, began to call out, "Good luck with the tips." The bridge attendants regularly came out of their cubicles to wave. Without fail, I saw the same retired gentleman sitting on the bank each day nodding in the sun, his fishing pole propped beside his chair. No matter how often I asked, "Catch anything today?" he always answered, "Nope, Fish aren't biting." I was sure he never bothered to bait his hook. On one of the many houseboats lived two chimpanzees. They played on the stern of the boat and would chatter and make faces at me as I passed. I never saw their owners and after a month, I wondered amusedly if they even had any.

I tried out my Spanish with the seamen on a Panamanian freighter; noted every new arrival of tankers from Colombia, Liberia, the Bahamas, and dozens of other countries; and always venturing close enough to the newly arriving sailboats to find out where they were from and where they were going.

The daytime rides were wonderful and a welcome respite from the hectic *Halcyon*, but the nighttime returns were even better. The river would get very still and quiet after dark. An occasional person could be seen sitting on the shore or on the deck of a boat, and if it was someone I knew, I would slow the motor way down and venture close enough to visit a minute. But mainly, I stayed well to the center of the river. The glow from the city provided ample light to navigate by and I didn't think it at all frightening, simply a beautifully serene place to enjoy.

One early September night, Roger and I were sitting on the deck enjoying a glass of wine and recanting the activities of the day. "Have you seen the paper?" he asked.

"No. What should I see?"

"The Bahamas have closed their waters to all American lobster boats. They claim the Americans are overfishing their waters. "He showed me the article and I felt sad to see the emphasis on "expected hostilities" between American and Bahamian lobster fishermen.

"I certainly would hate to see tension develop between the two countries. It could make it rough for the cruising people too. And speaking of cruising, how much longer are we going to be rebuilding *Halcyon*'s innards before we can get cruising again?"

"I think we're nearing the end. But we have another problem, and it may make a difference on where we decide to go next."

"Egads! Now what?"

"Sometime in the next six months she'll have to be hauled out of the water to have her bottom repainted. It's been over a year and the anti-foul paint is almost gone."

"So what! Is there any danger in letting her paint peel for another year?"

"Well, we have algae growing there now. In another couple of months, we'll have seaweed and barnacles. Follow that with some coral, and if we wait long enough, she might permanently attach herself to the bottom somewhere and become a new island. Halcyon Cay. Sounds nice."

"All right," I agreed. "If it's got to be done." I was becoming conditioned to *Halcyon*'s constant demands. "And there's no need to tell me how expensive this will be, I already assume a weekend of tips won't cover it. So where do we go for this operation?"

"How about New Orleans?"

I perked up—that was my hometown. A lot of my family still lived there and some of them I hadn't seen for years. "That's great, and maybe we can see the Mardi Gras." The idea gave me a real lift and having a goal in mind made the everyday living problems more bearable.

Over the next few weeks, work on the boat began to wind to a close. Tools disappeared into the cupboards to be replaced by supplies for another voyage.

The newspapers repeatedly ran stories about the "Lobster War" and it was obvious that tempers were flaring on both sides. An American lobster boat had been caught by some island fishermen sneaking into Bahamian waters. The Americans were escorted back to International waters, but not without threats to "get even." Then the conflict began to come home to us on the day a Bahamian trading vessel wound its way up the river. As it passed near our stern, we could hear fishermen from neighboring boats shouting obscenities at the foreign crew.

"Could this get out of hand?" I wondered out loud.

"I sure hope not," Roger answered. "But don't bet on it."

The kids continued to visit the park each afternoon, and I relaxed when they obediently stayed within easy calling range. Occasionally they told me of Sandy visiting with them but I never had an opportunity to see or to meet her. One day I asked if she was married.

"No, but she has a boyfriend named Homer," Janice told me.

As an image of one of the "Ladies of the Evening" seen along the waterfront crossed my mind, I asked, "How old do you think she is?"

"Oh, she's old," Ron said helpfully.

"Older than me?" I asked.

"Yeah, lots," he answered.

That could be anything from thirty-six to eighty-six, I thought, then forgot about it.

The day finally came when Periwinkle had to find a new home. We were far too attached to her while Sea Coral was becoming less so. The kids were playing on the dock and I was preparing for work when Sea Coral suddenly lashed out at Periwinkle, then she sat and hissed at the bewildered little kitten. When Roger arrived, I told him about the weaning process and together we suggested to the kids that they go over to the park and find a willing home for Periwinkle.

The next morning Ron announced, "Guess what, Mom! Sandy took the kitten!"

"And she just loves her," Janice said. "She told me Periwinkle was the nicest kitty of all."

"Didn't you tell me Sandy had lots of cats?"

"Oh yes—thousands!" Tommy proclaimed. "She even asked if we had any more but I told her we couldn't give away Sea Coral."

I agreed with Tommy that we had to keep our "good luck charm." I did wonder what kind of person this Sandy was, to put up with "thousands" of cats.

The first week in October, Roger resigned his job. The restaurant business had slowed down, and he had made the decision that we might get on our way faster if he devoted all his time to the boat. I hoped so; the more I thought about it, the more I wanted to see New Orleans.

With Roger home during the day, I postponed the kids' lessons altogether. There was just too much activity going on. Roger scoured the marine supply stores for more parts, then began assembling food from the lists I gave him each morning. Cabinets were emptied, refilled to capacity, then emptied again because someone suddenly needed an important item nestled at the bottom. The boat began to sit lower in the water as we loaded the provisions.

In exasperation, Roger asked, "Toni, are you sure you need this many cases of food?"

"Remember the Bahamas?" I asked. "This time I am not going to run out of food!"

"But we will be traveling the Gulf Coast of the United States, not the Bahamas, and I have never yet seen an American town without a supermarket."

"Then we'll be prepared for the next pork-n-bean shortage. Now help me move these floorboards and I'll stow that case in the bilge."

During the turmoil of provisioning, the kids told us Sandy wanted us to come to the park one afternoon to meet her. We promised we would tomorrow, but tomorrow was always too busy. Then Roger and I chose a hot afternoon to pack all the dirty clothes on the motorbike and head for the laundromat. When we returned, Ron said, "Sandy came to visit while you were gone. She said she was sorry she missed you, but she'll come another day."

"And we rowed her across the river," announced Janice with pride.

I was perturbed again. "You guys know better than to get out on that river when we aren't here to watch you."

"Aw, Mom, she walked here, and she said she was too tired to walk back," Janice explained.

I had to agree it was a very hot day and it was five or six blocks to the bridge that crossed the river, but I was concerned about them disobeying another rule.

"I helped her up the seawall," Tommy bragged.

It was two days later that I learned what a feat that had been. Roger had gone out shopping and I had emptied the tool locker trying to find more room for the latest purchases. A tiny voice called my name and I climbed over the debris and up the ladder to find a couple who were at least seventy-five years old standing on the dock. The kids proudly introduced me to Sandy and her boyfriend. Homer was bent over, gray haired, and utterly exhausted from their ten-block journey.

Fearing heat stroke, or something worse, I offered them a seat and some iced tea. But, once aboard the boat Homer simply refused to sit down. His china blue eyes twinkled, and his excitement was quite apparent; he wanted to see the deck, the cabin, up forward, the engine room, the rigging. He seemed lost in another era and explained that he had been a young boy sailing a trading vessel in the South Pacific, and he recalled sea stories and adventures for us as though they were yesterday.

But, as good as his memory was, his eyesight and mobility were not. He kept missing steps, bumping his head, and backing too close to the side of the boat while craning his neck to look up at the mast. As Sandy sat on the Captain's seat and chirped with great affection about the antics of her kittens and our kids, Homer kept appearing and disappearing from one corner of the boat or the other. Each time his head popped up, he was midway through another story of sharks, or typhoons, or beri beri, or rum smuggling, or whatever.

They were a positively delightful couple, but I felt immeasurable relief when they announced they had to leave. It was clear that Homer would hurt himself if he didn't get off our boat soon.

When Tommy piped up and offered to row them across the river, I gave him a swift kick in the shins and made all kinds of protesting noises. It didn't help; Sandy revealed that the kids had given her a ride on the previous visit and that cinched it. Homer rushed to the handrail where the dinghy was tied, and in a flash was dangling over the side of *Halcyon* announcing, "If Sandy can have a dinghy ride, THEN I CAN TOO!"

I looked across the river at the steep bank and the seawall and prayed for Roger to get home. Homer very nearly fell, getting into the wiggly little boat, but Tommy jumped in the bow and Ron into the stern, and together they steadied it while Homer sat down. Janice and I held on to Sandy and carefully lowered her over the side.

"I remember when we had a dozen men in a boat not much larger than this...." Homer said as they began to row across the river.

Janice and I stood at the stern of *Halcyon* wringing our hands and watching. I shouted at Ron to find the easiest place along the bank to let them off, but Homer was talking so much I was sure Ron never heard me.

They pulled up alongside the seawall, Tommy stood in the bow and Ron in the stern, both holding onto the wall to steady the boat. Homer found a foothold and slowly pulled himself up onto the wall. As he lifted himself over and sat down, I let out a very audible sigh. He then reached out and grabbed Sandy's hand to help her up. As soon as she braced herself against the seawall, she lost her balance and pushed instead of pulled. The little boat slid slowly away from the bank and in horror, I saw what was coming. We all shouted at once as Tommy and Ron tried desperately to force the boat back to the wall, but it was too late. Sandy went over the side without letting go of Homer's hand! It was a study in slow motion as Homer dove forward, then down into the water in a teeth-jarring belly flop!

I was sure the water was at least six feet deep along the wall, but still I was relieved to see the two old people surface for air. Ron grabbed their hands and jockeyed them alongside the dinghy but couldn't get them back in it. I shouted some ridiculous orders from the *Halcyon* and cursed myself that I hadn't learned to swim. Good Lord! Could that geriatric couple swim? And could their hearts stand the excitement? Janice blew the air horn and attracted the attention of a powerboat further down the river. As the boat pulled up to the dinghy, I was glad to see it had a diving platform on the stern.

The crew had no trouble helping the old couple up, and by using the powerboat's boarding ladder, Sandy and Homer were able to climb up safely. As the powerboat sped away, I shouted, "Are you all right? Do you need any more help?"

They sat there making funny kinds of noises. Finally, Sandy answered me, "We will be fine as soon as we can quit laughing!"

Moments later they stood up, waved, wished us a Bon Voyage, then holding hands and dripping wet, they walked across the park toward home. I could hear laughter all the way to the end of the street, and Homer's voice saying, "I haven't had so much fun in years! It reminds me of the time...."

And that, I hoped, will be Roger and me in forty years.

Roger was trying to convince me to give up my nightly rides on the river. I wouldn't listen. They were too enjoyable and besides, they were due to end shortly anyway. I had given notice at work. My husband was concerned that the tension on the river was growing with the Bahamian trading boat docked in the midst of the fishing boats. But I didn't agree; I felt sure the Cold War was easing, and I put him off.

Friday nights at work were always busy and the last one was a humdinger. It was at least an hour later than usual when I got out of the restaurant, walked across the parking lot, untied the dinghy, climbed in, and started the motor. As I eased slowly out to the center of the river, I noticed that the night was peculiarly quiet, then saw that none of the bright deck lights from any of the ships were burning.

The hulls of the giant ships loomed black and ominous on either side of me as I slowly traveled the canyon between them. For the first time I felt defenseless and uneasy. But I put my fears aside and concentrated on the job at hand. Great patches of hyacinths floated along in the inky black water, and to avoid snaring one large bunch in the propeller I veered closer to the side of one of the ships.

When the floodlights hit me full in the face, I knew the ship was the Bahamian trader.

"Who you be?" shouted someone from the deck. His thick island accent confirmed that they were Bahamians.

The lights were blinding. I couldn't see but sensed there were guns pointing at me. My voice shook as I answered, "I live on the river." And I gave him my name.

A voice I recognized as one of the fishermen from another boat, called out, "Hey man, she's all right. Let her pass."

As I moved away a second light flashed and someone else called, "You would be wise to hurry home, young lady." He didn't have to tell me twice. Revving the dinghy's motor, I fled and when I spied the granny squares in *Halcyon*'s portholes I began to breathe again.

Roger was waiting for me and he caught the dinghy line and helped me on board. I told him about the incident and his reaction was not unexpected. "That's it!" he roared. "For your last two nights at work I am taking you on the motorbike."

I didn't argue. It was plainly obvious I could have been shot.

At noon the next day Roger went out for the newspaper. When he returned, he dropped it into my lap and said with anger, "You were luckier than you think!"

On the front page was a picture of the Bahamian boat sitting where I had seen her the night before. But there was a difference: her hull had a jagged gaping hole in it, right at the waterline! The caption explained that someone using a small boat or dinghy had attached a bomb to the hull during the night. Disgruntled American fishermen were suspected. The article went on to say that no one had been hurt and there were no suspects, but the River Patrol was beefing up their staff to prevent any more such disasters.

Putting aside the paper, I felt sad. The river we had learned to enjoy so much had become a place of fear.

It was a crisp late October morning when we loaded the last of the supplies on board, then sat waiting for the kids to return to the boat. With our permission they had gone to Sandy's apartment to say goodbye.

"Did we forget anything?" Roger asked as he checked the lines securing the motorbike for the thirtieth time.

"Only the new carpet," I reminded him.

"What new carpet?"

"Oh, forget it."

Miami disappeared off our stern as *Halcyon* turned south and headed for the Keys. We expected to be in New Orleans by Thanksgiving. It would be the only time on the boat that we would set both a schedule and a destination and successfully meet them both.

Captain Roger Larson at the wheel

Anticipation ran high. We were eagerly looking forward to New Orleans, but we also had other pleasures on our agenda: the planned exploration of the Gulf Coast, and the company for a while, of another passenger. Before leaving Miami, Roger's shirttail relative from Minnesota (the brother-in-law of a sister-in-law) sent word he wanted to crew with us for two weeks and we agreed to meet him in Fort Meyers.

The weather could not have been more perfect, with moderate winds, clear skies, and temperatures in the seventies. We ran aground only twice, and both times were able to reverse and free *Halcyon* without a struggle. The fathometer was working, but very quickly we were learning the readings were taken too near the stern of the boat. By the time the instrument registered an obstruction or shoaling water, it would be too late. *Halcyon* would already be sitting on the bottom.

To prevent further such mishaps, I decided to construct a lead line. While Roger steered and the kids watched, I took a nylon cord and tied a three-pound sinker to one end. Measuring off two-foot intervals, I tied a knot, and every third knot I added a piece of red tape.

"Each six feet is one fathom," I explained patiently to Janice as she watched me. "And the red tape that marks the fathoms is easier to see than the knots. The cord now has seven pieces of tape, so it is seven times six, or forty-two feet long. Right?"

"I don't know," she shrugged.

I frowned at her, finished off the last knot, walked to the bow, coiled the line, worked up a good swinging arch with the lead, and let go of the line. It sailed forward of the boat in a perfect sweep and... kept going! I had thrown the whole thing away!

"Why'd you do that, Mom?" Janice asked.

Ignoring the question, I went back to the afterdeck, plunked down, and began to fashion another line. I could hear Roger chuckling behind my back. In the second line I put a loop in the bitter end and slipped it over my wrist. There was no way I was going to make a third lead line. It would be a year later when I would discover the foolishness of what I had just done.

Back on the bow I wrapped myself around the forward shroud to keep from falling in, coiled the line, then heaved the lead as far out as possible. The lead sank to the bottom, I tightened the line, and before the bow of the boat came alongside it, I had a very accurate reading of the depth. With lots of practice, I was able to develop a rhythm of throwing, reading, recoiling, and throwing again that gave us a reading approximately every fifteen seconds as we moved into shallow or unknown waters.

The lead line is probably the oldest aid to navigation. Columbus's crew used it, but theirs was over two hundred feet long. After a mere twenty minutes of throwing and coiling my forty-foot line with a three-pound lead I had to admire the sailor who had done this on the *Santa Maria*. He must have had arms the size of tree trunks by the time they'd finished discovering America.

I used my most nautical voice in calling out the depths while we moved along, after explaining to the kids that Samuel Clemens took the name "Mark Twain" from the readings shouted by the riverboat crews when their lead lines marked two fathoms in the Mississippi River. No telling who I might inspire.

"Fifteen feet!" I called.

"How many?" Roger called back from the wheel.

"FIFTEEN FEET! NO! TEN FEET!"

"WHAT?" from Roger

"LOOK OUT! GO TO PORT! " I screamed.

"STARBOARD! STARBOARD!" Ron shouted from the ratlines.

"Which way? Port or starboard?" Roger sounded testy.

"I see bottom!" Tommy announced from the bowsprit.

"BACK HER DOWN! REVERSE THE BOAT!" I was panicking again. THUMP! Too late.

"I think we ran aground," Janice observed as she looked over the handrail. "We ALWAYS run aground!"

After a half hour of backing, kedging, and waiting for high tide, *Halcyon* floated free.

Sometime along the way we smartened up and posted one of the kids midway between Roger at the wheel and me with the lead line. That kid would relay the calls, and finally tempers cooled. After all, it was not so easy to tell your child to order his or her father to go soak his head. The Little Darling would inevitably ask, "Why?"

We decided to take a day and go diving for lobster. It might be our last chance for a Florida lobster dinner, and we didn't want to miss it. East of Islamorada Key, the chart showed a likely looking reef and we found it quickly. Anchoring for a few hours, Roger and the kids jumped in and scouted around, but no luck. We pulled anchor, moved down the reef, and tried again. Nothing.

Discouraged, we prepared to leave when Ron spied a small lobster boat further out from shore. His favorite pastime had become examining the details of other boats and he ran for the binoculars to get a closer look. "Dad, someone is standing on deck waving something at us," he said.

Roger stood and glanced at the small speck of a boat in the distance, "Are you sure?"

Ron squinted through the binoculars. "I think it's his shirt he's waving over his head."

"Then we had better go see," Roger said. "That's a distress signal."

As we pulled alongside the boat, we found a very tired, middle-aged couple on board. It seemed their engine had quit on them during the night, they had been paddling continuously for over sixteen hours, and all the while the Gulf Stream had been pulling them further out.

I could tell how glad they were to see us when the wife said, "We came out last night to check the traps and I didn't think we'd need any food or water. We had some candy bars, but we ate those a long time ago. We drank the last soft drink about two this morning, and with that hot sun today, we were getting mighty weak."

Roger caught their line and towed them as far into shore as the *Halcyon* could manage. Then, while I taxied *Halcyon* along the shore, Roger and Ron got in the dinghy and pulled the lobster boat the rest of the way to the beach. As Roger cut their line loose and started to leave, they called him over, thanked him, then handed him a burlap bag.

Climbing back aboard the *Halcyon*, Roger handed me the bag. I looked inside and whooped for joy. There were ten beautiful lobsters!

"Wow!" I said, "Good Samaritanism certainly has its rewards."

We found Hobie and Emogene on the *Imagine*, Don and Madeline on the *Talisman*, and Max on the *Minnie*, and spent an evening trying to convince them to join us. They declined with the explanation that they were going to give up cruising and settle in the Keys.

I wondered if it wouldn't have been smarter to join them, but we promised to write, waved goodbye, and headed northwest toward the Everglades and into the Gulf of Mexico.

The shelter of a tiny island provided anchorage for one night, the mouth of the Shark River supplied a second. As we continued north for Naples the breeze changed and we knew a winter wind was approaching.

By noon the wind was on our bow, not cold, but strong enough to force us to start the motor. Our plans were to arrive in Naples by morning and we felt satisfied with our pace; our trip was going well. As the sun dipped low on the horizon we sat on the deck, a dinner of sandwiches in our lap when suddenly the motor coughed once then died.

"What's wrong now?" I groaned.

Roger looked in the engine room, checked the fuel tanks, and then casually reported, "We're out of gas."

It took very little figuring and remembering all the exploring and motoring we'd done the previous few days, to realize the obvious. We had been careless and grossly overestimated our supply.

When Roger came up from the cabin to report our latest position, I asked, "What do we do now?"

"Apply the Larson Theory," he said with a yawn. "When in doubt, drop anchor and get some sleep."

To lie at anchor completely exposed to the open Gulf in twenty-mile-an-hour wind and six-foot choppy waves is not in the least restful. I woke at dawn, if I'd ever slept at all, sore and irritable and more than eager to get under sail again. To make me feel worse, Roger and the kids informed me they'd slept like babies.

A new dilemma arose. How to raise the anchor without the motor to help move the boat. We were going to have to *sail up* on the anchor. Roger had talked, many times of trying it in case we were ever without an engine, but naturally I put him off. After all, I was the one who had to pull on the damn anchor line. Now we had no choice, and we spent the succeeding hour getting all the practice I hoped we would ever need.

The trick was to tack back and forth on a severely taut anchor line gaining a little on the line with each pass, until the boat was directly over the anchor.

Roger manned the wheel, Ron changed the sail sheets with each tack, Tommy and Janice stayed below out of the line of fire, and I pulled in the anchor line. *All one hundred and fifty feet of it.*

Each tack brought in a few feet of line, another blister on my hand, and achingly strained arm and shoulder muscles. By the time we got the anchor on board, I was ready to drop it again and go back to bed.

We traveled onward to Naples making about one knot. Very late that evening we sailed up the channel and hailed a motorboat to tow us the remaining few hundred yards to the fuel dock. Roger was proud; I was exhausted.

Two days later we dropped anchor on the river at Fort Meyers, dinghied to the docks, and found our new passenger, Bob, waiting for us.

I inquired about the family back in Minnesota, then Roger asked, "What made you decide to go sailing with us?"

Bob explained, "You guys are doing what we've talked about for years. The wife and I decided before we sold our house and bought a boat, we'd best get some practical experience. So here I am, ready to learn!"

I smiled, gingerly touched the blisters on my fingers, and said, "Oh, you are going to love it!"

Roger supplied the practical experience by putting Bob's natural talents to work helping to tune the engine, correct a loose steering cable, grease, oil, patch, repair, and generally have a wonderful two days at anchor amidst tools, grime, and spare parts.

While Bob and Roger merrily tinkered with *Halcyon*'s engine, the kids and I made a crab trap. We took some cord, two wire coat hangers, and fashioned a crude trap similar to those I'd used as a child along the Louisiana bayous. It worked. I showed the kids how to drop it, then left them on deck to catch supper.

The crabbing was excellent in the river. The kids quickly ran out of bait, coaxed some leftover chicken out of me, then pleaded for something more. Considering it an investment in dinner, I promised to buy some chicken necks for the trap when I went shopping that afternoon.

After lunch the kids and I left the two men in the engine room, climbed into the dinghy with the grocery list, and headed for the docks. As we pulled in beside several party boats unloading their catches, a thought occurred to me. "Ron, stay here and wait for us. And when those guides get through cleaning the fish, ask if you can have the fish heads."

Tommy, Janice, and I went on to the grocery store. When we returned, we found Ron waiting for us at the dinghy with a half dozen huge fish carcasses, as well as two nice-sized red snappers (whole!), and a gallon and a half of milk, a pound of salami, some bread, a jar of peanut butter, and a month's supply of jelly.

In amazement, I asked him how he'd gotten all that food when all we needed were a few fish heads.

"Well, the man gave me the carcasses, then asked me what I wanted them for. I told him you used them to make soup."

I started to giggle. I had failed to explain that the fish heads were for the crab trap and apparently, he remembered me boiling the carcasses of our dolphins in the Bahamas to make stock for the gumbos and stews. Trying to hold a straight face, I asked, "Where did you get the rest of the food?"

"After the man gave me the carcasses, he went over and talked to some tourists on the other boats. Then the tourists started bringing their ice chests over and emptying them into the dinghy. The man that gave me the milk, left, and came back with the two redfish. He even asked me if I wanted more. I thought I'd better say no."

I giggled all the way back to the *Halcyon* as I imagined those people feeling sorry for that skinny, young boy in raggedy cut-offs, whose mother sent him begging for fish heads.

I told Roger and Bob what had happened; Roger grinned broadly. "I think we have finally learned to feed ourselves! Nice going, Ron." After I explained to the kids that their dad was just kidding, we feasted on the redfish for dinner, and the carcasses lured two dozen hefty crabs into our trap the next morning.

With *Halcyon*'s motor reassembled, we headed north. The winds increased, the waters of the Gulf turned gray and choppy, and we chose to motor along the Inland Waterway. By the time we reached St. Petersburg the weather was terrible. If we had expected the tropical breezes of southern Florida to follow us all the way to New Orleans, we were being rudely awakened. The air turned nippy, and I hunted in lockers for warmer sweatshirts and jeans. With each drop in the temperature, I handed out another layer of clothes.

At anchor in St. Petersburg, we sat and listened to the rain, the wind, and the radio telling us the weather would remain the same for the next three or four days.

"I've got to get back to Minnesota," Bob informed us at breakfast.

Roger looked thoughtful. "But you haven't had a chance to sail at all; you can't go back without experiencing the best part of being on a sailboat."

"I really don't have much choice," Bob said.

"Then we'll sail for Carrabelle this afternoon!" Roger announced with conviction, as another gust of wind threw pellets of icy rain against our deck. "*Halcyon* can handle it and the experience will be good for all of us."

"Sure," I mumbled. "It'll be fun." Was it possible that Roger believed what he was saying?

We left the shelter of Tampa Bay and entered the Gulf with winds gusting to twenty-five mph. There was no place to duck in for shelter should the weather worsen, and I prayed hard that it wouldn't.

It rained. We buttoned up all ports, hatches, and the companionway, and below deck, living conditions became intolerable. *Halcyon* heeled over to port, the portholes on the low side dove underwater, and my head whirled dizzily when I looked up from the galley sink right into the ocean! I tried to tell myself we were on the submarine ride at Disneyland and any minute, a plastic octopus would wink at me. It didn't work.

When they weren't sleeping, Ron and Janice read and seemed totally unaffected by the crazy tilt of the boat. Tommy slept forty-eight straight hours! For me, sleep was difficult. A bunk board and pillows supported my back, but the simple act of turning over in my sleep forced me to wake up and reset the pillows.

Cooking and eating were juggling acts reminiscent of an old Lucille Ball movie. Anything not anchored down simply crashed to the floor. The smell of kerosene from the stove was strong, especially with no way to vent the fumes, but I thanked the "Powers that be" that our one-burner gimballed stove was working. At least we had coffee and hot bullion. "Otherwise," I announced, "It is cold sandwiches or nothing."

Roger, Ron, and Janice ate non-stop, I nibbled sparingly, Bob and Tommy gave up eating altogether.

The chaos below was escaped only at shift time. The first hour the wind came from the north, forcing us to sail on a westerly course. Then, at nightfall it shifted to NNE and we were able to point toward Carrabelle. But the further from shore we traveled, the stronger the weather, and at 10 p.m. we were pushing top hull speed with thirty-five-mile winds and ten-to-twelve-foot waves. Roger established a round-the-clock-watch. Bob, Roger, and I alternated through the night and Ron helped during the day.

At the wheel Ron and Roger seemed to share an affinity with *Halcyon* that baffled me. While watching Ron through the stern porthole, I witnessed an enthralled young man intent on holding a steady course, totally aware of his responsibility at the wheel. When he walked across the deck my once-clumsy little boy displayed all the grace and coordination of a very grown-up seasoned sailor.

When Roger took over, I felt more jealousy than admiration. His skills had originally been no better than my own, yet he seemed to instinctively grasp the finer points of sailing, where they continuously eluded me. My jealousy seemed to be extending beyond Roger's sailing abilities. As I watched him sitting at the wheel, I realized I hardly knew this eighteenth-century buccaneer with shaggy hair, moustache, and goatee, his eyes glowing rapturously as *Halcyon* responded to his every command. I felt if *Halcyon* had been human, I would have punched her in the nose.

Down below, Bob looked as though he would have gladly traded the whole trip for a thrilling weekend in a Minnesota blizzard. I kept telling him how much fun he was having, but he kept turning green and moaning. When he went topside for his turn on the wheel, his personality did a complete Jekyll and Hyde. Like Ron and Roger, he sat at the helm, enjoying every minute, even shouting with glee each time an especially hefty wave hit us. Was there some difference between men and women that eluded me?

Late the second night the winds increased to forty-five mph and every few minutes icy spray washed the deck. My watch came at 1 a.m. and inching my way carefully to the wheel, I sat down. It took only sixty seconds for a wave to ram us broadside, leaving me soaked to the skin and gasping for air. I behaved like the truly liberated, self-sufficient, capable, cool-headed sailor that I was and proceeded to cry.

Morning found us a very tired, beat-up crew tying up to the Carrabelle docks. We pulled in behind three extravagantly luxurious "big game" powerboats, and the weekend sailors came over to catch our lines. "Where are you folks coming from?" asked a flush-faced man, who looked like he'd had more to drink for breakfast than just orange juice.

"St. Pete," I answered as nonchalantly as possible while snubbing a line and directing Ron with the fenders.

"You came through that weather?" he asked in amazement, then he shook his head and took a sip from a plastic glass containing his 9 a.m. cocktail. "You guys are crazy!"

Looking up at him I stuck out my chest, and as off-handedly as I could manage, bragged, "Why? There was nothing to it. We had a great sail!" Somewhere behind me Roger made a muffled noise that might have been choked laughter. I paid no attention.

Some luxuries have a value that cannot be measured, and the luxuries of electricity and hot showers offered by the marina seemed more valuable than most. As soon as we were rested, bathed, and dressed in dry clothes we went ashore and did the most remarkable thing. In the first restaurant we came to, we ordered a terrific meal of fried shrimp and oysters. Less than twenty-four hours earlier some of us would have sworn we'd never eat again, and there we all were dining on raw oysters! Such recuperative powers our stomachs have.

The next morning, before he boarded the bus for the airport Bob asked, "What does Halcyon mean?"

"Peaceful," I replied with a slight sneer.

"Good name," he said with a nod.

We waved goodbye. I had wondered if his two weeks on *Halcyon* had destroyed his desire to live on a sailboat. I shouldn't have worried. A year later he and his family sold their home and moved to Florida where last we heard they were still sailing around. Occasionally I receive letters from his wife and when I read them closely, I can hear her bafflement at Bob's apparent obsession with his boat.

Of the entire southern coast, Apalachicola was my favorite. It is a true fishing town almost untouched by the tourist industry that has changed the face of every other coastal town.

We entered the harbor, pulled out of the channel just enough to drop anchor, and then retired for the night.

The next morning while sitting on deck eating breakfast, we looked at the scene around us. Quaint fishing boats with funny names were tied up to the fish and icehouses along the waterfront. Large shrimpers and scallop boats chugged back and forth; seagulls swarmed behind them, looking for a handout. One man seemed to be making or mending nets, and the nets were draped about him like giant cobwebs drying in the sun. There was not a luxury boat to be seen anywhere unless we counted our own. I didn't.

The entire scene of people loading or unloading one thing or another was just too inviting and the kids begged to skip a morning of schoolwork to join the activities. We dinghied up to the dock and tied next to a scallop boat. A burly giant of a man with a broad blade shovel tossed mounds of shells and miscellaneous other ocean debris, from the boat onto a conveyer belt. The shells were carried for thirty feet then a second man shoveled them onto the bed of a refrigerator truck. Along the belt at least a dozen people were lined up shorting through the refuse.

We watched for a few minutes and saw that each person had two or three buckets at his feet, and all hands were moving, darting back and forth from belt to bucket, sorting and gleaning until all that was left at the end were the scallop shells.

We inched closer and peeked in the buckets—what treasures! One was full of shrimp, another contained flounder. Most of them were loaded with shells, olive shells, beautifully marked tulips, pink-tinted murexes, and many others I'd never seen before. One bucket contained nothing except squid. I wondered if we could get bait for our crab traps and troll lines here.

We noticed the people sorting the shells. They didn't really look like dockworkers. A few men were apparently old enough to be retired. There were a couple of teenage boys, some housewife types with hair tied back in bright scarves, a well-groomed man who looked more like a stockbroker than a dockworker, and two rosy-cheeked gray-haired women in pastel-colored smocks wearing pink rubber gloves.

As the last of the shells were shoveled from the belt, the two ladies started to carry their buckets to a station wagon parked nearby. We offered to help, and they seemed to welcome the extra hands. As each of us lifted a bucket, we chatted with the ladies and learned they were widows from somewhere in the mid-west. They told us they had spent every winter for the previous five years vacationing in one of the nearby resort towns and on each trip, they had made almost enough money doing this work to pay for their vacation.

"This company must pay well for sorting scallop shells," I speculated.

"Oh, they don't pay anything for that," one of them chuckled. "They also don't charge us for the privilege. The scallop company just lets us keep anything we find on the belt, except for the scallops of course."

The second one piped up, "We come down three mornings each week and collect enough shells to meet our needs, then we clean them and take them home to sell in a gift shop. Some of the shells are real collector's items if you know what to look for. Amy once got thirty-five dollars for a very small one. Look in those ice chests."

We looked into the four ice chests and saw shrimp. Altogether there must have been a hundred pounds!

When I looked up with a stunned expression, Amy explained, "We trade shrimp and flounder to the hotel's restaurant for our room and board."

I turned to study the other people, who were loading their cars with buckets and chests, and realized they were all there for the same reason. What a fun way to have a vacation!

Later that day, we toyed with the idea of joining the group working on the belt the next morning. We never made it, the weather turned foul, and the scallop boats were stranded for a week.

After waiting another day for better weather, Roger looked out at the white caps and threatening skies over the Gulf waters then opted to go up the river and take the Intercostal Waterway to Port St. Joe. Sometimes, I thought he used good sense.

That stretch of the Waterway was one of the few parts we could navigate due to the height of the mast. Whoever designed all those fifty-foot bridges obviously didn't like sailboats with fifty-five-foot masts.

The Waterway is primarily a system of bayous and streams connected by dredged channels. High banks and thick vegetation protect the Waterway from wind, so naturally, the trip became another motorboat ride. The wildlife in and around the tea-colored, slow-moving water mesmerized us. Birds of intense colors roosted in the trees or waded along the root-tangled muddy banks; brown turtles sunned themselves on cypress logs; green and blue horseflies darted out to rest on our rigging. Hyacinths floated all around us, and sometimes the channel all but disappeared as a mass of the purple flowers spread from bank to bank. The songs of crickets, frogs, and birds mingled with the hum of *Halcyon*'s motor.

We couldn't resist. We dropped anchor next to a bank, shut down the engine, and enjoyed a lunch of fresh crabmeat with cold beer amidst the serene sounds of the surroundings.

From Port St. Joe, we ventured into the open ocean and experienced the last truly beautiful sail we would have for months. If we had known it then, we might have savored it more.

As we dropped anchor in Panama City a chilly north wind sent us below and to bed early. At daybreak the thermometer read thirty-two degrees! Why hadn't we remembered what winter was like?

I jumped out of bed, rushed to the lockers, and pulled out socks that didn't match, long-sleeved shirts that had been used to mop the floor, holey sweatshirts, jeans with legs too short or with holes in the knees and rears. We put on everything we could find, covered it all with windbreakers, and set out at a dead run for the nearest Goodwill store. A half hour later we walked out with every sweater, coat, and pair of mittens they had in stock.

From then on, we were miserable. We stayed in our bunks for three days, covered to the chins with blankets and trying desperately to stay warm. Even Sea Coral seemed bewildered. She slept day and night under the covers at the foot of my bunk and came out only long enough to find her way to the stern of the boat and her litter box. The decks were like ice and if a cat could be said to tiptoe, then that's how she walked.

On the fourth day the weather warmed up to the sixties and we set out for a bracing sail to Destin. Ron was at the wheel when we heard him shout, "Porpoises!"

We'd seen so many by then no one was particularly excited, but he became so agitated we went up on deck to observe a most incredible sight. Five or six porpoises were romping with us. They were lined up beside our bowsprit, racing along at the same speed as the boat. Roger took the wheel and the kids and I hurried to the bow to watch as one large porpoise swam into position below the sprit. His tail flicked a mere few inches in front of *Halcyon*'s onrushing bow, and he effortlessly held ahead of the boat.

I stretched out on the bowsprit and dangled my hand to just inches above the beautiful creature's body. He was so close I could see the breathing spout open and close when he broke the surface for air. His skin was covered with a very faint pattern of spots. Suddenly he rolled over, and I was looking directly into his eyes. Behind me, I heard Janice suck in her breath and say, "He's smiling at us!"

I thought she was right and added, "I don't think he's afraid either."

The porpoise dove, swam aside and we watched as another took his place and repeated the process of swimming, rolling several times, then diving out of the way to let the next one have a turn. It was a perfect rotation and no one porpoise seemed to use more time than the others.

"Mom! They're playing Follow the Leader!" Ron shouted.

We watched for half an hour and when they finally swam away, they did a few hearty leaps into the air while we applauded from the deck. Porpoises surrounded us all the way to Pensacola, and we felt safe knowing they were there. If any of us had fallen over, we were sure we would have been well cared for until help arrived.

A "crazy" is a fight that comes from nowhere, is over something that no one else understands, usually lasts long enough to generate a good cry, and makes everyone around wonder what hit them. Some people go crazy if they can't find their keys or if someone has the audacity to use their toothbrush, razor, or comb. More than one 'crazy' has been sparked when some insensitive jerk forgot to replace an empty roll of toilet paper.

Roger never seemed to have any crazies until he put on his Captain's hat, the kids were just developing theirs, and most people living on boats discover they have crazies they never knew about. I certainly seemed to have my share and one of them concerned my scissors.

We were anchored in a small lagoon on the edge of Pensacola, and I decided it was the perfect place to repair the jib sail. The stitching showed wear and needed reinforcing along the weak seams. I assembled all the necessary tools, then couldn't find the scissors. They were the only decent pair I had, and I was perturbed when I emptied the last locker and they weren't there.

On a hunch I went to Roger's tool locker and, lo and behold I found one pair of scissors, covered with rust and bent out of shape from being used as a crowbar. I saw red! Roger watched in utter bewilderment as I grabbed the scissors and went flying up onto the deck. Flinging them as far out into the water as possible, I turned on Roger and blubbered incoherently about "Nothing being sacred!" and "Thank God *Halcyon* doesn't eat food and wear clothes or we'd all be naked and starving to death!" By the time my wailing and shedding of buckets of tears had ceased, I had moved out.

Since there is absolutely no place to go to if one moves out of a boat at anchor, I found myself perched on the bowsprit with the jib sail draped in my lap, and there I sat, furiously sewing for the rest of the day. I refused to speak to anyone and took great pleasure in listening to Roger try to put together a meal for the kids. He spent a full half hour just looking for a can of chili, but it served him right!

By nightfall I had double-stitched two miles of sail using a rusty old razor blade to cut the thread (as well as two fingers and a thumb). I also found I was not as mad as I was hungry, cold, and sore from sitting so long on the wooden bowsprit.

Going below to an atmosphere of icy silence, I ate a peanut butter sandwich, climbed into my bunk with a book, and soon was asleep.

The sun streaming through the porthole the next morning woke me. The boat was unusually quiet and still. I jumped up to find that Roger and the kids were gone!

This time my "crazy" had gone too far. With repentance in my heart, I rushed on deck to see the dinghy approaching, and when Roger and the kids climbed on board the boat, they handed me a small package. Inside I found a shiny new pair of scissors!

Feeling thoroughly rotten, I hugged the kids, then Roger, and apologized for my behavior.

He grinned, we kissed and made up, and silently I vowed to do something to control my crazies.

Traveling by boat makes possible one of the greatest pleasures in life: the up-close visiting of new (or old) surroundings. When we fly from one place to another, we miss all of the in between sights and smells. Driving is not so bad, but often the trip goes too fast and if the windows are closed for the air conditioner, and if the country roads are never explored, and if food stops occur only along the highway, then what is the point? Trains are fun for the experience of riding the rails, but the scenery passing outside the window is still too far removed to produce that special tingle of excitement.

We saw the South in the Waterway between Carrabelle and Port St. Joe and heard it in the Southern drawls around St Petersburg. But it was the food that tugged us along, the shrimp and oysters in Carrabelle, catfish and hushpuppies in Pensacola, boudin sausage and spicy stuffed crabs in Biloxi.

Our anticipation at seeing New Orleans again grew as *Halcyon* slowly wound her way along the edges of the Gulf Coast. Roger and I used the quiet times to reminisce about our honeymoon in Biloxi, my growing-up years and his bachelor days in the French Quarter, and we answered questions for our kids about our destination: "What is Mardi Gras? Were people really buried above ground? Can anyone ride on a ferry? Does everyone speak French in the French Quarter?"

And as our excitement mounted, our charts slowly changed from the Native American names of Florida to the French names of the middle Gulf Coast, Dauphin and Petit Bois Islands, Pass Christian, Bayous Platte and Sauvage, Lakes Maisson, Antoine, Michod, and finally, Lake Pontchartrain. It was two days before Thanksgiving.

CHAPTER 9: ON A SCALE OF 1 TO 10, I'D RATHER HAVE A HOUSE

New Orleans was cold. The winter winds rolled in off Lake Pontchartrain to clang all the rigging in the marina in a ceaseless, cacophonous racket. The dampness chilled us to the bone, and in an effort to get warm and stay healthy, we bought a small kerosene heater. It helped a little.

Thanksgiving was spent in a real house amidst aunts, uncles, cousins, grandparents, and friends. The kids renewed an acquaintance with TV and Roger watched endless hours of football when he wasn't dozing contentedly in an overstuffed chair. For me it was wonderful to touch home-base again, but after twenty-four hours with family, I began to notice a left-out feeling. They talked of microwave ovens, food processors, the latest fashions, decorating trends, fad diets, religion, and child-rearing. And they looked perplexed when I talked of motoring to work on the Miami River, wanting to sort shells in Apalachicola, our new found sailing abilities, schooling with the kids, or Roger's conversion from a harried businessman to a completely relaxed and happy vagabond. I became increasingly aware of how out of touch with their world I truly was. I also noticed that the discussions did not make me envious, and I wondered why.

There was puzzlement etched all over my aunt's face when I raved about the hot shower I had just enjoyed in her bathroom. "Well, Dear, how do you shower on the boat?" she asked.

"In the head; on the deck; but usually at the end of a very cold hike down a very long pier."

She shivered. "Oh, that sounds difficult."

Then just for a moment, a picture flashed across my mind of me floating in a warm aquamarine sea, life ring around my waist, shampoo in my hair. "Only sometimes," I said.

They asked how long we planned to stay in New Orleans, and I couldn't tell them. Roger and I hadn't talked about it.

"Just long enough to have *Halcyon*'s bottom repainted," Roger spoke up. "And the kids would like to experience the Mardi Gras in February. After that we'll head south again."

That's nice, I thought. He could at least have consulted me.

"What are you going to do for wheels?" a cousin asked.

"The motor bike I suppose," Roger answered. "Although, if the weather stays this cold it will be rough."

Out of generosity and probably some pity, the cousin offered his second car to us for a month. And since pride was a luxury we could ill afford, we took it with lots of gratitude.

We began looking for a boatyard for *Halcyon*. For weeks we drove the entire southern coast of Louisiana and visited every yard around. We didn't expect what we found. Boatyards that were too small to lift our weight, too big to bother with us, too expensive, too busy. Yards located on canals too shallow, or canals with bridges or overhead cables that were too low for our mast. Yards that wouldn't let us do any of the work ourselves, others that wouldn't do any work for us, and yards that wouldn't let cats in, kids in, or any of us in. We kept searching.

The week after Thanksgiving, life aboard *Halcyon* reverted to the tumultuous norm. Cold weather forced us to keep the cabin closed tight and the kids were rarely allowed outside. On waking each day, they began fussing with one another and never stopped. They resisted schoolwork and I tired of trying to stuff fundamental facts into unwilling minds.

Then Sea Coral gave us an encore performance: four more kittens. In Miami we had talked of having her fixed, then rushed away too quickly, and too late. After speculating about her one fateful evening with C.K. and noting all the tiger striped kittens, we decided that true love obviously has its consequences. We named the kittens Barnacle, Binnacle, Compass, and Sprit and I vowed they would find new homes at the first sign of weaning.

The arrival of kittens filled me with foreboding. I was determined we would not spend another miserable month in constant turmoil. Roger and I had to have some time alone once in a while, I needed some peace. It was obvious we were going to be in New Orleans more than a month or two, so I took the kids down and enrolled them in school.

They thought it was great as they went off eagerly each morning to catch the bus and were filled with excitement over meeting new friends, wearing real clothes, eating in the cafeteria, even studying. The excitement lasted two days, in the end it seemed school is school no matter where it happens to be.

Another list of trinkets for *Halcyon* emerged: a new mainsail, sail covers, parts, and paint. And at the top of the list were the expenses of having her hauled and repainted. In addition, Roger wanted a used car to get around once we returned the cousin's, but nowhere on the list was a new carpet for me.

Roger looked at the estimated costs of everything, bit the bullet, and took another job waiting tables. I went out and bought some material, drug out my sewing machine, started making bedspreads for the bunks, and tried to shake the depression that kept recurring with each new cold front.

The bedspreads were finished before Christmas and the boat looked much less Spartan. Then Roger brought home a few strings of blinking, colored lights and fastened them along the portholes on the inside of the cabin. Then he took us all out on the dock to survey the effect.

Halcyon winked bawdily as the lights flickered behind the already colorful-granny squares on her portholes. "She looks friendly," Roger said as he beamed in admiration.

"Yeah," I agreed wryly. "On most days."

We bought presents for the kids, clothes for school, books, drawing materials, and games. It was our second Christmas on board, and I doubted that we would make a third. Fervently, I yearned for the warm, tropical isles, swaying coconut trees, white sand beaches, but they all seemed so far away. It was at that moment that I made the decision. Immediately after Christmas I would approach Roger and call a halt to the whole sailing experience. Cruising was fun but living on a boat was for the birds. And the living far outweighed the cruising.

On Christmas Eve, Roger had to work so the kids and I ate dinner alone. Their excitement kept them chattering and bubbly all through the meal and instead of lifting my spirits, their innocent anticipation simply reinforced my depression. As the evening wore on, we made cookies for Santa, read stories, and listened to carols on the radio, until eventually (and gratefully) they fell asleep.

Crawling into my bunk I lay there staring at the ceiling and tried, unsuccessfully, to ignore the constant drip of the rain on the deck. Why hadn't I remembered how damp and cold New Orleans could be in the winter? The bed covers felt as though I'd been storing them in the ice box, and I wondered for a moment if a fireplace could be installed on a sailboat.

It was midnight when Roger arrived and in his arms were the bundles he had been hiding in the trunk of the car. I helped him pile the chart table high with Christmas presents. As we finished, he turned to me, smiled, and handed me an envelope. I opened it to find a small piece of gold and brown carpet. Sitting down on the bottom rung of the companionway, I gave him a long look and whispered, "What is this?"

His eyes were smiling. "How do you think it will look on the floor?"

"Not bad, but it's awfully small." I glanced at the square of carpet, then back at him. "Is this a promise, a sample, or a tease?"

"Call it a bribe. Anyway, there is enough in the trunk of the car to cover the entire cabin floor and we can lay it in the morning, if you are ready to help." he spoke softly.

I wondered if he knew how ready I was to give it all up.

I leaped to my feet and nearly upended him as I threw my arms around his neck. "What's wrong with tonight?" I squealed.

Strangely enough the kids slept through the total operation. The first light of Christmas morning coming through the portholes found the two of us sitting on our heels, surveying the effect. It was wonderful. *Halcyon* had a bright new image, and I had a whole new outlook.

I kissed him soundly, and said, "The carpet is perfect. This is a wonderful Christmas present. Thank you."

He was watching me closely. "Do I detect a serious note?"

"It shows does it? Well, I was going to have a talk with you tonight."

"About moving off the boat?" He finished my thought.

"You knew?"

"Yes, I'd guessed. I've even thought about it." He paused for a minute, then put an arm around my shoulders and said, "You know how I feel about sailing, and I know it's been harder than we expected. All I can ask is that you give it a little longer."

Running my hand over the soft carpet I gave him a teasing smile, "This really was a bribe! You are more devious than I ever suspected. Okay, I'll try for a while longer. Now let's wake the kids and see what they think about my present."

Tommy and Janice responded to my calls by sitting up in bed, jumping down on the new carpet, and running straight for their presents. Ron rubbed sleep from his eyes, looked around at the floor, and asked, "What's for breakfast?"

Christmas Day was a day to play and for us to renew a love affair with a city. New Orleans is one of the places where the natives rave and rant about the 'modern changes', when in retrospect nothing ever changes at all. The many layers of history that make up the city are still there, and the newest layer is merely piled on top of the old.

We toured the French Quarter, then on Dumaine Street, we pointed out the picturesque, renovated slave quarter tucked at the back of a quiet, red brick courtyard. "Dad and I lived there right after we were married," I told the kids.

A few blocks away we peeked inside Lafitte's Blacksmith Shop. "It's a bar now," Roger explained. "But in the early 1800s a pirate named Jean Lafitte and his brother ran it as a blacksmith shop. In the back room they sold smuggled goods to the rich people and often illegally sold slaves."

"Do people still sell slaves?" Janice asked as she apprehensively watched a bar patron stagger past us and down the street.

"No, Dummy!" Tommy sneered. "Abraham Lincoln stopped that with the Silver War."

"With silverware? That's stupid!" Janice sneered back.

"Tommy, Janice is not a Dummy." I stepped in. "And Janice, Tommy is not stupid." And a lesson about history and the evils of slavery was taught right then and there.

Ron announced it was lunchtime, so we made our way to Jackson Square. Along the way we bought fat spicy Italian sandwiches from a neighborhood grocery store and carried them with us to the Square. Finding a park bench in the sun, we sat and ate. Andy Jackson sat astride his horse, oblivious to the ever-present pigeons in his hair and the cold winter day with the five of us at his feet.

We explored every inch of the French Quarter, rode the ferry back and forth across the mighty Mississippi, took a streetcar to Audubon Park, and then devoted an hour to browsing in one of the "Cities of the Dead." The kids learned that people really were buried above ground in vaults that resembled little houses. And while the three kids expended energy by dashing in and out of the "neighborhood" of multi-tiered granite crypts and mausoleums, Roger and I rested on a low stone wall and peered around the graveyard.

"It looks exactly as I remember it," Roger said as he scanned the cemetery, and the verandaed houses on the street beyond.

I nodded then said, "Do you know in another hundred years all the aluminum, plastic and glass will be covered with wisteria, ivy, and green moss, like these graves. And some buxom, fur-coated, Matron of Society will come along and hang historical markers everywhere to commemorate the twentieth century."

"As hard as that might be to believe I think you're right."

If it is nice to see that some things don't change, it can also be discouraging.

"What's a N****r?" Ron asked, after school one day.

"Ron!" I was as surprised at the question as I was at the word.

"But, Mom! What does it mean?"

How amazing to learn our children had been so protected, they had never been exposed to the racial slur. Ron and I sat down to a long talk about race and color that ended with him feeling confused and me, frustrated.

I knew it wasn't settled when, a few days later, Janice asked, "Is it all right if I eat lunch at school with somebody who is black?"

"Certainly. Why do you ask?"

"I sat with Emmy today and the other kids called me a 'N****r Lover'." Tears welled up in her eyes and spilled down her freckled cheeks. I cringed. It had been twenty years since the Civil Rights movement in the South and the insults were still being used. Would it take another hundred years to stop calling names?

We had another dissatisfying discussion that ended with Janice feeling only slightly less intimidated by the others in her school.

When Tommy asked, "Why do people like to smoke 'grass'?" I came close to dropping the coffee cup in my hands.

"Why do you ask?" I tried not to sound overly shocked, but it was hard—he was only eight years old.

"Some boys in my class say they like to smoke grass," he announced. "That sounds dumb to me."

"You're right, it is dumb. By the way, do you know what 'grass' is?"

"Sure, the stuff that grows in yards."

"And, as usual, you are partly right." I giggled.

It seemed that each day brought a new question, and though dinner discussions were enlightening, they were also disturbing. Before long the kids were feeling ridicule and laughter from their classmates, and for them, life was growing increasingly more difficult. I could see, they were as out of touch with their peers as I was with mine. Besides the jargon of drugs and ethnic insults; the current slang, rock stars, and TV shows were topics our kids knew nothing about. Janice showed her unhappiness by getting snippy; Ron withdrew into his books; and Tommy reverted to his "Class Clown" act, which eventually won admiration from the other boys in school, if not from his teacher.

Roger and I discussed it and realized the problems the kids were facing would not disappear by leaving New Orleans. It didn't matter where we went anymore, something had changed for all of us. I thought of a conversation from two years before, when we'd prepared to leave California. We had sought out the advice of a friend who'd done something similar with his family, and my questions then had been, "What will this mean for the kids? Won't they miss a lot in their social development?"

What he told me made me uneasy. He'd said, "Your children will be 'special people' when they come back. They will see life differently from everyone they know simply because their horizons will be wider. And because of the education they miss via Madison Avenue and TV, they may even be angry at their parents for 'depriving' them. But the experience is worth the pain. I promise you that someday way down the road they will understand what they gained."

I thought his answers were gloomy and even negative and I did not believe all that he said. Now, however, I was not so sure.

The weatherman on the radio announced January to be the coldest since 1927. The kids were elated to find ice on the deck when they left in the mornings and kept voicing their wishes for snow. I didn't care; the new carpet made the boat feel snug and warm as never before.

We returned the cousin's car and Roger resumed riding the motorbike to work for one night. A slow drizzle accompanied his trip back to the boat, and as he came down the companionway, eyes and nose red, hands blue, teeth chattering, and icicles in his mustache, he said, "Tomorrow we buy a car!"

Within twenty-four hours we had a beauty, and if it had been a horse it would have been shot on the spot.

In mid-February the weather broke. I opened ports in the afternoons to let spring and fresh air into the cabin. Our new sail arrived, all crisp, white, horridly expensive, and I certainly hoped *Halcyon* appreciated the sacrifice.

Finally, we found a yard that would haul the boat for us. As a rule, that particular yard-built oil rig tenders. After some pleading from us, the manager felt he could squeeze us in around the end of March and work on *Halcyon* in his spare time. With no other choice, we accepted the terms.

Mardi Gras is that insane custom of many Catholic communities around the world to prepare for the solemn arrival of Lent. Since Lent is a time of fasting, sacrificing, and repentance, the Orleanian feels he must do all he can in the weeks before Lent to prepare himself. If he intends to fast for Lent, then he gorges for Mardi Gras. If he must repent during Lent, then he does something worth repenting in the weeks before.

"Mardi Gras" translates "Fat Tuesday," and comes the day before "Ash Wednesday." If anything can be said about the virtues of Mardi Gras, it is probably that during the forty days between Ash Wednesday and Easter, there is less smoking, less drinking, more dieting, and the churches experience their best attendance of the year.

It was all I remembered it to be, and we enjoyed every minute. The first parades began a full three weeks before "Fat Tuesday," were held at night, and each one attempted to outdo the others in lavishness and excitement. The kids saw ten parades before the arrival of Mardi Gras, and they discovered the most exciting thing. The riders on the floats threw presents to the crowd! From the first parade they brought home five pounds of plastic necklaces, two sets of vampire teeth, forty-seven doubloons, one (or is it a pair of?) big red rubber lips, some whistles, and a wiggly green rubber snake. By the end of the festivities, they had enough trinkets to trade for Manhattan at current prices.

We prepared pirates' costumes the night before Mardi Gras. Each of us, using blue marking pens, drew wide stripes on five new white undershirts. I made eye patches from elastic and black felt, and to complete the get up, the boys drew on mustaches (Roger had a perfectly stunning one of his own), and each of us had one gold earring with a bright red scarf to tie around our heads.

Mardi Gras morning dawned warm and only slightly overcast. We donned our costumes, drove downtown to an area known as Lee Circle, and stood on the sidewalk with a half million natives and tourists to watch the first of many parades. By 2 p.m. we'd seen enough to last us for a while, and as we walked toward the French Quarter, the costumed crowds pressed around us. On Canal Street we met a family of plump red tomatoes waddling along on skinny green legs. We shook hands with them, smiled at Mr. and Mrs. Frankenstein, and took some pictures of a group of assorted clowns.

Approaching Bourbon Street, we saw an assemblage of nuns strolling solemnly by. One had a five o'clock shadow, another raised her outfit to expose a red lacy garter on a hairy muscular leg.

"Did you see that?" Janice asked with eyes as big as saucers.

Behind them came a couple dressed in all the splendor of a King and Queen from the seventeenth century, long satin robes, and jeweled crowns on elaborate powdered hairdos. I realized they were royalty from the gay world.

We bumped into a large cardboard box. The outside of the box was painted like a vending machine, and across the top was a sign, "Fortune's told." At the bottom were two slots, one for a penny, the other for the fortune. The kids begged for money, deposited it in the appropriate slot, and received their fortunes. Tommy's was the closest: "You are so lazy you are destined to a life of welfare." The box thanked us for the pennies, then lumbered away.

The crowd parted to allow a grocery cart to roll by. It was an unusual sight mainly because all vehicles were banned from the Quarter for the day. The cart was pushed by a pretty young man dressed like a court page, and inside the cart were piles of purple satin pillows. Seated in the midst with legs dangling over the end was an abundantly plump middle-aged woman with too much makeup, a slightly askew tarnished crown on her frowzy semi-bleached hair, a plumber's friend for a scepter in one hand and a can of beer in the other. She handed some beads to Janice and ordered majestically, "Pay homage to your Queen, Honey."

Janice giggled.

The crowd grew denser the further we traveled down Bourbon Street. We passed a couple from outer space. Snoopy passed us eating an ear of corn. So many people occupied the street we could hardly move. At one point, we found everyone looking up at a balcony and we stopped to see a lovely girl dressed in an elaborate antebellum hat and gown. She waved, threw necklaces and doubloons to the admiring crowd, then turned around, flipped her dress up, and exposed her bare bottom.

"WOW!" Ron gasped. I grabbed him by the arm, and we pushed on. At the edge of the masses I spied a young man with a solemn face carrying a sign that read, "The wages of sin are DEATH" and I couldn't help but laugh as I told Roger, "He sure has his work cut out for him."

In the next block we heard more cheers and looked up at the balcony to see dozens of lovely young ladies in mini bikinis, each posing, and in turn receiving adoration and applause from the crowds below. It took a second look to see that they were all male.

With relief we turned toward Jackson Square. The crowd thinned and the sights became a little less surprising. As we approached Pirates' Alley, we listened to a country-western band. Further on we spied a juggler, a folk singer, a rock band, some acrobats, a magician, and a con artist playing his shell game.

We crossed the Square and went into Cafe du Monde for café au lait and beignets (coffee and French doughnuts), then climbed the levee to watch the mighty Mississippi go by for a while. It was 4 p.m. and our feet hurt. We rested for an hour stretched out in the grass. The sounds of the make-believe world of the French Quarter floated out over the river to mingle with the occasional horn blast of a passing tug. I felt we were sitting on top of the world looking down at complete insanity on one side, peace and tranquillity on the other.

At 5 p.m. we turned back toward Lee Circle, elbowed our way through the mob, and arrived just in time to watch the Comus night parade, the last of the season. As the final band marched away to the sound of the bass drum, we searched out the car and went home to *Halcyon*.

The next morning the newspaper read, "The Best Mardi Gras Ever! Five hundred thousand people had been packed into fifteen square blocks and I was sure we had bumped into every one of them.

Amazingly, we had seen only one scuffle the entire day and I wondered if the attitudes of the policemen we'd met had helped to keep the carnival season festive. There were so many police they had to be transported in rental trucks. For two weeks they had worked around the clock (sixteen hours on and eight hours off), slept in converted buses parked in the Quarter, and the buses had been identified with signs the police had made that read "the Pig Hotel" or "The Pig Pen."

The policemen must have been tired, and tempers should have been short, but we never saw an example of it. They joked with the young people, gave us directions willingly every time we asked, and always seemed to maintain a sense of humor. One officer wore a grotesque mask full of warts and wrinkles with a sign that read, "This is what happens if you get a social disease!" But my favorite was the policeman in full uniform except for his mask—a huge plastic head of a PIG! Apparently, there is more than one way to deal with an insult.

March arrived and the weather warmed up so much we slept with the hatches open again, and it was wonderful. The kittens thought so too. They had grown so big and playful, it was necessary to put them out in the cockpit during the day or risk their lives under foot in the cabin.

Sea Coral kept trying to wean them, but they weren't particularly interested. Then one night we found out just how serious she was to end their dependency. We had been asleep several hours when a strange noise woke me. I crawled out of bed, turned on the light, and there on my new carpet sat Sea Coral, the kittens, and a six-inch-long LIVE fish flopping in their midst. The kittens were enchanted with the wiggling, smelly thing and kept trying to play with it while Sea Coral sat and watched, looking very pleased with herself and her charges.

I snatched the fish up marched to the deck and flung it into the water as Sea Coral ran up beside me. It was obvious she was upset as she watched the fish swim away.

I went back to bed and wasn't asleep more than a few minutes when I heard the same noise again. Was I dreaming? For the second time I jumped out of bed, and on the way to the light stepped, barefoot, on another cold slimy fish! Where was she getting them? In anger I simply picked up the fish and sailed it right out of the hatchway and into the water.

The next hour saw two more fish come and go the same way. At least I thought they were different fish. If not, then one fish must have been awfully dizzy by the fourth go round.

The following morning, we walked along the docks trying to figure out how Sea Coral had caught them. We couldn't solve the mystery, but realized those kittens had to go before we found ourselves living with fish on board.

The kids made signs asking for homes for the kittens and posted them near the showers. Since sailors like to have a cat on board for company and to keep the rats away, the first two went quickly. The last two were still around a week later when the kids came home and announced that the "Bionic Man" wanted them.

"Bionic Man?" I asked, knowing full well that was a silly question.

"He's our friend," Tommy explained. "And we just call him that."

When they insisted I go with them to deliver the kittens, I agreed. Mainly, I was curious to meet this "Bionic Man."

He was quiet and moody, in his late twenties, and had lost an arm in Vietnam. The prosthesis was fascinating to the kids and was the reason for the name. But I was shocked to see the open curiosity they displayed about the artificial arm. When I scolded them about their rudeness, the young man stopped me. "Please don't. They really aren't making fun, you know. Besides, I like being thought of as the Bionic Man."

He showed us his home, a dilapidated old wooden houseboat he shared with his hundred-pound shaggy dog, and our two kittens. I was surprised when, as we were leaving, he invited the kids to come and visit the kittens the next day. "I don't want the kittens to feel lonely," he explained.

When I hesitated, he must have seen my concern because he said, "I enjoy having your children around. They are so cheerful."

"Okay," I agreed. Then, as an afterthought I added, "If the dog and kittens don't get along, please let us know. I don't want you to feel pressured into taking them."

"Don't worry," he smiled. "They'll do just fine." I wasn't so sure; that dog looked like it could have swallowed those kittens whole.

After school the next day the kids stopped to visit the Bionic Man and the animals, then reported to me that the kittens were very happy.

"Mom, you wouldn't believe it," Ron said awestruck. "The dog and the kittens eat from the same bowl and at the same time!"

Janice was equally amazed. "And when they are all through, they lick each other clean!"

I received daily reports for a week, then began to worry that the kids were becoming a nuisance. They had been admonished to stay on the dock when visiting but I still thought they could be annoying for the shy young man. Finally, I told them to stay away for a while.

"But the kittens will miss us," whined Janice.

"Well, they have good care and your friend probably would enjoy some peace."

I was on my way to the showers when I met the young man again. "It's been almost a week since I've seen your children. I hope they aren't sick." He was genuinely concerned.

"They're fine," I said. "I'm responsible for them not visiting. I know they can be a little rowdy at times, and I didn't want them to become pests."

"Oh no," he insisted. "They are always welcome. The kittens miss them so much and so do I." Somehow I knew he meant it.

The visits resumed from then until we left New Orleans, and Ron summed it up for me at dinner one evening. "Mom, he likes animals and kids more than people."

The "Bionic Man" was certainly one of the "special' ones," I thought to myself.

Of all the special people in the lives of children, the most special are the grandparents. And the only person more special than a Grandmother, must be a Grandfather. Grandmothers spoil children, love them unconditionally, read them stories, and laugh at their elephant jokes. But Grandfathers do most of those things and more—Grandfathers buy candy, gum, and ice cream!

When my father came from northern Louisiana to visit, the kids were in seventh heaven. They made daily treks to the ice cream parlor, the objective being to try all fifty-seven flavors before Grandpa had to go home.

In between their visits to the ice cream parlor Dad and I talked, and he, like my mother, was entranced with our sailing experiences. But when I described any of the hardships of surviving and just plain living, he smiled and said such sympathetic things as: "You made it, didn't you?" Or "Relax, Toni, and enjoy it. The good things never come easy."

Hadn't Mother said something like that?

After dinner one night, Dad, Roger, and I were sitting at the table with our coffee while the kids lay in the forward bunk, listening to their nightly mystery stories on the radio.

The men talked of sailing. "What are your plans from here?" Dad wanted to know.

"Panama, I hope," Roger answered. "As soon as we leave the boatyard." He paused for a minute as though formulating the thoughts in his head, then added, "Along the way I would like to stop in Cozumel, dive off the coast of Honduras, then go through the Canal and back up to California."

Before he went any farther, I thought I'd better bring him back to reality. "Roger, you make it sound so easy! Judging by our track record, don't you think a trip like that might take a while?" He didn't answer.

"Which leads to my next question," Dad asked. "How long do you plan to live on the boat?"

Roger answered without hesitation, "I'd like to find some way to stay on it permanently."

I was aghast. "Roger! You can't raise three kids on a sailboat! Have you lost your senses?"

"Well, a few more years shouldn't be all that hard. Then maybe an island somewhere for a while."

When Dad said, "That sounds perfect!" I decided he was as crazy as Roger. My whole family was crazy!

The two of them talked into the wee hours of the morning, while I sat and wondered how I could turn this conversation around. They studied charts, chose good diving spots, discussed hurricane anchorages, and talked of the politics of the various countries in Central America.

"Do you have a gun?" Dad asked suddenly.

I jolted upright. "A GUN! No way are you going to put a gun on this boat! One of us would probably shoot himself with it."

"But I've been hearing a lot about drug smugglers in the Caribbean, Toni," Dad said with concern. "I would feel safer if you had a gun on board."

To me the idea was nonsense and I argued against it. "We hear the stories too and have met hundreds of sailors but none that have encountered a smuggler or a hijacker. I think our biggest enemies are probably ourselves. What we need to do is make sure no one leaves the sea valve open on the toilet. A gun wouldn't help then."

"Toni, your dad might be right. I'd feel a little safer with a gun on board."

It occurred to me that if there was that much danger, then why were we doing this?

Dad said, "As soon as I get home, I'll send you my shotgun."

It was settled.

The gun arrived a week later, and Roger stashed it away in the engine room, well secured above a beam. I smiled to myself as I thought about trying to get that gun out in a hurry. It would take five minutes of wiggling on one's tummy, past pumps, hoses, engine, and fuel tanks to reach it. Hijackers had nothing to fear from us.

We began processing five passports, bought a case of freeze-dried rations, and refilled our first aid kit.

Roger called the Mexican Embassy to find out what we needed to cruise in their waters and was told we needed to be inspected for rats.

"RATS! Not on this boat!" I was indignant.

Roger explained it was just a formality.

A very official-looking man in a dark blue suit came to see us, walked around the boat once, then handed me a certificate saying we were rat free. Whew! That was a load off my mind.

For the Panama Canal we learned we had to be weighed.

"Us?" I asked Roger.

"No, the boat."

"But couldn't we just tell them? The documentation shows our weight."

"That's too easy," Roger said, and he was right.

A second, very official looking man in a dark blue suit arrived, spent two hours measuring Halcyon from stem to stern, then handed me a certificate attesting to her weight.

Well, it keeps down the unemployment, I thought as I stashed the weight certificate away with the rat certificate.

We made doctor's appointments, endured complete physicals, and received enough vaccinations to make us sick for three days.

It took another week to replenish the bilge with canned foods and dried beans. And finally, we were ready to go, except for the boatyard.

Roger and the kids motored the boat five miles across the Lake to the boatyard, and I drove the car. Tying *Halcyon* to the dock we hurriedly went to work. It was the last week in March and we expected to be through in ten days.

To be sandblasted and painted meant removing all the metal and wood hardware from the deck winches, cleats, chrome, hatches, vents, hand, and toe rails. With help the job should have taken one day, but an emergency arose in the yard, the workmen disappeared, and Roger and I ended up doing the entire stripping job ourselves. It took a week. After waiting a day for the use of the crane, we lifted off the main mast and when I saw *Halcyon*, naked except for her steel, I wondered if we would ever get her back together again.

On the tenth day *Halcyon* was finally ready to come out of the water. We knew we had to vacate the boat, us and everything that was not part of the superstructure. We'd tried for days to find a place near the yard to stay, but the closest motel was over ten miles away and far too expensive. A motel also meant the logistics of driving the kids back and forth to school, me back and forth to the boatyard, and having Roger sleep under a tree somewhere. In exasperation, we put the housing problem aside, rented an enclosed trailer and began to empty the boat. She was going to get hauled and painted no matter what.

It took a full day of all five of us unloading food, clothes, mattresses, bedding, tools, and a billion other items before she was completely empty. As the last item disappeared into the bulging trailer, the yard manager, Mr. Simms, appeared.

"We will pick the boat up about 7 a.m. Can you be here then?" he asked.

"I'll sleep on the boat tonight." Roger answered with a frown. "But after tonight I just don't know where we'll be staying."

"You don't have a place to live until the boat's done?" Mr. Simms asked with concern.

Roger explained, "It looks like Toni and the kids will have to stay with a relative across town. I'd like for them to be here to help with the work, but there isn't anything available in this part of the city. For myself I'll just have to search again tomorrow for a bed somewhere."

Mr. Simms scratched his head, looked us over, then said, "See that houseboat tied up at the end of the yard there? It belongs to the boatyard and sometimes we let oil company executives use it when they are visiting from out of town. I'll see if I can get permission for you to stay there."

We thanked him profusely, held our collective breath, and within the hour we were moving aboard the houseboat. As I opened the door I gasped, I couldn't believe what I saw. A houseboat? It had two stories, three bedrooms, full carpeting, fireplace, double oven, dishwasher, bathtub, showers, and a television. Secretly I hoped *Halcyon*'s bottom painting would take at least a year.

The next morning, as the boat was cradled and made ready for the sandblasting, Mr. Simms walked over and handed us a dozen rolls of masking tape. "Cover every opening, seal the boat TIGHT or you will have one hellava mess when this job is done."

We went to work, sealing vents, openings, hatches, then wondered how we could protect the glass on the portholes. Roger thought a minute then went to the rental trailer and climbed inside. After rummaging around he came back with all my plastic dinner plates.

"What are you doing with those?" I was worried.

"They are the perfect size for the portholes," he said as he began taping a plate over the first hole.

The least he could have done was ask. "Is there anything else I can sacrifice to this goddess? My children? My wedding ring? How about a heart transplant? Mine's working."

"Aw, come on, Toni. Just think, your plates are going to be sandblasted, primed, then coated with a heavy-duty marine paint. You'll never have to worry about rust on your dishes again."

"You spoil me."

The sandblasting took one day; the first coat of paint took another. Then a dust storm blew in, lasted three days and when it finally blew south, *Halcyon* looked like a giant piece of blue sandpaper.

One day a broken-down crewboat arrived and the painting crew deserted us—for a week. When they returned it was another day painting, one more for first coat on deck, second coat on the hull, one for painting the boot stripe, last coat on decks, a third on the hull, then a wait of three days for the crane to put *Halcyon* back in the water. The entire operation should have taken a week, but it actually took more than three.

As *Halcyon* settled into the water we untied her from the crane, floated her backward toward the dock, then snubbed down the lines. The kids and I ran around the deck pulling off the masking tape covering the vents and removing the plates from the portholes. Roger stepped onto the dock to talk to Mr. Simms.

Ron peeled away the covering for the companionway, started down the ladder, then stopped midway and shouted, "Mom, Dad, WHAT HAPPENED?"

Joining him at the ladder, I looked into the cabin and couldn't believe my eyes. It looked as though the cabin had been spray-painted white from ceiling to sole! The walls were white, the counters, the bunks, and even the brass lanterns where white. My new carpet was white, and it was all SAND!

I turned, and in a daze, climbed back on deck and walked over to Roger just as he was saying goodbye to Mr. Simms.

"Roger, I think you better see this...."

He stopped me. "Just a minute Toni. Mr. Simms wanted to tell you, we have to be out of the houseboat by 4:30 this afternoon. He says some people are arriving ... Hey, what's the matter?"

I was crying, I couldn't stop, and not even a Pollyanna would have kept a stiff upper lip after all of this. Between hiccups and sniffles I told him, "We have a disaster in the cabin. We didn't tape it tight enough."

He headed for the boat in a rush, and I took a deep breath before turning and following him. We found the kids writing their names in the sand dust and laughing at the mini storms they created as they fanned the air.

"This is neat!" Tommy squealed.

It was 11 am, I stopped crying and got us organized. We divided into two crews. Roger and Ron cleaned the and packed our things while Tommy, Janice, and I cleaned *Halcyon*. We vacuumed the boat from stem to stern nine times.

At 4:30pm Roger moved our belongings back on board, shut the door of the houseboat, and officially we were home. Five minutes later the new residents of the houseboat appeared, and I was sorely tempted to go over and find out how much they would take to change places with us.

It was another week of cleaning before we stopped eating or sleeping in the gritty sand, and months before it finally stopped sifting into drawers, cabinets, and beds.

While the two youngest kids and I worked at returning all the belongings from the trailer to the proper lockers on the boat, Ron and Roger tackled the near-impossible task of reattaching all the hardware to the deck. It was like solving a gigantic jigsaw puzzle. Roger began to look distraught and worn before it was done. We were to the last step, raising the mast, when Mr. Simms announced the crane would be unavailable for three or four days.

Roger had reached his limit. "We will tie the mast to the deck and take it to the boatyard back at the marina," He told me firmly, "Maybe their crane isn't so busy!"

The idea seemed risky to me, but we used all the dock lines, sail sheets, and even the anchor lines to secure the mast to the deck. When we were through, I looked at the tangle of ropes and prayed that we wouldn't roll the mast off the deck into the lake, or worse yet, impale another boat with the ten-foot overhang protruding from the front of the bowsprit.

We left the car behind to be picked up the following day, started *Halcyon*'s motor, and headed out into the lake for the five-mile trip back to the marina. I was relieved to see the calm water, but a low ceiling of clouds soon opened up and we were accompanied four of the five miles by a drenching rain. As we traveled, I looked at Roger at the wheel and thought I detected a twitching of the jawline. Could he be gnashing his teeth?

It was dusk when we pulled into the marina, tied to the end of the first pier, and Roger went ashore to find the harbormaster for a slip assignment. The kids and I went below to change into dry clothes. At least the rain had stopped. They asked immediately to go visit their friends from the other boats and especially the Bionic Man. I agreed but admonished, "Don't stay gone long, we need you to help move the boat into the slip, and we'll wait here until you get back."

Ron on newly painted deck

I stretched out in my bunk and tried to relax. The worst was over and never did I want to go through another sandblasting again. I was starting to doze when the sound of voices and feet running around on deck aroused me. Climbing onto the deck I saw we had company: kids everywhere!

"Mom, this is Mr. Wilson," Janice introduced me to a pleasant-faced man in his mid-forties.

Mr. Wilson held out his hand, said, "How do you do?" then added proudly, "I'm a Cub Scout leader and this is my troop." He waved his arm around, indicating about a dozen boys all ten to twelve years old.

I half-heartedly returned his smile, and said, "I'm pleased to meet you. What can I do for you?"

Then I looked around and saw Ron leading three or four boys into the cabin, and Tommy escorting several others out onto the bowsprit. "Hey guys ...... "

"Mom," Janice interrupted me, they've never been on a sailboat before. I told Mr. Wilson you wouldn't mind. That's all right, isn't it?"

"Oh sure." I tried to sound as though I meant it. "Go ahead, Janice. Give Mr. Wilson a tour."

Even the kids think we are the E ticket at the fair. Step right up, folks. See how this crazy family eats and sleeps while sailing to Shang-ri-la.

Minutes later Roger returned, and a look of stunned horror filled his face as he took in the scene before him. Counting our three, there were fifteen squealing fidgeting bodies, and one cheerfully smiling man who grabbed Roger's hand, pumped it up and down, introduced himself, then said, "Thank you so much for letting us ride with you."

RIDE? Who, I wondered, *had said anything about a ride?* Roger gave me a "what in the hell is this all about?" look, and I simply shrugged my shoulders.

Mr. Wilson kept on talking. "This is so nice of you. The boys are thrilled. Did I tell you they'd never been on a boat before?"

Roger nodded, and for a moment I expected some kind of explosion, but then he began giving orders to get underway. I realized he was not putting Mr. Wilson and his boys ashore.

Our assigned dock space was none too easy to maneuver into, and we came close to skewering several other boats in the process. As we approached the slip, Roger remembered that most of our dock lines were tied to the mast, and he shouted orders to Ron and me over the chattering of the boys. When he wasn't heard the first time, he raised his voice louder and his language was very explicit. The Scout leader paled.

But the response was immediate—all fifteen kids rushed to obey. Unfortunately, they couldn't seem to do anything more than tangle the lines, stub their toes, and step on Roger's feet. It was no small miracle when *Halcyon* eased into the dock space without hitting anything.

I cinched down the last line, Roger turned the engine off, and abruptly a hush settled over our crowd. Then Roger began to laugh! We all stared at him as he laughed his way down the companionway to the galley, laughed as he poured himself a drink, and we could still hear him laughing as he made his way into the forward cabin and slammed the door.

With an uncomfortable and worried look Mr. Wilson called his boys together, thanked me again, and left.

Alone at last! The kids and I went below, and were just closing the hatchway, when I heard the telltale splash of water hitting the floor. That could mean only one thing! Rushing to the head I looked in and sure enough someone had left the sea valve open on the toilet and sea water was overflowing everywhere.

It took a half hour and three layers of skin off my knees to mop up the last of it, and as I crawled out of the head, Ron was waiting for me at the door. "What's for dinner?" he asked.

I felt a strong urge to reopen the sea valve, but instead handed Ron the loaf of bread and a pound of bologna, ordered all three kids to fend for themselves, then joined Roger in the forward cabin. Together, we laughed ourselves to sleep. Some days are just like that.

The car was sold, the mast remounted, we gave a farewell party for friends and family, and left New Orleans two and a half months behind schedule.

As the wind filled the sails and *Halcyon* responded, the tension flowed out of our bodies. Roger sat at the wheel once more master of all he surveyed, Ron rigged the troll line, Janice challenged Tommy to a game of gin rummy. And, as we skimmed across Lake Pontchartrain with the wind in our hair and the sun on our backs, it felt good. Whatever was coming, would definitely be better.

CHAPTER 10: MURPHY WILL GET YOU EVERY TIME

If we had left New Orleans before March fifteenth, there would have been warm days, cool nights, favorable currents, north winds to blow us to Yucatan, and no fears of hurricane season. But it wasn't March fifteenth, it was May fifteenth. The wind merely ruffled the sails in the warm spring-summer air. Even if we had wanted to, we could hardly motor fifteen hundred miles. *Halcyon* would barely make five hundred miles before running out of gas. Cursing our timing, we turned east.

As we pulled into the City Marina in Biloxi and tied to the concrete dock, the harbormaster approached us and the tone of his voice was coldly unfriendly as he asked, "Are you spending the night?"

After killing the engine, Roger answered, "We'd hoped to."

"Then you better lock up that cat!" The man indicated Sea Coral who was poised, ready to spring onto the dock. "We don't allow no animals in this marina."

"Can we walk her to the beach?" I asked while shading my eyes and looking at the wide expanse of white sand that came right to the edge of the marina.

"It's okay if you carry her, but if she walks it'll cost you a hundred bucks." There was no mistaking the fact that he meant it.

"We'll carry her!" I agreed and bent down and scooped up Sea Coral. She yowled, bared her claws, and made known she was not happy being held, nor did she want to be locked below in the hot cabin. I couldn't blame her; she had been cooped up on the boat for two days and was as stir-crazy as the rest of us.

We watched the harbormaster stroll away then Tommy begged, "Can I take her to the beach?"

"Sure." I said and handed him the cat. "We will go to the grocery store and meet you on the way back."

Tommy, carrying Sea Coral, skipped merrily away. Roger, Ron, Janice, and I hiked the three blocks along the quiet shady streets to the closest store.

It was invigorating to walk again. On our trip to New Orleans the previous autumn we had been hiking at least five miles a day just to collect groceries, parts for the boat, or to sightsee. But as soon as we'd put the bike ashore and bought the old car, we'd forgotten we had legs. We were always driving to the corner drugstore for a newspaper and could take ten minutes to search out a parking place as close as possible to the front door of the A&P. It made no sense--walking was fun.

An hour later we returned to find Tommy sitting in the sand near a crumpled sandcastle, and the look on his face spelled trouble. "I can't find Sea Coral." he whimpered. "I've called and called, but she won't come."

Roger and I tried to reassure him that we'd find her, then Roger said, "Worrying about it won't help." He pointed to the east saying, "Ron, you and Tommy walk that way; Janice and I will go the other direction. Keep calling her as you walk. We'll meet back at the boat in half an hour and there's an ice cream cone for the one that finds her first."

"I'll go put the groceries away," I offered. "Besides, she's probably waiting on the deck right now for her supper."

But she wasn't. By late afternoon we had searched the marina and the fish houses along the waterfront, got on our knees to peer under dozens of parked cars, and covered the beach for miles in either direction. No Sea Coral.

The next morning we did it all again. Trying to put ourselves in Sea Coral's paws, we followed the malodorous scents emanating from the restaurants and fish houses. It was then I realized how we'd lost her. By Tommy carrying her through the marina, she hadn't been able to smell along the way. After wandering away from him she probably grew confused and couldn't find the smells necessary to lead her back to the boat.

We called the ASPCA and the Humane Society, then questioned the other boaters and the harbormaster. No one remembered seeing a three-colored cat. We put cat food on the deck of the boat each night and were disappointed to find it drawing flies in the morning. It was hopeless.

As we motored away from Biloxi, the kids sat on the deck and scanned the beach in one last effort to spot our beloved cat. Watching them, I knew how they felt because I felt it too; broken hearted and strangely lonely.

"At least she'll have lots of fish to eat," said a tearful Janice.

"Yeah, and she'll get big and fat," said Tommy. "Just like you."

"Mom, make him stop!" Janice cried.

As I separated the two kids a thought flashed through my head, maybe Sea Coral intended to run away.

We continued on to Pensacola on a rare but freshening south wind. Under full sail, we literally skimmed across the tops of the waves, feeling pleasure as *Halcyon* stretched her muscles through the water. The sun dipped behind us; the red sky was the kind to inspire love songs. An Army helicopter appeared overhead, and we could see a soldier in the hatchway.

Grabbing the binoculars, Ron peered skyward and shouted, "Hey, he's taking our picture! Why?"

"Because we look so beautiful," I answered smugly, and at that moment felt as though nothing could go wrong for us. Where had I been the last two years? Mr. Murphy's Law had been written for us!

Dropping the sails the next day, we prepared to motor into the harbor inlet.

The shape and weight of the keel on a sailboat is designed to keep the boat steady and stable in the water, and the boat will stay steady if there is a sail on top to act as a counterweight.

Our first mistake may have been our smugness, but our second was dropping all the sails! The channel looked so calm from where we sat. What we did not see was that underneath the gentle four-foot waves ran a very strong outgoing tide, and it took only seconds to discover it. Before we could re-rig the jib, *Halcyon* was lurching so violently, and none of us could stand on deck.

"Can we turn her around and head out?" I called to Roger while clinging for dear life to the mast.

He pointed toward the bow and answered, "By the time we wait for those ships to pass we won't have room to turn. Besides, we don't have far to go."

Following his direction, I saw several of the Navy ships coming toward us and realized he was right. Well, we could ride it out. I ordered Tommy and Janice below and told them to sit on the floor. Roger revved the engine to full capacity, and we plowed forward, pitching first to the right, then to the left. The following waves laid shoulder to the stern while the outgoing tide acted as a wall against the bow.

A crash from the cabin made me flinch then Janice called up, "Mom, the sugar just jumped out of the cabinet."

Swearing under my breath, I called back, "Leave it alone, we'll clean it up later."

Lashed to the handrail were a dozen five-gallon plastic jugs containing fuel for the stoves, extra diesel, bleach, and vinegar. One big mistake was to tie them with one continuous line. As the first jug worked itself free, the others followed, and in a split second they fell like dominoes to roll, bang, and plop open across the deck. Ron and I tried crawling around on our hands and knees in an effort to retrieve them, but before we could get close several had burst open and covered everything with an oily, pungent film. Finally, we gave up, sat still, and prayed for a quick end to the trip.

Sailors from the passing ship waved to us and I wondered in embarrassment what they thought of the mayhem on the bobbing cork of a boat they were passing. To add insult to humiliation, their wake pitched us over in a heart-stopping roll and more noises came from the cabin below.

Janice's voice came again. "Do you want me to pick up the dishes?

"Heaven's no!" I yelled back. "Just stay put and hold on!"

Two seconds passed. "Mom?

"What is it?"

"Tommy doesn't feel good."

"Tell him to lie down on the floor!"

"But he says he wants to throw up ON ME!"

"As long as it isn't on the carpet!" I answered callously, and thought that if he could make threats, then he couldn't be that sick.

In that two-mile channel, the havoc had started unexpectantly and had lasted only fifteen minutes. And though it seemed like an hour, it was over the instant we cleared the point into the bay. Five minutes later we were tying up at the Yacht Club.

As Roger shut down the engine, I stared dazedly around me. The deck looked like it had been bombed! With reluctance, I descended the companionway ladder and found the cabin to be in much worse shape than the deck. The only blessing was that Tommy had not carried out his threat.

In the galley I saw that a shelf retainer had flipped off, allowing dishes and food to go sliding to the floor—and under it all lay five pounds of sugar! In resignation I began scraping grit out of the carpet and was on my knees when Roger came down the ladder pulling the hatch closed behind him. "We've got a storm coming," he said.

A loud clap of thunder boomed overhead, and *Halcyon* heeled away from the dock as a gust of wind hit with the force of a steamroller. The stretching dock lines creaked, and I voiced my fear that the boat might pull loose from the dock. "Don't worry about it. She'll hold," Roger assured me.

Returning to the matter at hand I wailed, "Look at this mess! Why is it that the worst always happens to us?"

As he stooped to help me pick up the dishes from the floor, Roger answered with a chuckle, "Toni, that's not so."

I sat back on my heels and looked at him in amazement, "Well, how do you figure THAT!" He had to be blind not to see the disaster.

His amusement was obvious as he answered, "Do you realize that if we had been ten minutes later coming through that channel, the storm would have hit us?" Then he was laughing. "I think our luck has changed. For once we didn't get rained on."

Dumping another scoopful of sugar into the garbage pail I stood up, put my hands on my hips, and gave him a disgusted look. "I suppose I should also be thrilled we weren't struck by lightning, or swallowed by a whale?"

ZAP! The flash of light and clap of thunder were instantaneous.

"What was that?" I shrieked. The air was tingling with electricity.

"The mast just got hit by lightning!" Ron announced excitedly, his nose pressed to a porthole.

In disbelief I looked at Roger, who was laughing so much he could hardly talk. "Don't worry, Toni," He blurted. "I think the odds are against tsunamis in Pensacola Bay."

"Don't bet on it!" I snipped.

The frightening storms had built in minutes, unleashed violent winds and rains, then blew quietly away an hour later signalling that summer had arrived. No wind, not even a breeze came out of the north to push us to Yucatan. We waited two days for favorable weather, then took advantage of a clear day to motor to Panama City.

When we arrived, the crowded noisy docks were teeming with tourists and weekend sailors. The steamy hot weather forced Tommy and Janice to seek relief in the cooler forward cabin where they read or played checkers. Ron and I sat in the main cabin laboring over English lessons, while Roger looked for refuge under the awning on the deck to work on one of the endless repair tasks. Occasionally I could hear him talking to one of the passers-by on the dock.

Ron and I were struggling through spelling rules when Roger descended the ladder, followed by a very pleasant-looking young couple.

"Toni, Ron, meet John and Peggy. They were curious about the boat and I invited them to have a look."

We shook hands and I learned they were schoolteachers from Minnesota on vacation in Panama City. John was a gentle giant with a bashful smile and a warm handshake, while Peggy was his opposite—petite, energetic, and talkative.

I gave Ron a recess from school, cleared the table, and invited the visitors to sit for a while.

"This looks like so much fun!" Peggy gushed enthusiastically as she gazed around our tiny home.

I kept quiet. I was not going to spoil her fantasy.

"We'd like to do this too someday," John spoke up. "We would love to live on a boat and just cruise around. Where are you going?"

"Yucatan," Roger sounded so sure of himself.

We talked for an hour about the places we'd been, the things we'd learned, and our present wind problems.

"Where's your next stop?" John wanted to know.

"If we don't get wind, then we'll have to stop in St. Pete for fuel," Roger told him.

"Well, great! We're driving that way tomorrow. We'll look for you at the docks, and maybe we can have dinner together."

We told them goodbye and as they strolled down the dock, I remarked, "There goes another innocent couple who think living on a boat is an endless cycle of margaritas, tropical sunsets, and balmy breezes."

Roger put his arm around me, smiling as he asked, "Well, isn't it?"

Two miles south of Panama City the wind died. We floated. Roger started the engine, but I fussed so much about it that he shut it down. "We aren't in any hurry," I pleaded. "We've got four months before the first north winds show up and we can't afford to motor all over the hemisphere. Let's at least have some peace and quiet while we wait." He relented.

We drifted south for two days on a slight current, just rolling around on a glassy sea, catching fish, chasing some floating object spotted on the horizon, and reading aloud about Columbus's discovery of America. The history was very alive for us as we read of the doldrums and looked out at our hazy, silver gray sky and water. At times the horizon line disappeared altogether, as *Halcyon* drifted through the warm cloudlike air. It was an eerie unreal world. Time had no meaning and often I felt as close to the fifteenth century as I did to the present. A passing galleon would have seemed no less normal than a passing gull.

We flew the jib to keep the boat steady, lashed the wheel in position to hold some semblance of a course, then established lookout watches in case of a storm or ship.

It was too hot to cook so we ate salads and fruit when we were hungry, slept when we were tired, talked, read, sang, and the kids even learned embroidery. The closest we came to a routine was when a radio station on shore aired the nightly *Mystery Theater*.

An hour before the broadcast started, Roger and Ron fixed popcorn, Janice spread all the cushions around on deck, and Tommy set the portable radio on top of the hatch cover. At exactly 8:00 p.m. we turned off all the 12-volt and kerosene lamps, stretched out on the cushions, gazed up at the hazy night sky and listened as horrid villains did despicable things to fair maidens until valiant heroes came to the rescue. TV was never this good.

On the third day a mild southeast wind appeared. We raised all the sails and made it into Tampa Bay by nightfall. Our acquaintances from Panama City were waiting for us at the St. Petersburg docks.

"How was the trip?" John called as he caught our lines.

"Perfect," I said and smiled contentedly.

"Slow!" Roger growled.

John and Peggy joined us for dinner, and we talked into the evening. Their interest in our lifestyle was clear and I was pleased when Roger asked them, "Would you like to join us to Sarasota? You can leave your car here and catch a bus back."

They said in unison, "We'd love it!"

The next day additional gear was stowed on board along with our two willing passengers, and by noon we were on our way.

It was while we were nearing the last buoy in the channel that a large shrimper approached our stern. Roger checked our bearings, then pulled to the edge of the channel to allow the boat to pass. An ever-familiar *thump* on the hull told us we had run aground.

"What was that?" Peggy asked with alarm.

"We're sitting on the bottom," I explained.

Roger sounded puzzled. "How did that happen? We're still in the channel."

"All the same..." I started.

Janice looked at John and Peggy and spoke in her witheringly tolerant voice, "We *ALWAYS* run aground."

Roger gave her a threatening look. "That will be enough young lady!"

The afternoon was spent practicing our standard futile ungrounding routine of kedging, winching, engine right, then left, sails up, then down, and as usual when high tide arrived, we quietly floated free. By then it was dark, so we dropped anchor and slept until morning. John was hardly impressed with our galloping speed of two miles in twenty hours.

The next day was not much better as strong wind and choppy seas forced us to motor slowly all the way to Sarasota. The jib prevented any rolling, but our guests turned green anyway and passed up the lovely lunch I'd prepared.

As they disembarked in Sarasota, Peggy looked at me with glazed over eyes and asked, "Is it always like this?"

"It seems to be, much of the time," I answered. "But you get used to it."

When Roger and John carried their gear up from the cabin, I caught the tail end of John's conversation. "Peg and I have always wanted to travel in a camper. You know one of those big sleek motor homes. We'd tour the States in it, and maybe spend a year in Mexico."

We waved goodbye and watched them disappear down the dock, then turning to Roger, I grinned and said, "Somehow I feel like we've just done a good deed."

We motored for a day, waited two more for a wind from any direction except on our nose, then motored again. It was while we were in Naples that Roger, Tommy, and Janice went ashore to do laundry. Ron and I stayed behind and worked on more spelling rules.

Ron's mind kept wandering from the lessons, and in exasperation, I snapped, "Please pay attention! This is not going to go away until you learn it!" Then, realizing we were both trying too hard, I gave up. "Put it all away, we'll finish it later."

Listlessly he picked up the books, then stopped and asked, "Mom, what's this?"

I looked. He had pulled his T shirt up and was pointing to an area on the left side of his chest. When I reached out to touch it, he flinched. "Does it hurt, Hon?"

He nodded and a chill ran through me. Ron was not one to complain about anything except hunger, and it had been years since he'd even had a cold. Gently, I probed with my fingers and felt a hard lump under the skin. "Did you bump into something?"

"I don't think so," he answered.

"Well, we will watch it for a few days, and if it doesn't get better then we'll see a doctor. But try not to worry about it, that won't help."

But I worried, and my imagination was running full tilt when Roger returned. He calmed me down by suggesting, "It's probably no more than a bruise."

We decided to head for the Keys and if the lump was not gone when we got there, we would find a doctor.

We anchored for the night at the foot of the Everglades, packed a picnic dinner and the kids into the dinghy, and struck out for a nearby island as the sun began to set. A quarter of a mile from shore the water shoaled sharply, and we realized if we wanted to picnic on the beach, we would have to wade in. It wasn't worth the effort. Spreading our dinner out in the dinghy, we sat back, dangled our ten feet over the gunwale, and toasted the sunset with lemonade and margaritas.

As we enjoyed our improbable picnic I looked out at the water and the reflection of an occasional heron or egret flying across the red sky. For a moment it was clear why we had set sail for parts unknown, in a relatively small boat, away from all the comforts of a suburban home. Here we were, a family alone, in a beautiful unpredictable sometimes dangerous world, but we had each other. And what in life was more important anyway? Perhaps living on *Halcyon* I was learning that, and the uncertainty of Ron's health reminded me not to forget it.

Hobie mixed us drinks while Emogene passed around some of her good bread, and the company and the bread gave us a sense of homecoming. We were sitting on the stern of the *Imagine* in a tiny harbor in the upper Keys. *Halcyon* lay at anchor at the mouth of the inlet a mile away, the channel being too shallow to accommodate her keel.

We asked about Don, Madeline, and Max, and learned they were in Michigan with plans to return to the Keys in a few weeks.

After an hour of conversation, Hobie inquired about our plans for cruising. Roger related our efforts in trying to sail south, then ended with, "Hurricane season's here and we've decided this is as far as we'll go until fall. Besides, we have a minor problem with Ron that needs to be looked at before we go any further."

"What's that?" Emogene asked as she turned to Ron, who was quietly and happily devouring the plate of homemade bread.

Explaining about the lump on his chest, I casually mentioned that it was slow in going away. I hoped Ron did not sense my worry.

She frowned. "I don't have any idea what it might be, but I agree you should see a doctor. Do you have one in mind?"

"I hoped you could give us some recommendations," I said.

"Well, we don't have a personal doctor yet, but there is a clinic not far from here. Why don't I drive you over in the morning?"

Agreeing to meet the next day, we loaded the kids in the dinghy and returned to the *Halcyon*.

The anchorage was not the best, and one of the summer storms might easily have drug the boat onto the beach. To prevent any problems, Roger, Tommy, and Janice chose to remain on board, while Ron and I met Emogene on shore the next morning.

Emogene drove us to the clinic, where a nurse ushered us into the examination room. The doctor entered, introduced himself, then quickly turned to Ron and asked, "What seems to be the problem?"

Ron shyly indicated the left side of his chest, and the doctor began to silently probe. When he frowned and asked, "How long have you had that?" my heart stopped.

"About two weeks," Ron answered quietly.

"Well, you can put your shirt back on and wait for your mother outside."

I could see by Ron's expression that the doctor's cold clinical manner was beginning to worry him too. "Go sit with Emogene, Ron, I'll only be a minute," I told him and smiled to reassure him.

Ron closed the door and the doctor spoke with no emotion in his voice. "It's a cyst, Mrs. Larson. Ron should go in the hospital immediately."

"A cyst!" My heart had started to trip wildly, and my voice shook. "Could it be malignant?"

"I can't possibly say without surgery, but I know the cyst must be removed." And he picked up a pen and a pad of paper.

Had I been dismissed? Tears welled up in my eyes, and I was thankful Ron was in the waiting room. Trying to calm myself, my mind turned to the more practical matters of the problem, and I asked, "Doctor, it will take us about a week to get located, either in Miami or Key West. Do you have a suggestion as to which place would be best to have the surgery done?"

He looked up from the desk, directly into my eyes, and I had the distinct feeling he was annoyed with me. "Please understand, Mrs. Larson. I strongly suggest you admit Ron into our hospital here tonight so we can operate in the morning."

"But we are only visiting here. We live on a boat, we don't have a place to dock it." I could hear myself babbling as I tried to explain that we had no car, I couldn't remember the name of our insurance company and I had to contact Roger—he had to know first!

When I stopped talking the doctor looked at me briefly, tore the top sheet from the note pad, handed it to me, and said, "Give this to the Admittance Clerk at the hospital and have Ron there in an hour." Then he stood, opened the door, and ushered me out.

Emogene drove us to the hospital. In attempting to explain to Ron what was happening I tried to hide my fears but could tell by the look on his face that I wasn't succeeding. We sat in the admittance room for an hour waiting for someone to sign Ron in and my heart ached at the fear I could see on Ron's face. My frustration finally came out at some hapless telephone operator at the front desk as I raged, "Isn't there anyone around here that can sign my son into a room?"

"I'm sorry you are having to wait so long,"

"But a staff meeting was called this afternoon, and no one is out yet. But if you will just wait a little longer..."

"That does it!" I grabbed Ron's hand. "Come on, honey! We're going home!" I turned to the surprised telephone girl and added, "We may be back tomorrow."

Emogene drove us to the dinghy, and Ron and I returned to the *Halcyon*. After sending Ron to fix himself a sandwich, I quietly told Roger about the sinister diagnosis, finishing with, "What are we going to do?"

"Well, first, I believe in second opinions. But most of all, I want us in a place safe enough to leave the boat with Tommy and Janice. If Ron is going to have an operation, then we are certainly going to be with him!"

My hands stopped shaking and I found myself calming down. "Where do you propose we go for this second opinion?"

"If we motor all the way, we can be in Key West in twenty-four hours. And that sounds like a nice place to spend the summer."

"It will be," I said. "If Ron is all right."

CHAPTER 11: WHY ANCHOVIES?

The Key West Clinic was a short bus ride from the docks, and within twenty-four hours of leaving Hobie and Emogene, we were sitting in the waiting room. Ron nervously fidgeted as he sat between Roger and me. I knew he would have bolted for the door if he thought he could have made it.

Every few minutes he blurted out, "It doesn't hurt at all! I remember now! I fell on the dock! Mom, it's getting smaller! Dad, I can hardly find it!" Our usually reticent son had found his voice.

A plump, cheery nurse ushered us into the examination room where we were greeted by the doctor's friendly smile and warm brown eyes. My spirits improved immeasurably from no more than his handshake.

Ron, looking paler than the sheet, sat on the table and suffered through a second examination. The probing ended as the doctor patted him on the shoulder and said, "You're a fine, healthy specimen if ever I've seen one. I bet you've grown a lot this year, am I right?"

Ron nodded warily, and I added, "It seems like a lot to me, too."

The doctor told Ron to put on his shirt, then started to speak to us, but Roger raised his hand and asked, "Would you like Ron to wait outside?"

"Oh no, I think he should hear this," the doctor answered. "First of all, you folks are worried over something that is really very minor and rather common. Your son is growing up." Ron looked uncomfortable at the sudden attention to his changing body.

The doctor carefully explained that our son was going through puberty, the sudden growth was producing an oversupply of hormones. The hormone level should begin to stabilize soon, he said, and the cyst would simply disappear on its own!

"You mean you don't think he should be operated on?" I hardly dared to hope. "Are you SURE?"

"About ninety-nine percent sure. Just to make it a hundred, why don't you bring him to see me in two weeks. If the lump is smaller or gone, that'll be it. If it is any larger then we'll worry, but the odds are with you so go home and relax."

Ron smiled broadly as he jumped down from the table, and he was still smiling when, on the way back to the boat, Roger bought him a hot fudge sundae with all the toppings.

For the following two weeks Ron got the third degree. "How does it feel, is it any larger, would you like another cup of hot chocolate, how about an oatmeal cookie?" He gave us looks that suggested he thought we'd taken leave of our senses, but he accepted all offerings anyway.

By the second doctor's visit the cyst was greatly reduced, and a month later it was gone altogether. Obviously, we were thankful we'd sought a second opinion, but not half as much as Ron was!

By July the weather was monotonously predictable: thunderous stormy days, and hot humid windless nights. We anchored to avoid the mosquitoes and to catch an occasional breeze from the water, but the first bad storm frightened us. In rough weather the area around Key West held little protection from the ocean waves, was overcrowded with boats, and a poor holding ground for anchors.

The local marina could have provided safety, but as was typical with most U.S. marinas, the management did not allow live-aboards for more than ten days. There were simply more boats on the water than there were dock slips to hold them. We knew we had to find something more secure, just what and where was our dilemma. And we had the old problem of money again, never enough.

While exploring the town, Roger and I talked about waiting tables. New Orleans had been great for tips, but we both doubted Key West would prove as lucrative. "Besides," said Roger, "that is a dead-end street. We need to find something we can do anywhere. Surely there is a way to consistently make an extra dollar with a boat."

"That is the main topic of conversation of every cruising sailor we've met, and I have yet to find one I'd call successful."

"Oh, I can think of several that do pretty well," he said teasingly, and I knew who he was thinking of. It was a couple from Panama City that cruised on a beautiful forty-foot ketch. The man professed to be an artist and whenever they pulled into a fancy yacht club, he would collect his sketch pad and charcoal pencils, and head for the bar. While perched on a barstool, the artist would proceed to do portraits of all the customers, who in gratitude, would buy him enough drinks to get him royally snockered.

The couple could have starved to death if the artist's wife hadn't developed a much more productive line of business. In her mid-thirties, she was extremely attractive and well-endowed with one of the most impressive sets of built-in flotation equipment ever tucked into a mini bikini, and her bikinis were hand-crocheted from approximately six inches of see-through yarn. Roger claimed I exaggerated, but I noticed that when we were docked next to them, Roger hit his head on the boom every time he went topside.

The wife crocheted the micro bikinis (such talent!), packed them in miniscule plastic sandwich bags, and sold them for $25 each to the male tourists. The men took the gifts home to their flat-chested wives, who I was sure, used the skimpy pieces of yarn for plant hangers on the back porch.

"Chesty" could whip one up in about fifteen minutes and seemed to sell all she made. Well, I could crochet and so could my great Aunt Harriet, but it was plainly clear to me that neither drawing or crocheting were the talents contributing to that couple's success.

There were other work and live-aboard sailors. In Miami, we met one that made a fair living writing pornographic books. When he bragged loudly of his riches, we decided to try our hand. One night, after the kids were asleep, I collected notebooks and pens, then Roger and I climbed into our bunks to begin. Within minutes we discovered I didn't know enough dirty words, Roger couldn't spell, and collaboration reduced us to giggles, horseplay, and cold showers.

Of all the "tycoons" we encountered, the most industrious appeared while we were at Tollgate Marina. That couple carried a heavy-duty sewing machine, as well as dozens of bolts of canvas and sail cloth, on a boat no larger than *Halcyon*. Within twenty-four hours of docking, the husband rushed around accumulating orders from every other boat around, for new sails, awnings, hammocks, water-spray dodgers, and ditty bags. I never met his wife; she was always sewing.

When Roger suggested I try, I sneered at him, "It took me a year and a half to make the bedspreads for the bunks. I don't think anyone is going to sit around that long waiting for a new ditty bag. Besides, my talents and my sewing machine are simply not up to such tasks."

"You may be right," he said.

"And you aren't a gentleman for agreeing," I said with a frown.

"Maybe we can charter!" he offered

I voiced my doubts, but we found the charter boat dock anyway and talked to the crews. An afternoon of conversation confirmed what we already suspected—there weren't enough customers to go around. I was also aware that chartering one's boat was akin to renting out one's house, then staying around to become maid, butler, and cook for the new occupants. And even if I'd wanted to do it, which I didn't, not even if we were starving, how would we charter a boat equipped with three kids? No matter how skillful we thought they were, no one else would ever mistake them for crew.

"Can we find something where I don't have to cook or sew, and the kids can be involved?" I asked.

"Well, we could dress the kids in their raggediest clothes and send them out panhandling," he suggested.

Ron heard and gave his dad a worried look, but said nothing. I think he would have walked on water if Roger had asked.

Tommy and Janice went flitting down the dock, with Tommy threatening to throw Janice in the marina. She squealed for one of us to save her, and as I looked at their faded cut-offs and straggly sun-bleached hair, I said, "Well, they are dressed appropriately, but I'm afraid they don't look listless and underfed enough."

Roger reached out, collared Tommy, ordered him to leave his sister alone, then continued, "You might be right about the clothes but there must be some way we can convert this excess energy to income."

The kids took off in the direction of the sportfishing boats and we followed. Some of the slips were empty, but most of the boats were tied to the docks, their Captains waiting hopefully for a tourist to wander by. We came upon the *Miss Lilly* and said hello to a heavy-set man with a bushy brown beard, ruddy cheeks, and a quick smile. He was lounging in the fighting chair situated on *Miss Lilly*'s afterdeck and introduced himself as Captain Smith.

If we entertained thoughts of chartering for fishing, he dispelled the idea with one remark, "Winter's the time for tourists around here. It's just too hot or too stormy in the summer."

We told him we were looking for something we could do with the boat and the family to earn extra money through the summer. He climbed off his boat, sat beside us, leaned back against a piling, and said thoughtfully, "That's a tall order. I don't know what you could find to do with a boat and them young'uns."

Looking down the dock we could see all three. They were watching a party boat unload the catch of the day. Janice was talking animatedly to one of the passengers, Tommy and Ron were observing a crew member clean fish in a trough beside the boat. By the look on the fisherman's face, I could guess the boys were bombarding him with their preponderance of questions.

"Fishing ain't for everyone," Captain Smith chuckled. "Nope, it sure ain't. That reminds me of another sailor I met. His name was Dingo. He lived on an old wooden hulk of a sailboat that he'd fixed up and he had great dreams of making enough money to sail around the world in it. He used to come around here to watch us load up the rich customers for an afternoon of fishing, and he was impressed by the cases of booze and all the expensive gear the customers would pile on board." The Captain's eyes twinkled as he said, "I could tell Dingo thought we were making a bundle.

"One day one of them big fancy powerboats tied up to the dock. On board were four Texans, dressed to the teeth, you know: them big hats, silver belt buckles engraved with the state of Texas. That power boat was their latest toy and they'd brought it all the way from Galveston to Key West to do some marlin fishing."

He paused long enough to reach over on the deck of the *Miss Lilly*, lift the lid of an ice chest, and bring out three frosty cans of beer. We accepted his offering and sipped on the beer as we listened to the rest of his story.

"Yep, that boat was something. Carpeted, wet bar with lots of mirrors, double glass sliding doors leading to the cabin. It even had a built in TV, stereo, and a galley with one of them new microwave ovens. The dishes actually had the boat's name printed right on them." Captain Smith stopped, wiped perspiration from his forehead with the back of his hand, then smiled broadly. "In other words, them Texans were roughin' it.

"When Dingo heard they were looking for a fishing guide, naturally he volunteered his services. 'Course Dingo didn't know a damn thing about fishing. I heard about the trip the next day. Everyone in Key West heard about the trip. Seemed them Texans were nearly to the Bahamas when one of them hooked a giant of a marlin. It took 'em over an hour to bring it alongside the boat, then they like to never got it on board."

Captain Smith began to chuckle, and his laughter was infectious. "What Dingo had never learned was to make sure the fish was dead, real dead, before bringing it on board. At first that giant just lay there on the deck tuckered out from the fight while them guys went running for their fancy cameras. As they began taking pictures, the fish's tail twitched, and one of them tossed a towel over it thinkin' it would help. 'Course the twitches just got wilder. Someone thought to try and knock it out, but by then, it was too late. When Dingo hit that fish with a bottle, it really woke up, and it was madder'n one of them bucking broncos and just about as destructive. The tail smashed everything on the deck—fishing gear, cameras, beer glasses, binoculars, everything. For a while Dingo and them Texans tried throwing things at the fish but finally realized their lives were in danger, and they headed for the cabin roof. There they lay, stomach down, looking over the edge of the cabin, and waiting for that fish to get tired and die. But they soon learned better: that marlin went right through them sliding glass doors and them doors were shut! A half hour later it was still flipping around in that cabin breaking mirrors, china, upending one thing then another."

We laughed at poor Dingo's plight, then the Captain finished the tale. "That boat was over a month in the boatyard before it could be returned to Texas. The owners hired a professional to do the captaining and they flew home."

"What happened to Dingo?" I wondered.

"Oh, he's still saving his money for that 'round-the-world cruise he's going to make some day."

"Surely he isn't guiding anymore?" Roger asked.

"Oh no. He's found a more suitable occupation. You'll find him in one of them places over on Duval Street tending bar."

We shared some of our own fish stories, then Captain Smith remarked, "That's vacation fishing you folks been doin'. It's fine, just not too productive. But if you know how to catch fish, you'll never go hungry, and the best folks to ever teach you how are the Cubans on the commercial docks."

He paused for a minute, scratched his head, then looked us over carefully. "If you're looking for a job and dock space, that's a place you might check."

Bright and early the next morning we were at the commercial docks talking to anyone who looked like a fisherman. In a very short while we learned the gear necessary to get started would cost about $20 (I found that hard to believe), a commercial license was $30, with a license we would get discounts on diesel, ice, fishing gear, and dock space was free as long as we caught fish. It sounded too easy.

When we went to the courthouse to fill out the forms, the clerk told us we were the first sailboat in years to hold a commercial fishing license, and at the time I wondered if there was a reason for that.

When I questioned what we were doing, Roger said, "Think of it as 'bringing back the Good Old Days', Toni. This is an exciting new adventure! You'll love it."

What he didn't tell me was how much work we were in for, and no matter what the dictionary says, I have come to learn that excitement is just another word for sheer madness.

In the beginning, the Cuban fishermen thought we were joking. Did a family with three kids really think they could learn anything about the profession of fishing? And on a sailboat, yet? But once they saw we were serious, they showed unbelievable kindness and a willingness to share their knowledge.

The fish house assigned us a slip space across the dock from the *Lucky*, an old, green, wooden fishing boat owned by three generations of the same family. Pepe was the Captain, but his father Abuelo was undeniably the leader.

We learned that "Abuelo" meant "Grandfather" in Spanish, and if he had any other name, no one used it. Abuelo's age was difficult to guess, however if the wrinkles on his face were like the rings on a tree, he was very old indeed. His gnarled hands showed scars from countless thousands of fish fins and hooks, but his eyes seemed alert and wise.

We listened attentively as Abuelo spoke in his low quiet voice; he was the expert. In broken English he told us to put away our fancy rods and reels, because they were too slow to be effective, as well as inaccurate in hooking and landing a fish. After he showed us what to buy, we dutifully headed for the tackle shop.

Our purchases included five hand reels known even at the store as "Cuban hand lines," 200 feet of nylon line for each reel, a few light lead sinkers, some swivels, and a box of small hooks. Altogether our bill came to a little more than $20. To me it seemed like a meager bit of equipment, but Abuelo had assured us it was enough to start.

We returned to the dock and sat at his side while he, his son Pepe, and his grandson taught us how to tie the hooks. I was hypnotized by the suppleness of Abuelo's arthritic fingers; he could grasp a hook and piece of line and connect both with the speed of light. Trying to do the same thing, I stabbed myself then swore and stuck my finger into my mouth.

Smiling, and looking much like an old native shaman, Abuelo said, "You will learn." He would tell me that same thing many more times that summer.

We waited three days for the moon to wane. "Fish don't like any light," Pepe explained. "When they see the shadow of the boat, they think it is a shark."

Finally, the *Lucky* crew announced it was time to fish, and invited us to go along. After lunch, we left Tommy and Janice in the care of some fellow live-aboards the kids had befriended, then Ron, Roger and I joined Abuelo's family aboard their boat. We motored away from Key West for forty-five minutes then Pepe steered in wild circles for half an hour. I had about decided they didn't know what they were doing when Pepe shouted the order, "This is right! Drop the anchor!"

Looking over the side of the boat I could clearly see the bottom fifty feet below us and noted we were floating above a ledge. The grandson cinched down the anchor, then walked to where we sat and explained in detail the importance of depth, ledge, currents, and vegetation. Obviously, they knew more than I had given them credit for.

Pepe shut down the motor, then went to the small galley and brought out cokes and beers. Passing them around, he said, "Enjoy these. If it is a good night, we won't have time for any more until morning."

When Abuelo began showing Roger how to mix something in a bucket, I edged closer to watch. Within five feet of the bucket the aroma hit me, and I gagged. "It smells like last week's fish innards!" I mumbled nasally with fingers pinching my nose.

Roger smiled and said, "You got it. That's exactly what it is, mixed with equal parts of cornmeal and sand. Guess what it's called?"

When I shrugged, he answered, "Chum!"

"You're kidding!"

"No, it really is chum. And if fish scraps are in short supply, Abuelo says we should use chicken livers and cat food instead."

"Boy, would Sea Coral love that!" Ron spoke from beside me.

I looked at the gray, smelly stuff, and was very thankful when the sea breezes dissipated the odor.

The crew sat on camp stools sipping their drinks, smoking cigarettes, and waiting for nightfall. At one point, Abuelo held up three crooked fingers toward the west and announced, "Forty-five minutes before sun goes."

Looking at my watch, I asked him, "How do you figure that?"

"Each finger between sun and sea is fifteen minutes," he answered authoritatively.

When he walked away, I whispered to Roger, "I think he's a braggart."

"I wouldn't bet against him," Roger replied. Forty-five minutes later the sun set.

The crew tied hooks to their lines, and we saw that no one used sinkers. Asking why, we were told they weren't necessary because the fish would be feeding on the surface. For once Roger's face showed disbelief and he asked, "How do you plan to coax those fish up from fifty feet?"

"Patience and chum," Pepe smiled sagely.

Ron helped the crew fill a large plastic garbage can with crushed ice and seawater while Pepe explained, "This is the chill barrel, it will keep the fish near freezing until we have time to clean and ice them."

As the last rays of the sun dissolved into the water, Abuelo appeared from the cabin with paper towels. He tore one sheet from the roll and spread it on the deck next to the chum bucket. Scooping up a handful of the concoction, he plunked it into the center of the towel, wrapped the paper around the chum, then dropped the neat little package over the side of the boat.

"When this hits the bottom, it will break open and spread around," Pepe said, continuing the lesson. "The current carries the oils from the chum out over the ledge, and the fish follow the smell."

Abuelo reached for his hand reel, took a small piece of mullet, and baited the hook. Tossing the line over the side he let it sink slowly, and we watched him count each arm length as he let it out. When the hook touched the bottom, he tightened the line slightly and I was startled to see his arm jerk almost instantly and begin pulling the line back into the boat. On the hook was a yellowtail snapper weighing about two pounds! Ron, Roger, and I gasped as we watched Abuelo flip the fish into the chill barrel, then we dove for our hand lines.

"Not yet!" Abuelo ordered. "We are not ready."

Sitting back, we waited patiently while Abuelo rebaited his hook. My stomach rebelled when he plunged his hand into the chum bucket, lifted out a fistful, and packed it tightly around the bait. Carefully he lowered the hook and mass of chum over the gunwale, letting it down slowly as he counted, " *diez, once, doce*...," he counted in Spanish. At five lengths less than the bottom he gave a sharp snap of the line, then paused. The fish took the hook with a vengeance, and in amazement, we watched another yellowtail emerge.

The process was repeated a third time, and Abuelo released the chum ten arm lengths from the bottom. When a third snapper appeared on deck, we reached for the hand lines again.

Pepe cautioned, "*Uno memento*! The fish are coming up. Every time abuelo releases the chum a little higher, and soon we will see fish swimming behind the boat."

He was right. In less than half an hour we were all fishing frantically, barely getting our line into the water before a ravenous yellowtail had the bait. I had never had so much fun in my entire life.

When the line began to slice into the joints on our fingers, Pepe advised us to find some old bicycle inner tubes and cut them to three-inch lengths for our fingers. "Always wear them," he cautioned. "If you ever hook a shark, or a fifty-pound grouper, you will be glad for the protection."

Rain stopped us for the night, but in only a few short hours we had caught over five hundred pounds of fish! Looking into the barrel at the mass of cold, limp, glassy-eyed bodies, we saw eighty cents per pound! Like the fish, we were hooked!

It seemed like a great way to make money until Pepe demonstrated how to gill and gut the fish. As though born to the trade, Roger and Ron hunkered down with the crew and went to work. I looked around the deck to see if I could sweep, dust, or swab something—anything except gut a fish.

But I wasn't going to get out of it. Roger offered me a spot next to him, and Pepe handed me a knife and cutting board. Damn Women's Lib! As the macho crew watched, I gritted my teeth and joined in. Never let it be said that I let my sex down.

The icy cold fish were instantly numbing to the hands, and the slippery bodies were nearly impossible to hang on to. When one slithered through my hands and careened across the deck, I tried using my knee to anchor it down. The crew snickered and Pepe came to my rescue by showing me how to grasp it under the gills with a thumb while slicing open the belly.

An hour later, we handed the last fish to Pepe to stow in the crushed ice and I sat back to rest my hands. My fingers were stiff, swollen, and sore from the many pricks of fins, and I moaned with pain.

"The hands will get stronger," Abuelo said to me with a slight smile. He was right about that, too.

The following night, we felt brave enough to try on our own, but first we had to find a way to carry crushed ice. The icebox in *Halcyon*'s cabin barely held two fifty-pound blocks, so Roger went to the store and returned with two massive styrofoam chests. Strapping them to the upper deck he said, "That'll give us three hundred pounds altogether, not much, but a start."

We motored in *Halcyon* across the harbor to the commercial icehouse and as we approached the dock, a red-faced, red-haired man in a dingy T-shirt came out on the dock to meet us. "This is a commercial house," he warned. "We only sell to the fishing boats."

We tied up anyway, then Roger stepped onto the dock and pointed proudly to the official sticker on our bow. "Red" looked at it, grunted, took in the kids climbing around on the boat, glanced at me, then crossed his arms and said, "Gotta see more'n that."

Roger sent Ron for the license and handed it to the man. Red studied the fishing license and obviously thought we were crazy but finally, he asked, "Where's your hold?"

"Hold?" Roger didn't follow him.

"Yeah!" The man's face flushed angrily. "Where do you want me to blow the ice?" He indicated the long hose that carried the crushed ice from the crusher to the boats.

"Oh," Roger said. "Right there in the cockpit."

"How much do you think you can get in there?" Red asked with sarcastic amusement. We knew most fishing boats carried ten or twelve thousand pounds of ice, and Roger sounded somewhat sheepish when he said, "We'll take six."

"You can't get six thousand pounds in there!" Red bellowed.

"No, I mean six hundred pounds."

The man started to say something, then shook his head in disgust and headed toward the icehouse to start the crusher.

Roger and Ron pulled the fat black rubber hose onto the boat, pointed it into the cockpit, and we stood back to watch as a mountainous snow cone appeared before our eyes. As soon as the machine quit, the five of us scurried frantically about with buckets to scoop up the ice and run it to the chests before it could melt.

Red watched, arms crossed, and mouth agape as though he'd never seen the like before.

We finished, smiled, thanked him, and waved as we pulled away. He glared at us in obvious distaste until we were out of sight.

The routine began. We sailed out and anchored on a reef five miles from Key West. As late afternoon approached, we cut mullet into small pieces, mixed the chum, fixed a chill barrel, had a cocktail, cooked dinner, then sat on the deck and watched the sun go down. The moment it was dark, we fished.

I could not understand why the fish cared whether it was light or dark. A week later we tried fishing during the day, and all we produced was sunburn and frustration. If the fish that brought the most money at the fish house were nocturnal, then we could be too.

Using a rotation system, four of us set up deck chairs along the handrails and fished while the fifth ran for snacks, drinks, aspirin, and more fishing gear. To help alleviate seasickness, we switched places every half hour. Roger raised the jib sail to keep the boat from rolling in the swells of the open ocean, and *Halcyon* sat steady as a rocking horse, all night. But, as long as the fish were biting, a hurricane couldn't have budged us.

Roger agreed to pay the kids ten cents per pound for their fish, and to help them calculate the weight, he bought a handheld scale. Each child kept a pad and pencil next to his chair and listed the weight of the fish. The results were miraculous. Even Janice's multiplication improved. Amazingly, she also lost her fear of handling the cold slick creatures, and soon was heartlessly prying hooks out of the mouths of all but the largest fish.

Tommy's seasickness disappeared completely the minute the fish began biting, and in addition, he seemed to have an ability to catch fish that defied reason. Once, in an effort to untangle the knots and snarls that were his personal nemesis, he threw hook and line into the water sans bait. Within seconds he had a prize yellowtail! We offered no sympathy when ten minutes later, and with the line still snarled, he moaned, "I wish they would leave me alone for a while—that's the fifth fish I've caught on a bare hook!" For the first time we regretted the sleepiness that overtook him and forced him to bed.

Ron shunned the smaller yellowtail and snapper feeding near the surface, preferring to let his bait settle on the bottom in hopes of attracting a giant grouper. Though he missed the excitement of constantly bringing in fish, he puffed with pride when he always caught the heaviest fish of the session.

As the clock chimed midnight, we would send Ron and Janice to bed, then Roger and I would fish and talk through the quiet night. During that summer we learned to enjoy those rare hours, and the opportunity they gave us to explore each other's memories, backgrounds, philosophies, likes, dislikes, fears, and pleasures. It soon became apparent to us both that we had not allowed enough time in our thirteen previous years of marriage to do just that: to know each other, and not only was it enlightening, it was also pleasurable, like meeting for the first time.

Sometime before dawn one of us would fish while the other began gilling and gutting. Since that chore was tops on my list of dislikes, I tried every dubious means I could think of to get Roger to do the dirty work, pleading, "My fingers hurt, my head hurts, my back hurts." or "The fish are still biting on my side of the boat."

Once I even tried bribery, but he was too stubborn.

Giving up the chair and my line, I fixed a cup of coffee and sat down on the edge of the cockpit to begin. After an hour of working, my bare feet were still buried to the ankles in dead fish, and my arms were covered to the elbows with fish blood. "What do you suppose Mother would say if she could see me now?" I wondered in disgust.

Roger chuckled. I would not get any sympathy from him or her.

"Do you know what is really ironic?" I asked as I viciously whacked open another fish belly. "The doctor tells you, that you are allergic to anchovies, and two years later I am up to my hip pockets in fish!" I sighed. "Why couldn't you have been allergic to rocks? Then maybe these fish would have been diamonds."

Packing away the last of the catch we stripped off all our clothes and dumped them into a bucket of bleach, soap, and water. After scrubbing ourselves with a strong soap, we poured seawater over each other to rinse, and washed down the deck at the same time.

At 8 a.m. we fell into bed for a few hours' sleep, only to have Ron wake us at 10 a.m. for the trip into Key West. In the weeks to come, our need for sleep became overpowering. In desperation, we often turned the boat over to Ron. What luxury! He would wake us only long enough to help pull anchor, then we were free to go back to sleep while he steered us toward port.

It was apparent Ron took pride in his role as temporary Captain: charting the course, dividing the shifts between the three kids, then seeing to it that Tommy and Janice kept a true course. If sails were raised, he woke us to change tacks, but otherwise he learned to trim sails without our help. As *Halcyon* approached the last marker in the channel, he would rouse us once more to assist in docking procedures. For a child just a few weeks older than thirteen, Ron was definitely growing up.

In Key West we did laundry, bought groceries, restocked with bait and ice for the next trip, and wedged in schoolwork wherever possible. The routine broke up during the full moon or bad weather, and only then did we go sightseeing, or laze around the docks.

Abuelo's family were unusually successful fishing with the *Lucky*. When comparing notes, if we did half as well, we felt proud. But it took only one week for us to realize fishing was not a way to get rich, or even to live comfortably. For many of the other small fishing boats on our dock, it was not even a way to survive.

As a rule, the family-owned working boats were old and mortgaged as heavily as the banks would allow, and it took only one serious storm, or engine breakdown to destroy a career that often spanned generations. For some victims of misfortune, there was a way out when the worst occurred. Money could be had for the asking in marijuana smuggling.

We saw it in the papers, we heard it in the rumors, but that was all it was to us, rumors, until a little red-and-white trawler from our dock demolished its engine one night trying to ride out a storm. The boat was towed into the harbor by the Coast Guard, and there it sat for a month while the other fishermen speculated about what would become of the family that owned it.

It was a warm Sunday afternoon when the owner appeared with his wife and several forlorn-looking small children. As they stood beside their boat talking, I could see the unhappiness on the wife's face and the anger on her husband's. Even their children were unusually quiet, as though they knew their parents were facing a crisis.

The next morning two young men arrived with bags of tools. They boarded the trawler and spent the day tinkering with the engine. Each morning after that, they returned to work diligently on the engine until they finally had it running.

When the owner of the trawler came again, we strolled over to congratulate him on the repair of his boat. The man merely smiled, then asked Ron to untie the lines. "I'm going to try it out," he said, then waved and sped away. We never saw him again.

The boat was tied to the usual place at the pier twenty-four hours later, but no one had seen or heard it return. Eventually the bank foreclosed, and the boat passed into new hands, but that was not the end of the story.

One lazy afternoon during the full moon all the trawlers were tied in the harbor, surrounded by flocks of squawking seagulls begging for handouts. Pepe sat drinking a beer with us on the *Halcyon* when suddenly he pointed over to the little red-and-white boat and said, "I saw that guy in Miami last week, he's doing very well, now."

"That's wonderful. Is he fishing?" I asked as I thought of the forlorn family I had watched a few days earlier.

Pepe looked down at his beer and began to rub his finger around the rim of the frosted can. "Oh no, I think he will never fish again."

"Why do you think that?" I asked with alarm.

"Once you have tasted big money, it is hard to go back to eating fish."

"Big money?" Roger asked.

"There is a lot more out there than fish," Pepe said enigmatically, and he looked out at the open sea. We could not get him to say anymore, but when the newspapers ran a series of articles on drug smuggling, I suspected we had the answer to the mystery. The papers reported that fishing boats were meeting freighters in the Gulf Stream, taking on cargoes of marijuana, then delivering the illegal goods to remote anchorages in the Keys or the Everglades. The going price for one night's run: $250,000!

No wonder drug smuggling was so difficult to control. The smugglers were not shady-looking characters with scars on their faces and guns strapped under their arms. They were more likely to be independent fishermen, down on their luck, and with nothing more to lose except their freedom.

The Coast Guard began an all-out war against the trafficking and by August, there was hardly a fishing boat around that had not been boarded and searched. Our turn soon came...

We were anchored on a reef ten miles out of Key West, and the only visible object was the *Lucky* with Abuelo and Pepe sitting about a half mile away.

The night before, a run of red snapper had hit with unbelievable ferocity, and by morning we were out of bait. Roger had tried radioing the *Lucky* to see if Pepe had any bait to spare and was told that their luck the night before had been as good as our own and their bait was almost gone. After signing off, Roger talked of heading back to Key West, but we knew we wouldn't be able to restock and return for two days. By then the snapper would be gone.

As we sat on deck and pondered what to do, a shrimper pulled up to the reef and dropped anchor. Suddenly Roger jumped up and smiled. "They've been shrimping all night! I think we've got our bait!"

Pulling the dinghy alongside, he dumped in all our plastic chum buckets, then he and Ron took off for the shrimp boat. When they returned, the buckets were overflowing with fish and Roger was clearly pleased as he told me, "I tried to buy shrimp, but they wouldn't sell any. They gave me five pounds instead, then told me to take anything I wanted from the trash fish on the deck. It was about to be thrown overboard! Look at this! We have enough bait and chum to last a month!"

"Don't count on it," I said and held my nose.

While Janice and I cut the best of the fish into bait, Ron and Roger ground up the rest into the chum bucket, then put the bucket into the dinghy and let the line out as far as it would go so we wouldn't have to smell it.

That night the fishing was the best ever, and we felt very grateful to the shrimpers for their generosity. At dawn we were staggering with exhaustion, but still had clean-up to do. Thinking of sleep, we hastily stripped and scrubbed, rinsed the deck once or twice, and threw on some clean clothes.

I started breakfast while Roger woke up Ron and gave him directions for the morning. "The deck needs a good scrubbing. Mom and I barely rinsed it off. As soon as the three of you finish eating, I want you to get up there, fix some soapy water, and wash it down."

Remembering that the chum was still on deck, I told Ron, "Empty the bucket and wash it out. We'll make some fresh for tonight."

I hoped he wouldn't forget—the weather felt close to 90 degrees already and it was only 8 a.m. Since chum started out smelling rotten, cooked chum surely would not get any better. Silently, I thanked the designer of

Halcyon for putting the huge forward hatch on her. The ocean breezes cooled the cabin, but more importantly the hatch kept out the smells from the afterdeck.

Roger called the *Lucky* and arranged to store our fish in their hold so we could stay another night since our chests were filled to capacity. While he talked, I put breakfast on the table. As I looked at the bowls of oatmeal, I wondered how the kids could eat it in the hot weather. To me it looked a lot like chum, but they loved it any time of year.

Shaking Tommy and Janice awake, I gave them a last-minute warning before following Roger to bed: "We want to sleep for two hours. If you must wake us, you better have a good reason or you'll be in the chum bucket tonight!" Roger was already snoring when I fell across my bunk. I'd never been so tired in my entire life. Unconsciousness had barely taken over when someone was shaking me. Burrowing under the sheet, I tried to ignore the intruder.

"Dad! Mom! Wake up!" Ron was agitated.

"Leave me alone, I know I haven't slept two hours yet."

"Get up!" he insisted. "The Coast Guard wants to board us!"

Sitting up, I looked over at Roger. He opened one eye and mumbled, "They're going to have to search without me, just let me know if we're going to jail." Then he covered his head with the pillow, and in seconds was snoring.

Trudging slowly up on deck, I arrived just as Tommy and Janice were catching the lines from the eighty-foot patrol boat that was twice our size. The smell that accosted my nose told me the kids had not started the deck cleaning. The Coast Guard officer noticed the same thing when he stepped from the patrol boat to our own. He inhaled once and sat down quickly with the color in his face noticeably paling. Too late, I saw the chum bucket beside him, and the smells emanating from it were as ripe as a garbage dump.

"Wouldn't you prefer to sit down below?" I asked hurriedly.

"Oh no!" the poor man nearly shouted.

I tried to explain to him that the cabin didn't smell at all and it was much cooler, but I could tell the officer was not convinced. Pulling out a handkerchief, he wiped his forehead and said, "This is fine, just fine! I'll only be a minute. I need to ask some questions."

Hoping he meant what he said, and this "search" might end soon, I sat back and tried not to resent Roger sleeping peacefully in his bunk.

The officer was young, boyishly towheaded, very uncomfortable, and very eager to get the necessary procedures out of the way. He probably would have forgotten the whole thing if there hadn't been a half dozen of his fellow officers leaning over the rail of the patrol boat nearby watching us. Dutifully, our officer snapped open his briefcase, pulled out a raft of papers, and began to ask questions about the boat, crew, equipment, and cargo.

Our tiny bit of breeze died, and *Halcyon* gently rolled from side to side in the soft swells from the shimmering glassy sea. *Please end this before I doze off right here.* I prayed to myself, and as if in answer to my prayer, Tommy came roaring up out of the cabin with a banana in his hand, flopped down beside the officer, and leaned over to look at the papers. The officer gave an alarmed glance at the banana and slid closer to the chum bucket.

I started to order Tommy below, then stopped and smiled wickedly. *Sleep might be near after all.* The officer mopped his forehead again, and there was evidence of a slight green pallor under his eyes and around his mouth.

Next Janice appeared, munching on a piece of toast. Sitting beside me, she proceeded to swing her foot, barely missing Tommy's shin. Tommy retaliated by reaching out and smacking Janice, and in the process, he smeared a tiny bit of banana on the officer's lovely, crisp, clean, regulation Coast Guard shirt. Janice squealed, jumped to her feet, and took off running with Tommy right behind her. The boat rocked some more.

Dabbing at his jacket with his handkerchief, the officer stammered another question about tonnage just as Ron strolled up the companionway with a bowl of cereal in hand. Sitting where Tommy had been, he lifted the bowl up to the officer's nose and asked, "Would you like some oatmeal?"

In a blur of speed, that young man shoved the bowl aside, stuffed the half-finished forms into his briefcase, leaped to his feet, turned, and began waving frantically for the patrol boat that was drifting alongside.

"Do you want to search the boat?" I asked sweetly.

"Humpf!" His answer was muffled by the handkerchief covering his mouth.

When the patrol boat was within five feet of *Halcyon*, the officer literally lunged from deck to deck, and we watched as he dove through a door into a cabin. At that moment I would have been willing to wager the proceeds from our trip, that he was on his way to the head.

We smiled and waved as the patrol boat moved away, then I patted Ron and praised him for being so polite as to offer our guest breakfast.

Ron looked puzzled, then shrugged and said, "I thought you wanted me to."

"Oh, I did. You were wonderful!" He accepted the praise, then joined Tommy and Janice in deck clean up as I staggered below to crawl back into bed.

"Are they gone?" asked Roger.

"Um hum," I mumbled as my head touched the pillow.

"How'd it go?" he asked and I detected a touch of guilt in his voice.

"Just fine," I answered sleepily. "By the way, let me know if you want to go in the smuggling business—I've found a fool-proof technique."

"Huh? What are you talking about?"

But I was already snoring.

The Coast Guard was not our only visitor on that fishing trip. That night the waves were choppy, the weather threatening, but stars peeked out of the fast-moving clouds to let us know the thunderheads were in a hurry to move on. It was one of those nights that a hurricane could have hit and we wouldn't have quit fishing. The yellowtails and red snappers had been so plentiful, that when the ice bucket was full, we simply threw the fish on deck. By midnight the cockpit was alive with them, slapping and sloshing about our feet.

Roger elected to be the first to clean and ice the catch. We couldn't see how many we had on the dark deck, the only light came from the kerosene lamp in the galley, but we knew there were many more fish than usual. We had to begin cleaning them soon or we wouldn't get any sleep at all. Before starting the dreary job, Roger went to the galley to fix a fresh pot of coffee. Ron and I sat quietly, he in a deck chair on one side of the boat, me in a camp stool on the other, and each holding a nylon line between our fingers. Tommy and Janice were asleep in their bunks. Suddenly, Ron let out a yelp, and his line tensed more than usual. Reeling in a moray eel he fell backward pulling the eel into the pile of neatly coiled fishing line. It was impossible to rescue it as the eel writhed around in the line and neatly tied itself up tighter than a Christmas package. Roger arrived to our rescue in time to cautiously hoist the squirmy ball of fishing line and angry eel over the side of the boat.

That was enough for us. We cleaned up and called it a night. In the morning, we made our way back to Key West.

September arrived with no relief from the heat, afternoon thundershowers, or long nights of fishing. The only change seemed to be that the yellowtails and snappers had found feeding grounds other than on our favorite reef. We tried staying out two, then three nights, but were catching fewer fish with every trip.

When Abuelo and his family prepared for a trip to the Dry Tortugas eighty miles to the northwest, they invited us to go along. Roger was willing, but I declined. The threats of bad weather scared me, and I preferred to stay near safe harbor. Besides, the kids and I enjoyed getting off the boat as often as possible. But it was discouraging when a week later, the *Lucky* returned with two thousand pounds of fish! We continued to go out at night, and sleep or struggle with schoolwork during the day. But more and more, I found myself sitting on the reef and looking back at the tiny speck of Key West in the distance, yearning for the end of one more fishing foray.

When I wasn't complaining about feeling tired, then I harped about the constant encroachment of fish scales into the cabin, into our bunks, and onto my Christmas carpet. "Why can't you wash your feet before you come below?" I groaned at Ron one day.

"I do," he answered defensively. "Every time."

"Then do it better!" I snapped. "It's bad enough we have to live with that mess on deck. I won't live with it down here!"

My outbursts left me feeling truly ashamed, but I seemed less able to control them with the passing of each frustrating day.

That night Roger sent all the kids to bed early, and we were anchored on the reef and sitting on deck fishing when he said, "Toni, if we made one trip to the Tortugas, we might catch enough fish that we wouldn't have to go out again for several weeks, then you could live for a while without fish scales and chum."

It sounded appealing, but I raised my usual argument, "There isn't a good harbor there in case the weather turns bad, and the Tortugas are eighty miles out in the middle of the Gulf! What if a hurricane brews up?"

"I think we would have enough warning to get back in time, but I am more concerned about the ships that ride the edge of the Gulf Stream than I am about hurricanes. Have you noticed how close they are coming to this reef? Like that one over there. I've been watching it and I'd swear it is headed right for us."

Looking to port, I could make out the white lights, one atop the other. "Roger, that doesn't look right. Can you see the running lights?"

"I'll get the binoculars." He reached below to the chart table, picked up the binoculars, then focused on the ship. Very calmly he ordered, "Turn on all our deck lights."

"What do you see?" I asked.

"Now! Turn on the lights NOW!"

Rushing below, I began switching them on, all of them. Ron sat up in his bunk, blinking in the bright light, just as Roger bellowed, "Ron, get on the radio and try to raise that ship, he's coming down on us!"

Ron dove for the radio, as I ran for the deck. "Are you sure?" I squinted toward the ship. It did look a lot closer.

"Do you see the running lights?" Roger asked.

"No, not yet."

Roger was still looking through the binoculars.

"What does the piloting book say if you see both the red and the green lights?" he challenged.

"Get out of the way, of course. Do you see ...? Oh my God! I see them!" I could also clearly see the ship outlined against the horizon.

Roger ordered me to start the engine as he picked up a spool of fishing line and headed toward the bow.

"Can we get the anchor up in time?" I called to him, but he didn't answer. After starting the motor, I grabbed the spotlight and began flashing it in the direction of the ship, but a sinking feeling in my stomach told me I was wasting my time.

"Just stay at the wheel!" Roger commanded. "When I give the order, rev the engine as high as it will go and head straight for the reef!" I could see he had tied the fishing line to the anchor and was in the process of attaching a plastic milk jug to the end of the fishing line.

"Why the reef?" I had to ask.

"That ship won't follow us into shallow water. Just do as I say!"

I glanced over at the ship. There was no doubt, the running lights were clearly visible. That ship was coming right at us.

Ron's voice came from the cabin and we heard him talking to the Coast Guard. At least someone would know we were about to be sunk. And then I saw it! The bow of the ship emerging from the darkness and it was HUGE!

"Roger, we are out of time!" I screamed. "We're about to be hit!"

"Go!" he ordered, then picked up the anchor line, plastic jug, fishing line and hurled them all into the ocean.

I went wide open for the reef! Ten seconds later Roger yelled, "That's it, turn her to starboard!" The fathometer read twelve feet and rising.

Slowing the motor, I turned the wheel and looked back in time to see the ship pass within inches of the bobbing milk jug that marked our anchor. "We could have been killed," I whispered to myself. I was shaking like a leaf.

New voices emerged from the radio. The ship was finally responding to the Coast Guard. "Yes, of course we can see the sailboat," someone was saying. "It is at least a mile away!"

Roger had heard it too and was down the companionway in a flash. He grabbed the microphone from Ron. "The Hell you are! If you are a mile away, then how did you manage to run over my anchor line!" He was furious.

A three-way conversation yelling match set in for some minutes, then Roger gave up and returned to the deck. Obviously, right-of-way belonged to the big guys.

Halcyon had been circling through it all, and I was beginning to feel uncomfortable about the proximity of the reef. I willingly turned the wheel over to Roger, picked up the spotlight, and found the plastic jug in the beam of light. Ron took a position at the handrail, and as *Halcyon* made a pass over the anchor, he retrieved the jug and line with the gaff hook.

"Pull in the anchor." Roger sounded weary.

"Where are we going?" I asked.

"Back to Key West—I need a good night's sleep!"

I did not argue, and we headed back to port and the docks.

"It would be safer than being run down by ships!" Roger was trying again to convince me that we should do a run to the Dry Tortugas. "We'd only be gone a week and Abuelo says the groupers are huge along the outside of the islands."

"I don't think it is a good idea," I answered stubbornly.

"Well, how about stopping at the Marquessa Keys for a day?" He had a mischievous twinkle in his eye as he spoke. "The Keys are deserted, and the kids would enjoy a day building sandcastles."

My interest picked up. The thought of a few hours of play, and a romantic interlude were too enticing. "I'll go to the store for groceries, and we can leave in the morning."

While Roger and the kids prepared the boat for the trip, I went shopping, and feeling a little reckless I bought us a treat: spareribs! Our fish diet had become very monotonous, and a special barbecued dinner would be a welcome change.

Returning to the docks, I found the harbor filled to overflowing with small boats and tourists. When I inquired of a fellow fisherman about what was going on, he explained that it was the combination of opening of lobster season and Labor Day. Looking around at the sudden overpopulation of boats and people, I wondered if there were enough lobster to go around. Just then the Island Tour Boat cruised into the harbor and a booming voice from the loudspeaker directed everyone on board to look in our direction.

"Ladies and Gentlemen, this is our fishing fleet," the voice proclaimed. "And there's a fisherman now." Tommy waved as he hung by his knees from the ratlines, his head dangling four feet above the deck. And so the tourists took pictures of Key West's youngest fisherman. Janice danced a jig, then turned, dashed below, and reappeared with the air horn. Blowing a salute, she received cheers from the tourists.

I giggled and thought, *we'd better get out of here before the kids start signing autographs.*

Chapter 12: Dry Tortugas, Wet Boat

It was still early. I was deep asleep in my bunk when I felt a rude poke to my ribs followed by a soft whisper in my ear asking, "Can we go swimming now?"

Turning my head, I opened one eye and found myself nose to nose with Tommy. "She's awake!" he blasted loudly for the benefit of Ron and Janice, who were standing behind him.

All dreams floated away to join miscellaneous other junk in my head while I sat up in the bunk and tried to remember where we were. The view from the porthole reminded me: we were at Boca Grande, one of the Marquessa Keys.

"Can we go swimming please?" Tommy begged again.

"Not until your dad wakes up," I said through a yawn. "You can't go without him."

Tommy directed his attention toward Roger, who protested mildly, but rolled groggily from his bunk anyway, pulled on a pair of swim trunks, and still half asleep, felt his way up the ladder to the deck. Staggering to the handrail, he stepped over, leaned out backward, and allowed gravity to do the rest. The kids joined their dad, splashing into the water with squeals of pleasure as the warm blue-green water swallowed them whole.

Fifteen minutes later they returned to sit in dripping puddles on the deck and wait expectantly for me to carry the coffee thermos and breakfast up from the galley. Roger, with sun glistening in his wet hair, stretched out on a cushion, munched on a piece of toast, sipped on his coffee, and sighed contentedly. "I think this is the only time in my life I've actually enjoyed waking up in the morning."

Ron chattered about the live coral he'd seen under the boat and begged to go back in the water after breakfast.

"Schoolwork comes first," I insisted.

Roger gave me some back up by saying, "You can swim later, and maybe we can row to the island this afternoon."

That placated the kids long enough to settle them down with their books. Roger retired to his bunk with a spy novel. I took the spareribs out of the ice chest, covered them with marinade sauce, and happily anticipated a fishless supper.

After lunch we rowed to the island and walked in the clean white sand. The kids skittered about like frisky colts, chased each other in and out of the water, got into a pushing fight, then sat down to play on the beach.

Birds circled overhead, but there was not another boat or person in sight anywhere, we had a corner on one part of the world.

Roger found a scrub tree and we plopped down in the shade for a rest, while a bird screeched wildly from the tree behind us. Resting on my elbows, I watched *Halcyon* rock gently at the end of her anchor line and grudgingly admitted to myself that she was an attractive, graceful lady. Sometimes I even liked her when—she wasn't making voracious demands on my husband's time and money.

"It's nice to be so alone for a while, with no one around except the birds," Roger mused.

"And three kids," I said as I looked along the beach to where they were building sandcastles. They needed the day off as much as we did and were obviously enjoying it.

"I see what you mean," Roger said as he glanced their way then turned back and whispered, "We could send them back to the boat."

I gave him an innocent look and asked, "Did you have something special in mind?"

He smiled. "Do you ever have fantasies?"

"Sure, like living in a real house again. Why? Do you?"

"That's not the kind of fantasy I meant. Do you remember From Here to Eternity?"

"Vaguely. Why? Do you want to bomb the island?"

"I wasn't thinking of the war scenes," he said—but I already knew that.

When the kids finally tired of their sandcastles, we hustled them into the dinghy, and rowed back to the *Halcyon*. After fixing a snack, I gave them a few school assignments, put a blanket in the dinghy, then instructed, "We'll be back in an hour. Just blow the horn if you need us."

Roger pushed the dinghy away from the boat, and shortly, we were truly alone on the island. Several hundred yards down the beach we found a cove out of sight of *Halcyon*, and Roger shook out the blanket. To avoid the wet sand, we undressed and draped our clothes on a clump of bushes under the mangrove trees. Running nude into the water, we played like the kids, splashing, dunking, and giggling; then returned to the blanket to bask in the warmth of the sun and each other.

We had barely settled back on the blanket when I became alarmed. "Roger, do you hear something?"

"No!" he answered impatiently. "And the kids are all right too! Now just relax for a while!"

There was a definite sound of a motor, and when I looked over Roger's shoulder, I gasped. A powerboat was rounding the end of the island and there were two dozen holiday divers milling about on the deck. We had no time to run for our clothes. Pulling the blanket over ourselves, we could do nothing but lay, bare behinds in the sand, and wait. I started scratching first, then Roger swore and scratched. The sand fleas had us, and they were hungry.

It was absurd, and we scratched and moaned for an hour while the powerboat anchored, and the passengers dove and swam a mere hundred yards away. Unfortunately, when the intruders finally departed, our romantic notions went with them. We put on our clothes, picked up the blanket, and headed for the dinghy. Scratching my legs as I walked, I asked Roger if he thought Deborah Kerr and Burt Lancaster's passionate scene included sand fleas.

"Funny how the movies miss things like that," he said with a laugh.

On board the *Halcyon*, I started dinner while Roger and the kids took advantage of one last hour of swimming. Despite the brief excitement on the island, it had been a lazy day and I was beginning to feel the effects of it as I filled the alcohol cup in the bottom of the oven. We had declared it a day of rest, and I vowed to myself to take a nap as soon as the ribs were on.

Lighting the primer, I watched it burn brightly for a moment, and hoped it would not give me any trouble. The oven was seldom used. It overheated the cabin and took so much longer than the pressure cooker, but I was determined the spareribs were going to be perfectly baked and the oven was the best place to do it.

As the flame flickered down, I heard Roger call from the dinghy, "Toni, bring us the spears. I see a lobster under a coral head."

A tiny voice warned me to wait a moment longer, because the element was not yet hot enough to catch, but impatience won out. Grabbing the pan of ribs, I shoved them in, turned on the oven, then ran up on deck to find the spears.

Digging in the deck box, I located a shaft, but the sling was lost under inner tubes, dock lines, and an odd assortment of flip-flops. Frustration boiled up. "Roger, why can't you keep this chest straight?" I yelled.

Roger was sitting in the dinghy, holding on to *Halcyon*. "Just keep looking, it's there."

I spied the rubber sling, untangled it from the lead line, and started toward the side of the boat. As I came abreast of the hatch, my heart stopped. "Do you smell something?" I sniffed the air, then shouted, "Oh my God! My ribs!"

Looking down the companionway I could see the smoke—the cabin was thick with it! Roger climbed on board as I plunged down the ladder and we were shocked at the sight of flames leaking out from around the oven door. My eyes watered, and coughing seized me as I reached for the handle to the oven. It was so hot I couldn't even touch it. Roger grabbed the fire extinguisher and positioned it while I snatched a potholder and flung open the door.

Swoosh! In a split second the cabin was white—completely white! When the cloud settled, the fire was out, and everything, EVERYTHING, was covered with a quarter inch of fine white powder.

"These things are powerful!" Roger sounded amazed as he looked at the spent extinguisher in his hand.

I pulled the ribs out of the oven, not only were they charcoal-broiled, but they were frosted too, and the skillet resembled a small volcano as a wisp of smoke floated out of the mound of fine white dust. In disgust, I carried it to the deck, called the kids back to the boat, then joined Roger in the cleanup. Using the whisk broom and dustpan, Roger attacked the worst of the dust under the stove, and listened to me complain, "We can't even vacuum until we return to Key West and have electricity!"

The carpet was a shamble, and my earlier pleasant mood turned sour. "It seems as though we can't get cleaned up from one catastrophe before another one hits!" I whined, wiped the walls, and thought about the sand from the shipyard in New Orleans that had lasted for months. Then the sugar on our disastrous trip into Pensacola (there were still stains in the carpet from that one). Now a summer of fish scales, topped by a deluge of white powder. "Why is it so hard to keep this place halfway liveable?"

Roger sat back on his heels, blew a puff of powder from his mustache, and calmly stated, "You know, this would be a lot easier to clean up if we didn't have the carpet."

"I will pretend I didn't hear that!" Then I shut my mouth and returned to the wiping.

After swimming around the boat for an hour, our somewhat shriveled and ravenous kids climbed on deck as we were discussing dinner. "When do we eat?" they asked.

"I think that's only baking soda," Roger said as he looked at the skillet of ribs.

"Let's read the label on the fire extinguisher," I suggested and picking it up, studied the fine print but it didn't help. The instructions were for use, not ingredients. Obviously, they didn't expect people to eat the stuff. I went below, looked in the cupboards, then reported back, "We can have canned tuna, chicken noodle soup, or oatmeal."

Roger gazed longingly at the skillet, then stood, filled a pot with water, and dumped the ribs in. Two or three rinses later he tasted one. "Not bad," he said. "A little salty, but not bad." And he began to eat. Mumbling through a mouthful, he added, "If this is going to be my last meal, it's worth it."

We ate every bite and slept soundly that night. There wasn't a bellyache in the bunch—but the flea bites were a nuisance.

Halcyon at Fort Jefferson

I had always believed the Florida Keys ended with the highway at Key West, but there are many more little islands extending beyond Key West for as much as eighty miles. The first grouping is called the Marquessas, and sixty miles beyond the Marquessas are the Dry Tortugas.

We could scarcely believe the sight of Fort Jefferson on Garden Key in the center of the Tortugas. The one hundred-thirty-year-old fort seemed to be floating in the emerald green water, and if I'd been a heavy drinker, I would have quit, then and there due to apparent hallucinations. Like a mirage it rose in the water, an edifice of earth-colored stones, eerily beautiful on the western horizon.

The illusion of floating was created because every square inch of the island was covered by the fort, and in some places the structure even extended into the water. It had been built in the middle 1800s to serve as a protection against invasions along the coast, but it had become obsolete as a viable defense post even before it was completed. To save face and probably to placate the taxpayers, the US Government turned it into a prison and used it as such for many years. In 1865 four conspirators in the assassination of Abraham Lincoln were imprisoned on the island.

The vacation was over. After spending a day exploring the Marquessas, and another day playing tourist in the Tortugas, it was time to go back to work. We found the *Lucky* at anchor in the lee of the fort and received directions from Pepe on a likely reef for fishing at the edge of the preserved waters of the National Park. Agreeing to meet them the next morning, we sailed out and anchored on the reef.

The porgies and yellowtails were too small for the fish house but, they were the first fish we caught. Roger decided to keep them; he put them in a mesh bag then hung them over the stern of the boat to be used for bait the following day. After an hour of chumming, an active school of large yellowtails came to feed behind *Halcyon,* and we settled in for a very productive night.

My excitement peaked when a particularly hefty fish hit my line, and as I started working it toward the side of the boat, the pull on the line abruptly stopped. "What's this?" I yanked hard, and just as suddenly the line slackened. Roger turned on the deck light as I pulled in the line, then we gaped in wonder at one very large yellowtail HEAD! The body was missing, sliced neatly away below the gills.

Examining the head, Roger guessed it was a shark or a large barracuda feeding under us.

"I've got one too!" Ron exclaimed and he held up a fish head.

Whatever it was, it was hungry, and I shivered. We began a game of speed, hooking a fish and furiously pulling while attempting to get it into the boat before the predator ate it. Whatever was down there was fast and picky too. He took only the big ones. Admitting defeat, we rested and hoped our unwelcome guest would move on.

It was Ron who noticed the string on the fish bag hanging from the stern of the boat. "Look, its moving!" he whispered. "There's something down there!" We crept over, peered into the water, and saw a shark to rival *Jaws* chewing on the nylon mesh bag.

"My God!" I gasped, and as Tommy leaned over the stern rail, I blanched and grabbed for him.

"Aw, Mom!" he shrugged me off. "I won't fall in."

Ron untied the bag and commenced a game of tug of war, but the shark got the fish bag, and a foot of line. Reaching for the heavy-duty hand line, Roger rigged a steel leader on the end, baited the hook with a small yellowtail, and dropped the line over the side. He kept the plastic spool in his hand. A shark that size could exert enough pressure to cut through the pieces of inner tube protecting his fingers.

Jaws swallowed the bait and hook immediately, then Roger coaxed the creature to the surface. In total fascination, we watched as the pectoral fin sliced back and forth through the water. The shark was obviously unconcerned with the hook in his mouth. There was no fighting. He simply slowly swam and for a minute it looked as though Roger was out for a leisurely stroll with his "pet"—or vice versa.

The thought made me giggle nervously, then I stopped as a vision of Dingo entered my mind. "Roger, you aren't going to bring that thing on board, are you?"

Before he could answer, the shark gave one good jerk of the head, and was gone. The steel leader had snapped in two!

A chill ran down my back as I looked into the inky black water. There seemed so little protection between us and the monsters down below, and the words of an old salt from Miami came to me, "To become a good sailor, you must always feel fear. If you ever get so sure of yourself that the fear goes away, then you've had it." Right then and there, I had the makings of a very good sailor. There was no way I wanted to visit that shark in his territory.

An hour later we were still feeding Jaws our choicest yellowtails and as a storm gathered, we called it a night, and went to bed.

The morning sky was overcast and ominous. We returned to the fort and dropped anchor within easy rowing distance of the *Lucky* and later, when Pepe told us how productive their night had been, we realized the shark had cost us a lot. Before the trip was over, the storm would cost us even more.

Fourteen boats spent the night in the lee of the island, rocking in the wake of the suddenly angry weather, and one of the boats was a sloop named *Bewitched*. During a lull in the storm, we rowed over to meet the crew and were delighted to discover a family with children! Ron and Janice were excited. At last they had playmates: a girl Ron's age and a boy Janice's age.

The children's father was a banker from California named George who had "chucked it all" to grow a mustache and live a life of leisure on the bounding main. His wife, Peg, thought the whole idea stunk! It was instant camaraderie. The kids played, Tommy sulked, Roger and George discussed the virtues of their respective ten-ton mistresses, and Peg and I swapped notes on the recklessness of our respective husbands.

Over a cup of coffee on *Bewitched,* Roger asked, "Where are you going from here?"

"Back to California," George confidently proclaimed as he preened his unbanker-like mustache. I noticed his blue eyes displayed the same mysterious gleam that Roger's did when talking of "Great Voyages."

"As quickly as possible," Peg added, and I guessed she was as uncomfortable with George's world as I had been with Roger's. They had sailed for only six months, how much longer would Peg hold out?

George continued talking, "We're doing the same thing, waiting out the hurricane season. Why don't you join us when we leave?"

"That sounds great!" Roger said enthusiastically.

"Now wait a minute," I interrupted. "We need to talk about this!"

Roger seemed to want to argue his case, then unexpectedly he backed down with, "We'll think about it, George. I'll let you know."

But there was not going to be any talking, I had made up my mind. California was over three thousand miles away by water, and I was no longer in the mood to spend the rest of my life getting there.

Later in the day the stormy weather eased, but the pressure was on us. We had to catch more fish, or the entire trip would be wasted, and we had to do it fast—our ice was melting.

Pepe suggested we try a reef fifteen miles from the Tortugas. "A beacon sits on the shallowest part," he explained, "but it is still twelve feet deep, and you don't have to worry about shoals."

The reef was interesting. Either it was an island in the making, or one that had eroded away and was visible only by the rapid changes in the color of the water. Four miles across, it fell away quickly around the edges, and provided a perfect spot for fishing. Going to the outer perimeter, we dropped anchor in eighty feet of water, then watched as the wind drifted us out over the ledge. I scanned the horizon and felt uncomfortable; there was no land to be seen anywhere, only that beacon flashing two miles away.

"What if the weather kicks up again?" I wondered out loud.

"We can ride it out," Roger said confidently. "And we have fifty feet of chain at the end of the anchor line—we're not going anywhere."

I listened to the weather report on the radio, and felt somewhat reassured to hear, "Only occasional thunderstorms are expected."

We fished for three hours, when one of the "occasional thunderstorms" dumped on us. We put the leftover chum in the dinghy, let the line out to avoid the smell, cleaned off the deck, went to bed, and rocked to sleep in the softly churning sea. The last thing I saw when I looked out of the porthole was the flash of the beacon two miles down the reef.

It was just daylight when Ron's voice woke me with, "Should we put a bumper over the side?"

Roger sat up in bed and blinked sleepily. "Bumper?"

"I think the boat's going to start hitting in a minute," Ron answered.

I came wide awake. "What are you talking about?" I asked as I peered out my porthole. There was nothing there but ocean.

Turning his head Roger looked out his side then spoke in apparent shock, "What the Hell?"

We both hit the floor at the same time and in the tiny space we collided instantly. It was a Laurel and Hardy routine as we headed for the companionway, pushing and bumping each other in our haste to reach the deck.

And there it was, skeletal in its shape, awesome in its size, and just inches from the boat! The BEACON!

It took only seconds for us to get safely away. The kids reached out to hold us off the footings, I ran to the bow, and Roger started the engine. But when I pulled in the anchor line, I discovered the anchor and chain were gone! Obviously, a switching wind during the night had wrapped us in the sharp coral, and the line had been easily sawed by the wave action working against the boat. But why, in all that ocean had we drifted straight for the beacon? Was the *Halcyon* a giant magnet attracted to steel ships, tankers, and lighthouse towers? I was certainly beginning to wonder.

Taking a compass bearing on the wind, we retraced our steps the two miles to the ledge, and had no trouble spotting the white plastic jug marking our anchor.

Roger donned the SCUBA gear and dove, and once he and the anchor were back aboard, he described what he had seen. "This reef is solid coral and drops off quickly. And it's downright spooky hanging on to the side of the ledge and looking into that purple pit where the ledge falls away. But you won't believe what is there. That ledge is covered with anchors! Some of them are so encrusted with coral that only the shape is left!"

"Then we aren't the only ones to have our line cut." I said but somehow that wasn't at all comforting to know.

"Not only that, but I would also guess some of those anchors are well over a hundred years old. I thought we might dive some of them up."

Roger was ready to dive again, but I wasn't having it, and put my foot down. All I wanted to get back to Key West before something else hit.

By late afternoon a gale was blowing, and we rocked in the lee of Garden Key and played cards with the *Bewitched* crew until midnight.

We were having breakfast the next morning when Pepe rowed over to discuss the situation. "Our ice is melting rapidly now," he said. "The other fishing boats have the same problem, and we are all carrying fish. Another day of this weather, and we'll lose it all."

It was very apparent by the tone of his voice he was worried, and I could understand why. The wind was gusting to fifty miles an hour and the weather reports said it would last at least two more days.

"We'll lose our catch as well," Roger said, "if we don't get back to Key West by tomorrow."

Pepe ran a hand through his hair as he said, "Manuel on the *Cassandra* tried to leave this morning, and almost swamped his boat in the waves. One more bad trip like this and the bank will foreclose on his boat. At least my father-in-law will help me out, I hope."

Roger sat forward and his voice was suddenly excited. "We've been fishing so much I've almost started to think we were a round-bottomed fishing boat as well. But we're a sailboat! We can handle this weather."

Halcyon might make it, but I was worried. I protested, but to no avail.

Roger asked Pepe, "If we collect the ice chests from all the boats, can we get all the fish on board the *Halcyon*?"

"Maybe. We can try." Pepe looked hopeful.

"Roger, we can't go out in this weather! Are you crazy? It's a gale out there!"

"Sure we can," he said. And by his excited expression, I knew there was no changing his mind.

Within an hour the deck and cabin were covered with ice chests, gunwale to gunwale, and Roger used every line we had plus spare lines from all the other boats to lash the chests securely. With butterflies in my stomach, I filled the thermos with hot soup, made several dozen sandwiches, ordered the kids into their life jackets and, as *Halcyon* cleared the channel, I helped Roger raise reefed canvas.

We sailed away from Garden Key to the sound of cheers from all the fishermen as they urged us on, and it was then I realized how important our trip was to all of them. They had entrusted us to save their catch and possibly even their boats. I sincerely hoped we would not disappoint them.

Halcyon heeled over hard to starboard as the fifty mph winds filled her sails. The first hour was the hardest with waves relentlessly bashing at our stern quarter, but *Halcyon* took them in stride, and I seemed to be the only one who noticed as I inched my way back and forth while clinging to the rails and bulkheads. Tommy slept, Ron and Janice read, and Roger sat happily at the wheel.

Some relief from the wave action came when we entered the lee of the Marquessas. The islands blocked the sea, and with the smoother water and the high wind, *Halcyon* literally screamed along. From then on, Roger and I alternated shifts at the wheel. Every hour he took a speed reading, and when the scale consistently showed eight-plus knots, I was disbelieving. But Roger assured me we were doing it easily. He was right. We rounded the beacon into the Key West channel less than nine hours after leaving the Tortugas! The boat had averaged eight knots, and Roger was beside himself with pride in both he and his beloved *Halcyon*. I was mostly relieved.

Taking the cargo to the fish house, we had it weighed and the monies credited to the appropriate accounts. That done, we spent the afternoon vacuuming up the rest of the fire extinguisher powder, and at the first break in the weather the next day, we loaded up with fuel, bait, and ice.

The look on Red's face when we pulled into the icehouse with all those ice chests was easily worth the whole trip. Through the summer Red had become increasingly less friendly, but he was downright hostile that day. Grudgingly, he fed us ice in four separate series of crush, blow, scoop, and fill again, and by the time we were through and pulling away from the dock, he was pacing back and forth and mumbling obscenities under his breath.

Looking at the color of his face, I wondered when he'd last had his blood pressure checked.

On the return trip, we found the storm only slightly improved, but I still felt uneasy about leaving the secure harbor and said so.

"We promised we'd bring the fishermen more ice," Roger argued. "Besides, the trip yesterday was nothing, and the weather is calmer now. We won't have any trouble."

Looking out at the gray sky and white-caps, I said, "You're right, the small craft warning is up, the wind is still blowing a gale, and we are carrying two thousand pounds of excess weight in ice. It'll be duck soup!"

My sarcasm didn't dampen his mood at all, but I couldn't have been happier when, nine hours later in the last glimmer of daylight, we spotted Fort Jefferson. Unfortunately, night was fully upon us when we entered the channel, and the wind was blowing hard against our beam.

Ron and I lowered main and mizzen, then he went below to sleep while Tommy and Janice stayed on deck to help drop the jib and bag it. Pensacola had taught us to keep that jib up until the last minute and it certainly helped steady us.

I held the spotlight on the markers and Roger gingerly steered *Halcyon* in the direction of the anchored boats.

"Toni, I can't see a thing! Will you please keep the light on the markers?"

Quickly I flicked the beam around, pointed out a buoy, then panned the light back to the anchorage. I was searching for the boats we'd left behind. "There's the *Lucky*!" I shouted. "Janice, get the horn and let them know we're here."

She ran below for the horn, while Roger yelled, "For God's sake! Will you shine that light at the shore! I know this wind is blowing us in that direction."

The *Lucky*'s horn sounded, and the waiting fishermen saw us. A cheer went up from the fishing boats, we were getting a hero's welcome. When Janice blew the horn, five others answered.

The heart-sickening screech of metal against metal was followed by a very sudden stop that knocked us all to the deck. Gasping, I grabbed up the spotlight, and with Roger beside me, scrambled to the side of the boat. The powerful circle of light illuminated our predicament. We were rammed neatly into an abandoned coaling dock, and were cradled between two rows of ragged, long-rusted, steel pilings.

Roger released the jib sheet, then turned and gave me a thunderous look. I couldn't deny it, it was my fault, and the only thing that saved me from his wrath was the immediacy of the situation. Every little wave or gust of wind was forcing us further up onto the spikes of steel, but we noticed that as each wave lifted us *Halcyon,* momentarily floated.

"Tommy, you and Janice go forward and try to hold us back;" Roger shouted. "Toni, get Ron up, and the two of you stand on either side of the stern and push us backward each time a wave comes through."

Rushing below, I shook Ron from a sound sleep, then back on deck I showed him where to stand and told him to push hard against the piling whenever Dad ordered it.

"Where are we? What happened?" He seemed in a trance.

"Just do as I say, I'll explain later," I said, then took my position on the opposite side of the stern.

"Now!" Roger shouted, and the four of us heaved shoulders against the pilings while he gunned the motor in reverse. *Halcyon* floated backward into the channel. Picking up the spotlight, I held it as steady as my shaking hands would allow and gave full attention to my job of guiding us into the anchorage.

As soon as the anchor was down, Roger donned snorkel gear, and while I played the light along the waterline, he went into the water to survey the damage.

"We have a foot-long dent on the starboard side about two inches below the boot stripe," he announced as he climbed back on deck. "Otherwise, there's some paint scratches but nothing else." Then he gave me an obviously angry glare. "If *Halcyon* had been anything except steel, we would have sunk!" I was grateful he said no more than that.

The most amazing revelation that resulted from the incident was the behavior of the kids. They had taken the crisis seriously and performed with a strength I never suspected they possessed. Clearly, we would not have escaped so easily without them. But it was the next morning when I learned just how acute Ron's sense of responsibility had become.

The kids were splashing around in the water beside the boat, when I heard Ron ask, "Where did we get this dent?"

"From the coal dock last night," Janice told him.

"What coal dock?" He looked genuinely puzzled.

We thought he was kidding, but over breakfast we quizzed him at length. The only thing he remembered was going to bed about dark, then nothing until morning. He had spent at least ten minutes on deck, followed directions to the letter—all while soundly asleep!

Dawn brought a red sky, and I reminded Roger of the old sailor-take-warning adage, but he was determined to go out fishing anyway. Conceding that the wind was much lighter, I extracted a promise from him that we would stay close to the lee shore of one of the Keys in the event the gale whipped up again.

As we were preparing to leave, George rowed over to share a cup of coffee and try to entice us once more to join them. "We're planning a quick run through the Bahamas, then we'll strike out for the Virgin Islands on the tail end of a norther. From there we can turn east, head for Panama, then sail up the West Coast to California."

It was amusing how simple he made it sound: just raise the sails and go. But if there was any lesson I had learned in the two years on the *Halcyon*, it was that the only wind to be had appeared with the fishing gear and disappeared the moment someone said, "Cruise!"

All the same, Ron, Janice, and Roger were ready to go. Tommy wasn't sure, especially with those two new kids around. Once again, Roger promised George we'd think about joining them to California.

After we anchored and fished until midnight, the storm returned, churned up the water, and set *Halcyon* to rocking. Rough weather had become the norm for us. The kids slept as Roger and I wearily cleaned the fish, put the chum in the dinghy, scrubbed the deck, moved the boat closer to the shelter of the island, and finally fell bone tired into bed.

It was a toss-and-turn night, as I dreamed of a world covered with fish. Everywhere I walked I stepped on cold, slick, scaly snappers. I saw fish, smelled fish, tasted fish—they were even in my pockets, in my bed, on my plate, and in every direction. As far as I could see were dead fish, white bellies raised, and waiting to be gutted.

In the morning the dinghy was gone. There wasn't even a frayed line to prove how this had happened, and the only conclusion we could reach was that one of us had failed to cinch down the line securely. We searched for hours with no luck, and the loss was devastating. The dinghy had been much more than our car—it had been our recreation, our occasional escape from the confines of *Halcyon*, the kid's toy, a swimming platform, our friend.

"Roger, we are all too tired!" I was trying to explain the catastrophes we'd had and convince him to turn back to Key West. "There are too many accidents to blame them on weather or chance. I know I am not thinking anymore, and I feel that you and the kids are just as tired. We need a break; we need a rest!"

"Okay, you're right. But let's fish one more night, then go back with the *Lucky* in the morning. And if you are worried, we can inflate the life raft until we get the dinghy replaced."

It was only a partial concession, but I relented. After lunch Roger took the wheel. Ron pulled anchor and we started out for what I hoped would be our very last night of fishing—EVER!

There was no sign of the storm from the days before, but the smothering heat was back. The cabin felt like an oven in the noonday sun and the island effectively blocked any wind, but *Halcyon* was headed out to sea. Soon she would be away from the island and we could cool down.

In the meantime, Roger and the kids sat on the deck while I finished fixing a pot of coffee for the thermos. As I worked, I could tell we were moving further out because a freshening breeze gave speed to the boat and the air flowing through the portholes was supplying some relief to the cabin. It was against our boat rules to have the portholes open, but the air felt too good on my hot sticky skin, and the sea was calm for a change.

But as we lost the protection of the island, *Halcyon* bounced momentarily in the new chop, then rolled slightly in the surge of unbroken ocean. Dropping the coffee pot into the sink, I rushed to close the ports on the low side, and had just finished the ones over the bunks, when I heard Roger's voice. "I'm coming about!"

"No!" I screamed. "Not yet!"

But he didn't hear me. As the wind caught the back of the sails *Halcyon* slid over to the opposite tack, and the three remaining open ports plunged down toward the onrushing waves.

My legs simply wouldn't carry me fast enough as I dove for the open ports, but it was too late anyway. When the roller hit the side of the boat, the water came gushing in like three wide open fire hoses ten inches around! It shot across the cabin with staggering force, struck the opposite bulkhead, and sloshed down into the bunks. All I could do was duck.

The kids came to the rescue, together we tightened the last hatch, and as Roger brought the bow into the wind, calm settled over the boat.

I looked around the cabin and saw that the mattresses were floating on their frames! Water dribbled out from under a drawer, and opening it, I stared at the soggy mess of clothes inside. The gurgling sounds under the floorboards told me the bilge was full. But worst of all as I walked across the cabin, the carpet slipped and slid under my feet. It was ruined.

The kids went to work wringing out their clothes while I climbed the ladder to the deck and, with hands on hips, confronted Roger. "Why didn't you give me more warning?" My anger was fueled with months of pent-up frustrations, but his anger matched my own.

"What in the name of sanity were the portholes doing open?"

"I wanted fresh air!" I bellowed.

"Have you forgotten? You live on a *boat*, not in a house! When you want fresh air, you get up on deck!"

"But you aren't supposed to change directions without giving me fair warning!"

"And you don't leave portholes open underway!"

"Well, you don't have to worry about it anymore, because we are getting off this boat at the very first chance."

His voice dropped very low as he said, "I think you have always hated this boat. From the very first you have tried to make her into a house, and it just doesn't work that way." Then he ended the scene by turning on his heel, going below, and starting the bilge pump.

We worked in a tense silence as we tried to put some order back in the boat. With the kids' help, we pulled all the mattresses and bedding up on

Sailing Against the Wind – Toni Larson 189

deck to dry. I filled plastic garbage bags with the soaking-wet clothes from the drawers, and as the mound of bundles grew, I knew we would be a week in the laundromat getting everything washed and dried again. The kids carried all the books onto the deck and spread them about, and as I looked at all our soggy possessions, I thought it had to be the most discouraging moment in my life.

But something happened to my depression as we rolled up the Christmas carpet. Clearly that carpet had become my symbol of what we'd left behind: the comforts of a home that didn't bounce around, become covered with sand, food, fire extinguisher powder, fish scales, and sea water. But when I looked at the damp floorboards, I was surprised to find no regret, only a sense of freedom. Suddenly there was nothing left to worry about or develop hysteria over.

Roger and I declared a truce, apologised to one another, then miraculously he agreed we needed a night's rest more than another hundred pounds of fish. Returning to Garden Key, we made plans to head for Key West at sunup. As we said goodbye to George, Peg, and their kids the next morning, they promised to stop by when they reached Key West. George tried one last time to talk us into going with them, but Roger surprised me by saying, "I don't think so, George."

During the trip back I had ample time to think about the fight. Was Roger right? Had I really given the cruising life a chance or had I resisted it from the very beginning? Looking back, I wondered if any of the last two years had been worth it. Of course, much of it had been fun, but ....

How about the kids? What was this doing to them? Okay, their schoolwork hadn't suffered, we had proof of that in New Orleans and they were progressing on a steady basis now. Plus, I had to admit I truly enjoyed teaching them. Tommy and Janice continued to fight, but more and more it was playful fighting. And would that be any different anywhere else?

Ron was blooming. He was charting all the courses with perfect accuracy and knew much more than I did about the fine points of setting the sails to gain the most from the wind. He also seemed far more contented than any other child I had ever met at the same age and appeared to yearn for nothing more than to stand attentively at his father's elbow.

Were they healthy? Beyond a doubt! Were they happy? Well, no one had said, "I'm bored" in more than a year.

As for Roger, it was eminently clear to me he could spend the rest of his life sailing from pillar to post, unless I put my foot down. Wasn't two years at this enough? I watched him sitting on deck, entirely focused on Janice while she taught him how to tie a Turk's head-knot. And she glowed when he admired her handiwork. Tommy had my sewing basket out and was embroidering a picture of the *Halcyon* on the back of one of his T-shirts. The colors were vibrant, his stitches tiny and mostly passable. He enjoyed sewing so much that a lot of what he owned was now dotted with hand-embroidered artwork—usually sailboats. No one told him embroidering was "girl's work."

None of them missed TV. They wrote dozens of letters to friends from every city we'd visited, and they consumed books at the rate of one a day per kid. They had their father's attention, more than any they'd experienced ashore, and Roger enjoyed it as much as they did.

So, what was wrong? I knew the answer and Roger had been right: it was me and my attitude. On board *Halcyon* I seemed determined to live half my life in fear and the other half yearning to get off.

Ron interrupted my thoughts with a shout. "We're back!"

I looked toward the bow and saw we were approaching the bell buoy that marked the entrance to the Key West Channel. I also noted that another storm was gathering to the southeast.

Three days later it was still raining, a dull, ceaseless pounding on the deck. Each morning we turned on the radio to hear the cheerful forecaster proclaim it was over, only to learn we had a tropical low overhead with no clearing in sight.

Time was spent below decks doing schoolwork, reading, or listening to the radio. Roger and I had ample opportunity to discuss the future, but he avoided the subject. He did agree we would take the boat back to Miami and sell it as soon as the weather let up and promised we would spend a few days visiting with Hobie and Emogene. Beyond that he would say nothing. I knew he was not happy about the decision to sell and steeled myself against the arguments I expected from him, but they never came. I hoped he would get over the disappointment as soon as we began to make other plans.

When the rain finally let up, Roger took the motorbike into town and when he returned, he announced he had rented a motel room for the two of us on the beach. "A sort of holiday," he called it. He also made arrangements for Tommy and Janice to spend the night with a family on one of the neighboring fishing boats, and he assigned Ron to stay on the *Halcyon* to watch it.

"What if something happens?" My natural worries surfaced.

"I trust Ron to take care of everything, and he has the phone number of the motel if he needs us. Besides there are a dozen occupied boats on this dock right now, we know everyone here, and he has more than enough help if he needs it."

I didn't argue, and whatever his motives, I was ready for a night away from the boat.

It was wonderful. We were sitting in the middle of a queen-sized bed, munching on popcorn and flipping TV channels every five minutes as we giggled at the novelty and groaned at the quality of that magic box. "Has it gotten worse?" I asked as I watched a policeman shoulder his way through a cardboard door.

"It certainly seems so," Roger said and flipped the channel to a sitcom that had nothing to offer except a blatantly phoney laugh track. "Or maybe, when we watched it every day, we became conditioned to mediocrity."

Licking the buttery salt from my fingers, I jumped up to take a bath, and as I turned on the light, I sighed, "They go on and off so easily! We have spent so much time away from land this summer that even electricity impresses me."

What I found the most delightful rediscovery in the bathroom was that the toilet flushed with only a flick of the wrist, and from a faucet hot water instantly appeared to fill a bathtub the size of *Halcyon*'s head. Dumping bubble bath into the water, I climbed in and soaked so long I dozed off. When I woke, I was very clean, but my skin was slightly shriveled. Would I ever take these things for granted again?

We turned off the boring T.V. before the news came on and went to sleep with the sound of rain gently falling on the roof. We should have listened to the weather report. The only hurricane to touch the shore of Florida that summer, was forming over Key West that night as we slept in our queen-sized bed.

At 7 a.m. there was a loud banging on the door and the first thing I saw when I opened it was our dripping wet son. The second was the wind, it was roaring so much we could barely hear Ron shout something about the boat. Pulling him inside I forced the door shut, then Roger and I fired questions at him with such haste the poor child could hardly answer.

He told us that the wind had picked up during the night and by 4 a.m. the waves were crashing over the seawall. The harbor was a thrashing sea and *Halcyon* was tied on the windward side of the dock jammed hard against the pilings with the pressure of the wind and waves.

I breathed a little easier when he said, "Tommy and Janice are safe in the fish house."

"Why didn't you call us?" Roger demanded as he pulled on his pants.

Ron's eyes filled with tears at the angry tone of his father's voice, but he went on to explain, "I did call over and over, but the switchboard operator said she wouldn't ring your room before daylight. I told her it was an emergency, but she wouldn't believe me. Finally, she told me not to call again, so I started walking."

"My God, Ron!" I couldn't believe it. "Did you walk all the way?" When he nodded, I stared at him in amazement. The motel was more than twenty blocks from the docks! And in all that wind and rain!

"I'm going to take Ron on the motorbike, Toni. Do you want to wait here until I can get back for you?"

I shook my head. "Stay with the kids and the boat. You don't know what you will find, and you don't need to worry about me" A sick feeling filled my stomach as I thought of *Halcyon* being pummeled against the dock. "I'll follow as soon as possible. The buses will be running in another hour, and if they aren't, I'll find a cab or walk. If Ron can do it then so can I." I gave him a hug. "Ron, no matter what else happens, you did the best anyone could do."

I insisted Ron put on my dry windbreaker, and as they rode away in the rain, Ron perched on the seat behind his dad I marveled again at his growth. He was becoming an adult before our eyes—and a terrific one at that.

The wind died a little by the time I collected our gear and began the long hike back to the boat. I had traveled less than two blocks when a bus came along, and, waving it down, I climbed aboard and settled into a seat across from an old gentleman carrying an umbrella. Shaking some of the water off my hair, I nodded to him and commented, "I wish I'd had the foresight to carry an umbrella."

"On this day, I always carry an umbrella," he announced.

"On this day?" I asked, thinking I'd misunderstood.

"The big storm hit on this day in 1936. I got wet. I have carried an umbrella ever since." He spoke very matter-of-factly, and I looked at him closely to see if he was putting me on, but he didn't seem to be.

"I think I'll mark my calendar," I answered.

His accent told me he was a rare species known as a "Conch," someone born in the Keys. He was about five feet two, had few teeth, brown leathery skin, and he looked to be near seventy years old. We talked for a while about the island, the weather, the tourists that were ruining the Keys. I told him I was married, had three kids, and lived on a sailboat.

He frowned. "That's too bad."

His reply startled me. Did he mean the condition of being married, living on a boat, or the weather? I glanced quickly out the window at the trees whipping in the wind and could see the storm was finally weakening.

"I'm so unlucky," he stated mournfully. "Every pretty girl I meet is either married or likes boats, and you live on one! I was hoping you and I could be friends," he said in his singsong accent.

I was amused at his approach, and curious too. Thanking him for the compliment I asked, "What's wrong with boats?"

"It start with the Second World War. I was on a battleship in the South Pacific, and the ship sink. I live for fourteen days on pieces of floating wood from the ship. I pray to St. Christopher: if he save me, I will never get on the water again. He did and as soon as I get back home I buy a St.

Sailing Against the Wind – Toni Larson   193

Christopher's medal that I wear around my neck." And he patted his chest to indicate it was hidden under his clothes.

"I can certainly understand your fear of boats," I said.

"Oh, that is not all. When my son get grown, he want a boat, so I buy him a little speedboat. Every day he ask me to go for a ride and every day I say no. One day I say yes. We go out and we hit something and the boat sink." He patted his chest again. 'Another boat save us."

Once more I told him I understood, but he didn't stop there.

"Long time ago, I was with a friend who is a fisherman. He always asking me to go fishing with him and I always say no. One day he call me chicken! There are women there. I cannot let him call me 'chicken' in front of women, so I have to say yes. We was only three blocks away from the dock when the boat begin to leak. We turn around and come back, and we almost make it. You can still see the boat sitting on the bottom of the harbor. A nice young man pull me out."

He began opening the top button on his shirt. "The Virgin Mary save me that time." And he pulled five medals out to show me. "I buy two extra for good measure." He was deadly serious, and I had to bite my lip to keep from smiling.

"So, you see, it will be hard for us to be friends because I will never come to visit you."

I gave him a solemn look and said, "I hope you don't change your mind." then I smiled at him.

He broke out in a broad toothless grin. "Oh, but I like you anyway!"

The bus coasted to a stop in front of a Cuban restaurant at the lower end of Duval Street, the awning over the front door had been torn from its frame and was flapping wildly in the wind. I waved goodbye to the "Conch" as he stepped onto the sidewalk, his umbrella tucked securely under his arm. Then I smiled to myself as I thought of that umbrella and the five religious medals—the ultimate in being prepared.

Sitting back in my seat, I watched the rain sheet on the windows. The Bahamas and the Keys had taught me that the island folk see life differently than those on the mainland. It is hard to pinpoint the difference, but it is there all the same. A line from a favorite poem crossed my mind: "Once you have lived on an island, you'll never be quite the same...."

Anyone can recognize the more noticeable differences of a slower pace, more casual dress, a talent for finding more time for living and less time for working. But there is more to it than that. Like looking at life through a prism, then selecting out those things worth keeping and leaving the rest for someone else to worry about. It occurred to me that it really isn't the experiences in our lives that make us different nearly as much as it is the parts of the experiences we chose to hang on to or insist upon worrying about.

"Where are you going, Miss?" the bus driver was speaking to me.

"To the fish docks," I answered and was surprised to see the driver turn away from his scheduled route and drive the two extra blocks to the fish house.

As I prepared to step off the bus, he remarked, "The weather report says this storm is moving north and will be gone by afternoon. I sure hope so; tomorrow's my day off and I want to go fishing. Have a nice day." And he smiled, closed the door, and drove away.

Rushing through the fish house, I emerged out on the dock and was shocked to see the turmoil. The seawall was obscured by the crashing waves that poured over the top, and the churning waters of the harbor carried the debris of several boats that had not survived the onslaught of the storm. But I could see *Halcyon* was securely tied to the lee side of the dock.

At the moment I stepped on her deck, I felt very grateful we were not out in the ocean somewhere. But if we had been, I somehow sensed that she would have survived. I meant it when I said out loud, "*Halcyon*, it feels good to be home."

Roger and the kids were below playing a wicked game of Monopoly. (Tommy was cheating, but Roger was winning anyway). Ron greeted me with a description of what had happened when they got back. "Dad tried to move the boat, but the wind was too strong. *Halcyon* put a big hole in the dock, but she hardly even got scratched!"

Roger finished with, "The Coast Guard arrived and pulled all the boats, including *Halcyon*, around the dock. The *Lucky*'s fine, the *Bewitched* is over at the marina. They're safe. They came in yesterday before the worst of it hit."

I took off my wet outer layer of clothes, put on a terry cloth robe and curled up next to Roger at the table. "When are they leaving for the islands?" I asked.

"George says he's headed for Miami as soon as this last weather clears, then to Bimini about a week after that. It's less than two weeks before November gets here, and this should be the last of the tropical storms for the year. I told him to write to us in care of the Miami Marina when he gets to the Virgin Islands."

I started brushing the water out of my hair and off-handedly I asked, "Do you think you could call him back?"

"Sure, why?"

"If we're going to the islands, too, I think we'd better go with a Buddy Boat. Don't you?"

"Are you serious?"

"Yes, I am, but I have one request."

"Anything you want." He was smiling.

"I want to find a store that sells religious medals."

The color of the sea changed abruptly from deep purple to peacock blue as we approached the entrance to a Shangri-la like cove east of Nassau. *Halcyon* rounded the sandspit into a postcard-perfect lagoon. Sails fell to the deck like limp laundry while the engine roared into life.

We could see small coral cays surrounding the isolated anchorage, shielding it from the waves. A larger island, covered with thick stands of coconut and sea grape trees, protected us from the wind. The intrusion of our boat was jarringly noticeable as *Halcyon*'s droning motor pierced the tranquil setting. I tossed the lead line and watched as it arched out from the bow to shatter the surface of the aquamarine water.

Roger shifted the transmission to neutral. The propeller churned to a stop and remaining forward thrust carried us closer to the shore. Coiling the unnecessary lead line, I laid it aside. In the lagoon the depth was as simple to read as if I'd been looking through a clear window.

A momentary breeze brushed by and painted a kaleidoscope of blue, green, and purple octagons on the otherwise undisturbed surface of the water ahead of us. Ron, Tommy, and Janice sat quietly at the handrail, enthralled by the underworld of sea creatures, shells, brightly colored brain and fan corals that unfolded beneath their dangling feet. A spotted ray swept past the bow, seemingly unperturbed by our invasion of his domain.

Standing ready, we dropped the anchor several hundred feet from the shimmery white sand beach. Roger shut down the engine, Ron and Janice raised the awning. Within five minutes by a stopwatch, Roger and I were lounging in the deck chairs with rum punches, and the kids were swimming in the water with belly flops from the bowsprit and challenging each other to races around the boat.

It was our first time to enjoy an afternoon cocktail since leaving Key West, and taking a sip of the sweet punch, I sighed with relief that the ordeal of the previous two weeks was over.

Once the storm had cleared and the fateful decision to continue cruising had been made, we said a hasty farewell to Pepe, Abuelo, and the other fishermen. Then we set out on a breakneck motorboat run for Miami. George and Peg were waiting for us, and George made it plain that he was impatient to set sail for the islands. With no time to waste, we began to provision as soon as we reached Miami.

Our previous island cruise made restocking easy. Without the guesswork on the scarcities of the Bahamas, provisioning went quickly. We doubled the amount of food we'd carried the first time. For trading on the islands, we added ten cases of beer and one case of large fishhooks. Experience taught us that those were items that had value when banks or money-changing facilities were not available.

Ignoring George's protests to hurry, Roger took time to look for a new dinghy. But our hunt was fruitless; we found nothing affordable or towable. George became so impatient he offered his spare two-man life raft to use as a car until we could find something better. Reluctantly, we accepted the offer but paid him for the dinghy and breathed easier about having a backup, no matter how unserviceable it was as a dinghy.

Charts were a problem. The marine store nearby was out of many of the charts of the lower islands and everything south of Cuba. The proprietor offered to order some for us, but when he said it would take a week, George hastily assured us we'd find more along the way. Buying the charts that were available, we hoped George was right.

I wrote letters to the family telling them where we were headed. Roger sent a message to our bank in California requesting the next two months allotments be wired to a bank in Charlotte Amalie, Virgin Islands. As we finished our purchases, we discovered we were down to only three checks, and Roger quickly dispatched a second letter to the bank requesting a new supply.

Old fears cropped up as I watched our fishing money disappear on food, emergency spare parts, and charts. I protested when Roger cashed one of the precious checks to empty the remainder of our bank account telling him, "It doesn't seem like enough money. What if we have another engine breakdown, or one of the kids gets sick?"

He shrugged me off as he folded the small handful of bills and stowed them in a niche over the freshwater holding tank. "We'll have more by the time we get to the Virgin Islands. Besides, we are well stocked this time, so stop worrying. Nothing is going to go wrong."

It did seem reckless to me to be starting out on a three-thousand-mile trip without sufficient dinghy transportation, or enough charts or money. But I shut my mouth and made two commitments on the spot: to stop worrying so much, and to remember my marriage vows to love, honor, and never say, "I told you so."

We left Miami, motored across the Gulf Stream with all the skill and accuracy of old salts, spent twenty minutes in Bimini clearing Customs and refueling, then took off in a mad dash for Nassau. The entire way we beat into southeast winds! George and Peg drove us on; they were anxious to meet family in the Virgin Islands by Christmas and they weren't about to be slowed by unfavorable weather or our dragging feet.

Following a second fuel stop at Chub Cay in the Berry Islands, we rested for the night, and in the morning, we were dismayed to find the wind blowing stronger, and right on our nose. It was too much, and I put my foot down, "Roger, do you realize we have motored all the way from Key West?"

He could hardly argue the point. Besides, by continuing to burn fuel so haphazardly, he could see we would use up our money very quickly. It was a small victory when he said, "I'll tell George we'll meet him in Nassau in a day or two, and we'll wait for a better wind."

As the *Bewitched* motored toward Nassau, we journeyed a few miles east to a cove we'd found on the chart, and indeed it looked perfect for providing a little rest, relaxation, and privacy.

After their swim, one by one the kids climbed aboard the boat, disappeared below to change clothes, then willingly settled down to read and nap. All of us were unwinding, but the surroundings and the rum punches certainly helped to untie the knots in my stomach created by hurried preparations and days of running to catch up to George and Peg.

Roger stretched out on a deck cushion and dozed off in the late-afternoon sun while I sat in a chair and peered at the closest island, watching for any signs of wildlife in the thick growth of coconut thatch palm and sea grape trees along the beach. Then I heard the noise! Sitting forward, I poked Roger in the ribs, saying "Wake up! Do you hear that? It sounds like a motor! Didn't the chart show these islands are uninhabited?"

Roger raised his head and listened. "It sounds like a bulldozer, probably a mile away. Someone must live here." I frowned as he dismissed me by returning to his nap.

The sound of any motor in the Bahamas is unusual, but this one seemed even more so, though I wasn't sure why. We were in a very remote spot, vulnerable, with no buddy boat around, but it was no time to start worrying about pirates behind every palm tree. Shrugging off the uneasy feeling, I told myself that Dad's gun was stashed somewhere in the engine room, at least I hoped it was. We hadn't seen it in months. And pirates didn't use bulldozers.

The noise was no more than an annoying intrusion, but it continued until sundown, and was rumbling again when we awoke the following morning. With the warm clear day, I seized the opportunity to wrestle all the bedding onto the deck to air. Once the chores were done, the kids and I settled down for a few hours of schoolwork. Being always in need of relevant topics, I assigned essays for them to write about that unseen machine.

Tommy said the Bahamas were building another Disneyland, and he described all the imaginary rides. Ron declared it was a UFO and wrote about going ashore and being swept away by Martians. Janice wrote of an enormous, hungry, green-eyed cat that was eating up all the trees and animals, and soon it would come after us. I thought her image was closest to my own.

With my curiosity whetted, I prodded Roger. "Let's go see what it is."

He was probably planning an afternoon nap when he answered, "Forget it. I'm sure this is a private island."

"But what could they do to us for exploring?"

"Arrest us, for starters."

"Well, there aren't any 'Keep Out' signs. Anyway, I think you are just trying to get out of exerting any energy."

He gave me a smile that said, *you guessed it*, but I won anyway. We left Tommy and Janice playing Scrabble, Ron reading a science fiction novel, and climbed into the small rubber raft to row ashore.

The hot sand burned through the soles of our tennis shoes as we drug the raft away from the water's edge and tied it to a low-growing bush. Clambering a few yards up a sand-and-coral ridge, we found a trail, then a narrow winding road that looked to be thirty years old and unused for twenty-nine.

The droning bulldozer tugged us along. Trees and scrubby vegetation closed in on the edge of the road, and thorn bushes scratched at our bare legs. A skittering, curly tailed lizard crossed our path. Hermit crabs dressed in pilfered shells rustled around in the tangled underbrush. Mosquitoes buzzed our ears. The air weighed heavy and still, and smelled strongly of dust, dry seaweed, and wild sage. Rivers of perspiration trickled down my neck and cooled my skin.

We trudged for half a mile, then stepped into a clearing and gaped in wonder. Before us lay a village that could have been plucked intact straight from the Swiss Alps! A dozen tiny stone houses sat before us, deserted, unkempt, and as strangely out of place as coconut trees would be in Switzerland. How long had they been empty? The shutters on the windows were nailed tight; the doors were secured with chains and padlocks; and any paint was cracked, peeling, and faded to a nondescript beige. Heidi had been gone for some time.

A green patch of unruly vines, dried flowers, and thistles marked the location of a small village square. Peeking out of the rampant growth of vegetation was a marble pedestal, vacant except for a small brown lizard warming in the sun.

At the edge of the village and closest to us, stood a two-story house noticeably larger than the others, and apparently in use as well. A lawn encircled the house, and expertly pruned fruit and flower trees provided an umbrella of shade. Double doors on the second floor opened onto a balcony, and the balcony commanded a view of the deserted Alpine village and the square.

A tingly sensation played along my spine as we walked toward the town. Until that moment there had been no sign of life except the lizard, no sound except the machine in the distance. Then we saw the man standing in the shadow of a house watching us.

He was a light-skinned Bahamian, neatly but casually dressed, and clearly unhappy to see company. Stepping into the sun, he demanded, "How did you get here?"

Roger coughed nervously, then explained where we were anchored. I added that we were curious about the island.

Our host frowned, and the firmness in his deep bass voice made me squirm. "You will have to return the way you came!" There was no misunderstanding his intent when he finished with, "I'll walk with you too, and make sure you do not get lost."

"What'd I tell you?" Roger whispered into my ear.

The man stepped between us and we obediently did an about face and began to retrace our steps. For a moment we walked along the dusty path in silence, but my nervousness brought out the chatter and I pointed at the gingerbread village. "Do you live here?"

"No."

I waited but when he didn't say anything else, I asked, "Do you live there?" and I nodded toward the big house. Roger gave me a look that indicated he thought my nosiness was out of order, but I ignored him.

"No." The man must have sensed my next question because he added, "I live on the other side of the island."

"Does the island belong to you?" He shook his head and I pushed on. "I'm sorry but we didn't know it was private, or we would never have come ashore. Who does...."

"It belongs to a man from Canada. I am the caretaker." I thought he was going to stop again and was surprised when he offered more information. "My boss bought it last year from the estate of an American woman."

"An American? Was she the one that built the village?"

"Yes and lived here too for almost forty years."

"Well, I can't blame her. It's a lovely place. But why did she build a whole village?"

The man smiled and his amber-colored eyes warmed with amusement. "I think she was unhappy in the States and wanted a place to practice her particular lifestyle."

"Really? What kind of lifestyle was that?" The prying surprised even me, and Roger looked ready to throttle me. Anyway, my questions paid off.

"Well, she preferred the company of beautiful women. She dressed like a man and ruled this island as a man would have. The main house was hers and she liked to stand on the balcony every morning to review her troops."

Roger looked at our host in disbelief. "Her troops?" I smiled to myself; he was hooked too.

"Yes, she had a private army of two hundred Bahamians. They lived here and on neighboring islands with their families, and she supported all of them. Every morning the army paraded fully uniformed around the plaza for her inspection. The pedestal in the center of the square held a statue of her and the statue was ten feet tall." His voice faded off for a minute. "I don't know what became of that."

"Did the army live in the village of houses?" I asked. "The architecture is certainly unusual for the islands."

"Oh no. Those belonged to her favorite women friends," he explained. "She built a different house for each one. Some of the ladies were very well known." He named a few and I was surprised to recognize two famous names from films in the '40s. "She brought them here by private plane, to the airstrip on the other end of the island."

"She must have been interesting." The descriptive word hardly seemed adequate.

"Different I suppose, but everyone liked her. She was very good to the Islanders. She often gave big parties, and those that worked for her had free beer and food."

As we reached the beach, we thanked him for the history, and without another word our escort turned and disappeared through the trees.

Roger looked at me and sneered, "Well, are you satisfied now?"

"No," I pouted. "I forgot to ask about the bulldozer."

As if on cue, the machine stopped. A heavy stillness enveloped the island, then the natural sounds returned to fill the void. Birds chattered overhead, a land crab rustled in the dry leaves, a gentle wave swooshed onto the sand beach.

"Do you hear that?" I whispered.

"I don't hear anything!" Roger spoke impatiently then bent to untie the raft from the bushes. "Now climb in this boat before we get shot."

I did as he ordered but was sure I'd heard a sound in the distance: the cadence of marching feet, and a faint, "Hup, two, three, four."

We sailed away from the Berry Islands, tacked back and forth, and two hours later found ourselves a mile from where we'd started. *Halcyon* stubbornly refused to sail upwind. Roger started the motor and burned up another valuable tankful of fuel getting us to Nassau before nightfall.

Anchoring beside the *Bewitched* and off the beach from the Sheraton Colonial Hotel, we sat in the same spot we'd anchored two years before. Looking at the setting I wondered if we, like *Halcyon*, were tacking through life against a head-on wind.

After dinner on the *Bewitched*, the kids swapped Hardy Boys mysteries then fought their way through a game of Monopoly. Roger and I played bridge with George and Peg while we plotted the next part of the trip. The two sea Captains agreed to leave for the Exumas the following morning. They planned to stay in radio contact all the way, then somewhere before Georgetown we would rendezvous and strike out for the Virgin Islands.

The *Bewitched* pulled anchor at dawn and headed out of the harbor. Roger talked to George over the radio, promising to follow as soon as we ran a few errands and fueled up.

As their boat disappeared beyond the Paradise Island bridge, Roger said, "I'm going to run ashore and see if I can find some charts." He began untying the two-man raft. "Do you need anything?"

I gave him a list. "If you pick up some fresh fruit and vegetables then I think I'm all set."

A half hour later he returned with everything on the list, as well as a stalk of slightly green bananas, which he tied to the end of the mizzen boom. Standing back, he admired the effect. "Now I feel like a bona fide cruiser."

The kids attacked the stalk and peeled off three nearly ripe pieces of fruit. "Well, you might feel like a cruiser, but I think we look more like a boatload of monkeys," I said. Hear, See, and Speak No Evil sat in a row happily stuffing their cheeks with the sweet fruit. "By the way, did you get the charts?"

"No, but the marine store gave me an address of a possible source. I thought we'd move the boat to the docks, and while I track down the store you and Ron can fuel up."

We motored the two miles to the fuel dock and inched our way to the pumps. The kids readied the lines while I worried about the reading on the fathometer. "Roger, there is only six and a half feet of water under us and we're at high tide!"

Checking the fathometer, then the time, Roger concluded, "We have about an hour before the tide turns. But just to be on the safe side, I'll catch a taxi and be back here before all the water drains out."

I wasn't satisfied. "What's the drop in the harbor?" Our keel was five and a half feet down so I knew we might have trouble.

"About a foot and a half. Right here will probably drop to five feet. I know we'll be trapped if we don't get out in time, but don't worry, I'll be back before then."

We tied up and Roger hurried off down the street. The kids and I topped the fuel and water tanks, then waited. Tommy and Janice left the boat for a while to explore the water's edge and to feed pieces of bread to the minnows and hermit crabs. Ron sat beside me on the deck and together we watched the tide reverse, then slowly begin to flow out of the harbor.

"Mom, Dad's been gone over an hour now. Do you think we can move the boat?"

"Let's wait a little longer." I didn't want to tell him I was scared. I'd never moved the boat by myself before and wasn't sure I could.

The dock manager walked up and asked for Roger. "He's not back yet," I stammered. "But I expect him any minute."

"Well, Lady, he's gotta get this boat out'a here—it's using up most of my dock!"

He was right. We were covering over half of the dock and in another thirty minutes we would be anchored there for the rest of the day, stuck to the bottom.

I was pacing the deck as a small speed hull came roaring alongside. When *Halcyon*'s keel bumped the bottom in the wave action, I ordered Ron to start the engine. Picking up the air horn, I signaled for Tommy and Janice to return to the boat, then surveyed the situation. We were head into a horseshoe; parallel to the dock on our starboard side, the seawall at our bow, and a line of expensive powerboats were tied off our port. Open water lay beyond our stern.

With each minute, the current picked up speed and pushed us harder against the dock. I was sure if I tried to back *Halcyon*, the tide would force the stern around the end of the dock and into a bank of mud that had probably been left by a dredge when the dock was first built. Then we would really be stuck. But if I could pivot her, turn her forty-five-foot length in the sixty feet of space and point her out to the channel, we would be free. Even I could see it was impossible.

"Your husband back yet?" The manager leaned on a piling beside the boat, and clearly, he was annoyed that he had to deal with a nervous wife.

"No, not yet." My heart was sinking as fast as the water table.

"You plannin' to move this thing by yourself?" The smug grin on his face was just what I needed to give me momentum.

"Certainly. Why not?" And I ordered Tommy and Janice to start untying the lines. A couple of dockhands joined the manager, and it was certain they were lining up for the show.

After sending Tommy to the bowsprit to let me know if I was getting too close to any of the powerboats, I gave Janice the boat hook and instructed her, "Start in the bow, and when I give the order, push against the dock, and as you push, walk toward the stern of the boat."

"Huh?" She looked puzzled. Carefully I repeated the instructions.

"You better wait for the Captain, Missy," some sidewalk smart aleck offered. I looked up to see several more sideline supervisors in the audience.

"Come on. Roger," I prayed under my breath, but he was nowhere to be seen.

Ron and I walked the boat back to the last piling on the dock; I wrapped a line around the post, secured one end to the boat, and gave the other to Ron. "Stand on the stern of the boat and hold the free end of the line as tight as you possibly can. When I tell you, release it a little, and when we are turned around, pull the whole line on board." If it worked, I figured, that line was going to be the hinge for *Halcyon* to pivot on.

Someone from the dock called, "Just back the boat up, Lady. She'll get out all right if you just back her." Hadn't anyone ever told him a sailboat can't back a straight line, (especially with me steering)?

A male chauvinist put in his two cents, saying, "That's no work for a lady." He turned to a companion and said, "She don't know what she's doing."

That was all I needed—this boat was going to turn on a dime if I had to lift her around on my shoulders! I revved the motor and backed hard on the stern line, all the time shouting at Ron to hold tight and for Janice to push. The bow inched out as the stern eased a few inches around the rear piling.

The onlookers began to loudly share their directions. I spun the wheel back, shifted the gears to forward, and poured on the gas at the same time, instructing Ron to release about six inches of line. The bow eased forward and out another few inches. Backed up again, I gained another foot.

My hands were shaking and the shouts from the dock began to drown out my voice. Two more maneuvers and *Halcyon* moved some more. Janice grew red in the face from straining against the boat hook, but she didn't let up and I knew she was as determined as I was to prove to those jerks that we could do it.

The bow slid past the seawall and pointed toward the powerboats. Confusing the gears, I came close to ramming Tommy and the bowsprit into a hundred-thousand-dollar Hatteras but corrected in time. Then I felt it: the currents were applying pressure to the opposite side of the bow! We were free! Backing her once more, I shouted to Ron to release the line.

With the gears in forward, we had started to pull away when noises from the dock and Tommy and Janice pointing, made me turn around and look. Ron was standing on the dock! Throwing the motor into reverse I backed so hard, that I hit the piling before the boat stopped. From their expressions, I knew I had jarred the teeth of my audience, but the only damage was to my ego. Ron jumped aboard, I gunned the engine, and we struck out for open bay. Cheers and laughter followed in our wake.

We taxied in circles for another hour before Roger showed up, riding in a native fishing boat. As he climbed on board, he breathlessly explained, "The store was miles from the dock, and I couldn't find a taxi or a bus to get back. I must have hiked ten miles."

He stopped his explanation, then grinned broadly. "I had to ask one of the fishermen on the dock for a ride. You should hear them talking about you back there. You got their respect. How did you do it?"

I was glad my knees and teeth had stopped quivering, but my hands were going like butterflies. I tucked them under my rump while I described the method I'd used to turn *Halcyon*.

"That's amazing," he said when I had finished. "Well done!"

"There was nothing to it!" I was fairly bursting with pride.

The kids took turns on the wheel as we motored away from Nassau and across the Banks for the Exumas. Roger and I spent a lazy afternoon lying on the deck. After all, we'd had a strenuous day. We were both stretched out on the deck cushions when Roger informed me, he'd been unable to find the charts we were missing. I knew he was trying to reassure me when he said, "Maybe we can trade with a boat coming from the other direction."

He seemed surprised when I answered, "Don't worry about it, we'll make out all right."

Raising up on one elbow, he gave me a long look. "Where did you get this sudden burst of confidence?" he asked.

"Maybe I just learned how easy it is to handle this boat."

Janice had to choose that moment to tell him how I hit the dock.

We spent one night at Norman's Cay, then decided to renew a pleasant memory with the natural well water of Shroud Cay. Entering the mooring, we found a wooden yawl anchored near the beach, and three people, wearing snorkels and masks, swimming beside it.

Choosing a spot as far away as possible, we dropped the anchor and Ron dove to secure it under a small ledge of coral. Roger shut down the engine, then raised the awning, and we settled in to enjoy an afternoon of leisure on the deck.

I had collected discarded socks all summer for a craft project, and Tommy and Janice gathered them together along with bright scraps of material, glue, and marking pens, spread the equipment out on deck, and began to create hand puppets for a play Ron had authored.

For a while we watched the kids, then our attention wandered to the other boat, and the neighbors who were just climbing aboard. As the two men and one woman stepped onto the deck there was no denying their sexes, they were nude.

One of the men went forward to raise the anchor, the second started the motor and walked to the wheel. I couldn't help but wonder about working on a sailboat without clothing. It seemed a risky business. The woman stood amidships, arm around a shroud, long blond hair draped wetly over one shoulder. The boat moved forward slowly, then turned in a wide arc and headed in our direction. As it drew closer, I could clearly see, that the three occupants had spent most of their time sans clothing.

Feeling a twinge of jealously, I thought of the white streaks decorating our own bodies, the result of various styles of swimsuits, halters, and cut-offs. Roger's torso was the funniest: the whiteness of his backside glowed in the dark! As the three approached us, we could see there wasn't even a change of shades on their bodies.

Suddenly it dawned on me they were coming alongside *Halcyon*! Catching Roger's eye, I silently signaled a question. *What about the kids*?

He grinned as he read my thoughts. "Your Protestant ethics are showing," he said, then stood to wave at the sun worshippers passing within yards of us. "Where are you headed?" he called.

"Miami," The girl leaned out over the handrail gifting Roger and Ron, who had naturally joined his dad at the gunwale, with the full benefit of her pulchritude.

"What kind of boat is that?" Ron asked.

The answer came from Adonis as he coiled the last of the anchor line. "One-of-a-kind, made in Scotland."

Janice turned her head and appeared momentarily interested before looking back at me. "Mom, they don't have any clothes on," she said.

Before I could answer, she resumed drawing a mustache on one of the socks.

Tommy stood and gave the boat a long look as it motored past our stern on its way toward the Banks. "Theirs isn't as long as ours," he announced.

"Their what?" popped out of my mouth before I could stop it.

Tommy looked at me like I'd lost my marbles. "Their boat! What did you think I meant?"

Roger was obviously amused by my discomfort. "Yes, Toni. What did you mean?"

"Nothing." And I sat down in my chair and shut my mouth.

The boat disappeared around the end of the island, and the kids returned to their activities with no further comment. Roger pulled a banana off the stalk, propped his feet on the binnacle, and peeled the newly ripened fruit. "Yep, she sure had nice lines," he said.

It took him a half hour to get all the banana out of his nose.

That night we packed dinner in a basket, loaded the water jugs into the five-man life raft, and rowed to the beach. After filling the jugs at the well, we ate dinner, then roasted marshmallows and sang sea chanties while the sun dipped beyond the Banks. As twilight faded to night, we loaded our picnic remnants into the raft, and let Ron flex his muscles by rowing us home. Nine o'clock found every one of us, peacefully and soundly asleep.

The cabin was pitch black. I blinked but the darkness remained. Evidently something woke me, but what? Roger was breathing softly from the other bunk. I listened for the kids and the boat was still.

Where were we? As I peered out of the porthole, I tried to remember. The night was a curtain, drawn close around the boat, and it blocked out any clue of our location. *"That's north,"* I thought, then wondered how I knew.

The tide was slack, *Halcyon* hardly moved. No whisper of water passing along the steel hull, no wind clanging in the rigging. *Halcyon* slept as soundly as the people on board her.

The noise came again, a tiny swish alongside the boat. Alerted, I sat up, leaned toward the porthole, and rested my chin on the narrow ledge. The night was impenetrable, and my eyes wouldn't adjust. Unexpectantly, I felt a moving wave brush six inches below my chin, and a loud whoosh of air swept past my face. Someone was there—and close!

The noise was human, exactly as if someone had released a long pent-up breath. Covering my mouth, I swallowed a scream. Immediately, a flash of sheet lightning illuminated the water and revealed the back of a porpoise as it dove beneath *Halcyon*. My pulse returned to normal as I relaxed and listened to the wild creature in our midst. It surfaced, blew air, then dove again.

A second burst of lightning outlined the island, and I realized I'd been right about the direction the boat was facing. What primitive instinct told me which way was north?

From the day we'd moved on board *Halcyon*, Roger had displayed certain senses that somehow eluded me. For a long time, I couldn't even understand what they were. But lately, I found myself sharing a few, and the porpoise outside my porthole was a good illustration of one of them. How did the soft blowing of that animal wake me?

Roger and I could and did sleep like the dead at dockside, when boats were racing their motors all around us, or the kids were running across the deck with no regard to noise. But the moment we left the safety of the harbor to anchor in the precarious shelter of an island, or in a spot like this so remote and uninhabited that we could disappear from the face of the Earth and no one would be the wiser, something happened. Our bodies became tuned to any subtle variation in the boat, and even during sleep our minds reacted to an unusual sound—a quickening wind, the tides, the change of rhythm in the songs of *Halcyon*'s rigging.

It was as though my senses had awakened. I had a oneness with the surroundings; even the phases of the moon were as much a part of me as my own heartbeat. This feeling of oneness with the world was new, something I never would have believed a city girl could develop, and it was such an exciting feeling that I silently vowed never to lose it when we returned to land.

The porpoise moved away. Stretching out in the bunk, I closed my eyes and Roger suddenly mumbled, "What time is it?"

I made a guess, "About 4 a.m." Quiet settled around the boat and I drifted toward sleep as the ship's clock chimed the watch change. I was right about the time, too.

Staniel Cay turned out to be a homecoming. Bringing the boat into Happy People Marina (a wonderful and appropriate name), we anchored and went ashore. While re-exploring the dusty streets, we passed a little girl about ten years old playing in the shade of an almond tree.

When Janice spotted her, she beamed with pleasure, dashed over to the girl, and said, "Hi, Cynthia."

We were surprised to hear the girl respond in kind, "Hi, Janice." It had been almost two years since our first trip, but they recognized each other and even remembered names.

The same was true of many of the villagers who smiled, waved, and greeted us warmly. The shopkeeper recalled that Roger was the sailor with the "coppers," and proudly showed us the pennies, sitting for "safe keeping" in a jar on his counter.

"There still be exactly eight dollar and twenty cent dere," he said as he pointed proudly. "I be keeping it for emergency." And he smiled broadly at the link that would connect us until some unknown emergency came along.

Returning to the boat, we heard an inordinate amount of noise and activity on the docks and went on deck to investigate. Dozens of people were seated on the rough boards, cleaning fish, lobster, and conch, and all the time chattering excitedly in the almost indecipherable Island lingo.

Janice translated for us. "The schoolteacher and his wife are having a birthday party tonight."

A pleasant-faced old fisherman dressed in straw hat, T-shirt, and enormous gray britches held securely by a length of rope, stood, hefted a straw basket full of raw conch meat to his shoulder, and approached us timidly. "Captain, you and your Lady be invited to come too. The teacher would like it."

We thanked him and said we'd try. Later, on the boat as I put our purchases away, I asked Roger, "Do you think we should go?"

"Why not? I'm sure the man meant the invitation, but if you feel uncomfortable, we'll skip out early."

Thinking it might be an "Adults Only" party, we settled the kids down for the night, dressed, then started for the schoolhouse where the fisherman had told us the festivities would take place. The entire town of one hundred people was there, as well as several other sailors. And not only did we feel comfortable, but we were also sorry we had not brought the kids.

I noticed that the school desks had been relegated to a small back room to make space for all the people, the band, and the bar. Several dozen metal folding chairs lined the room, but no one was using them. People either danced or milled around in the yard, swapping gossip, jokes, smokes, and booze. The band was crowded into one corner of the room: five young men who made up in enthusiasm what they lacked in skill or equipment. Within five minutes we heard their whole repertoire of two songs, but they played both remarkably well. All that practice, I decided.

The schoolteacher and his wife came up and shook our hands warmly. They were an attractive young couple and seemed most anxious that we enjoy ourselves. They led us to the two-sawhorses-and a-board bar, offered drinks, then informed us food would be served at 10 p.m. "In the meantime, please dance." Smiling, they went away to greet more guests.

Dancing was not Roger's favorite sport, but we tried a beginner's reggae through the two selections of the band, and afterward he slipped away to a corner to join another sailor. Expecting to be able to sit and watch, I settled into one of the chairs by a window, but soon found out no one was allowed to sit.

A very bright-eyed and bashful twelve-year-old boy appeared before me. I hesitated over his invitation to dance before I noticed four or five of his friends watching us. I could hardly rebuff so vulnerable a suitor in front of his peers.

We shuffled around the floor for a minute, bumping into more people than any one-room schoolhouse was ever meant to hold, when a sixty-five-year-old grandmother type, sporting a T shirt emblazoned with, "Try it, you'll like it," sashayed up to us, grinned broadly, and spoke to my partner, "Sidney, you be a gentleman now!"

Sidney nodded, looked at me through lowered lashes, then broke loose to show me how much he knew about the fine art of reggae dancing. Before the evening was over, I had danced with every twelve- year-old on the island, five more times with Sidney, and enjoyed a rest only when I stumbled out the door and down the path to the outhouse. I was ashamed of my breathlessness after the first two hours of dancing. After all, the grandmother had danced as much as me, and she didn't even look like she needed the outhouse.

Roger pried himself away from the sailors when the food was served. More sawhorses and boards filled the dance floor, then elaborate dishes began to arrive, carried in proudly by the wives and mothers who had prepared them.

We feasted on raw conch, lobster salad, pigeon peas and rice, fruit salads, conch fritters, and mounds of fresh fried grouper. An Out Island birthday party is worth any price!

At midnight, the band burst into a very island version of "Happy Birthday." Though the party went on and on, we said good night and strolled home through the deserted village.

I awoke the next morning to a backache. Over breakfast, the kids begged to go to church, and Roger agreed we would go. When I tried to beg off, he goaded me by saying, "Is it possible that you are out of shape?"

Snapping to attention, I denied the obvious through clenched teeth. "Not on your life! It must have been the way I slept." And in agony, I silently dressed.

About half the town made it to the church. Those that didn't had rum hangovers or backaches worse than mine. Mrs. Schoolteacher was there, but Mr. wasn't. "Too much rum," she explained with a rueful smile.

Sidney and his friends flirted with me across the backs of the church pews, the T-shirted grandmother sat down in front of us, and when she nodded, I realized I hadn't recognized her in her Sunday dress.

The service was a replay of our first trip, a very vocal choir, the man with the switch, the entire congregation filing by to shake our hands afterward. The whole world may be changing around us, but I believe Staniel Cay will always be the same. At least I hope so.

Roger raised the *Bewitched* on the radio, and found it sitting in the Georgetown Harbor impatiently waiting for us. George was none too happy to learn we were still two days away, but Roger appeased him with promises we'd leave Staniel Cay at sunup, and sail or motor nonstop for Georgetown.

We started at dawn with good intentions of keeping our word, but an hour out of Happy People Marina, the brisk wind turned into a rainy gale. Tucking tail, we ran for the protection of Farmer's Cay Harbor.

On the first trip we'd skipped Farmer's Cay, but when we entered the anchorage and saw the tiny village of white clapboard, tin-roofed houses nestled along a beach of craggy coral and sand, we knew we were not going to miss it again.

By afternoon the wind had died down and the boys were asking to swim ashore. Janice showed her fear of the stormy murky water and by asking, "Why can't we row to shore instead?"

"You're just chicken," taunted Tommy.

"Am not!"

"Are too!"

"Am not!

I stepped in and asked Ron to row instead of swimming. When he protested as loudly as Janice had, Roger came up with an idea. "Janice can ride in the raft, Tommy and Ron can push it."

That pleased everyone and they left for the beach, Janice sitting regally in the tiny boat, Tommy and Ron pushing on the stern, their legs churning up water like two 100 hp Evinrudes.

After an hour of romping with a variety of island children and frisky dogs, the kids returned, each with a new playmate. As we met them at the rail, doled out towels, and helped all six aboard, Janice volunteered the introductions. "Meet Jeff, Simon, and Marie," she announced proudly. "They wanted to see the boat."

Picking out the oldest, a tall skinny boy with amethyst-colored eyes, I asked, "Do your parents know where you are?"

He grinned the ever-quick island grin, and answered politely, "Yes'm. That's my father over there." He was pointing to the beach where a fisherman knelt and cleaned conch at the water's edge. As if the man knew we were talking about him, he looked up and raised his hand in a salute. I waved back, then wrapped a towel around Tommy's blue body and sent them all below to get warmed up. Within minutes the puppet show was set up, and our three were happily performing a modern Punch and Judy for their guests.

Roger and I sat on deck and listened to the chattering voices coming from the cabin and I couldn't resist observing, "I think it is amazing the way our kids can make instant friends and it doesn't seem to matter anymore about status, race, background, or which one knows the latest rock group."

Roger nodded. "I bet you're thinking about New Orleans."

"No, not altogether. It's more than that. Even age doesn't seem to matter to them. Remember the Bionic Man, and Homer and Sandy? Our kids are simply more receptive to people than they used to be. They truly enjoy the differences." I paused as I tried to put it into words, then I gave up and said, "Whatever it is, I like it."

"Agreed," Roger said, then something caught his eye and he looked toward the village. "I think we are about to have more company."

Skillfully sculling the small wooden boat against the persistent wind, the fisherman came alongside, and we caught his line. "I'm Mark. I come for my children; I hope they not trouble."

We assured him they weren't, then Roger invited the athletically handsome islander aboard. The two of them talked while I descended the ladder to gather up Jeff, Simon, and Marie.

Obviously, the children had a true friendship going. Ron and Tommy gave Jeff and Simon several of their prized comic books, and Janice gifted Marie with a string of Mardi Gras beads. As they were preparing to leave, Janice begged, "Can they come back tomorrow?"

Sailing Against the Wind — Toni Larson   211

Looking at the six eager faces, I answered, "If we are still here, but don't count on it. I suspect we'll be gone by then."

We weren't. The weather report that night warned that the storm would last at least another day, and small craft were advised to seek shelter during the morning hours. With all due respect to *Halcyon*, I considered her to be small craft.

Mark returned that afternoon with his children and his three joined our three for a rerun of the puppet show. And even with the wind blowing to forty knots and the water beyond the harbor whipped to a white chop, Roger and Mark went diving for lobster. Perhaps the harbor was safe enough for the small fishing craft to handle, but I knew it would take a hurricane for Roger to pass up an opportunity to dive with an "expert." As I watched them leave, I could see that Roger had made a friend as quickly as the kids.

It may not have been too cold to swim, but it was clearly too cold to sit on deck. Descending the ladder, I settled into an upper bunk, and from there watched the kids around the table.

Jeff was bragging that he was the only one in his family to ever have seen a TV. The earthshaking event came on a trip to Nassau with his father, and in his brother's and sister's eyes, that made him a hero.

Mark's children were fascinated by the tiny metal cars Ron and Tommy pulled from the bottom of a drawer, and Marie shook her curls and lamented, "I've never seen a car, only pictures in a book."

It was amazing to us to discover communities with no roads, only footpaths that wandered, mazelike through thick underbrush, and were the only connections to family and friends. At the crossing of two or more paths, stores appeared, and I had to chuckle at the contrast between those quiet, hidden little centers of commerce, and the meeting of two interstate highways. What would Marie think of a Los Angeles traffic jam? Or a shopping mall?

The kids were describing their respective schools when Jeff asked, "Why don't you go to school with us in the morning?"

They all begged but I warned, "I don't think the teacher would appreciate three unexpected visitors."

"We can find out," Simon offered. "She is my aunt."

When the rest of them joined in with the pleading, I used the standard mother answer: "We'll see."

Roger and Mark returned with four nice lobster, and we divided the catch. When the kids asked Mark what he thought of the school idea, he agreed it would be fun for them all, and he offered to ask his sister that night. Then he said, "If she says it be all right, I come for your children in the morning."

Roger argued, "We hope to be gone. But if we're still here, I can take the children ashore."

"No, please. I will be at the beach all day tomorrow to wait for the mailboat." Then he smiled warmly. "Why don't you stay for the party?"

I perked up. The arrival of the mailboat was a big event for the Out Islands. The whole town would turn out to welcome the mail, supplies, friends, relatives, and crews that the boats carried from island to island. Depending on the weather, it could be weeks between visits, and except for the occasional sailboat, the Islanders had no other contact with the outside world.

It was worth a try, so I tried. "Roger, one more day couldn't hurt. We've never been around for a mailboat, and this might be our last chance."

"We are supposed to be meeting *Bewitched*," he reasoned.

"Aw…please?" I whined.

"We'll see." He too gave the standard mother answer.

That night Roger called *Bewitched* on the radio. After talking for half an hour, he and George came to terms: George and Peg were going to motor straight for the Virgin Islands, we were going to sail slowly eastward and meet them in St. Thomas sometime before Christmas. And if the winds weren't favorable, we'd call them on January first and plan another rendezvous.

It sounded reasonable. After all, that gave us from six weeks to two months to catch up. Surely that would be enough time.

The kids and I were happy—we had another day at Farmer's Cay. The sky was clear when Mark appeared alongside the boat to pick up the kids. We stood on the deck and watched as he taxied them to shore. They joined Simon, Jeff, and Marie, then the six children skipped away, five brunettes and a blond, swinging lunch bags, laughing, and teasing as they went.

"I wonder if that teacher is prepared for the invasion," I mused.

"Only if she's an Army drill sergeant," Roger said as he put his arm around me and asked mischievously, "Do you realize we have the whole day to ourselves? How about making use of it?"

"Roger, are you sure you didn't instigate the whole thing?" I asked suspiciously.

"What do you mean? I thought you did!"

While I dressed for shore, Roger sat down and wrote a letter to the bank in California requesting that our money be recalled from the Virgin Islands and held in California until further word from us. With letter in hand, we rowed the five-man raft to the beach and visited with some of the townsfolk while waiting for school to let out. Soon after the last bell sounded, three excited kids came galloping down the road.

"It was so much fun!" Janice exclaimed.

"I answered all the questions," Tommy jumped in.

Roger said, "That's great, Tommy. What were the questions about?"

"Miami, New Orleans, and California," he said smugly. "And I knew all the answers."

"I got hungry." Ron was not to be left out.

"Yeah, and he ate one of my sandwiches!" Janice tattled.

"He tried to eat one of mine, too," Tommy squealed. "But I wouldn't let him."

"They got in a fight," Janice continued to snitch. "The teacher had to stop them." She hardly took a breath before asking, "Can we go back tomorrow?"

"I think the teacher may be running out of patience," I said. "Besides, you have lessons of your own that you are neglecting."

They fussed a little, then raced away to join several new friends in a game of King of the Hill.

The village had turned out *en masse* for the mailboat's arrival. It was a noisy festive affair as everyone waited expectantly on the beach. Kids and dogs chased each other around the legs of the parents, who stood in small circles sharing the events of the day. We were introduced to everyone, made to feel welcome, and I decided it would take all of twenty-four hours before we would no longer be "outsiders."

A group of teenagers formed a band comprised of a drum, whistles, bamboo sticks, and plastic jugs filled with dried beans. The throb of the makeshift music blanketed the island, and soon we were tapping our toes to the beat along with everyone else.

By nightfall the mailboat still had not appeared, but the storm returned, and a sudden shower sent us all scurrying for cover. Roger and the boys joined Mark's family; Janice and I accepted an invitation into Maggie's house.

Maggie was a friendly lady beyond the age of sixty, skin the color of soft suede, eyes hazel brown, voice the soft singsong of the island. Her home was obviously her pride and joy and she seemed happy for the chance to show it off. She offered us chairs in her small kitchen/living room, and we sat at the table and talked about boats, babies, the States, and the Out Islands. She told us her husband had died the year before, and her only son lived in Nassau. As she talked, she picked up some palm fronds and began to plait the long strips of straw. As we watched her fingers deftly flick the strands of straw, I asked, "Do you make this into baskets?"

"No, I make only the rolls." And she indicated four large bundles of plaited straw, in a corner of the room. "I sell those to the crew on the mail boat, and they take them to Nassau for me." Her fingers did not let up as she explained her livelihood. "The crewmen will sell the bundles to a woman in the straw market. That woman will sew the plaits into purses, basket, or dolls."

"How long are the rolls?" I asked. "And how much time does it take to make one?"

"They are each twelve yards long. Sometimes I do one roll in three or four days, but mostly it take me almost a week."

Janice picked up some of the straw and began to imitate Maggie's hands. Within minutes she had a neat strip about one inch in length. "Mom, maybe we can make baskets on the boat and sell them to the tourists when we get into a port!" Eagerly she turned to Maggie and asked, "How much do you sell one of those rolls for?"

"I make five dollars per bundle," Maggie answered.

"Wow!" Janice looked pleased at the prospect, but I marveled at the miracle these island women performed. Many of them fed their families on five dollars for a week's work.

We continued to sit, listening to the rain pelt against the corrugated tin roof, watching Maggie plait straw. About 9 a.m. the clouds lifted. I thanked our hostess, found Roger and the boys, and we returned to the *Halcyon*.

As soon as the breakfast dishes were cleared away, I put the kids to stowing their toys and securing the cabin for sailing. Roger and Ron worked on deck, lashing down loose gear, checking the rigging, readying the sails. As they worked, they searched the horizon for the mailboat. There was no sign of it.

With the last detail completed, Roger decided to make a quick trip to shore to give the letter for our bank to Mark, and I chose to go with him and say goodbye. The kids packed a small box with a few toy cars, some plastic vampire teeth, and a book for Jeff, Simon, and Marie. Tucking the gifts under my arm, I joined Roger in the raft.

Mark was on the beach waiting for us, and Roger handed him our letter. "We'll be leaving shortly—would you mind putting this letter on the mailboat?"

"Not at all. But why do you not stay? The boat be sure to come today."

"We really must move on." Roger shook his head. "The longer we stay, the harder it is for us to leave. But your island and your friendship has been the highlight of our visit to the Out Islands."

"I agree," I said and we both meant it. The harmony and serenity of Farmer's Cay were not going to be forgotten.

Mark paused a moment before saying softly, "When my wife and I were first married, I built a house for her beyond the hill over there." He pointed to a small, wooded rise on the far side of the village. "As our children come, she be begging for a house closer to her mother, so we move into the village. But the house still be there, a good house with a generator and even a refrigerator." He smiled proudly and I knew that the refrigerator was a very important status symbol to these people. "The house be yours anytime for as long as you like."

Mark's offer, and the sincerity that went with it, touched me. Obviously, Roger felt the same as he stammered, "That is certainly generous. We appreciate it, really we do."

"It is tempting," I added. "I think our three children would love it here too. But I'm sorry. We have to turn it down. we can't stay."

"I understand," said Mark. "Just remember the house be yours if you want to come back."

The kids were waiting as we climbed out of the raft and hoisted it aboard *Halcyon*. I went forward to raise the anchor, Roger and Ron started the motor, Ron took the wheel, and soon we were moving toward the inlet. We looked one last time at the village. Mark, his children, and a dozen others stood on the beach waving. Janice grabbed the horn and blew a final farewell.

If we hadn't set a date with the *Bewitched*, I wondered how long we would be willing to stay right where we were. And as I pondered that thought Roger surprised me by asking, "Wouldn't it be interesting to live on an island?"

Before I could respond, a loud horn sounded at the harbor entrance and we looked to see the mailboat just rounding the point. A new cheer went up from the islanders on the beach and we joined in waving, cheering, and sounding our horn as we passed each other. The temptation was great, but we didn't turn back.

Halcyon rocked on her anchor line from the wild hustle and bustle of her crew. We were preparing for a real night out! True, we had been to a birthday party on Staniel Cay, and an island get-together while waiting for the mailboat, but this was different. Perhaps it was because we were homesick. I wanted to hear an American accent, the Southern drawl, the Midwestern twang, even the New York sneer. Roger was craving a cold Budweiser, the kids wanted hamburgers and French fries. And hopefully, the very American luxury resort on the south coast of Cat Island would relieve all our yearnings.

With razor and scissors in hand, I lined up Roger and the boys, converted the deck to a barber shop, and performed major surgery on an overgrowth of hair. Then, as Roger, Ron, and Tommy alternately soaped up and dumped cold buckets of seawater over each other's heads, I scrounged through the lockers and put together a well-coordinated set of dress-up clothes. After a teacupful rinse with fresh water, the men returned to the cabin to dress, while Janice and I took their places. With the grooming completed, we stood back to admire the results: at least we looked a cut above the beggar class.

A white stone path bordered with gardens of hibiscus and conch shells led from the resort pier to the yacht club. As we strolled along, it became apparent that the owners had run out of steam or money. Weeds grew in the flower beds, a chipped plaster statue guarded a dry, cracked, cement pond. Stakes marked building sites, and a few even showed signs of construction, though nowhere did anything appear to be current.

A rambling, cabana-style hotel sat on a rise overlooking the harbor, and a rusty air-cooling system hummed away at one end. There were no cars around, but that was to be expected. Tourists didn't arrive in cars in the Bahamas, and seldom needed them once they got there. Beyond the hotel lay a dusty airstrip where a small two-engine plane sat at one end.

Between the hotel and the harbor was the yacht club—all glass and mortared coral stone, and in every way a carbon copy of forty others we'd encountered throughout the islands.

Entering the ice-cold air-conditioned bar-game room, we approached the only other occupant of the room at the moment, a bartender dressed in jeans and a sport shirt. After he took our order, I asked where he was from. "Florida," he answered. "I've been here six months and thank God. I'm going home next week, FOR GOOD! I can't wait—this place is a drag!" Well, so much for my first American.

The kids gravitated to the ping-pong table, Roger and I fled to a spot in the corner, to luxuriate in the mosquito-less, refrigerated environment. As the front door opened, we glanced up to see a couple walk in, and they didn't have to speak for us to guess they were American. He was wearing an electric green silk shirt spattered with yellow flowers, beige linen Bermuda shorts, and an expensive pair of spotless new deck shoes. His much-sunburned balding head exactly matched his beet red face and knees. The lady at his side was immaculately white: white carefully coifed hair, white linen dress, white sandals, and slightly wrinkled powder-white skin. The starkness was relieved only by a necklace of shiny green beads and bright pink lipstick.

As they approached the bar, the man spoke with a midwestern twang, "Two pina coladas, please."

Then his companion turned to him and whispered loudly, "I sure hope they are better than the last ones he made. Those were too sweet. You remember, Dear?"

And if we could hear her, it was clear the bartender did too. He gave a sneering smile as he plunked the drinks down on the bar and sloshed fifty cents worth over the sides of the glasses.

Taking the fruity concoctions, the couple turned and started to look for a table when the man spotted us in the empty room.

"Well, hello there. Are you folks just arriving? Mind if we join you? Over here, Josie."

We could hardly say no; they were already seated by the time he'd asked permission. And he continued. "Where are you from? Are those your children? I didn't hear your plane, did you come in on a commercial?"

It took five minutes to complete the histories. He worked for an insurance company in Chicago, she played tennis. "The tennis courts in the islands are so—well—primitive," she informed us. "They aren't lighted so we can't play at night, and it is just too hot during the day. I can't bear the sun, but Ernie loves it. Don't you think he's getting a marvelous tan?"

I winced as I looked at the overcooked Ernie and wondered if he had insurance to cover second degree burns. They were fascinated by the idea that we lived on a boat, but Josie said, "I just couldn't do it. I'd be scared to death of sharks."

Roger asked Ernie how they'd reached Cat Island and he replied, "We flew. That's our plane out in the back. We are here for the Treasure Hunt, of course." When we looked puzzled, he went on, "Josie and I signed up back in Illinois. A real estate company back there thought up the idea for people who fly their own planes."

I was having trouble following the conversation and asked, "What are you looking for?"

"We don't know yet, but the prize is supposed to be something really big. I think we're almost there, too. We only have one more clue to go."

"Clue?" I felt like I was questioning one of the kids.

"You see," Ernie tried to explain, "we picked up the list of clues in Nassau, and the first one led us to a resort in the Berry Islands. The next one was a resort in the Eleutheras...," and he paused as though he'd forgotten something.

Josie reminded him by saying, "The third one was in the Exumas, Dear. You remember that dreary little restaurant with all those rude waitresses."

"Oh yes. Why don't these islanders learn to be a little friendlier? The Bahamas would dry up if it weren't for the tourists, yet these people do everything they can to run us off."

I thought about the people of Staniel and Farmer's Cay, then realized that the only time we had met a rude native in the Bahamas was back at Cat Cay on our first trip (and that had been at another resort.)

Ernie continued, "The last clue brought us here. I don't know where the next one leads..."

Roger finished it for him. "But I bet it's another resort, on another island."

"Yeah, you're probably right." Ernie was catching on. "Maybe they're trying to sell us some land in one of these places."

Josie bolted. "Oh no! The Bahamas are too remote for me. Don't get me wrong-I'm enjoying the trip, but well I prefer Fort Lauderdale. Have you been there?"

Roger and I nodded, but I didn't think we'd seen the same city she was talking about. Fort Lauderdale from a sailboat is an entirely different place than Fort Lauderdale from the Hilton.

Ernie was expounding upon the laziness of the Bahamian when the door opened again, and two extremely bedraggled, unshaven young men walked into the bar. One of them carried a limp bundle under his arm, and when he reached the bar, he unwrapped the package and deposited a fair-sized dolphin onto the bar and beneath the bartender's nose. The bartender cringed, but Roger came to attention like a hunting dog with the scent of a possum. Excusing himself from the table, he left me at the mercy of Ernie's wanderings and Josie's complaints while he gravitated toward the newcomers.

"Where did they come from?" Josie asked, as though she worried they might somehow soil her white dress.

I was relieved when the kids tired of ping-pong and appeared on the scene to beg for food. I introduced them to Ernie and Josie.

"Have you ever been in a plane?" Ernie asked Ron.

"Once, when I was six years old," he answered shyly.

"Would you kids like to take a ride in my plane tomorrow?"

Of all the dumb questions in the world, that one took grand prize. Ron grinned from ear to ear, Janice quivered in excitement, and Tommy wanted to know if he could sit by the window.

They made a date for the next morning, then I gave the kids some money for hamburgers, and they galloped happily toward a door marked, "Restaurant."

"We'd better eat, too, Ernie." Josie looked at me and asked, "Would you like to join us?"

"I think I'll wait for Roger, and he might be a while," I alibied. The homesickness had mysteriously vanished, and I found myself anxious to part company with my fellow Americans.

As Ernie and Josie departed, I walked over to Roger at the bar. He introduced his new friends, two sailors in their early twenties on a return trip from Haiti to South Carolina. One was a tall blond named Joe, and the other a shorter brunette called B.J. Both were lean and wiry and had beards that looked like the result of not shaving rather than cultivation.

Roger filled me in. "B.J. caught this dolphin on the way from Aklins Island and the bartender says they can't have it cooked here. I told them you'd do it." And Roger hastily added, "They don't have a stove on board their boat."

"Hah!" I registered my disbelief.

But he grinned and said, "I knew you wouldn't mind."

Hoping the National Organization of Women wouldn't snatch my membership card, I gave in. We gathered the kids, the fish, and the sailors, and hiked back to the boat. I didn't want a hamburger, anyway.

While we prepared the dinner, the sailors told their story. They were from a tiny town on the East Coast, had built their own boat and sailed it to Haiti without an engine. They also had no food, except a jar of peanut butter and a loaf of bread when they'd left the States, and oranges and the one fish on their way back. And if that wasn't Spartan enough, they had no money, no radio, fathometer, charts, stove, refrigerator, head, or anything else except two bunks and themselves.

When they had reached Haiti, they'd been arrested and detained in jail for four days for being destitute. Roger was amused at the irony. Both of us thought about the stories in the U.S. newspapers about destitute Haitians coming ashore on the Florida beaches.

"The jail was an experience," B.J. said. "We got pretty scared, but the guards were nice enough, and on the fourth day they passed a hat, collected twenty dollars and not only did they give us the money, but they drove us back to our boat."

Joe continued, "We were rich! At a penny a piece, we were able to buy enough oranges to last two weeks, and hopefully we have just enough left to get us home. By the way, that food looks wonderful."

He was all but drooling as I served up the fried fish, about five pounds of fried potatoes, mounds of hush puppies, and four cans of cream-style corn. Never had I served a plainer meal to more appreciative guests.

"How did you survive on only oranges?" I asked as I watched the food vanish from the table.

"The oranges were great," the blonde said between mouthfuls. "The tough time was getting to Haiti. We ran out of our peanut butter and fresh water three days before, and when the wind died, we couldn't get into a port for more. If a norther hadn't come through, we might not have made it at all."

Roger gave them a questioning look and asked, "But why would you do it to begin with?" I thought that was a strange question coming from him.

They glanced at each other, then B.J. spoke. "I don't really know. It happened the day we put the boat in the water. When we saw it sitting there, we just couldn't wait until we could afford all the trimmings. We wanted to go somewhere right then." He smiled slightly. "We began talking about where we'd like to go, when I looked up and Joe was untying the lines. I guess if we'd thought about it, we wouldn't have gone."

"It was worth it," said one.

"I'd do it again," said the other.

They talked for an hour about Haiti. The kids asked dozens of questions and were as enchanted with the two sailors as Roger and I. Ron summed it up for us: "I'd do the same thing, but I'd take more than just peanut butter and bread."

The kids woke us at dawn, dressed and ready to go flying. We held them at bay for four hours, all the time trying to force-feed them a dose of math before rowing them ashore and handing them over to Ernie. We watched the plane take off, then Roger and I retired to the bar for a peaceful game of ping-pong. An hour later Roger had chalked up eleven wins when we heard the plane on the runway. As we walked outside, the kids came across the yard in a dead run.

Ron did not suffer for lack of words telling us, "We saw the Exumas, and the horizon, and all of Cat Island, and ......"

"I saw the *Halcyon*!" Janice spoke up.

"I got sick, but I didn't throw up!" Tommy's blue eyes glowed.

We thanked Ernie, who shrugged it off with, "Glad to do it. Kids really get a kick out of airplanes. I'm trading this one in on a newer model when we get home, larger and with more range..." He spent fifteen minutes describing his toys, and he was still talking when we said goodbye.

At the dock we discovered the two sailors had left. *Halcyon* sat alone in the tiny harbor, and suddenly it seemed very empty. Climbing on board the boat, I tripped over a small brown paper bag, and lifting it, looked inside to find a dozen oranges and a note.

"Thank you for the wonderful dinner. If you ever come to South Carolina, please look us up. We'll be there if we aren't sailing for the South Pacific. Have a good trip. P.S. Hope you enjoy the oranges.

The kids each took a piece of fruit, sat down, and began to remove the peelings while they chattered about the airplane trip. In mid-sentence, Ron stopped and looked at me. "Do you suppose they have enough food to get home?" I knew he meant the sailors.

"I sure hope so," said Janice, who seemed worried.

"We should have told them to go to Farmer's Cay," Tommy said. "Jeff's dad would have fed them."

Janice eased her mind. "Maybe they'll catch another fish."

I sat back and listened with pride as the kids worried about the sailors. They had received two gifts that day: an airplane ride and a bag of oranges, and a dollar value on either could not come close to signifying the worth. Certainly, the gifts were as different as the people who had given them—four individuals from the same country, converging on this remote island, relating experiences to us that were similar only in geographical miles. One American had seen a Haitian jail as an;" another saw a Bahamian tennis court as "primitive."

The contrast was not much different than living on a sailboat: it could be primitive, or it could be an experience. How would I describe it when it was all over?

Roger joined me on the cushion. "Where to next?" he asked.

"Hadn't we better catch up with George? We're into December now."

"There are two ways we can do it: sail day and night against the trade winds, or motor."

Picking up an orange, I ripped into the skin before asking him, "How about Haiti? We can wait for George there, and if fruit is a penny a piece, it must be a cheap place to eat."

Christopher Columbus was an interesting explorer, not only for what he explored, but for what he wrote. Of all the fourteenth and fifteenth century travelers, Columbus's diary was the most readable, and the most graphic. He described smells and tastes, sights and sounds, conflicts and fears. And all of his worries seemed to match our own by the time we reached Rum Cay.

Rum Cay was Columbus's second stop in the New World, and according to his log, the only thing separating his anchor from our own, was five centuries. Gathering the kids on deck, I opened a copy of the log and read aloud as we looked out at precisely the same view. Except for the coconut trees and the dogs romping on the beach, all else was as he described, the low rolling hills, the fine stand of hardwood trees, a bay of water as clear and clean as a mountain lake. He had smelled wood fires, the drying kelp, and the salt bed, and we did too.

Toni, Tom, and Janice on picnic

He found the farming to be a curiosity, done "pothole" style in the natural indentations of the coral. The diverse crops were a welcome treat to his sailors after weeks of eating salt meat, hardtack, and drinking water "gone bad." For the first time he tasted; corn, pigeon peas, sweet potatoes, and the unmercifully hot peppers. We added the same to our own larder.

Columbus stumbled into the New World looking for spices and gold—and found very little of either. However, as an afterthought he stashed away on the *Santa Maria* something of perhaps even more value, the cotton plant. And we found bunches of it growing wild along the beach. The kids willingly filled their pockets with the white fluffy balls (to be used later for stuffing sock puppets).

The galleons, and the *Halcyon*, sailed together to Crooked Island, where Christopher (we were on a first-name basis by then) described a peculiar bed slung between two trees, the first hammock seen by civilized (?) man. I'm not sure what criteria was used to measure civilization, but any culture that could invent the hammock could not be that backward.

Christopher described the Arawak Indians as, "Brown-skinned children that invite you to share anything that they possess and show as much love as if their hearts went with it." History tells us that these explorers were not as generous with their love in return.

Sailing uphill is the slowest form of travel invented by man. It is also exhausting. *Halcyon* beat hard against the southeast wind as we aimed for a gunkhole or shallow cove on the south tip of Acklins Island. We wanted desperately to get there before dark because our charts showed coral heads and shoaling sand bars everywhere, and we knew we needed as much light as possible when we entered the anchorage. We didn't get it.

Every cruiser knows that when the sun sets in the Out Islands, he had better be ready. As we approached the lee shore, we had the fathometer on, Ron rode in the bow with the searchlight, and I stood at the handrail with the lead line tied to my wrist. Janice was training the flashlight into the water beneath my feet to give me enough light to read the knots on the line.

I tossed out the line, gathered it in, and called to Roger at the wheel, "I found bottom!"

At the same moment, Tommy picked up a blip on the fathometer. "Forty feet!" he yelled.

Ron was scanning the edges of the darkness with the spotlight, searching for any suddenly exposed coral heads.

I tossed the line a few more times, then felt uncomfortable about being perched so precariously on the side of the boat. Wedging myself between the two forward shrouds, I hooked a leg around a stanchion post. No matter what, I didn't intend to fall into that inky black sea.

The lead showed twenty feet, and Roger slowed the engine. Another toss, and I called, "Eighteen feet."

The line snagged! Adrenaline surged as I yanked on the line, but it wouldn't come. A chill like ice water traveled all the way through my body as I fought to free the loop from my wrist, and the screams came automatically, "Stop the boat! Roger, I'm caught! My God! Stop the boat!"

Roger threw the gears into reverse, but the boat had too much speed and *Halcyon* slid forward; her movement pulled the line through my fingers. The loop tightened. Abandoning the efforts to free my wrist, I made a decision—I was going in the drink! Drowning may have been my nightmare, but the alternative was unthinkable. The pressure against my arm and wrist were rapidly becoming unbearable.

I tried disentangling my legs, but they refused to work fast enough. The lead line stretched out and my arm and the top half of my body jutted out over the water, while my lower limbs remained wrapped in the rigging. Fear gripped me and my mind raced wildly, and the reality of the situation was all I could think of "*I was going to lose my arm!*"

Janice threw her flashlight down on the deck and reached for the lead line to help me pull, while the beam of the spotlight in Ron's hand focused on the scene. We could hear the motor laboring as Roger desperately tried to slow and reverse the boat.

And at the very instant that I knew it was over, the lead line rose to the surface, and the lead shot five feet into the air, followed closely by an enormous barracuda!

We watched in fascination as Ron's light caught the arc of the fish. "What is that?" He gasped.

Quickly, I coiled the line, sat down on the deck, and clutched the lead against my chest. My laugh had a tinge of hysteria. "That was a very hungry fish," I choked out. "Hungry enough to swallow three pounds of lead!"

Roger left the wheel and came to make sure I had survived. But he sounded as angry as he did relieved when he asked, "Why in the hell didn't you have a slip knot on that lead line?"

"Because I never thought about it getting snagged," was all I could answer.

It was another lesson well learned, and I did wonder how I had not foreseen the possibility of that happening in all the two years I'd used the line. One week later, the lead snagged in coral instead of a fish's belly, but thankfully it was tied to a shroud with a slip knot. We lost the line, but it could have been worse. There had to be a Fairy Godmother watching over us somewhere.

We waited patiently at Aklins Island for the wind to get off our nose, and after three days, we set out on a gentle westerly breeze. Great Inagua was our destination, a hundred and fifty miles to the south.

It was just another typical day in paradise. The breeze died, *Halcyon* floundered, the currents ran opposite to those shown on the charts, the winds shifted, gusted to thirty knots, died, and we floundered again. By afternoon we were no longer sure where we were. To check our position, Roger set up the often-repaired Radio Direction Finder on the chart table, but the static (due in part to *Halcyon*'s steel-encased cabin) made reception impossible. He then set it up in the hatchway, picked up one station, and was working on the second when Ron's turn came to relieve me at the wheel. As Ron emerged from the cabin, his size twelve foot clipped the top of the set, and sent it flying down the companionway to lie in pieces on the cabin sole.

Roger started to berate Ron, then noted his pale expression and said instead, "Forget about it. The damn thing never worked anyway." Then muttering something about Murphy, Roger discarded the mangled instrument and went searching for the sextant.

As he spread the charts out next to the sextant, he sighed hopefully, "If the sky stays clear enough, we might be able to get an accurate fix."

Naturally the sky didn't. Within the hour the westerly breeze shifted to a northerly gale, and storm clouds rolled overhead to completely block out the sun. Roger put the sextant away, and we watched as the sea turned from a soft dove gray to an angry blue black.

If we suspected we were off course, then it was confirmed for us when Roger went looking for his windbreaker. Opening the binnacle cabinet beneath the compass, he found a dozen of the kid's metal Hot Wheel cars stashed inside, and with the removal of each one, the needle on the compass flitted spastically. A compass, calibrated with Hot Wheel cars, is not likely to be honest-to-God accurate.

Gathering them all up, Roger stomped to the companionway and dumped them down the ladder, where they came to rest in approximately the same spot that the RDF had, two hours earlier.

The string of bad luck was too much. In disgust, Roger left Ron and me on deck and went below to join Tommy and Janice in a nap. But once there, he found a decidedly green-faced Tommy just stepping out of the head. "Dad, I need to throw up and the toilet's not working!"

There was panic in Roger's voice when he called, "TONI! What can Tommy throw up in?" Dashing to the rescue, I shoved the garbage bucket under Tommy's nose, just in the nick of time while Roger lunged for the companionway.

Tommy's eyes were dull and lifeless, and he looked at death's door as I tucked him into the forward bunk, wedged a clean bucket between him and the bulkhead, and left him to fend for himself. Feeling a wave of guilt, I closed the cabin door. After all, no one has ever died from seasickness...they just wished they would.

On deck, Ron was holding the wheel and a steady course to who knew where, and Roger was reclining on a cushion, eyes closed and the sea spray and mist soaking his clothes and hair.

I sat down next to him. "Are you all right?"

"I'm fine!" he barked. "I just wonder where we are, and what's going to happen next!"

"I thought I was the worrier."

He opened one eye and gave me a half-hearted groan.

I should have left him alone, but I could foresee an approaching disaster. "What do we do about the toilet?"

"Pray for constipation!" he answered flippantly.

I gave him a "get serious" look, and he continued, "Well, surely you don't expect me to work in that closet-sized head with the boat rolling around like it is. Use a coffee can. I'm not going to do anything about the plugged toilet until this boat is anchored, and THAT'S THAT!"

"Boy, are you getting testy. Forget the toilet. What are we going to do about our course? We might be sailing around out here for days if we don't get a position soon, and without a toilet, I'd say we are in the midst of a crisis."

"I guess we keep going south until we hit something." And he closed his eyes again.

Suddenly Ron spoke up. "Maybe we can get a fix from that ship over there."

Roger leaped to his feet, and I turned quickly to see Ron pointing off the port side. There was a ship on the horizon! Running to the radio, Roger began calling repeatedly. There was no answer. Back on deck, he took a sighting on the ship, then checked the compass twice more. He was bewildered when he said, "It hasn't moved! Not at all!

I agreed—that was strange. The large cargo ship was about a mile away and looked like any of the hundreds we'd seen on the Miami River that worked the trade between the U.S. and South America. It was infuriating that no one answered the radio. The unwritten law of the sea was to respond to any transmission from another vessel, and surely there was someone at the radio. Even more curious was why any ship would be moving so slowly?

Roger gave Ron the order, "Alter course and head straight for it."

As Ron turned *Halcyon* to port, Roger tightened the sheets, and I went below and started calling on the radio again. With any luck, the closer we came the more likely we were to be seen, and someone would surely answer my call.

"Would you look at that!" Roger's voice carried a hint of alarm. "Ron, turn into the wind! Right now! Toni. Bring me the binoculars!"

I steadied myself against a bunk as *Halcyon* wallowed helplessly, her sails suddenly spilling the wind. Handing the binoculars up to Roger, I called out to Ron, "What does he see?"

"A coconut tree!" came the answer.

"Did he say, a coconut tree?" Janice asked as she sat up in her bunk and peered out a porthole. "Where are we?"

"Who knows?" I climbed back on deck to check out the latest revelation. There was nothing, only vast ocean and that ship, still a half mile away. "What do you see?" I called to Roger where he was perched in the ratlines, the binoculars to his eyes. A slow-rolling wave slid under *Halcyon*'s bow and lifted us high into the air, and then I saw it! A slight tinge of blue green water and one straggly coconut tree! That ship was wrecked on a reef!

Fifteen minutes later we cautiously eased into the lee side of the ship and dropped anchor at the very moment the gray day faded into a black, stormy night.

"How long do you suppose it's been here?" I wondered aloud as we stood and watched the last rays of light play across the huge rust-covered steel wall before us.

"A long time," Roger guessed, "If that rust is any indication."

I shuddered. It was an exceedingly uncomfortable feeling to see something so large, and seemingly impervious to the elements, stranded like a beached whale on so tiny a speck of coral and sand. Rain began to fall, and we escaped into the kerosene warmth of the cabin, closing the hatches against the unfriendly demons of weather and sea.

Ron had the table extended and was studying the chart. "The reef is called Hogsty. At least we know where we are now." He sat back and his eyes glowed with adventure. "I wonder how many ships have hit this reef. I bet we could dive up all kinds of treasure.

Roger squelched the idea quickly by saying, "Even if the weather improves by tomorrow, the first thing we do is unplug the toilet. Diving for treasure will just have to wait."

I had to raise an eyebrow. Roger was declining to hunt for treasure. I thought it best not to question it. At that moment Tommy stepped from the forward cabin, rubbed his eyes, and yawned. As he looked around at us, he grinned, and asked, "What's for supper?" Then he took a swipe at Janice and challenged her to a game of checkers. He had fully recovered.

The weather didn't improve. Daybreak found the kids and me sitting in agony on deck as the surging waves swept around both ends of the reef to converge unrhythmically against *Halcyon*'s ribs. None of us had slept well; just staying in our bunks had been accomplishment enough.

And if we were in agony, then Roger was in hell. With the boat rolling and pitching, he had torn the toilet apart into a mess of smelly pieces on the cabin floor and was working to dislodge the cap of a shampoo bottle from the pipes. How the cap had found its way into the toilet was a mystery only slightly less puzzling than the fact that nowhere on the boat could we find a shampoo bottle without a cap.

Lunch was exhausting to prepare, to eat, and to clean up afterward. Plates lurched across the table, soup slopped out of the pot, juice flipped out of glasses as though alive. As soon as the remnants of the meal were mopped up, we pulled anchor and took off again for Great Inagua. No matter how bad the ocean was, it couldn't be worse than that anchorage.

It wasn't easy. The seas were the highest we'd sailed to date, and the wind shrieked wildly in the rigging. It took every muscle in my arms to hold the wheel steady, and the final two hours, Roger and Ron dismissed me altogether, and then they spelled each other every fifteen minutes. Though feeling useless, I grudgingly admitted to myself that the men, and *Halcyon*, were tougher than I was. And *Halcyon* was too.

Mathewtown, the capital of Great Inagua, is purely a company town owned by the Morton Salt Company. We found it to be clean, neat, and charming with its white Victorian houses, colorful flower gardens, and seaside setting.

A particularly friendly young island boy helped us pull the dinghy up onto the beach, and soon he convinced us that we needed a walking tour and a guide.

As we wandered the quiet streets, he proudly pointed out the company store, the school, the town hall, and while speaking in a steady stream of island English patter, he said, "That house be for shipwrecked sailors."

We looked across the tidy little street to see a small well-kept gingerbread house in the center of a freshly mown yard.

"Shipwrecked?" Roger sounded uneasy.

"Yes. If your boat go down in the water, we rescue you and give you de house to live in 'til you go home," he explained.

"Do many people use the house?" Roger asked.

"Oh yes. Often. The last family have two boys the same age as me." By the tone of his voice I surmised that he had become friends with the stranded family.

Roger started urging us on down the street and as we walked, he whispered, "That is not the best way I can think of to get a free room."

I agreed.

We had a boatload of dirty clothes. We always had a boatload of dirty clothes and I was determined to get them washed before leaving the island. The town did not have a laundromat, so we moved *Halcyon* to a cove near the city water storage tanks and took the clothes to the beach. The kids hauled jugs of fresh water from the storage tanks while Roger and I filled the rubber raft with soapy seawater. The styrofoam ice chest was used to hold the fresh-water rinse.

Using the plunger, the kids took turns agitating the dirty clothes in the makeshift washing machine while Roger and I rinsed and squeezed. Very soon we had an audience of curious island children.

Ron plunged his two hundred strokes and didn't miss a beat, Janice cheated by half by counting the upstrokes separately from the downstrokes, Tommy just quit after twenty-five by claiming a headache, backache, and stomach-ache, (in that order). Knowing that Tommy made a career out of resisting work, Roger insisted he keep at it. But Tommy's whining grew so annoying I finally put his dirty clothes in a bucket and marched him, with bucket and plunger, to sit under a tree and finish the job.

As we continued to work, I noticed that our audience of children had wandered away to stand around Tommy. A few minutes passed when Roger interrupted our work and noted, "Would you look at that!"

Glancing up from my pile of wet clothes, I saw Tommy with his own laundry spread out all over the sand, and he was skipping over the wash in a wild imitation of the latest dance craze. It took him less than a minute to entice a dozen kids to dance with him. But when the Islanders began to fall by the wayside, a new idea entered Tommy's head. He grabbed up the bucket, rushed to where we were working, and filled the pail with fresh water. Then racing back to the tree, he scooped up all the clean, but sandy clothes, deposited them into the rinse water, then lined up his helpers to take their turns at plunging the sand out.

"Do you suppose he's charging those kids for the privilege of doing his wash?" Roger asked in amazement.

"He wouldn't dare!" I replied—but I wasn't so sure.

Our laundry was done in record time that day, with only minimum complaining from "Tom 'Sawyer" when it came time to fold and put away.

The cabin had developed a strong smell of exhaust fumes over the previous few days and Roger spent an afternoon crawling around in the engine room, checking out the fittings. He found a small crack in the exhaust pipe and went ashore to pay an outrageous price for a tiny can of metal glue to repair the crack.

When I grumbled about the cost of the repair and he answered that he would never pay a US dollar for a wilted head of lettuce, I knew we were back to worrying about money again. Once we filled the fuel tanks with diesel, paid for water, bought a few groceries (including the gold-plated lettuce), and one treat of ice cream cones, we were nearly out of money. So, Roger cashed a small check at the company store, and I complained, "What if we are slow getting our money to Haiti? That was our last check."

"Don't worry. It never takes more than a day for a wire." he said, but I had the feeling that he was far more worried about the situation than I was.

My lack of concern about being destitute may have been due to the cruisers we'd met when we first arrived at Great Inagua. Angela, Gilbert, and Zack were Europeans traveling together from Miami to Haiti on a small fiberglass sloop. And though they were struggling with English, we found communication to be no problem at all.

On that first day soon after we'd dropped anchor, we climbed into the raft with a gift of a six-pack of beer and rowed over to meet them. When Angela learned we were low on food, she presented me with a pound of rice and some alfalfa seeds for sprouting.

The second day, Roger took Zack diving and together they speared three groupers and three snappers. As Roger delivered Zack to his boat, Angela gave him a pound of coffee, then invited us for dinner.

While we ate, we learned they had lost their dinghy and a winch handle in a storm off Rum Cay. The next morning, Roger took them a spare winch handle that we had no use for. We also loaned them George's two-man raft, with the promise that we would retrieve it when we reached Port au Prince.

They gave us a bottle of rum, another pound of coffee, and Gilbert serenaded us with his guitar.

Our last day in Mathewtown, Angela rowed over in our two-man raft to give us five pounds of onions, some more rice, beans, and her recipe for Hungarian goulash. We promised to look for them in Haiti, said goodbye, and felt strangely lonely as we watched their small boat sail away toward the southern horizon. In three short days we had become fast friends, and like the sailors at Cat Island they had reminded us of what cruising was all about.

We traded the last of our ten cases of beer for some fruit and vegetables but decided the deals we had made with the beer had not been worth the space required to carry it. But we still had most of the case of fishhooks and thought that maybe they would come in handy in Haiti. Provisioning done, we pulled anchor and sailed away from the Bahamas for the very last time.

The kids took turns at the wheel through the day. The wind was so light that the sails filled, then spilled as soon as the boat pushed forward, and the only advantage to having insufficient wind was that we were able to raise the awning against the merciless tropical sun.

In the early afternoon we sat on the deck with the binoculars and viewed the mountains of Cuba far to the west. "Maybe, someday, we can sail there, too," I said as I passed the glasses to Roger.

He took them and focused. "I'll always remember Abuelo and Pepe talking about the beautiful waters around their island. Somehow it seems unfair that politics can interfere with sailing."

Soon the sun was dropping away off our stern quarter as we lounged on the deck. We sipped fresh orange juice cocktails, and Roger toasted, "Here's to Haiti by noon tomorrow."

I looked up at the limp sails against the pastel pink and gray sky and teased, "With this wind, don't count on it." A flying fish skimmed across the smooth as silk water, water that seemed to stretch forever. "But if the weather holds, I don't care. What's the hurry?"

"None I guess," he conceded.

Going below, I scrounged up six cans of vegetables from the bilge, chopped up an onion, and threw it all into a large pot and added enough water to call it soup. After dinner, the kids and I went to sleep with the water rustling a beautiful lullaby against the hull.

It was 1 a.m. when Roger brought me a steaming cup of coffee.

"Your turn, matey," he whispered quietly as he nudged me awake.

Sitting up, I looked through the overhead hatch and saw the jib flopping back and forth listlessly. "How are we doing?"

"Not too well. A ship passed about an hour ago and I checked our position. My calculations were only a few miles off, I'm sure it was because of the currents. We are drifting west about as fast as we are sailing south."

Slipping off his shoes and outer clothes, he climbed into his bunk, and I took his place on the floor. As I began to dress, he said, "At least it's nice to know where to put our dot on that enormous chart. Maybe the wind will pick up later."

I pulled on my pants, slipped into a sweater, then a life jacket, hung a police whistle around my neck, and gathered up my sewing kit. "See you in the morning," I said and bent to kiss him. He was already snoring.

On deck, I reached for the end of the lifeline and hooked it to the life jacket. The reverse end was securely tied to the mainmast, and even in the calm seas, I felt good about the precaution. The boat moved only when someone walked from one side of the deck to the other, but any fool could slip and fall overboard. I didn't want to be that fool.

Although knowing that it wasn't necessary, I still checked the compass. With the wheel lashed, we hadn't adjusted a sail in fifteen hours. And with no one else to talk to, I told *Halcyon*, "Sailing is either boring or terrifying. Why isn't there anything in between?" Then I thought I had better add, "But if I have to choose, I'll take boring any day." She gave me a playful nudge.

Using one cushion for a backrest and another to sit on, I picked up my sewing, and went to work hemming the red-and-black Haitian courtesy flag. I was determined to see it flying before we entered their port.

Every few minutes I glanced up to check in the distance for lights, but the horizon remained an unbroken line of black water meeting starry sky.

And after an hour, I switched off the deck light and stretched out to look at the heavens. It was truly "Halcyonic"

My body felt no conflict with the world around it. It was a condition I often thought of as my "Natural Clock" and it was why I was there: to be in tune with the tides, the moon, and the ocean, to be a part of nature instead of a casual observer. But it was more than that, too. It was the chance to spend time with my children watching a flaming red sunset, or a hermit crab dig a hole in the sand. To read to them from Columbus's diary, to talk with my husband about feelings of God, nature, and love. To share as a family homesickness, loneliness, fear, anger, pride, discovery, and even the crazies.

Had the stars always been so close? And so many? Was the smell of the sea always so clean? Had I ever been able to tell a storm was near before the first clouds gathered? Was it spring, or fall? What year? Had we been a week in a port, or a month?

Einstein had been right—time, speed, and distance were relative and finally I understood that as we drifted peacefully into space.

The rays of the morning sun spread pink and yellow on a bank of clouds resting along the southern horizon. Ron came up on deck rubbing his eyes in the bright light. It was still an hour before watch change, but he was always the first up.

Pointing at the colorful panorama, I told him, "Look at those colors. Don't those clouds look almost like mountains?"

He peered for a moment, then turned, vanished into the cabin, and re-emerged with the binoculars. Adjusting them to his eyes, he shouted, "Mom, those *are* mountains!"

Tommy and Janice poked their rumpled heads through the hatchway. "Where?" they asked in unison.

Ron handed Janice the binoculars and directed her where to look. Tommy sat beside me and gazed sleepily to the south. "Oh, I see them," he said casually. "There are some houses and trees, and two people walking their dog. He looks like Lassie. That's Haiti."

Knowing Tommy often hallucinated after one day at sea, we ignored his descriptions, but he was right about one thing, it was Haiti. "Happy birthday," I told him, and kissed his freckled nose. It was December seventeenth, and he was all of ten years old.

Tommy and Ron went below to get dressed and wake their dad, while Janice came and sat beside me to whisper in my ear. "Mom, I've decided what I'm giving Tommy for his birthday."

"What's that?" I asked, knowing none of us had planned anything special.

She was satisfied with herself as she revealed, "I'm going to let him win at checkers today and he won't have to cheat!"

"That is terrific!" I couldn't help but smile. "That is an absolutely perfect gift, and I promise not to give your secret away."

After breakfast, the kids began their rotation on the wheel. The faint outline of Haiti on the horizon teased us into believing the island was closer than forty miles and combined with the frustration of the still water and windless air, Roger was forced to resort to the engine.

I napped through the morning, then woke to spend a couple of hours cooking Tommy a birthday dinner on the one-burner gimballed stove. Using the pressure cooker, I alternately made cornbread, chicken and dumplings, and a birthday cake that sagged in the middle. But the birthday party was a success, and Tommy won at checkers, (without cheating).

Our charts on Haiti were good, but we feared entering a strange country in the middle of the night. As darkness approached, we killed the engine and allowed a light breeze to carry us slowly toward Cap Haitien—and a vastly different world.

CHAPTER 14: CHRIS, CHRISTOPHE, CRISIS, AND A SEWING MACHINE

During their fruitless search for the Emperor of Japan, Christopher Columbus and his crew wandered the coast of Cuba for a month before turning south to Haiti, and it was there they sailed into a protected little harbor, known today as Acul Bay. A gold-and-feather-bedecked Arawak Indian Chief welcomed the explorers to his shore. On the night of December 23, 1492, the Indians entertained Chris and his men, offered them all the virgins in the tribe, and fed them an impressive array of exotic tropical foods. During the revelry the Chief, using sign language, revealed that the "greatest of all Chiefs" resided only a few miles to the east. Naturally the overanxious Chris thought that was none other than the Emperor himself.

Breaking up the party, Chris collected his men and forced them back aboard the galleons, to weigh anchor and push on. When they were in sight of Cap Haitien harbor, the wind died, and the three ships wallowed helplessly. A discouraged Chris went to bed.

The disgruntled, hungover crew were none too happy about having to leave the all-night party and all those virgins, but to work on Christmas Eve and to then sail the whole day without any sleep seemed the last straw. When the Captain retired for the night, the *Santa Maria* crew stole away to bed also. That left, as the only man on the wheel, an eleven-year-old cabin boy. Unfortunately, he wasn't a sailor.

During the night a gentle breeze came out of the north and floated the flagship up onto a coral reef. The frightened young lad alerted the Captain, but it was too late. Before Chris could wake his men and free the ship, the breeze had turned into a hearty wind, and the *Santa Maria* splintered on the reef.

Being a very religious man, Chris saw the catastrophe as a message from God to stop looking for the Emperor, and to start a colony instead. Thus was the birth of Villa de la Navidad, named for Christmas Day.

Chris needed men to settle the new town and he had no trouble finding eager volunteers. It can be assumed that the prospect of countless parties, brown-skinned virgins, and mountains of gold were more enticing than cruising around indefinitely in uncharted seas. Chris selected two dozen of the heartiest men, gave them a large supply of hawk's bells and glass beads for trading with the Indians, left them a small stock of food, and bestowed upon them his blessing.

A year later Chris returned to find every Spaniard gone. It was a dismayed Chris that heard of the demise of Navidad from the Arawak Chief.

In less than a month after the founding of the town, the feasting had ended, the virgins were worn out, and the natives had traded for more bells and beads than they knew what to do with. The settlers grew hungrier each day, and being a mixture of noblemen and seamen, they simply took whatever they wanted. After all, common work was beneath the nobleman, and the sailors were not expected to do anything except know how to sail. Even fishing was a trade too lowly for the Spaniards to bother with.

But food was not the Spaniards main hunger—gold was what drove them to kill the first Indian and with that mistake came the downfall of Navidad. Arawak justice was swift. Before the passage of one full moon, twenty-four white men were dead, and the age of innocence was over.

It was visions of food, money, and letters from home that danced in our heads as we entered Cap Haitien (Navidad), eight days before Christmas.

"Shouldn't we declare the gun?" I whispered to Roger. We were standing on the deck, watching a company of officials climb out of a taxi at the end of the pier. Our boarding party had arrived.

"Not unless you want it confiscated," Roger quietly warned. "Private guns are illegal in Haiti."

"But what if we are searched?" My stomach churned uneasily as the officials neared the boat.

"We won't be," Roger reassured me but I wondered how he could be so certain.

Trying to still the fears, I turned my attention to the crowd of young boys milling around the boat. They had been there from the moment of our arrival a half hour before. They were a barefoot, raggedly dressed, and very noisy lot. Some spoke Pidgeon English, and persisted in asking if we needed a guide, oranges, a souvenir straw hat, or a taxi.

I answered them all without hesitation, "No, thank you."

Tommy was an easier mark. Looking at me, he pleaded, "Can we buy an orange?"

Our audience understood him perfectly, and six hands popped over the handrail, each holding a piece of fruit. Startled at the eagerness of the vendors, I stepped back and shook my head, then gave Tommy a stern warning, telling him, "Wait until we go to the market!"

That brought another young lad to life. "You need a guide, Lady? I get good prices for you in market."

"No, thank you," I dismissed him firmly. But it was harder to dismiss the sad little group of children sitting on the wharf beside the boat, their eyes listless, their bodies covered with a gray dust, their clothes as tattered as any I'd ever seen. Unlike the older boys, the gray children didn't talk, beg, or try to sell anything. They merely watched.

The yellow quarantine flag and the new Haitian courtesy flag, both snapped briskly in the ratlines to announce our need for clearance. Not only did the flags we were flying, and the strange group of people near us convey the message that we were in another country, but the Mediterranean-style town and the soft green mountains soaring behind it were far different than anything we'd seen or experienced before. I recalled the two sailors on Cat Island and their reminiscences of the pleasures of Haiti, but I also remembered the political and economic woes reported by the newspapers back home. Which Haiti would we find, and would we be sorry we'd come?

The boarding party, led by a bald man in a business suit, marched up to the *Halcyon*. Roger had unhooked the handrail and was stepping back to welcome them aboard, when a youth from the crowd of hustlers jumped forward, grabbed the bald man by the arm, and began speaking rapidly. The boy shook an accusing finger at Roger, at the boat, then pointed to himself. A second boy leaped out and repeated the gestures, followed by a third and a fourth. Then everyone began to shout at once.

I looked at Roger, he looked at me, and we both shrugged. Maybe it was a crime to refuse to buy souvenirs. Abruptly one of the soldiers entered the arena and barked an order that sent a dozen boys scattering to the end of the pier.

In the sudden silence, I murmured to Roger, "The Gestapo lives!"

"Shhh!" he hissed.

The four original noisy youth were still standing beside the bald man as he turned, and in precise English, asked, "Did these boys catch your lines and tie your boat?"

"Two of them look familiar," Roger agreed.

"They say you owe them each one dollar."

"I do?" Roger looked surprised and I could guess why. In all our travels, no one had ever asked for money to catch a dock line.

Roger started to protest. "All four? I don't remember..."

The soldier stepped menacingly toward the boat; the bald man stared coldly. It was clear Roger had no choice. He meekly descended into the cabin, and returned with four one-dollar bills, which he handed, one to each boy.

Everyone smiled, Roger scowled, and as if it were my fault, he hissed in my direction, "From now on we tie up our own boat!"

"Aye, aye, Captain," I saluted.

The bald man stepped onto the deck and introduced himself. "I am the interpreter," he said. We nodded and smiled.

Behind him came the business suit, and the formalities began. "This is the Customs Agent." We shook hands and I instructed Janice to show the official to the cabin.

Next came a uniform. "This is the Immigration Officer." We smiled, nodded, and handed him over to Tommy.

I thought that had to be enough people when two more uniforms stepped from the dock to the boat. "This gentleman is with the Army, and this one is with the Police."

"How do you do?" Smile, smile. Shake, shake.

Ron led those to the cabin, and I turned to follow everyone below, when the interpreter's voice rose again. "This is the Harbormaster."

Looking around I saw a man in a sports shirt shaking hands with Roger. A second sports shirt came up the rear. "*That must be the Mayor*," I thought, then the Interpreter introduced, "This is the taxi driver. You owe him five dollars."

"You're kidding!" Roger blurted out in irritation. "We did not take a taxi! And we don't intend to take one either!"

"Ah, you do not understand, Monsieur. You must pay the taxi that brings the officials to the docks."

Roger gritted his teeth and shelled out another five bucks. I gave silent thanks that everyone had shared the same cab.

Muscling my way down the ladder, I squeezed between the Customs Agent, the Immigration Official, the Army, and the Police, to stand in the galley; while Roger, the Interpreter, the Harbormaster, and finally the taxi driver, descended the ladder behind me. Every square inch of the cabin was occupied by bodies, and the closeness was made even more uncomfortable by the inquisitive brown faces peering in through the portholes. The hustlers from outside had ringside seats for the show.

Our kids settled into the upper bunks—Ron and Janice on the side away from the dock, Tommy opposite them alternately giving his attention to the faces in the portholes, and the seven strangers sitting below him at the table.

Somehow Roger found our passports and documentation papers, and holding them in his hand, he turned to the Interpreter. "Who gets these?"

The Interpreter indicated the business suit positioned next to him. From there our papers moved silently from hand to hand, were studied carefully, stamped, initialed, stamped again, then passed along. Even the taxi driver had his turn.

The Customs Agent spoke to the Interpreter, who translated, "Do you have firearms on board?"

My attention went to a fly buzzing around in the galley as Roger shook his head. "No."

From the corner of my eye, I could see the Customs Agent studying Roger suspiciously for an eternally long moment, then he added one more stamp to one more document, folded everything, and handed it to Roger just as I smashed the fly to smithereens.

The Sport Shirt spoke next, and the Interpreter translated, "The Harbor Master needs twenty dollars, please."

"TWENTY DOLLARS!" Roger's voice was much too loud, and dropping it a decibel, he asked, "What for?"

"Dock fees," the Interpreter explained.

"What if we anchor?" Roger asked.

"Still twenty dollars." Somehow, I had anticipated that answer.

Roger took a twenty from his wallet and I heard him mutter something about preferring to go to jail, but he handed over the money anyway.

That ended the ceremony. The officials stood in unison, shook hands all around, smiled a lot, and departed one by one. The taxi driver was the last, and he stopped to ask, "You need taxi?"

"No, no!" Roger growled as he waved him up the companionway and off the boat.

With relief, I plunked down on the settee and asked, "How much money do we have left?"

"Thirty-two dollars and eighty cents," he said, and I could tell he was worried. "We'd better call California today before one more official shows up to collect another fee."

"Well," I offered brightly, "at least we weren't searched."

He thought for a minute then chuckled briefly. "Do you have any idea how guilty you looked when that guy asked about the gun?"

"Okay, so I make a lousy smuggler."

At that moment the kids asked to go to the market. We were all eager to get on land for a while, so we closed the portholes against the faces on the dock, locked the hatches, and assembled above deck.

Roger signaled to one of the hustlers, "Do you speak English?" When the boy nodded, Roger asked him, "Where can we find a telephone?"

"I show you for a dollar." And a smile split the boy's face.

Looking resigned, Roger turned to me and said, "Correction. We now have thirty-one dollars and eighty cents."

"Such wealth!" I giggled. "Now what do you suppose it will cost us to dump our garbage?" And I indicated the large plastic bag stashed on the stern of the boat. It was all our trash from the previous four days.

Without warning, the pathetic gray children came out of their stupor and began shouting, "I take it for you, lady! I do it for free! Please, Missy, let me! Let me!" A dozen eager hands waved in my face, and for the second time that day I was bewildered by the eagerness of these people.

What was the harm I wondered as I picked up the bag, carried it to the handrail, and offered it to one of the youngest boys. Snatching it greedily, he dashed toward the end of the dock, and a half dozen others chased behind him. Shouts rose from the remaining crowd and we realized the hustlers were cheering the little guy on. We watched, our mouths open, as the boy dropped to the ground, savagely tore open the bag, and scooped out an armful of empty cans and plastic bottles. With the others closing in on him, he leaped to his feet and fled for the edge of the town, the treasures clutched tightly against his chest. Like vultures, the pursuers fell on the garbage, and it took less than ten seconds for them to sift through it. Then, one at a time, they ran—and all that was left on the dock were a few pieces of crumpled paper. Even the plastic bag was gone.

My kids' faces mirrored my own horror. Janice spoke first saying, "Mom! One of them ATE the potato peelings!"

Roger sounded baffled when he said, "I think this is going to be quite an experience."

Our guide's name was Garry, a bedraggled, barefoot, fourteen-year-old boy, and the only honest guide in all of Cap Haitien. (At least that's what he told us.) Looking at his enormous brown eyes, and the smile that stretched from ear to ear, I didn't doubt him. Garry led us swiftly through five blocks of traffic, people, dogs, pigs, street vendors, and hustlers, to the telephone company where we found Ma Bell sitting behind a long wooden counter. She was a sour-faced crone whose job description seemed to include manager, supervisor, receptionist, operator, and probably even the repair lady.

With Garry translating, we tried for fifteen minutes to convince the woman to place a collect call to the banker in California. She finally agreed—for twenty dollars CASH!

"How much does it cost if we don't call collect?" Roger pestered.

"Twenty dollars, plus the cost of the call," came the answer.

We gave her the twenty dollars, and one hour later our call got through.

Roger shouted into the phone, "You say you did not get my letter requesting the money be returned from the Virgin Islands?" There was a long pause. "Are you sure?" Another pause. "You want me to what?" He swore under his breath, then said, "That may take two years, and in the meantime, we are going to starve to death!"

He listened for a moment before speaking louder than before. "If I could afford to fly to the Virgin Islands, I wouldn't be calling my banker collect!" Then he spoke through clenched teeth saying, "Somehow that money has to be wired here as soon as possible. And if you think it can't be done, then just remember, we are stranded in a VERY strange country, with three little kids—hungry little kids—and eleven dollars and eighty cents to our name!" He wiped his forehead and glared at the floor. "Okay, I'll check the Cap Haitien bank day after tomorrow. Thank you. Goodbye." And he dropped the phone into the cradle.

Haitian girl.

"What's wrong?" I really didn't have to ask.

"He wants us to drop by the bank in California and sign a form in person!"

The idea sounded so absurd, I had to laugh. "He's been our banker for almost eight years. He's been sending our money to us, every month since we moved onto the boat. And now he wants us to drop by! Doesn't he know where we are?"

"Of course he does." Roger looked more concerned than I felt. "He finally agreed to make an exception to bank rules; the money will be here in a few days he says." Roger finished by growling, "It sure as hell better be!"

"Let's not worry about it—the money will get here. Now how about the blank checks?"

"He said he mailed a second set several weeks ago."

"Okay, we'll check the mail tomorrow. Now let's go find the market."

Collecting the kids from the front steps of the telephone office, we told Garry to lead us to the penny oranges.

Cap Haitien had clearly been marked by the French and the Spanish with the pastel colors, the wrought iron balconies, and the wooden shutters on the doors and windows. One- and two-story buildings crowded against the sidewalks, and with common walls, they gave the illusion of being one structure from corner to corner. Separation of storefronts was achieved visually, only by the abrupt changes in the colors of the paint.

Each street was a copy of the one before it, a crazy melange of shops, restaurants, homes, furniture stores, church missions, brothels, and bars. At each corner the line-up repeated itself, and everything looked so alike I found myself searching for the mountains behind the town to get my bearings.

If there was a center of town, a business district, it was the market and we smelled it before we saw it. Wrinkling my nose, I asked Garry, "What's the odor?"

"Charcoal," he answered, and I saw what he meant as we neared a slump-shouldered woman in a grease-stained dress hunkered down by the side of the road. Beside her on the ground sat a makeshift, tin can stove; a tiny mound of red coals glowed in the bottom of the can and on top of it teetered a small enamel bowl filled with a greenish broth.

I turned away as Janice grabbed my arm and directed my attention further down the street. "Mom, look at that!"

A young girl goose-stepped toward us, seemingly unaware of the load balanced effortlessly on her head: a flat basket, fully one yard across, and heaped to the limit with small flat loaves of bread. Seeing our interest, the girl drew closer, raised her hands to the basket, lifted it, and presented it for our inspection. When she asked something I could almost understand, I shook my head. Even if I'd wanted bread, I could not have brought myself to try it. As the girl shuffled away, Janice shivered and asked, "Did you see the flies?"

"Honey, those weren't flies they were raisins," I lied but I could tell by her expression, she wasn't convinced.

The streets teemed with humanity as we wove our way into the heart of the market. The smell of the burning charcoal hung in the air and mixed with the stench of fruit peelings rotting in the gutters, plus the odor of too many people in too small a space. Wooden stalls lined the streets and displayed an array of fruits and vegetables: grapefruit, papaya, bananas, but mostly oranges at a penny a piece.

On the ground between the stalls were spread dirty gray blankets laden with herbs, handcrafts, and used clothing. Intermingled with the stalls, the blankets, the people, the dogs, and the children were the tin can stoves that heated miniscule portions of food, liberally seasoned with street dust and flies.

Ron, Tommy, and Garry stopped at one blanket, and I stepped up behind Garry to peek over his shoulder. He caught my quizzical expression and whispered, "Voodoo!"

Before us on the ground were an assortment of items laid out for our inspection: pieces of carved wood and bone, ground powders, various lengths of knotted cord, tiny bottles of liquids, a bouquet of rooster feathers, and even a cross and a St. Christopher medal. Surreptitiously, I studied the vendor. The woman's dull brown face was marked with age, or a rough life, and her teeth were jagged black nubs in a mouth that did not give a smile. Her wiry yellow- gray hair stood out wildly from the edges of a faded red bandana, and when her eyes caught my own, I turned away with an uncomfortable feeling.

Joining Janice and Roger, I found them watching a woman winnow wheat with the use of a screen-bottomed shallow basket. The woman worked fluidly as she whirled the kernels on the screen and allowed the wind to carry the chaff away. At the woman's feet was a girl about Janice's age, whose job it seemed was to collect the wheat kernels and wrap them in tiny scraps of dirty newspaper, one handful at a time. When the young girl sold one of the bundles for a great deal more than I thought it was worth, I wondered what anyone would do with a quarter cup of wheat kernels, and even if I knew how to grind them, there wasn't enough to make even a small loaf of bread. A picture snapped into my mind: row upon row of clean shelves filled to capacity with five-pound bags of immaculately sanitary, bleached, enriched, self-rising white flour. We were a long way from a U.S. supermarket in more than just miles.

On other blankets along the street were newspaper-wrapped handfuls of rice, cornmeal, sugar, salt, and beans. We found cooking oil sold in small plastic medicine vials; milk and other liquids were ladled from buckets into shampoo or hand cream bottles supplied by the customers. And the prices were high by any standard, and ridiculous in a country as seemingly poor as Haiti.

I took hold of Roger's arm and said, "My God! Now I see why our garbage had value."

Sensing my discomfort, he asked, "Seen enough?"

"I think so. Let's get our oranges and go home."

We searched for the kids and spotted Ron and Janice immediately, but Tommy and Garry had vanished. Stretching on my toes, I peered anxiously over the mass of brown and black heads. Roger had less trouble. "There's a group of people at the edge of the market," he said, "and they're looking at something. He's probably there."

I felt a slight twinge of alarm as we dashed to the corner and pushed our way into the knot of people. And there in the center stood Tommy, looking baffled at all the attention he was receiving. A smile of relief lit his face when he saw us, then unexpectedly, one young girl reached out and patted his head. He jerked back in surprise, and the girl giggled then said something to her companion and they both giggled while others from the crowd joined in.

Grabbing Tommy's hand, I led him away from the people just as Garry appeared at my side. "What was that all about?" I asked.

Smiling, Garry looked at Tommy, then reached over and rubbed his hair. "It's different," he said.

Tommy frowned and pushed Garry's hand away and it was obvious what he was feeling. Being blond had never been "different" before.

Buying our oranges, we returned to the boat, said goodbye to Garry, and retreated below decks for an evening in our secure, protected little home. Dinner was beans, rice, and oranges, and it seemed such pitiful fare until we sat down at the table. As I looked up, there were brown faces in the portholes silently watching our spoons as they traveled from plates to mouths.

In my head, the Universal Mother nagged the Universal Daughter: "Be grateful for what you have to eat. Just remember all the starving children in the world." I had only to look at the portholes to see the Universal Starving Child.

Food stuck in my throat and dropping my fork, I stood, said, "Goodbye, Good night," and closed the ports against them. Then I turned to Roger. "If the money doesn't come tomorrow, we move the boat to anchor!"

"I think they are only curious," he said.

"I know. But they look so hungry."

"Why can't we feed them?" Janice asked, her mother instincts coming to the surface.

"Because we hardly have enough to feed ourselves," I answered. Besides, I realized it would be like trying to empty the ocean with a teacup.

The cabin was unbearable all night with the heat and by morning it was hell, when a noise on the deck brought me to a sitting position. I grimaced as I felt the soaking-wet bedclothes and the perspiration on my forehead and upper lip. Leaning over the three feet of space between bunks, I shook Roger's shoulder.

"What time is it?" he mumbled into the pillow.

"What difference does it make? Someone is banging on the deck and I'm not dressed. How about seeing who's there?"

"Don't worry about it, it's probably just another hustler." Instantly, he lapsed into sleep. The banging came again.

"ROGER!

"Okay!"

Grumbling, he pulled on his pants and stumbled out of our quarters, and within seconds voices were coming from the main cabin. Reaching out, I closed the door, then reluctantly got up and dressed. Company at seven in the morning?

As I stepped into the galley, I found Roger and our sleepy-eyed kids. They were sitting at the table with Garry, and two other boys. And like Garry, the new visitors were raggedy, shoeless, and smiling brightly.

Roger gave me a rueful grin as he introduced them. "Toni, meet Garry's brothers, Jean and Nicky. They came for breakfast."

I gave a half-hearted laugh, then sighed and turned to Janice and said, "Today your math lesson is to figure out how many teacups of water are in the ocean."

"Huh?" she responded.

For breakfast we had rice pudding, using the leftovers from the night before, as well as my last raisins, all of the remaining powdered milk, and the final two precious eggs. While I cooked, the kids took turns dressing in the forward cabin, Nicky and Garry cheerfully scrubbed the deck, and Jean talked to Roger and me about his family. Nicky was thirteen, Jean eighteen, and they lived with their mother and two sisters. Their mother took in laundry, their father was "gone." Nicky and Garry went to school, but were on vacation for the Christmas holidays, and all three worked on the docks as interpreters for tourists from the cruise ships.

"How did you learn your English?" Roger asked Jean.

"The mission taught us. We are Jehovah's Witnesses."

As the conversation turned to religion, I remembered the market and said, "We saw a woman selling Voodoo charms and potions yesterday. Is Voodoo very common?"

"Many people practice it." Jean paused a minute, then added, "I do not, but I know it works. I see it work."

I asked about the Catholic medals and learned that Voodoo also incorporated much from the Christian religions. Jean revealed that the Haitian philosophy toward religion is one of acceptance, total acceptance. If one religion is good, then three must be better, and for an instant I was reminded of the "Old Conch" in Key West and his five good luck medals.

We squeezed around the table and as we ate, Garry offered to take our laundry to his mother for washing. Roger answered him sternly, "You boys must understand this. We have no money. We cannot pay any more dollars for guides, or laundry, or anything else until some more money arrives from the States, and that may take a long time."

"You can pay us later," Nicky offered.

I winked at Roger saying, "The credit system has even reached Haiti." His frown made me uncomfortable. Why was he taking our predicament so seriously? Money would come sooner or later.

After breakfast I shooed the six kids up on the deck and tried to cheer Roger. "We have lots of oranges. Besides, the mail will surely arrive today, the money by tomorrow, and we'll be on our way."

"I hope you're right."

I wasn't. The bank didn't have our money, and the Post Office revealed that our mail had arrived the week before and had been promptly returned to the States! It seemed that Cap Haitien didn't have a "General Delivery" system, at least none that we could figure out through the hodge-podge of translations between Garry and the Postmistress.

No money, no blank checks, no Christmas cards from friends, no letters from family. My depression over the loss of the mail lasted through the oranges and bean soup dinner, but the six noisy kids kept the conversation lively, and soon my thoughts were diverted from our problems.

Not so with Roger. While the kids cleared the table and started a relay system of washing, drying, and playing catch with the dishes, I poured a cup of coffee for him. He had hardly said a word all evening.

"Roger, we have enough beans to last at least another week, and ten dollars will buy more oranges than we can eat in a month. And I am sure our money will get here soon."

It didn't help. He groaned, "I don't think I can look at another bean, and the smell of oranges is beginning to turn my stomach!"

It truly startled me to hear him complain. For so long he'd made light of my fretting. Always his optimism had been there to lift me out of my blue moods, and I never realized how much I needed it.

As if struck by a great idea, Roger's face brightened, and he sat forward. "What's the matter with me? We can feed ourselves! We can FISH!"

It was my turn to groan. The thought of fishing was somehow more distasteful than beans and oranges, but we did need food.

Jean interrupted the drying of a skillet to interject, "Captain, do not forget, you must get police clearance."

Roger brushed him off. "We'll do it first thing in the morning, as soon as the sun comes up."

By noon the next day, we'd been searching for three hours and were still unable to find a police chief with the right rubber stamp to clear us out of the harbor. In frustration, we stood on a street corner somewhere in the maze of Cap Haitien streets while Roger summed it up by saying, "I think we

Sailing Against the Wind – Toni Larson   245

could have had our clearance hours ago if only I were willing to grease a palm, or at the very least hire a taxi."

In disgust, he turned to Garry and asked, "What would happen if we just took off?"

The look on Garry's face startled us—he was aghast at the idea. "You can't do that!" he answered vehemently.

"Why not?" Roger was certainly considering it. "All we want to do is go fishing."

"Please do not go. It would be dangerous." That was all Garry would say.

"He's probably right, Roger. The interpreter was very clear about police clearance. I don't think we need to make the bureaucrats unhappy with us, we have enough problems. Speaking of that, let's go by the bank now. Our money is probably there, and we can forget about fishing."

It wasn't. We made another stop at the market to buy more oranges, then returned to the docks and moved *Halcyon* out to anchor.

Roger, Jean, and I were sitting in deck chairs after dinner watching a cruise ship regurgitate tourists all over the dock. The lineup of taxis and the mass of hustlers greeting the daily arrival of free-spending Americans gave testimony to the fact that tourism was the lifeblood of Haiti.

"Why do the ships stop here?" I questioned Jean. "The town is pretty, but there aren't any casinos or even a decent beach nearby. What do all those people come to see?"

Jean answered without hesitation, "Le Citadelle, Henri Christophe's Fort. You must see it too, before you leave."

Roger resisted. "A fort is a fort is a pile of rocks. If I never see another one, it will be too soon."

"But this one is different from all the rest. You will see," he insisted.

Roger gave him a suspicious look. "Does it take a taxi and a guide to get there?"

"Yes, and also a horse." Jean smiled at Roger.

"A HORSE! Now I know we won't be going."

Chuckling, Jean tried his sales pitch. "But Captain, the horse is cheap, no more than the guide, and I am the cheapest in town."

I sat and listened to the moot argument. With less than eight dollars in our pockets, it didn't matter if we needed a limousine or a rickshaw, we couldn't afford it. Finally, I had to admit, the financial situation was worrying me too. Naively I had expected the bank to whisk our money to us post haste, and our problems would all be over. But we had only one more day before the banks closed for the holidays, and we were feeding eight people on a regular basis. Our beans couldn't last forever, and how would we get enough cash to hold us until relief arrived?

The younger kids finished with their card game and joined us on deck as the last rays of the sun turned the harbor a fuzzy, smoky pink. "Roger, it's time for the boys to go home," I said, interrupting the discussion on the high cost of the guide business.

Roger turned to Ron. "You row them ashore but stay well clear of the cruise ship. The engines stir the water up, and you might get swamped."

That reminded Jean of something and he spoke up, "Be sure and watch your anchor tomorrow when the ship leaves. The thrusters boil up the bottom of the harbor, and the anchored boats sometimes break loose."

We assured him we would, then said goodnight and watched the four boys as they headed ashore. Tommy and Janice clambered below to get ready for bed. Roger and I sat in our chairs luxuriating in the cool breezes of the evening.

"Listen to that," I whispered.

"What do you hear?"

"The quiet. Isn't it nice?" I sighed and he knew what I meant. Life aboard the *Halcyon* had been a three-ring circus of late with all the added noise and confusion. Jean, Nicky, and Garry were helpful, interesting, and fun for the kids to play with, but three extra bodies in our tiny living space was just too much. And after three days with the commotion on the docks, the ever-present hustlers, the tourists, the fishermen, the faces in the portholes, we were worn out.

"I agree, it's certainly nicer out here." Roger yawned.

Ron rowed back to the *Halcyon* under the lights of the harbor, his strong arms pulling effortlessly against the oars. After he climbed on deck, we hoisted the raft on board and tied it down—we couldn't afford to lose our only transportation to land. Ron went below to bed. Roger secured the last knot, then returned to his seat. Stretching out his legs, he asked, "Do you suppose we'll ever see George's two-man raft again?"

"Sure we will, it's waiting for us right now in Port au Prince. An even bigger question is, do you suppose we'll ever see George again?"

Roger looked pensive and I frowned to myself. Just as he seemed to be relaxing, I had to bring up another problem. After a moment, he asked, "Toni, do you realize that Christmas is only three days away?"

"Shh, I haven't told the kids...maybe they won't find out."

"Are you kidding? If you ever need to know what the date is, just ask a kid how long until Christmas."

"Well, the money will be here tomorrow, and we'll splurge on a huge Christmas dinner this year. In the meantime, I am grateful for one thing. We won't have any faces peeking in the portholes when we wake up tomorrow."

He chuckled. "You're right! And there's something else we'll have: a cool night's sleep, for a change."

And it was cool. The breezes from the ocean worked into the harbor to push away the smells of the town. Toward morning I tugged the sheet up over my bare skin and slept like a baby.

Cottony dreams vanished with a peculiar sound somewhere near my head. Opening one eye, I observed a nose, a wide grinning mouth, and two jet-black eyes. Quickly I blinked, and there it was—A head! A face! A strange face suspended just inches above my own and I screamed the loudest, most blood-curdling scream I could produce.

The smile vanished from the face, the head jerked backward and thunked nastily as skull met steel before disappearing out of the porthole.

"What in the hell?" Roger sat up in his bunk.

"Somebody is next to the boat. He had his head INSIDE the porthole! Roger, he was watching me sleep!" I clutched the sheet under my chin as Roger fell out of bed and reached for his pants.

Mumbling something about "Don't these people ever sleep around here?" he headed for the ladder. The kids, awakened by my scream, had rushed up on deck and were talking to whoever was out there.

Roger reappeared, a gunny sack in his hand and a satisfied smile on his face. "Well, your peeping Tom was only an over-eager fisherman trying to sell us his catch."

I propped up in the bed. "You bought a fish?" I couldn't believe he would spend any money.

"It only cost a dollar and a fistful of fishhooks. And now we have Christmas dinner!" He opened the sack, and I leaned over to see what he had: a dozen lobsters!

"But they're so tiny!" I wailed. "Isn't there a legal limit on the size here?"

"I didn't ask. All I could think of was for once, we wouldn't have to eat oranges and beans!"

It was not a quiet day, or even a pleasant one, anchored though we were. Roger made his daily trek to the bank, returned empty-handed to sit on the deck and glower with envy at the money-laden tourists. Being really broke was a new, frightening, and very unwelcome feeling for him.

Jean's warning from the night before proved prophetic. When the massive engines of the cruise ship revved to their fullest, the harbor water boiled a thick, bubbling, black sludge cauldron, and our anchor popped like a cork.

We jockeyed in position until the ship cleared the harbor and the water settled down, then we reset the anchor on the murky bottom. Once the excitement was over, Roger withdrew to his chair, and pulled his moody shell around him. I tried schoolwork with the kids, but before we were barely started another skiff appeared.

It was Jean, accompanied by a young man. "It's out of the question," Roger was saying. "We aren't going back to the States for months."

"He will go anywhere you want, Captain," Jean argued. "He works hard. He can cook and clean. He wants only a ride."

I studied the subject of their discussion. The young man was no more than twenty-five, very tall and thin, with eyes that shyly made contact before glancing quickly down at his shoes. Looking down I saw the shoes had no laces, and it was no wonder, his feet were noticeably arched and obviously too large for the shoes. But the young man was clean and neatly dressed, though he wore a shiny, colorfully patched, threadbare suit that was as much too big for him as his shoes were too small.

"He say he have seven hundred and fifty dollars for passage, Captain," Jean insisted. "And he can swim for one mile. You put him in the water on the coast somewhere and he will swim to shore. He will go anywhere—Jamaica, Puerto Rico, Panama—anywhere."

"Absolutely not." Roger would not even discuss it further. Jean turned to translate the verdict, but it wasn't necessary. The young man understood what had been said. Tears glistened in his eyes as he stood, said thank you in broken English, and settled into the skiff to wait for Jean.

We watched in silence as they rowed ashore. The young man climbed from the small boat and dejectedly walked away. Jean returned to the *Halcyon* to have lunch with us.

When I had the chance, I asked him, "Why is it so important for that young man to leave Haiti?"

"He was chosen by his family," Jean answered simply.

"Chosen?"

"Yes, he is the strongest, the smartest, the best worker. His family have nothing, they sell all the furniture, all they own, to give him passage money away from here. In Haiti there is no work for him. "

"But seven hundred and fifty dollars is a lot of money. How did they collect that much?"

"There are twenty or thirty in his family that give him all they have. The parents, grandparents, aunts, uncles, brothers, and sisters. They save money for years."

"I still don't understand. Why can't he immigrate through the legal channels?"

"The line is too long. Some wait for years and still do not go. Then only the ones with the most money can pay the Tonton Macoute for permission to leave."

"The TONTON MACOUTE! But Jean, the Tonton Macoute are not supposed to exist anymore. I thought they were done away with when Papa Doc died."

He smiled ruefully. "Baby Doc say that to bring the American tourists back. The Tonton Macoute is everywhere."

I thought about what Jean had just revealed. The Tonton Macoute, the Boogie Man, the secret police, the Haitian equivalent to the Nazi Storm Troopers, really existed! The political Haiti was no longer something we'd read about in the papers. It was very real and feeling very close around us. I asked one more question: "What will happen to that man, Jean?"

"He will probably buy passage on one of the fishing boats that stop here. If he is lucky, the boat will take him and a hundred more like him to someplace in the Bahamas, or Florida, and put them on the beach in the middle of the night."

"And if he is not lucky?"

"The Captain will collect his money, take the passengers into the Gulf Stream, kill them, and throw them to the sharks. Many fishermen become very rich that way."

"Good Lord, Jean! How many actually get away safely?"

"Maybe one in five. No one knows for sure, there are so many no one hears from again. And for those families, they become people with no more hope. Their hope dies in the Gulf Stream."

Roger listened quietly to Jean's narration then went below to the cabin to dress for another trip to the bank. He was clearly worried about our situation. In an effort to instill sympathy in the bank personnel, he took all the kids with him for one more try at getting our money.

While they were out from underfoot, I plunged into preparing the lobster dinner. Dumping the creatures into the sink, I frowned. They were hardly larger than good-sized shrimp, and my conscience reacted as I severed the tiny heads from the bodies. I had to smile as I realized how typically "white" American it is to feel anger at the immature size of the lobster, in a land where many people ate food no better than garbage. While I worked, I thought of the young man seeking passage out of the country. We could make a small fortune if we filled the boat gunwale to gunwale with passengers. We also could be shot, put in jail, or have our boat confiscated. Smuggling marijuana into Florida had not tempted us; smuggling people out of Haiti did not seem a sane way out of our predicament either.

But what was? Being stranded in a strange country with no money felt akin to being stranded on a spaceship with no fuel to get home. And the possibility of our finding a job in a country of another language was not even worth thinking about. We had enough beans, oranges, rice, and some odds and ends of canned goods—nothing to make a balanced meal with, but certainly more than most around us were eating. And more than any of the Haitians had when they swam ashore to some country even more foreign to them than Haiti was to us.

My thoughts wandered from the unhappy young man to all the gray children we'd seen on the dock, and from them to the tattered beggars, and the tiny bundles of food offered for sale like gold in the market. It was the closeness of true poverty that brought fear to my mind, the helplessness of it, and the feeling that it could touch us.

Stop it! I shook away the feeling. Roger was right; we could fish if we could ever find the right policeman to stamp our exit visa. Would the Tonton Macoute insist we pay for permission to leave? If so, then we'd go to the Embassy. Was there an Embassy in Cap Haitien? What if one of us got sick? Broke a leg? I wondered if our insurance company would pay a Haitian claim if the hospital here would take us. My head seemed determined to run into walls.

How did Jean say the young man raised seven hundred and fifty dollars? The family sold everything. Maybe we could sell something.

I had dinner waiting when the family swarmed aboard the boat, and I started to ask Roger about the money when I saw his expression. We would not be having Christmas this year. The bank would be closed for the Christmas holidays and would reopen after New Year's Day—over a week away! Changing the subject, I said cheerfully, "Wait till you taste dinner, filet mignon never tasted so good."

Roger didn't think I was funny, and Jean looked puzzled.

"Okay, we can't sit around for a week moping about this! Jean, look around the cabin and tell me if there is anything here that you think we can sell quickly."

Roger gave a start, then sneered at the idea. "There is hardly enough here to fill our needs," he said.

"Well, we have a dinghy motor stowed on deck, and no dinghy."

"But we are going to find a dinghy one of these days, and the expense of a new motor in the islands would be ridiculous."

"As I see it, we can continue to eat beans until our money arrives, or we can sell something. But I am not going to sit here and feel bad."

Jean perked up. "Anything with a motor, anything from the U.S. is very valuable here. The motor, the motorbike, any electronic equipment."

"How about a sewing machine?" I asked.

"Toni! You wouldn't sell your machine!" Roger simply refused to cooperate.

"I've hardly used it since I made the bedspreads, it's not heavy-duty enough to mend sails. And it is certainly no help sitting in that locker, corroding from the salt and moisture, so why not sell it?"

Jean was enthusiastic. "With one sewing machine a man can become a tailor. In the morning, I have a buyer for you."

Before Roger could object further, I said, "Great! We'll meet you at the dock at 8 a.m."

After Jean and the boys left, Roger asked, "Toni, are you sure you want to do this? If we must, we could sell the motorbike or the motor, or something else. Maybe we should think about it."

"Nope, I've decided the sewing machine goes!" And my decision was final.

It had been our last Christmas before leaving Santa Barbara when Roger had presented me with the sewing machine. It was a wonderful piece of equipment, the most expensive, elaborate, intimidatingly complicated model ever manufactured by the Singer Company, and my most prized possession. I kept it polished, well oiled, wrapped in a clean dry blanket, and stowed in the highest, driest locker on the boat. It was my talisman, the last solid undeniable proof that I had once been a bona fide suburban housewife.

From the very first day I'd promised myself that I would learn how to use all those complicated attachments, but somehow, I had never found the time. The machine could perform miracles: zig, zag, hem, swirl, do loop-de-loops, monogram, buttonhole, tack, fagot, and possibly even whistle "Dixie." I never learned how to use it all and now regretted that there was no longer a need to learn. I searched out all the pieces and assembled them on the table along with the instruction manual and a swatch of muslin for demonstrating to the customer.

Roger and the boys moved *Halcyon* to the dock and tied her up while Janice and I scrubbed up the breakfast dishes. We were barely through when Jean arrived, accompanied by a very serious young man dressed neatly, though far too warmly in a dark brown suit.

I shooed Janice up on deck with instructions to keep the boys out of the cabin until the demonstration was over. "It won't take long," I promised. "And as soon as the machine is sold, we are going out for a celebration." She danced away glowing with anticipation, as were we all.

Roger ran an extension cord to the dockside electric pole. I was plugging in the sewing machine when Jean descended the ladder and introduced his customer saying, "This is Monsieur Romain. He speaks no English, so I will translate."

We shook hands and I offered coffee, then inwardly kicked myself when they asked for cream and sugar. Opening the last can of cream, I watched in horror as they each poured a quarter of it into their cups and followed the cream with four heaping tablespoons of sugar. Roger popped into the cabin, then stopped when he caught my expression of despair. Understanding the crisis, he turned and disappeared up the ladder in search, I hoped, of a cream and sugar store.

The brass ship's clock announced the time was 8 a.m. Praying the demonstration would go quickly, no more than fifteen minutes if I hurried, I sat down with Jean and Mr. Romain. Surely, they were anxious to get on their way. Jean's shirt was already wet with perspiration, and Mr. Romain's forehead glistened from the morning heat.

"May I take your coat?" I asked when I noticed the customer looking decidedly uncomfortable.

Jean translated and Mr. Romain shook his head vigorously. *The man was a masochist*, I thought. Then I looked at the portholes and saw that they were full of curious brown faces lined up to watch the show. No wonder the cabin was a pressure cooker...we had no air.

Deciding to get the show on the road, I began, "This is the 'on/off' switch."

Jean translated. Mr. Romain nodded, then indicated I should sew something. Picking up the muslin, I executed a passably neat seam then handed it to him. He studied my work, scowled, reached for the instruction book, and leafed through a dozen pages before he found what he wanted. Satisfied, he pointed at Figure #173, an applique of Donald Duck!

I flinched. "You're kidding!"

He wasn't. Crossing his arms, he stared at me silently. Clearly, he had no intention of backing down.

Reading the instructions quickly, I shuffled through the pile of metal and plastic attachments, found the right needle, foot, and stitch adapter, then went to work. A half hour later I was rounding the end of Donald's beak when the machine STOPPED! DEAD!

I closed my mouth against something very unladylike, then pointed at the ceiling and said to Jean, "The electricity is off."

"I will get it back," My gallant knight promised, then Jean jumped to his feet and dashed up the companionway. He returned with wonderful news: "The Harbor Master is working on the generator, so the electricity will be off all day!"

I was elated. "Aw, that's too bad." Did I sound convincing? "I guess the demonstration is over, Mr. Romain. But you can see, the machine works just fine." I started to rise from the table.

"No!" Mr. Romain grabbed my arm. Sternly he patted the wheel on the side of the machine, then he motioned for Jean to turn it by HAND!

"Noooo," I groaned.

"Oui!" he ordered.

A half hour passed before I proudly presented a lopsided Duck with a chicken's beak. Jean was even more pleased than I was. His arm visibly shook from the continuous effort of turning the wheel.

"How about some coffee?" Roger asked as he bounded down the ladder with a brown paper bag full of cream and sugar. The men nodded. On his way to the galley, Roger leaned toward me and whispered, "One dollar and fourteen cents!"

Fear leaped into my head again. If I had any doubts about what we were doing, they were gone. The machine had to be sold...now.

Roger fixed a fresh pot of coffee while we waited. Sitting back on the settee, I prayed for relief from the heat, and glancing up the hatchway, I saw no less than ten little black heads peeking down at us. Our kids were having a field day and with Mom and Dad occupied below, they were inviting every waif in town to tour the deck of the boat. *If we are lucky, Tommy is charging admission*, I thought then closed my eyes against the throb of an approaching headache.

Roger poured coffee while pressing Jean to find out whether Mr. Romain liked the machine. I hoped he could find out something, I had been unable to gauge anything by the man's expression. During a long conversation in French, Jean turned to me and said, "Missy, Monsieur Romain wants to see Figure 63." Looking at the book, I saw the reverse-stitch designs.

Moaning inwardly, I asked, "Which one does he want, Jean?"

After another barrage of French, Jean looked sadly back at me and said, "All twenty of them."

"ALL?"

"Oui!" snapped Monsieur Romain.

Jean turned the wheel, I made the adjustments, and together we sewed neat little rows of fish, cats, birds, and pine trees. Mr. Romain was mildly impressed, I was amazed. "Look at these, Roger! Aren't they cute! Wouldn't Janice look darling in a blouse decorated with tulips?"

Roger flashed me a "the heat is getting to you" look, and Mr. Romain began waving something called a double needle presser foot under my nose while demanding I get back to the business at hand.

It was noon by the ship's clock and 107 degrees by the ship's thermometer. Roger poured the seventy third refill of coffee, and I jumped up to adamantly announce, "That's all! The demonstration is over!" After four hours, my head was reeling with the intense concentration, not to mention the aroma of body odor, the bedlam of a multitude of feet on the deck over our heads, and the smells from the constantly burbling coffee pot.

Jean's eyes looked glazed as his mind converted the thousandth word of French to English. "Monsieur Romain wishes a pen and paper, please."

Roger scrambled through the kids' school supplies and produced the requested items. Looking disturbingly like an undertaker, Mr. Romain accepted the pen, wrote something on the paper, folded it in half, and solemnly handed it back to Roger.

Roger scanned the note, furrowed his brow, shook his head, scratched through the message, added his own, passed it over, then turned to me and winked. They were discussing price, and if I'd been in better condition, I might have objected. After all, it was my machine! But I sat back, sipped a glass of water, and just hoped the ordeal was over.

With great concentration, the bargaining proceeded for ten minutes without a sound. Each in turn, pored over the paper, stared the other in the eyes, picked up the pen and wrote, refolded the paper, then pushed it back across the table. And finally, it was one last pass of the paper from Roger's hand to Mr. Romain's. He examined it briefly, graced us with a smile for the first time that morning, then stood, clicked his heels, and skipped the translator. "Oui, Monsieur," he nodded.

He had accepted the price! I laughed with relief, Roger beamed, Jean shook my hand, and the kids on the deck cheered. It was over!

Abruptly Mr. Romain spoke to Jean, then turned, and marched briskly up the ladder. I stopped smiling. "Where's the money?"

"He says his wife must see the machine first," Jean answered.

"Oh." I didn't like the delay but understood the reason. "Okay, when will she come?"

"She will not come here," Jean said. "You must go there."

"Oh no." My shoulders slumped. Another day of waiting for money seemed an eternity, but we had no choice. "Okay, I'll go tomorrow morning."

"No, he says this afternoon at two o'clock."

"Please, Jean! Roger, help me! I don't feel well: my head is splitting, and this heat is getting to me. There is no way I can sew another stitch today."

Roger started to defend me when Jean softly said, "Missy, he is a Tonton Macoute." The words fell like a bomb.

My heart stopped beating, then began tripping wildly, but Roger recovered first, "Jean, is this illegal?" Jean nodded.

"Why didn't you tell us?" I squeaked.

Jean looked uncomfortable. "I think it safer for you not to know."

"Safer! If I am going to be a criminal, I want to know about it beforehand!"

Roger was quiet for a second, then asked, "Can we do this legally?"

"Yes, but it take many weeks to get permission and you must pay the right people. But if a Tonton Macoute buy the machine..." His voice trailed off and I guessed the rest. We were skipping the middlemen in a government system based on payoffs.

Roger tried to tell Jean to cancel the deal, then I remembered the one dollar and fourteen cents. "I think we are out of options," I sighed.

"Please don't worry, Captain," Jean reassured us. "It will be all right."

Roger gave in. "Okay, we'll do whatever Mr. Romain asks." Then he added as an afterthought, "I'm glad I didn't know he was the Secret Police when we were bargaining over the price."

Sailing Against the Wind – Toni Larson   255

Because the smell of peanut butter sandwiches and oranges aggravated my already uneasy stomach, I left Roger and the kids eating lunch, dug two aspirins out of the medicine cabinet, and retired to the forward bunk to wonder. *What if Mr. Romain's wife doesn't like the machine? What if we end up in jail? What would happen to the kids? What if I'd married that pimple-faced encyclopedia salesman back in Louisiana and never met Roger Larson, the* Halcyon, *or an island called Haiti?*

The headache was measuring eight on the Richter scale when Roger informed me that it was time to go. Dragging myself to the head, I did a half-hearted spit and polish, sprayed most of a can of deodorant under my arms, then joined everyone on deck.

Roger was instructing the kids to stay on the boat and keep everyone else off. Then Jean gave the kids a map to Mr. Romain's house in case there was an emergency.

"We won't be gone long," I promised.

It was a procession as we marched down the street. At the head of the parade was Jean, behind him came Nicki laden with the sewing machine. Garry was next, with the box of attachments, Roger and I followed him, and coming up the rear were one dozen of the curious in an assortment of ages, sizes and colors.

Seven blocks from the dock we rounded a corner and found a crowd of people outside the door of a modest yellow stucco house. Jean turned to us and indicated that we had arrived. "Why all the people?" I whispered to Roger. He shrugged, but it took only seconds to learn the answer. The crowd parted, and we looked inside a tiny, airless, living room. It was filled with people wall to wall! As the crowd on the sidewalk pushed aside, we stepped in the door and the pathway widened to reveal a three-by-three-foot white table and straight chair, set up against the far wall—as far from the fresh air as possible. A dim, bare lightbulb hung over the table and provided the only light. There wasn't even a window.

Nicki carried the sewing machine in and set it down on the table as though making an offering at an altar. Garry followed with the box of attachments. Jean walked to the chair and held it out for me to sit. I hesitated. The room was church quiet, and I felt foolishly like a sacrificial lamb. Turning, I searched frantically for Roger, but saw only a wall of bodies between me and the door. Stretching on tiptoes, I finally spotted his head. He gave a smile and a slight wave, then disappeared completely from sight.

"This is Mrs. Romain," Jean introduced a young woman with hard brown eyes, and the same undertaker's expression as her husband. She also spoke no English.

"Please don't leave me, Jean," I begged as I slipped into the chair.

"No, No, Miss Toni," he promised. "I stay here."

The demonstration began anew, and the only thing better than the morning was that now we had electricity. Mrs. Romain was even harder to please than her spouse had been. She wanted every picture in the book duplicated to the last stitch, and every word in the book translated into Creole as she watched my hands perform the operations. When we ran out of material, she vanished into another room and returned with more.

I felt near panic when Jean left my side for a while, but Mrs. Romain didn't seem to notice. She merely jabbed at the book, then pointed at the machine and said something that undeniably conveyed her wishes: "Keep sewing, Sucker!" I read the book, adjusted the forty or more dials, closed my eyes, and prayed.

The sewing went on, and on. No one in the room spoke or moved. Every time I looked up, I saw the inscrutable brown faces close in around me, all silent and unsmiling. "They're just curious..." Roger's voice came back to me. I hoped he was right.

Sweat tickled my neck and ran down my shirt front in little rivulets, my stomach growled angrily from hunger. When Jean reappeared beside me, I asked him the time. "Five o'clock, Missy," he answered.

THREE HOURS! No wonder I was hungry! I was probably dehydrated, too. My hands shook and I asked for a glass of water, then gulping it down, I turned off the machine and instructed Jean, "That's enough! I must go home. Please tell her I have to feed my children their dinner!"

Jean translated and Mrs. Romain never moved her eyes from my face. Nor did she smile, not once, even though I smiled and smiled until my face felt pinched and sore.

"Okay," Jean translated. "She say you can go after you show her how to make a buttonhole."

Plunking down at that table, I snatched up the cloth, and whipped out something that resembled a "Z." When I handed it to her, she tossed it back. "NO!" she spit out.

"She say...," Jean sputtered.

"I KNOW WHAT SHE SAID!" I could feel the tears welling up in my eyes, but I blinked them back, sat down, and tackled the machine one last time. It took seven tries before the buttonhole passed muster.

She nodded approval over the crumpled, sweaty cloth, but I could tell she was not yet ready to let me out of her clutches. Standing up, I grabbed Jean by the arm. "Find Roger and let's go!" Tonton Macoute's wife or not, I had decided I would rather go to jail than to sew another stitch.

But the woman grabbed Jean's other arm and spoke something, Jean turned and said, "She wishes to know if she can have the scissors now."

"Scissors?"

"She say you owe her one pair of scissors."

"No Way!" And turning, I pushed my way toward the door. Jean stayed behind in a heated discussion with the woman, but I didn't care. The Romains were not getting my scissors, or one more ounce of my blood, sweat or tears!

Outside, I found Roger on the sidewalk. He was shaking hands with a smiling Mr. Romain. "Can we go now?" I begged. Roger nodded, and I clutched tightly to his arm as we headed toward the *Halcyon*. In a few moments, Jean ran up behind us.

"They are happy," he said, beaming. "Tomorrow they will be in business as tailors. Someday they will be rich!"

I marveled at Jean's enthusiasm. "I don't doubt it," I said. "They certainly know how to do business. By the way, what was the nonsense about scissors?"

"It is a Haitian custom to give a pair of scissors when a sewing machine is sold."

My giggle was a little shaky. "Well, next time I sell a sewing machine, I'll know better."

Roger thanked Jean for his work, paid him a fair percentage, then asked, "Tomorrow will you and your brothers join us for a real dinner in a restaurant?"

Jean grinned broadly. "We would like that. Now I must go." He waved as he dashed away.

The harbor water glistened, smooth and shiny in the early-evening light. *Halcyon* rested against the dock, quiet except for Janice, who sat at the handrail talking to one of the street urchins. The boys were out of sight somewhere in the cabin below. Roger and I paused under a coconut tree at the edge of the water, taking pleasure in the view, the quiet, the first moment all day without a crowd.

"Did you get the money?" I broke the silence.

"Right here," Roger patted his pocket. "And in case you are wondering, it is American money, not Haitian."

I liked seeing him smile again. "May I see it, please?" I held out my hand.

"I guess that's the least you should expect after all you've been through today." He reached into his pocket and produced the thick wad of bills. There was a touch of awe in his voice as he said, "You were great. I didn't know you could do all those things with a sewing machine."

"Neither did I," I grinned. Then, holding the money in my hand, I reflected. "Do you remember a time in the Keys two years ago when the tide was out, and we went shelling?"

His smile faded and he looked puzzled as he nodded. "The time you nearly drowned?"

"That's right. You saved me that day, and later I told you I owed you one. Now, put out your hand." He did and I placed the money in it. "Well, I just paid you back."

He hugged me and laughed. "You're right! The debt is paid in full as long as I never have to eat another orange!"

From the time we woke up the next morning there was a festive air on the *Halcyon*, not the traditional holiday atmosphere perhaps, but certainly better than the "blue funk" we had just come through.

Jean and his brothers appeared in early afternoon to join in the excited planning of a dinner at the hotel, but when Garry offered to stay and watch the boat while we celebrated, Roger strenuously objected. "*Halcyon* is tied to the dock. It can be locked and there is no reason to worry about vandals. So you are coming with us, Garry! You deserve a party, too!"

It took a few minutes of arguing to learn that Garry did not own even one pair of shoes, and the hotel would not let him in barefoot. When the kids heard of his problem, they had no trouble following their better instincts. Drawers flew open, lockers emptied, and amazingly, a pair of shoes were found with soles intact, and in Garry's size.

Donning them, Garry rushed up on deck and strutted proudly from one end to the other. But he clunked so loudly I had to beg him to forget the shoes until it was time to leave.

Ron gifted Nicki with a pair of jeans, a perfect fit if Nicky only breathed in, and Roger handed Jean his favorite shirt with the embarrassed remark, "It itches in this heat." He'd never mentioned that before.

Using buckets of fresh water, and a full bottle of shampoo, the three brothers noisily and happily bathed. Since they had diligently carried jugs for us all week, and kept our tanks filled, we felt they deserved the right to dump half of it over their own heads. Besides, their pleasure in doing so was fun to watch.

It was a Good Ol' American dinner—hamburgers with dill pickles, French fries slathered in ketchup, frosty cold milk shakes, and chocolate cake. Our vote was unanimous: it was the best gourmet meal we'd ever eaten.

Acting silly and feeling free, we left the hotel and skipped through the streets to the tune of "Jingle Bells." All except Ron, who looked extremely uncomfortable as he dropped back a block to gaze with sudden deep interest at the architecture of the buildings along the way. I suppose, if I had been a teenager, I wouldn't have wanted to be associated with such a family either.

We exhausted all the singalongs, then Roger and Janice joined arms and marched in rhythm, Tommy and Nicki played a game of kick the rock that lasted for four blocks. At a souvenir stand we bought gourd maracas, straw hats, and a bottle of rum. A Christmas present to ourselves.

People smiled and waved, and several greeted Tommy by name saying, "Bon soir, Toe mee." He responded with a bright freckled-face smile.

Overnight, Cap Haitien had become a nice place to visit. It was surprising what a little money in the pocket could do for the spirit.

At the boat, Jean asked, "Do you need any help tomorrow?"

Roger looked at me questioningly. "Tomorrow is Christmas Eve. What would you like to do?"

"Something relaxing, different, and definitely off the boat." I said.

Jean suggested, "How about Le Citadelle?"

Roger gave him a sideways glance. "I suppose you would like to be our guide?"

Catching Roger's inference, Jean laughed. "No, Captain. I have to be with my mother tomorrow, but you should have a guide, and Garry has been to the Citadelle before."

The arrangements were made. Garry and Nicki would arrive at six in the morning, we would move the boat out to anchor to make room for the large quota of cruise ships expected at the dock. Nicki would stay on *Halcyon* to guard her, and we would set out to search for the ghost of Henri Christophe, first King of Haiti. We didn't know it at the time, but a second ghost was waiting in the wings.

During the sixteenth century, the Spaniards poured into the New World. The Arawak Indians welcomed them, gave them hospitality, many new foods, spices, and gold. The Spaniards gave the Indians smallpox, repression, enslavement, and finally extermination to the last Arawak.

According to the history of the era, the Spaniards took more than fifty million pounds of gold out of the islands alone. Their greed for the yellow rock was insatiable. And if the Spanish were too high-born to fish, then they surely weren't going to dig around in a dirty mine. Men were needed to do the mining, to melt the ore, and to load it on ships. And the Indians made terrible slaves because they tended to die too easily.

A new source of labor had to be found, thus less than twenty years after the first white man had set foot in the New World, the first black slave arrived—and was followed by twenty million more.

When the gold played out, the Spaniards had no more use for Haiti, and at the end of the century they ceded the western end of the island to the French. The French, being more inclined to farm, turned the island into coffee and sugar plantations. In the following hundred years Haiti became France's single wealthiest colony.

But, to the African slaves, the French were no more fun to have around than the Spanish had been for the Indians. As the whip forced many of the slaves to flee to the mountains, guerrilla bands sprang up and by the end of the 1700s, a revolution was underway.

The French fought desperately to keep the Island out of the hands of the troublesome slaves, but in 1804 after twenty years of fighting, Haiti became the second independent nation in the Western Hemisphere behind only the United States.

With independence, Haiti was divided into two sections: the southern part to be ruled by an ex-slave named Petion, the northern part to be ruled by another former slave, Henri Christophe.

Henri Christophe proved an even greater master at the art of tyrannical rule than the Spanish or the French had been. Declaring himself King, he took the weakest of his subjects as slaves (though he had been one himself) then went about building a kingdom.

A kingdom must have a castle, and Christophe wanted his to be the most beautiful in the world. Atop a mountain, fifteen miles inland from the sea, a site was chosen, and the palace was built: a near- replica of Frederick the Great's of Germany and identical even to the name—Sans Souci.

Henri's Sans Souci was something to behold, with grand ballrooms, luxurious sitting rooms, mirrored dining rooms, and countless state and meeting rooms, all lavishly decorated with fine marble statues, mahogany carvings, tapestries, and silks. Hand painted tiles covered the walls, highly polished marble served for the floors. There was even indoor plumbing and air-conditioning, provided by underground springs, fed through an elaborate system of conduits beneath the castle. The columned front entranceway commanded a view to the ocean, and terraced gardens that rivalled any in France filled the mountainside.

King Christophe grew steadily more despotic, and more insane with the building of his castle. Perhaps it was his years of slavery under the French, but for whatever reason he grew obsessed with the need to be the greatest, the most cultured, the most kingly. And certainly, in surroundings and in appearance, the Royal Family was second to none. The Christophes dressed in the most up-to-date fashions: massive, powdered wigs, velvet and silk gowns, perfumes, and face rouges, and strangest of all—silk stockings! (No one in their right mind would want to wear silk stockings in the tropics!) To complete the trappings of royalty, Christophe organized a court of Lords and Ladies in waiting, attendants, footmen, jesters, and entertainers. And sadly, fellow countrymen that Christophe had once shared a kinship of slavery with, became his servants and his slaves.

Soon Christophe had accumulated more wealth than he knew what to do with, and in the process, he became increasingly convinced that someone would take it from him. He feared the return of the French, a revolt of his own people, a takeover by Petion from the south, or an invasion by anyone and everyone else. In response to his most imaginary fears, he formed an army, then sent the army into the mountains to "recruit" more slaves for the next item on his agenda: a fort, big enough and strong enough to resist any outside attack.

Fourteen years later, Le Citadelle adorned the highest mountain peak on the coast and the structure still stands four hundred feet high, seven hundred feet long, with walls twenty to thirty feet thick. It was built at the cost of twenty thousand human lives!

There was an early-morning haze in the quiet harbor when we rowed the raft to the dock. Garry and Nicki were waiting for us, and we turned the raft over to Nicki for his transportation back to the *Halcyon*.

Nicki's parting words told us he was proud of his assignment of protecting our home. "Do not worry, Captain, the boat will be A Okay."

Indeed, we felt *Halcyon* was safe. Nicki would repel any invaders. Our double anchors, one of which was an eighty-pound Danforth that would hold against any storm were also in service.

With the kids in the lead, we struck out for the bus stop, ten blocks away. As we walked, the city rumbled with the first of its wakeup sounds. Church bells tolled, a vendor whistled while filling his stall with coconuts, a rickety car blasted its horn at a scrawny dog nosing in the gutters, shutters on shop fronts banged open, a sidewalk vendor asked if we would buy his shells.

Outside the door of a pastry shop, we came upon a kindly faced old man hard at work making peanut butter. As he sat in his chair, he held between his knees a massive wooden churn filled to midway with fresh-roasted peanuts. Clutched in his hands was a flat-bottomed mallet that served as the pestle. Slowly and rhythmically, he raised the mallet, plunged it into the three-foot depths of the vat, then raised it again, and each fall of the mallet produced a loud PLOOP, followed by a rush of nut-scented air.

With mouths watering, we inched closer and watched him pulverize the peanuts to a thick creamy paste. But when he added a goodly portion of coarse ground pepper to the churn, Ron gasped. The man looked up at our puzzled faces, chuckled, then jumped up and disappeared inside the shop to return with spoons for us to taste.

Roger and I exclaimed over the unique flavor, Garry grinned, nodding enthusiastically. But Ron grabbed his throat, bugged his eyes, and demanded water. Janice and Tommy voiced their vote: "Skippy's is better!"

We bought some anyway, as well as a loaf of bread and a bag of cookies. Next door to the pastry shop, we bought some cheese, and further down the street, Roger stopped a girl carrying bananas in a basket on her head and paid for a fat, ripe bunch.

She smiled, said, "Merci, Blanc," touched Tommy's head, and added, "Bon Jour, Toe mee." Then, with a ramrod-straight back, she walked away from us, her steps evenly measured under the load.

At the city limits, Garry pointed to a large weather-worn desk, crazily positioned in the dust on the shoulder of the road. A soldier in uniform sat behind it. "You must show him your papers," Garry said.

Approaching the outdoor office, we presented our passports, and answered a dozen questions about where we were staying, where we were going, when would we be back, the purpose of our outing....

The officer rubber-stamped our visas, and we thought we were through when he spoke sharply to Garry. The usually smiling boy jumped as though struck, then looked at the ground and responded in a barely audible voice. There was no doubt, Garry was afraid.

Their Creole-French conversation lasted for some time, the soldier speaking loud and long. Garry answering in muted, single-syllable words.

"I wish I knew French," I muttered with annoyance.

"If you did, what would you say?"

Roger's sensible question didn't make me feel any better. "Not much, I suppose." I was relieved when the soldier dismissed Garry and allowed him to rejoin us.

"What was that all about?" Roger asked.

"It is always so," Garry answered simply.

I wanted to know more, but Garry purposely changed the subject by saying, "There are the buses!"

We looked to see a lineup of flatbed trucks, each with a wooden lean-to compartment built on the back. Garry indicated a bright blue truck near the end of the line. It was colorfully painted with red and yellow roses decorating the hood, a stylistic Madonna adorning the driver's door. The sign mounted on the cab read, "Milot" the town nearest Le Citadelle.

Roger went first, climbing up onto a wooden crate step and into the gate of the lean-to, then he turned and announced, "No more room. Let's wait for another bus."

Garry rushed forward. "No, there is room," he said as he took Roger's place to lead us aboard. We followed.

Rough-hewn boards formed the sides of the cabin, nailed unevenly from the truck bed to window height. There was no glass where the windows should have been. The flat roof was a piece of tin, tacked over more planks. And the entire structure looked as though it had been tossed together by a couple of nine-year-olds as a Saturday afternoon treehouse project.

Serving as seats, five pew-like splintery benches were lined up and nailed to the floor, and thirty people filled the space designed for twenty bodies at most. Passengers groaned, pushed, and made room for the six of us, two inches per rump, but I felt less intrusive when after us came a woman with two children, then a man carrying a chicken. Somehow, we all squeezed in.

Once settled I found myself alone at the front of the cabin, pinioned between two women no older than myself. They appeared to be engaged in a heated discussion that had barely skipped a beat with my arrival. As the bus bounced down the road, their voices rose to a pitch that competed admirably with the racket of creaking boards, the clattering of the tin roof, and the thumping of wheels with no springs hitting ruts with no bottoms. To emphasize some important point, the woman on my left grabbed a wooden crucifix from a chain around her neck, leaned across my lap and waved the religious symbol under the nose of the lady on my right. That brought on a return volley of spitting remarks as "Righty" angrily shook her finger under the nose of "Lefty." Eyes flashed and both began to shout at once.

Turning in the seat, I looked desperately for Roger, and spied him in the back row. He was amusing himself by feeding a cookie to his neighbor's chicken. I tried but couldn't catch his eye.

Maybe one of the kids would change places with me. But Garry and the boys were sitting near a window, chattering excitedly about something on the road outside the bus, and Janice was playing "This Little Piggy" with a baby in the seat beside her. It was hopeless—I had nothing of enough value to bribe any one of them to take my place. I faced forward, accepted my fate, prayed the two women wouldn't come to blows, and tried to ignore their verbal duel.

The bus rambled inland. Occasionally, by turning far to one side or the other and peering over the heads of the passengers, I would catch a glimpse of a cane field or a grove of banana trees.

It took an hour of bouncing, stopping, reshuffling, and starting again, before we reached Milot, and my ears were as relieved as my rear end when the final stop emptied the bus. As my two traveling companions departed, side by side and still arguing, Roger asked, "What's wrong with them?"

"Probably exchanging recipes," I answered as I rubbed all the sore places.

Our first impression of the modest mountain town was its cleanliness. The paved streets were free of orange peelings, the air had only a slight tinge of charcoal, like burning leaves on a summer's day.

Garry led us into the police station, and our passports were stamped again. We learned the police were the coordinators of the trips to the fort, and so the bargaining began.

A bored officer with sleepy eyes informed us we needed to rent horses ($5 each), a guide ($5), the guide's horse ($5), entrance fees to the fort ($1.50 each), whips to beat the horses ($1 each), and a boy to walk behind each horse to keep it moving ($1 each). Counting Garry and the guide, that was seven horses and fourteen people! I refrained from asking why the whips and the walkers were the same price.

Roger and I put our heads together and tried to figure the bill; the sewing machine money was going to disappear fast if we weren't careful. Before we had a total, the officer added the kicker: we would have to buy soft drinks for everyone when we arrived at the top, and again when we reached the bottom.

I said, "Let's see. Twenty-five cents times two times fourteen... Roger, I've lost count!"

He was always better at math. "That's seventy-one fifty! Garry, tell them we'll walk, thank you."

Garry looked aghast as he said, "Captain, it is a three-hour walk, one way!"

When Roger seemed uncertain, I suggested we haggle. It took half an hour, but in the end, we accepted the guide, argued down the price of the horses, hired one walker to care for the horses at the top, said "NO DICE!" to the whips, agreed to the soft drinks, and ended up at half the original price. Later we learned we could have dispensed with the guide since he refused to talk to us anyway.

The horses, tethered behind the police station, were the most underfed, forlorn-looking creatures we'd ever seen. If they had been on display in front of the station, we could have saved a half hour of bargaining, and a lot of money. But they were paid for, and we decided to take it easy on them by walking all the steep parts.

It took another half hour to mount the horses, who were more than a little reluctant. Finally, in single file, our procession moved through town. Children and dogs appeared from all sides, and hustlers begged us to buy every kind of fruit, or basket, or bead, or wood carving. Voices shouted, "Very cheap, lady. On sale today only, usually one dollar, but I give to you for fifty cents."

I answered them all by saying, "No speak English," which confused them sufficiently enough to give us time to move on. Once beyond the town, the horses clomped slowly up the crude dirt road, past thick stands of fruit trees and tiny windowless one-room stucco huts with walls that bulged at the middle and with Chinese straw hats for roofs. Everywhere the yards were bare earth, packed hard as cement and swept clean as bleached bones. A charcoal fire smoldered from a hole in the front of each house, and every fire was tended by a bent-over, work-weary woman who seemed to be either cooking food or boiling laundry. *Why*, I wondered, *were the houses and people so poor, when the land seemed so rich and the trees so full of fruit?* The answer should have occurred to me, but it didn't come until later. The people did not own the land; the government did.

We reached the ridge, and the view was spectacular. The valley twisted and turned below us on its way to the sea. The mountain peaks loomed unexpectedly above us, then faded away behind filmy cotton clouds.

Near the outer edge of the ridge were ruins that reminded me of something I'd seen before: a photo from a travel magazine of an ancient Greek temple. Garry rode up beside me to explain what we were looking at. "It is Sans Souci, the palace. We will stop on the way back."

We plodded on, beyond the palace, up the mountain. The dogs, children, and hustlers dropped away as the road grew steeper. Our horses snorted then slowed. When the walker began running from horse to horse and snapping boney rumps with his switch, I protested, "Garry, tell him to stop! We can walk now."

Garry relayed my message, but the walker ignored the order and slapped the legs of Tommy's horse. Roger shouted, "Garry, tell that twerp he's fired if he touches another horse with that whip!"

Twerp sullenly fell back to walk beside the guide, and the rest of the way they consoled each other—and steered clear of us.

Tommy and Ron had no trouble keeping up, but Roger lagged far behind. His sway-backed steed seemed to dislike walking with or without a rider.

Janice spent a lot of the ride crying. Her horse obviously adored her, and when she tried to lead him, he expressed his love by nuzzling her in the back. That convinced her he was a man-eating horse, and she decided it was safer to sit on him. The horse didn't mind her light weight. When she remounted, he spurted forward in pursuit of a blade of grass at the edge of a deep precipice. Her reaction—screaming hysterically and pulling wildly on the reins—led him back to the middle of the road. But that didn't satisfy her. Not Janice. She rode the rest of the way, pestering the poor nag to distraction with admonitions: "Don't step on that rock! Watch where you're going! Don't fall in that hole! Don't step in the water! Slow down!"

The last hour of the ride was over a trail carved into the face of the mountain, a goat trail that threatened to disappear altogether with the first good rainfall. We were beginning to wonder if we were on a wild goose chase when suddenly, there it was.

Le Citadelle was a structure so immense, so spectacular, so sinister looking it took my breath away. With several hundred feet still to climb we stopped to rest, and to stare in awe at the sight above us.

It was a hundred and seventy years old and built of stone blocks that had been carried for miles up the trail we had just followed. And from what we could see, every block remained intact. Impervious to time, it was an engineering feat to rival the pyramids of Egypt, but as I studied it, I could sense the aura of madness. It reminded me of a prison.

We left the horses with the walker at the base of the fort and entered through a creaky wooden door into the dark inner chambers of Christophe's monument. The rooms and corridors echoed with our footsteps, and the sounds of scurrying creatures in the shadows told us we were not alone. No one had to warn the kids to stay close.

In every room we found tools of war. One bronze cannon, covered with ornate figures and Spanish inscriptions, caught my eye. I found a date on the side: A.D. 1687. The cannon was old when Le Citadelle was built.

An hour of exploring brought us into the center courtyard at the top of the fort, and the fresh air smelled good after the musty aroma of damp floors and rat droppings. Around the perimeter of the courtyard were dozens more cannons guarding against Christophe's imaginary enemies. Altogether I estimated we had seen over fifty of the weapons, and our brochure told us some weighed over five tons. Beside each cannon sat a small hill of cannon balls all precisely stacked by the hands of the slaves. The pyramid piles were as high as my head.

Ron found one of the balls lying loose from the rest and decided to lift it. He started with "I could carry one of these up the mountain!" and finished with "Oomph!"

I tried my hand and concluded I couldn't have carried it down the mountain.

We walked to the edge of the wall and looked over. The equivalent of forty floors separated us from the ground; our horses were no larger than puppies in the grass. Beyond the fort, the trail snaked across the face of the mountain and the valley where we'd started seemed a mere haze in the distance.

"How in the world did Christophe get all this up here?" I wondered aloud.

"We learn in school," Garry explained. "King Henri make the slaves carry everything in one long line that go from Milot to here. When the slaves walk too slowly, King Henri begin to count from one to ten. Each time he say ten, he shoot somebody."

Roger grimaced. "I can see how that would speed them up," he said.

Garry was anxious to share what he knew of the history of his people. "Everyone in Haiti knows the stories of King Henri," he went on. "Do you see where we stand?" We nodded and he recited, "One day a white man come to San Souci. The King want the foreigner to see his power and go out and tell the world that Christophe is the strongest ruler of all. So, he bring the man up here. He make all the slaves line up and march to this very spot on the wall. When the slaves stop at the edge, Henri shout, 'March!' And they march."

I leaned over and looked at the rocks below. "All of them marched?" I could hardly believe it.

"Only one thousand walked off the wall—all of them died," Garry answered.

"But why? Surly there were enough men to overpower Christophe."

"The soldiers were all around the courtyard. They have the guns. The slaves know they die if they march, they die if they don't march."

A tingly sensation played along my spine, and I sensed an invisible hand poised and ready to give a push. Grabbing for Janice, I put another arm around Tommy, and moved us gingerly away from the edge. "I think it's time for a break from history," I said. "Are you guys hungry?"

We spread our lunch in the shade to one side of the courtyard and ate. The guide we'd hired (then not seen for over an hour) arrived to share our bananas, cheese, and peanut butter sandwiches.

Garry took some lunch to the walker, and when he returned, Ron asked, "Whatever happened to Christophe?"

"He shoot himself," Garry answered matter-of-factly. "He was crazy."

"Did the slaves go free then?" Janice asked and I heard a note of sympathy in her voice. History had become very real to all of us that afternoon.

"No. Christophe's son was made King. He was a bad ruler too." Garry paused to make sure he had our attention. "He did not live very long, and he died right there." He pointed at a pile of rubble a few feet away. "That was a room where all the guns and powder were put."

"The armory?" Roger asked.

He nodded. "The son walked inside the room with a cigar, and everything go BOOM!"

We had to laugh, and Garry, his eyes sparkling with pleasure summed it up. "He not very smart man." That opinion was unanimous

The sun had reached its peak and was falling toward the horizon when we remounted and started on the long trek home. Soon the trail led into the shade, then deep into the coolness of the trees, and we rode quietly, each with his own thoughts of an era of cruelty that could hardly be imagined. When the horses began to huff and blow, we dismounted and walked on wobbly legs, enjoying the respite from the rubbing of the saddles.

Stopping at Sans Souci, we wandered around in the crumbling ruins, but our senses were too numbed to take it all in. There were faint drawings still apparent in the tile walls, and clumps of weeds and moss grew through the cracks in the marble floors, but the ghosts had moved away. Sans Souci was not going to last as long as Le Citadelle.

The bus to Cap Haitien was much like the one we'd ridden that morning, and we were overjoyed to find we were the first on board and quickly claimed the window seats.

As the bus meandered through Milot, it took on passengers at every corner, most of them laden with produce for the Cap Haitien market. Bags of potatoes, bunches of bananas, and sacks of charcoal were piled on top of the tin roof, and once all the seats in the cabin were filled to capacity, additional passengers shinnied up the sides of the cabin to ride on top of the food.

A thin-faced woman in a faded and torn dress wriggled into the space next to me and deposited a large kettle on the floor at her feet. My first reaction was horror. The kettle resembled an old-fashioned chamber pot. But I needn't have worried.

The woman shouted out to no one in particular, and a passenger in front of us responded by turning while handing her a small coin, and a cup with no handle. The woman lifted the lid of the chamber pot, scooped out a cup of vegetable soup, and handed it to her customer.

At that moment the bus jerked to a stop, and a great cloud of dust poured in the windows and peppered the soup. The man drank it anyway.

When the woman looked at me to see if I wanted to buy a cup too, I vigorously shook my head. But others were not so squeamish. She sold six more cups (actually two cups, two jars of different sizes, a chipped bowl, and a tin can—(Haitians seem always to carry something to eat out of), plus a refill for the first customer. The soup must have been good.

With each bump in the road, sprinkles of coal dust fell from the roof and settled in our clothes, hair, and eyes. As I dusted my face with a grimy hand, I was reminded of a summer as a child when I'd stayed with my Grandmother. She was a strict woman with standards of cleanliness that often seemed silly to my eight-year-old mind. Her voice was scolding in my ears as I looked around and wondered what she would say about all the "filthy germs" on the bus. Quite certainly, she would have boiled us all in lye soap, and soundly chastised me for exposing the children to such conditions. With a somewhat guilty conscience, I checked the kids. Janice, her hair matted with tangles, was dozing peacefully in the crook of Roger's arm. Ron, his clothes sweaty and stained, was gazing, wide-eyed out the window. And Tommy, looking normally soiled, was amusing Garry with elephant jokes that Garry could only half understand. I settled back in the seat. Even with the filthy germs, they would survive.

From the bus to the harbor, the walk seemed interminable. Our heads felt dull, our legs like lead. Even Garry had to rest his feet. We stopped at the side of the road and waited for him to remove the new shoes he'd worn so proudly all day. After wiggling his toes, he tied the shoelaces together, slung the shoes over his shoulder, and we continued on.

With a block to go, our pace quickened. Each of us had visions dancing in our heads of baths, clean clothes, and bed. Rounding the corner, we hurried toward the harbor. In the early evening all was quiet. A few fishing boats sat at the dock, but the noisy cruise ships had gone. Searching for *Halcyon*, we peered toward the anchorage, then stopped cold. Panic passed through us like a jolt of electricity: *Halcyon* was gone.

Roger swore, Janice whimpered, my legs tried to buckle under me. But it took only a second, though it seemed longer before Ron shouted, "Is that the boat? Over there!" We strained to see where he was pointing in the gray light. "Right over there!" he tried again.

"I see it!" The rush of relief at the sight of *Halcyon*'s raked masts made us all cheer.

"Captain! Captain!" Jean called; he was approaching in a dead run from the far side of the harbor. "I have been waiting for you." He was breathless. "I have my friend's skiff that can take us to the boat."

Roger's voice was icy with anger as he asked, "Jean, how did *Halcyon* get out there? Where is Nicki?"

"He is on the boat, Captain. Waiting for you." Jean spoke nervously. "He did not leave the boat all day. Honest. And he tried hard, but he could not stop the boat."

Roger raised a hand to slow the excited boy. "Hold it! Start over and explain what happened."

"There were too many cruise ships. When the first and second ones left the harbor the *Halcyon*'s anchors were okay, but the third time was too much. The boat started to float away. Nicki tried to pull in the anchors, but the lines were all twisted together...the water must have turned the boat around."

We quickly followed Jean to the skiff and climbed in. Jean continued to talk, saying, "Nicki got both anchors on the boat, then he dropped one back in the water. He was by himself and not so strong, so it took him a long time. That is why the boat is way over there."

How had he done it? Nicki weighed little more than Janice, and the anchors, combined with thirty feet of chain at the end of the heavy rode would have been difficult for someone twice his size to handle.

Jean took a long breath before finishing. "I came to the docks in the afternoon to see if Nicki was all right, and when I saw where the boat was, I borrowed my friend's skiff to go and see what happened."

Nicki was waiting for us when we pulled alongside. He caught the line from the skiff and held it steady while we boarded *Halcyon*. His face looked so troubled; the message was clear: he felt he had let us down. Roger quickly praised him for the fine job he'd done, and we all added our reassurances that he had performed magnificently.

"I tried, Captain," he said.

"We know you did, Nicki," Roger said. And finally, Nicki smiled.

Roger started the engine, then took the wheel as Ron went forward to raise the anchor. Looking around, I could see shoaling water everywhere. We had been lucky. *Halcyon* was afloat and rocking easily in the riffles coming from the open ocean. Thank God she had missed the reef. Then I shuddered. If Nicki had not untangled the anchors in time...If he had not been able to reset the anchor... If there had been a storm ... Then I remembered a cabin boy of long ago, and turning to Roger where he stood at the wheel, I asked, "Do you know what today is?"

"I'm afraid to guess." He sounded as though he was expecting me to announce the sky was falling.

I giggled. "Roger, its Christmas Eve!"

"Am I supposed to say Ho, Ho, Ho, or Bah Humbug?"

He wasn't following my train of thought, but it was certainly clear to me. "Somewhere out here on this reef are the remains of the *Santa Maria*!" When he still looked puzzled, I asked, "Have you ever wondered if you were the reincarnation of Christopher Columbus?"

As it dawned on him, he said, "Either that, or this place is jinxed."

Roger's romance with his wonderful mistress was changing. Of course, our lack of money had upset him and that was understandable, but it was not the reason for the change. I could trace the first signs of trouble to the plugged toilet in the Bahamas. But a plugged toilet will undo the greatest of love affairs for any sailor, at least temporarily. At the time I'd dismissed his foul moods, but there was no denying when the cruise ships had stirred up our anchors and nearly put *Halcyon* on the reef, Roger began to act like someone whose one and only love had tried to run off with the milkman.

Even after we moved *Halcyon* back into the harbor and securely set the anchor, Roger wasn't satisfied. Each hour through the night he climbed out of his bunk, went up on deck, and checked the line as if he expected her to bolt and run again.

There was one more incident that made me wonder about Roger's changing feelings. It came the day the bank reopened, and our money finally arrived from the States. In the process of making plans to get to Port Au Prince and meet George, it was decided I would do the market shopping and Roger and Ron would work on an important repair job we had been delaying: to replace a frayed transmission cable.

I left the boat after lunch and rowed ashore with Tommy and Janice. Jean and Garry were waiting for me, and together we left for the market. Tommy and Janice stayed on the dock to play Frisbee with a coffee can lid they'd found in the bilge. Roger and Ron were back on the boat, Roger in the engine room working on the cable, and Ron passing tools to him with the efficiency of a surgical assistant.

We were gone several hours and returned to find *Halcyon* tied to the dock. I called to the kids to help me get the groceries on board the boat, and Janice came running up first. "Mom! Did you see the scratch?" She was pointing at the hull on the port side, and I looked to see a streak, two inches wide and two feet long, where all the paint down to the bare steel was gone.

"What happened?"

Ron snapped at Janice, "Dad told you not to say anything!"

"What happened?" I demanded.

No one alive had ever been able to prevent Janice from spilling the beans. "Dad hit the dock!" she announced with glee.

Sailing Against the Wind – Toni Larson 271

Garry and Jean reminded me of the boxes of groceries, and I instructed Ron and Tommy to take them to the cabin. Thanking the brothers, I sent them on their way, then followed the kids below.

Roger was sitting at the table, glowering into a coffee cup. "The kids said you hit the dock," I said. "How did it happen?"

He gave them a threatening look, but it did no good, Tommy jumped in first by saying, "Janice told!"

"No, I didn't. All I said was..."

"Ron can't count," Tommy teased further.

"Well, it sounded like two bangs," Ron defended himself.

"Two bangs?" I couldn't understand any of it. "What happened?" I asked Roger again.

Looking uncomfortable, he explained that he'd taken the old transmission cable out and had the new one to replace it. "I could not make the connection to the shift on the deck. The hole wasn't large enough for the new cable, and I needed to drill it out. So, I decided to move the boat to the dock and get some electricity for the drill."

I was a step ahead of him. "And you didn't reconnect the old cable to move the boat?" My mouth started to twitch, but I suppressed the chuckle,—I had a feeling it wouldn't be appreciated.

"I couldn't; I had cut the old one when I took it out. There wasn't enough left to splice."

He stood and began unpacking one of the boxes, but I wasn't going to let him off so easily. "How did you manage to shift the gears?"

"Ron did it from the engine room. Now let's put the groceries away and...."

"Oh no you don't. I want to hear all of it. What is this about two bangs?"

"That was the signal," Janice said. "Dad was supposed to hit the deck with a hammer, one bang for forward, two for reverse, and three for neutral. But Ron can't count!"

Our usually peace-loving Ron looked ready to strangle his sister. "Well, it sounded like two bangs. How was I to know Dad had dropped the hammer?" he said.

Roger didn't think that was funny either, but I couldn't suppress the giggle any longer. When Ron saw my amusement, he relaxed and told his side of the story. "I put the gear in reverse, then I heard more bangs. I put it in neutral but there was some more banging. I put it back in forward, that's when we hit the dock."

"Couldn't you hear Dad yelling *neutral*?" Janice goaded him.

"I couldn't hear anything but the bangs," Ron answered.

"Well, you should have heard him!" she blabbed. "He was yelling loud enough."

"Were there people on the dock?" I was enjoying the mental picture immensely.

"Yeh, some policemen," Tommy offered. "And a whole bunch of other people." With that, I grabbed my sides and doubled up with laughter.

"What in the hell do you think is so funny?" Roger slammed down a sack of onions.

Composing myself, I tried to explain saying, "The Haitians already believe Americans are strange people. But can you imagine what they thought when they saw this boat barreling toward the dock, guided by a wild-eyed Captain with a hammer in his hand, and that Captain is pounding on the deck and ordering the boat to stop? When you hit the dock, you simply confirmed their deepest suspicions."

By then the kids were laughing too, but our amusement wasn't infectious enough. Roger didn't even crack a smile when he said, "I should have hit it harder!"

Something was changing.

It was sad when the three boys came to the dock to say goodbye.

They untied our lines, and stood waving and shouting, "Bon Voyage," and "Come again." But we were not even clear of the harbor before they were catching the dock lines of a newly arriving sailboat and offering their "very honest" services as guides.

The acrid smell of burning charcoal receded into the distance as *Halcyon* rounded the last marker in the Cap Haitien harbor. Soft green mountains that served as buffers from the easterlies rose majestically on either side of the channel. As we passed the last mountain I turned from the wheel and looked back to see a setting that would rival a Norwegian fjord in magnificence and beauty.

I sighed with relief. It felt good to be on our way again under a steadying jib. We cleared the channel and *Halcyon*'s weighty lethargic body heaved up and over the strong onrushing surge of the ocean. Coaxing her bow into the wind, I held her steady, Tommy released the sail ties on the main, Janice did the same for the mizzen, Ron and Roger applied their muscles to the winches. The two sails billowed free, then rose to snap like great white flags on their respective poles.

With the halyards locked in place, Roger and Ron took positions at the sheet or line winches, I eased the bow around to course, and Janice worked the jib line. Tommy killed the idling motor, and in the abrupt silence the winch ratchets clicked loudly. The sheets tightened, the sails ceased fluttering, and *Halcyon* heeled her body to port.

My eyes were on the compass as Roger, Ron, and Janice stared upward at the slackness of their respectively assigned sails. They pulled, released, then tightened the lines until each sail lay in perfect alignment to the others.

Halcyon's clumsiness fell away. She lifted with the wind and moved weightlessly across the top of the waves with all the litheness of a ballet dancer. Water rushed along the hull and churned out behind us faster and faster. We were a world-class skier on a downhill run, A.J. Foyt on the last lap of the Indy. The sensation was breathtaking, exhilarating, a freeing of the soul. (It was also relative. We were topping the speedometer at six miles per hour.)

"It's going to be a beautiful day," Roger said as he came to sit beside me at the Captain's seat. He was smiling and looked as relaxed as I felt.

Ron joined us and asked his dad to help rig the troll line. It took a half hour for them to locate all the gear, bait the yellow feather lure, and let the line out with expectation of catching a near-sighted Wahoo.

Tommy challenged Janice to a game of Hearts, and they clamored down the hatchway while arguing over who would decide the rules.

Leaning back in the Captain's seat, I hooked a heel on each side of the wheel to steady it and let the early-morning sun warm my body. *Halcyon* held the course as if she had a mind of her own and she knew where she was going. I smiled at the thought. From the beginning we had set deadlines and destinations that never panned out, but maybe *Halcyon* had been getting her way all along and we weren't aware of it. Well, it was all right with me—I was ready to let her take charge.

And before we were out of Haiti, she would do just that.

CHAPTER 15: GUNS AND GIFTS FROM THE AMERICAN PEOPLE

Two hundred years of history separated Christophe and his son from another father-son combination of "Papa" and "Baby Doc" Duvalier. But those two hundred years had done little to change the living conditions of the Haitian.

Other self-proclaimed kings and emperors followed King Henri. Then political reformers replaced the kings. But to no avail—their reform was negligible. It did not help that one politician after another kept fleeing the country with the national treasury.

In 1915, the U.S. became concerned that the Germans might gain a strategic foothold in the poverty-stricken island, and with that as an excuse the Marines landed in Port au Prince. They stayed for twenty years! When the American military finally left the Island, they also left an empty treasury and no viable government.

Early in the 1950s, a quiet, near-sighted, country doctor came down from the hills and claimed his place in the nation's history. The incredible power of Francois "Papa Doc" Duvalier came from a source that previous politicians had never thought to develop or to us: religious superstition.

Papa Doc took several years to work his way up the political ladder, but he made use of that time by carefully spreading, then nurturing rumors of his magical powers. Upon winning the presidency in 1957, Papa Doc declared himself "Leader for Life." Then he formed a group of secret police that the Haitians aptly nicknamed the Tonton Macoute, or "Boogie Men."

The Tonton Macoute were everywhere and seemed to be able to hear even the slightest grumbling of discontent. If an unhappy subject dared to speak out against Papa Doc, chances were he would abruptly, and mysteriously disappear (or better yet simply lie down and die). With such evidence, it didn't take long to convince the highly superstitious or woefully uneducated that Papa Doc and his Boogie Men were superhuman.

Papa Doc's mind-control form of oppression continued until he died in 1971. He was succeeded by his chubby spoiled nineteen-year-old son, Jean Claude, who was duly christened, "Baby Doc."
Following in his father's footsteps, Baby Doc performed his first official act by declaring himself,
"President for Life." Then he went about improving the lot of his countrymen by investing in flashy race cars and the company of beautiful women. The Tonton Macoute continued to exist, and the treasury emptied again in 1976 when a member of Baby Doc's cabinet made an unexpected move to

Switzerland with all the money. The populace secretly hoped Baby Doc would take up cigar smoking inside the National Armory.

Sadly, the worst of Haiti's present problems does not stem from the terror-filled reign of the politicians, the appalling heritage of slavery, or the insane rule of the Christophes or the Duvaliers. Neither are the Spanish, the French, nor the American occupations entirely to blame for the economic distress of modern Haiti.

If there is one single cause that can be pinpointed, it must be the charcoal.

Charcoal is the only cooking fuel used by ninety-five percent of the population, and therefore it is constantly in demand. Everywhere trees are cut and burned to make the coal, which then is sacked in the villages throughout the country, carried to the coast, loaded on boats, and shipped to the markets in Cap Haitien and Port au Prince.

For centuries the island was so fertile that charcoal was a cheap and easily available resource, but two things happened during the 1930's to change that: drought and overpopulation.

The growing numbers of people, who had little or no knowledge of crop rotation, terrace farming, or irrigation, over farmed the small country. When a drought cycle began (coinciding roughly with the droughts that brought about the dustbowl conditions in the U.S.) the already-overworked land stopped yielding. To support themselves, the Haitians cut, burned, and sold more charcoal than ever before, and when all the trees disappeared, the people began to dig up the roots to burn. In no time at all the land was stripped bare. Great erosion gullies sliced down the once-lush mountainsides. Whenever there was rain, the land was washed away to the sea. The deposits of soil and silt began to cover the reefs, smothering the coral and killing it. With nothing to feed on, the tiny fish vanished, and the larger fish soon followed. Now the coastal waters are as barren as the land. The life cycle of Haiti has been broken.

Halcyon cleared the point, and the kids began their shifts at the wheel as the green mountainsides of Cap Haitien faded away on the horizon to be replaced by the stark, skeletal-like terrain of a land with no water.

Roger and I went below to work out our course. The compass read west by northwest; we were headed for a tiny inlet ninety miles from Cap Haitien on the extreme western end of Hispaniola, a place called St. Nicholas Mole. The chart showed the Mole as a mere village, but it had a secure anchorage and looked like a promising place to spend a night on our five-day trek to Port au Prince.

Before leaving Cap Haitien, Jean had warned us we would see few towns and no lights along the way. We had purposely chosen a full-moon night to navigate by, while praying for good weather.

Our course was straightforward except for a twenty-five mile stretch of water lying between the mainland and a smaller island known as Ile de la Tortue, or Torture Island. When I saw we would be approaching Torture Island at nightfall, I was concerned that the five-mile-wide channel would not give us enough room to maneuver. "Time is not all that important," I reminded Roger. "Why don't we go to the outside of the island and play it safe?"

He didn't like the idea. "That would just put us another day at sea. Besides, we have a full moon to give us light."

I wasn't convinced and told him so. Compiling a complete picture of current flows and compass deviations, he carefully laid out the course, then announced, "It's an easy route. I can pick my way, blindfolded, through that channel." He may have thought he was being optimistic, but he turned out to be prophetic.

After dinner Roger took the wheel, and we watched as one by one all the lights on shore twinkled out. The moon came up to spread a silver glow over the tops of the mountains, and I went to bed in anticipation of a very pleasant night of sailing. At 1 a.m. Roger blew the whistle to summon me to the wheel.

Stumbling up onto the deck, I looked around in amazement. "It's so dark! Where are you?" I could see neither Roger at the wheel, nor the wheel itself!

"I'm here," he spoke from the inky blackness, but he didn't sound very confident when he added, "I think we're still on course."

"You think?" I looked around and felt a creeping fear.

He explained, "A bank of clouds moved in right after we reached the lee of Torture Island, and the wind has been very unpredictable the last few hours. But I'll get a fix on one of the islands as soon as the clouds lift. In the meantime, all we can do is hope my adjustments to the wind and currents are accurate."

I could tell he was worried and was glad when he stayed with me for a while. But the clouds didn't go away. The wind died to a mere ruffle, and a slow drizzle began. Then the wind quit altogether, so that the sails flopped around, and *Halcyon* bobbed helplessly in the sea. Roger started the engine and tried to maintain a steady speed, then the wind picked up. He turned off the engine and we tried to sail, then the wind died again. Except for the occasional raindrops, the night was silent, the water smooth. But there was an undercurrent, and it was pushing us onward.

After an hour, Roger gave up waiting for a break in the weather. He left instructions for me to maintain the slowest speed possible until the moon came out, then said, "Wake me if anything changes." With that, he disappeared into the cabin.

The old niggling worry forced me to turn on the fathometer, and I was relieved to see no reading. Our charts showed depths of over five hundred feet, right to the shoreline, so a blip on the screen would have been distressing.

I tacked back and forth for an hour, all the while scanning the sky for any sign of a star. The darkness was absolute, and the feeling was one of floating around in a damp cave. I had a distinct impression I could walk to the handrail, reach out, and touch a wall.

Several times, lightning lit the night enough to outline the mountains of one island or the other, but soon it vanished, too. Hoping the storm was indeed moving on, I tightened the limp sheets, then made myself comfortable.

I used the flashlight to amuse myself by looking over the side of the boat and watching debris pass the hull: small bits of wood, flashes of phosphorescent plant and animal life. A dead beetle bobbed alongside the boat, and I studied it for a minute. We were floating together, fellow passengers in the currents.

The night was eerily quiet, there was no longer even the rumble of thunder to listen to. A faint swish sounded, and I flashed the light up to the sails to see if they were catching any wind. Nothing.
The swish came again a little closer. I turned out the light, and the blackness returned. Another swish made my skin tingle, was I hearing more ghosts? And then it hit me, I COULD HEAR THE SURF!

"ROGER!" The scream should have carried ten miles, and just to make sure he had heard, I grabbed the police whistle from around my neck and began blowing!

Roger appeared in seconds, rubbing the sleep from his eyes and grumbling, "Whatinthehell...?"

"We're about to hit the beach!" I bellowed.

That galvanized him into action, and he had the engine going in record time. Turning the boat away from the deceptively gentle sounds of surf washing over rocks, we motored safely back into the middle of the channel, (which is a cinch to find when one knows where the beach is.)

Roger gave up any further sleep until dawn, and we were two very tired sailors when we entered St. Nicholas Mole.

The harbor of the "Mole" was so deep the entire length of the lead line could not find the bottom on our approach for a landing. Within fifty feet of the beach, Ron dropped the anchor and at a hundred feet of anchor line, it dangled like a fishhook. The same occurred at twenty-five feet, but ten feet from the beach we found a ledge, and the hook grabbed to a chunk of rock.

After snubbing the line around the stanchion post, we watched a small rowboat came alongside *Halcyon*. As the kids dashed to the railing, I stood to see the boat loaded with soldiers, and each one carried a very fearsome-looking machine gun! This boarding party meant business!

Without waiting for the formal invitation, the General—I assumed he was the General because of his much-decorated uniform and jaunty hat—leapt aboard *Halcyon*. Behind him came five more soldiers, and I had the feeling they were not pleased to see us.

Somewhere, we had learned that the Mole was the most sensitive spot in all of Haiti because of its proximity to Cuba, and that thought was on my mind when I whispered to Roger, "Surely they don't think we're invaders."

He gave me one of his more tolerant looks then turned to the General, extended his hand, and asked, "Do you speak English?"

The General responded with a barrage of Creole, so Roger tried again. "Habla Espanol?" The response was the same, and totally unintelligible to our ears. Roger looked puzzled for a moment, then shrugged and said, as if he expected the soldiers to understand, "Follow me!"

We all marched below, and Roger produced our ship's papers. The General took the passports and growled something at us. I offered him coffee (in English). It surprised me when his expression hardened, and his eyes narrowed as he barked another question. Had he asked, "Where to" or "Where from?"

Roger made a guess. "Port au Prince," he said.

It wasn't the answer the General wanted, and when he scowled, I tried another tack. "Cap Haitien!"

That wasn't right either. He motioned to one of his underlings and issued an order. The assistant snapped to attention, marched into the forward cabin, and began pulling out drawers and dumping books from the overhead shelves. Roger, also looking angry, watched the search from the galley. The kids and I sat quietly on one of the settees.

Even Ron was concerned. "What are they looking for?" he whispered.

I shrugged and glanced across the table at the unsmiling, unfriendly faces. Did Haitians take training in "Intimidation through staring?" When someone shifted his gun, I jumped.

The stares were diverted when the Assistant shouted triumphantly from the forward cabin, then rushed into the main salon and thrust out his hand. Dangling from his forefinger was a small muslin bag that I had sewn and filled with one of the chlorophyll type kitty litters. The bag had been stashed in a locker to absorb the moisture and smell of mildew.

Roger recognized it and gave me a this-should-be-interesting look, which caused me to burst out in nervous laughter. But the soldier didn't see any humor. He waved the bag at Roger, and I could tell he wanted an explanation.

"Kitty litter," I rushed to explain.

"Huh?" The man whirled in my direction.

"Meow, meow," I tried, and made scratching motions on the table. Roger chuckled but the soldier looked even more confused.

"I don't think he understands," Janice whispered from my side.

Naturally he didn't. On an island where the chief resource was sand, who would know what a litterbox was? I squirmed uncomfortably. Would we get a fair trial? Who would take the kids? What would my mother say when she found out we were spending twenty years in a Haitian jail for smuggling kitty litter?

The soldier gave up on the questioning, but not the search. Obviously, he thought we were carrying something illegal; he just didn't know what it was. With the others joining in, drawers and lockers were emptied onto the floor, flour and sugar were probed, mattresses and pillows were poked, the floorboards were lifted, and all the books were held out at arms-length and shaken.

Roger came and sat beside me on the settee, took my hand, and we watched apprehensively as the men tore the cabin apart. The kids were quieter than they'd been in months.

The temperature in the room climbed noticeably, and at first, I thought it was due to my nervousness. Then I saw that we had not opened the ports or the hatches in the confusion of the boarding.

I was on the verge of ordering the kids to get at it when I felt Roger tense. Glancing at him sidewise, I followed his stare to see one of the soldiers reaching for the doors of the engine room. *DAD'S GUN!*

Panic finally struck. Smuggling kitty litter might be excused, but smuggling a gun was another matter—and we knew it! Roger was still as stone. He didn't even seem to be breathing. I wasn't so well under control. My hands went clammy, my stomach rolled over, and when the room began spinning, I dropped my head between my knees.

Noticing my behavior, the General arched an eyebrow at Roger. Evidently Roger was thinking fast, he clutched at his stomach, blurted out, "Flu!" and gargled a very descriptive "AGHH!"

Tommy got the message immediately, and doing what he'd been trained to do, he dashed to find me a pot to throw up in. Grabbing one from the counter, he thrust it under my nose.

The General's reaction was instantaneous: he recoiled in horror, then motioned for the other soldiers to clear out. As I lifted my head out of the pot, I saw the backs of six sweaty behinds go flying up the companionway, while Roger and the kids followed to help them off the boat. It seemed best that I stay put, since my giggles were barely under control.

When Roger returned to the cabin, he wore a triumphant grin. "Well, you sure sent them on their way in a hurry," he chuckled.

"Can you blame them?" Sitting back, I took a deep breath. "This cabin must be 120 degrees. The thought of someone losing his lunch in here would make me run, too."

Roger studied me for a minute. "You know, you ought to consider taking up smuggling. You could become a millionairess. Besides using tricks no one has ever thought of, you are a remarkable actress."

"Who was acting? I was scared silly!"

"So was I." he smiled, and his hand shook slightly when he poured us both a cup of coffee.

We began the task of putting the mess back together again, and the kids opened the ports to let in the fresh air. Tommy seemed stirred up by all the excitement. "Did you notice those guns?" he asked, his eyes were huge.

"Who could miss them?" I cringed.

Ron wasn't so impressed. "They wouldn't have worked! There were parts missing, and two of them had safety pins holding them together."

Somehow that piece of information did not make me feel any better, and all of a sudden, I was very tired. I gave the kids a lesson assignment then, going forward, I climbed into my bunk for a much-needed nap. As usual Roger was already in bed, and asleep. Without any doubt cruising was strenuous work.

Haitian house

Cap Haitien had been poor, but not exceedingly so. The people enjoyed an abundant supply of tourist dollars from the cruise ships, and rain was not as scarce as in the rest of the country, but the haunting gray children who had appeared on the dock from time to time were a reminder to us that Haiti needed help. And though we knew it, we were not prepared for the poverty we found in St. Nicholas Mole.

An oppressive heat radiated off the powdery white earth and burned through the soles of our shoes as we walked up the street from the docks.

Sailing Against the Wind – Toni Larson 281

The gray children were everywhere. They sat on the sides of the road, or in the shade of their huts, and displayed little or no curiosity at our presence.

Beyond the children were the huts—hovels with dirt floors, no doors, no screens, no windows, and no furniture. At one a mother sat crumpled against a wall, a young child sprawled on her lap. Feeling a need to make some kind of contact, I stepped closer, then winced at the sight. The child's eyes followed my movements, but he didn't blink, even when tiny gnats swarmed across his face, and fed on his eyelids. Janice stopped, and I heard her suck in her breath as the scene registered, then she turned to clutch at her father's hand as if seeking his protection.

At the head of the street was the market. A tin roof, supported by four gnarled tree poles, providing a meager shade for the dozen women squatting on their dingy, faded blankets. The wares they hawked were pitiful: tiny mounds of beans and peanuts, hard juiceless oranges, salted and dried fish the size of sardines, and several foods with labels reading, "A Gift of the American People, Not to be Resold." The "gifts" of oil, powdered milk, and soybean powder were ladled out in miniscule portions, and the cost was dear.

It was finally clear to us, that food was not only scarce, it was expensive, and the entire wealth of this village combined did not equal what we spent in one month. Feelings of rage washed over me. Why couldn't someone DO something? Get organized? Find a way to store water and irrigate with it? It was an old Southern cliche, but it came to me then: These people were far too beaten to pull themselves up by their bootstraps.

Tommy tugged at my arm, and looking down, I saw I had been holding onto his hand so tightly his fingers were turning red. Dropping his hand, I searched around for Roger, Ron, and Janice. We'd seen enough. It was time to go back to the boat. I spied the others a block away, heading for a church at the edge of the village.

"Let's catch up," I urged Tommy, and we had started after them when a tiny boy of three or four stepped from the side of the road and directly into our path. The child's face was lifeless, a gray-brown mask as though carved from the earth. His severely distended stomach magnified the unusually small arms and legs, and his dull brown eyes were fixed, intently, on my blond, blue-eyed, very healthy son. The contrast in the two children was shocking.

"Hi," Tommy spoke first.

As if by magic, the child smiled, and I was moved to see his face come alive with pleasure. "*Maman!*" he shouted weakly. "*Le Blanc!*" Then the rarest of sounds emerged from his throat, a full-blown chuckle!

His mother rushed over, swooped the child up, muttered something that sounded like an apology, then skittered away into one of the huts.

Tommy gave me a peculiar look and I rumpled his hair. "He likes it," I tried to say, but my throat closed, and my eyes filled with tears. "Let's go," I mumbled and pulled him on toward the church.

As we walked, I glanced back over my shoulder. *What if my children had been born in St. Nicholas Mole?* Would it have been any different for them than it was for that sadly malnourished child? And if my own had begun life struggling merely to survive, would I have had any energy left to find the bootstraps, much less to pull on them? A twinge of shame for my earlier thoughts made me uncomfortable. How easy it is to have all the solutions, without ever having to face any of the problems.

Tommy and I stepped into the cool peace of the tiny Catholic church and found Roger and the kids talking to a priest not much older than thirty. We were introduced, and homesickness nudged when I heard his brisk Eastern Seaboard accent.

The pleasant-faced, sandy-haired man seemed anxious for us to stay a while, and to make sure that we would, he invited us to join him for a glass of lemonade. We gathered on the small patio outside the church and shared the pleasantries of getting acquainted. When a scrawny dog came close to sniff at our toes, the kids ran off with it to play a game of pitch and fetch.

With the kids gone for a while, our conversation turned to Haiti, and Roger asked the question that was foremost in my mind: "How do you like working in the Mole? I would think it would be very difficult."

He looked out toward the village and said, "Difficult? Yes, I suppose it is. I've been here five years and, in that time, nothing has changed, so I try not to think of it as difficult. That would only make it harder to get up each morning."

We asked him about the area, the people, and the church's role in the town, and he told us, "Haiti can boast about very few things. It is the poorest country in the Western Hemisphere, and it has more missionaries, and more prostitutes per capita than any country in the world. That should tell you something.

"As for the church's role here, I was a registered pharmacist in New York before I joined the priesthood. I'm able to use my small amount of knowledge to run a first aid station, and that is what takes most of my time. People come down out of these hills looking for a cure for their diseases—tuberculosis, cholera, typhoid, and malnutrition. But the most the government will allow me to do is supply band aids and say Mass for their dead.

"We run a small school, as does the Protestant mission on the other side of town, and together we teach them hygiene, to read and write, and to speak English. Hygiene is minimal with no water or toilet facilities. Reading and writing are worthless with no books or newspapers. And I'm not sure what they will ever use English for, other than to talk to the occasional sailor like yourselves."

The priest did not sound angry as I had felt earlier. He seemed instead to merely be relating the symptoms of a terminally ill patient, one who was taking a very long time to die. We sat for a while, looking out over the treeless, grassless, dusty town that surrounded the bay. We could see *Halcyon*'s masts above some of the rooftops. A native boat with tattered sails was tied to the makeshift dock and men, naked to the waist, loaded sacks of charcoal onto the deck of the boat.

"What do these people eat?" Roger asked, and I could hear my own frustration in his voice.

I added, "We stopped at the market and there wasn't enough food there to make one decent meal. And why is American food being sold? I thought that was given as aid."

"The packages marked, 'Gift from the American People' come mostly by way of the United Nations hunger relief agencies. We get some of them here at the church, and when we do, we announce it to the parishioners. They come by the droves. We divide up the food, but we never have enough to supply more than a meal or two per family. The bulk of the food seems to fall into the hands of one government official, or another, who in turn sells it under the counter for whatever he can get, and that is what you see in the markets. Eventually it ends up in the stomachs of the hungry, but at a very high price. And when you consider that the average Haitian earns less than sixty dollars a year you can imagine how dear that food is.

"The parent churches send food and clothes, too, and it helps, but that is not the answer. I am not sure if there is an answer."

When the kids joined us, we thanked the priest for his time and left.

Roger and I walked, side by side, while the kids raced ahead to the boat. No one had to tell us how lucky we were that they were healthy, happy, and well fed. I knew Roger's thoughts were following mine when he said, "That priest is doing a job that would tear the guts out of most people. I don't know if I could do it. It seems so hopeless."

The weather was calm, and the sky was robin's egg blue as *Halcyon* rounded Haiti's northern peninsula and entered the Windward Passage. The water beneath her hull changed from a murky brown to a royal purple streaked through with brilliant crystals of sunlight.

The soft wind pushed us slowly along as the kids and I sat at the handrail, our legs dangling over the side of the boat, our arms resting on the handrail.

"How deep is it?" Janice wondered.

"Twelve thousand feet," I answered but I had no more concept of the depth than she did.

She cocked her head and wrinkled her nose. "Is that a mile?"

"That's more than two miles!" Ron answered proudly.

We played a game of trying to illustrate twelve thousand feet of water, six thousand dads balanced on each other's shoulders, ten Empire State Buildings stacked like blocks. It was deeper than the Grand Canyon, almost as high as Pike's Peak, and when we were through, our minds still had not grasped the enormity of the depth, any more than we could imagine the vastness of space, how many teacups it would take to empty the ocean, or how much food it would take to feed all the "gray children" in the world. Some questions just don't have answers, but maybe they should.

Less than a month after that day, the priest from the Mole was arrested by the Haitian authorities under the charge of illegally dispensing medications. His trial was still pending when we left Haiti.

CHAPTER 16: A BIRD IN THE HAND IS A BIG MESS!

Two days of sailing brought us to the main docks at Port au Prince. Tying up behind a freighter out of Miami, we left the kids on board to guard the boat and went looking for someone to stamp our passports.

It took an hour of waiting in line before the necessary immigration officer with the proper rubber stamp saw fit to cover three more pages in our booklets with black smudgy ink. A few blocks from the harbor, we found the post office and spent a second hour trying to learn if we had any mail. It was useless. No one spoke English and our guidebook French produced giggles, but no mail.

At the telegraph office Roger dispatched a wire to the *Bewitched* in the Virgin Islands to let George know we had arrived in Port au Prince and would await word from him. With that done, we headed back to the boat.

The city was hot, dirty, and frighteningly noisy to our unaccustomed ears. Horns blasted, people shoved and shouted from every direction. Walking was made more difficult by the crowds that traveled with us— peddlers selling their straw baskets, beggars pleading for money, people wanting to guide for us, and the "just curious." My head ached with the confusion of it all, and when we passed a tiny house that appeared to be operating as a restaurant, I urged Roger, "Let's stop in here for something to drink. It looks like a very clean restaurant." He didn't object.

We entered and chose a table by the door. It was covered with an oilcloth so worn that the original pattern was no longer discernible, but it appeared clean and the room was comfortable. A large Casablanca-style fan hummed overhead in an attempt to cool the hot humid air. Humphrey Bogart would have fit right in.

A young girl in a brightly flowered dress approached, her soft cafe au lait cheeks painted with two bright spots of rouge. When she reached our table, Roger held up two fingers and ordered. "Beer, please."

The girl returned quickly, set the ice-covered bottles down in front of us, then took a seat herself. Roger looked amused. I was startled at the familiarity, but nodded politely when she asked, "Are you American?" Her accent was almost as heavy as her makeup.

"What you like?" She gave us a too-friendly smile.

"These are fine," Roger held up his beer. Noticing a twinkle in his eyes, I wondered what he knew that I didn't

"You go together?" the girl asked, pointing at both of us.

"Yes, we're married," I answered quickly. The situation was uncomfortable, but I still wasn't sure why.

Then she asked, "You want one girl or two?"

"We don't want ANY girls!" I spoke much too loudly.

Roger made a gargle sound into his beer, and when I glanced at him, he was laughing! Not only did he know where we were, he'd known all along!

Our table companion spoke again, saying "If you want boys, we have."

I shook my head vigorously. Roger made another choking noise. The girl went on to explain that her rooms were clean, that all her girls had had their penicillin shots (she pronounced it "penny see leen"), and that we could see her license. I just kept shaking my head and signaling for Roger to finish his beer. He seemed to be in no hurry.

The girl talked on and on, offering services that I wasn't sure of, and certainly did not intend to ask about. Finally, Roger drained the last swallow from his bottle, and we got up to leave. As we stepped through the door, she called out loudly, "Only five dollars! I give a good time!"

I answered by grabbing Roger's arm and dragging him down the street. He chuckled all the way to the boat.

The next morning, Roger, the kids, and I walked over to the Yacht Club to find Angela, Gilbert, and Zack, our cruising friends from Great Inagua. It felt like family as we hugged, kissed, and shared our experiences of the previous few weeks. Angela assured us that the raft was in good shape and waiting for us to retrieve it. Gilbert said they had just bought a small sailing dinghy to replace the raft, and naturally, Ron and Tommy volunteered to test it out for them.

Later in the afternoon we moved *Halcyon* to the Yacht Club and tied her next to their boat. It was so welcome to have them for neighbors. Though Angela was fifteen years older than Janice, they struck a friendship that could not have been closer than if they'd been the same age. Angela took Janice everywhere with her, taught her things about shopping, sewing, and cooking. Janice taught Angela English.

And for the boys, the common denominator was that sailing dinghy. No day went by that half of it wasn't spent racing that dinghy around the harbor. Age or language differences meant nothing—it was skill that counted most. A measure of true friendship lies in the trading, and ours was the truest as we traded knowledge, recipes, tools, spices, clothes, sail thread, as well as our native customs and folk songs.

Each morning, Roger continued to check the post office, but there was never any mail for us. Gilbert volunteered to go with him once, but they had no luck. Another day we resorted to hiring an English-speaking guide, but that didn't help either. Roger guessed we were getting the run around, but more likely there was something that eluded us about dealing with the Haitian Civil Service.

Whatever the reason, we thought we'd try the American Embassy. Maybe they could clue us in. Besides, we were eager to explore the city.

Leaving the kids in the hands of Andrea, Gilbert, and Zack, Roger and I set off in search of the Embassy. An American flag on the front of a large white stucco building told us we had arrived, and as we entered the sparsely decorated, tiny waiting room, we found a Marine sitting behind a glass partition. Looking up from his newspaper, he frowned when we introduced ourselves. When we told him what we needed, he shrugged us off. "I can't help you," he said.

Startled by the cold shoulder, we waited for him to say more, but he returned to his paper. We'd been dismissed. But Roger would not give up so easily. "Where are you from?" he asked in an effort to break through the impersonality of the glass.

"The States," came the bored reply.

"Is there anyone here that might help us?" I tried, and at the same time, I wondered if this was the usual reception for visitors.

He gave me a long cool look, then sighed, stood up, and disappeared through the door to return with another American, dressed in suit and tie. "'What do you need?" the man asked curtly.

We explained for the second time, but he wouldn't let us finish before he answered with, "I can't help you." And without further word, he exited through the inner door, slamming it in his wake.

As we stepped out onto the hot sidewalk, Roger swore, "I sure hope we never have to call on them in an emergency!"

"I know what you mean." My blood was boiling. "If I could say, 'Yankee go home' in Creole, I'd start an anti-American demonstration right now!"

Roger liked the idea and promised to keep up the kid's schoolwork while I served my time in jail. Then he stopped teasing to quickly point across the street and ask, "What is that?"

I looked to see a very modest, white stucco building with large black letters painted on the window. It was the Spanish word for "help" or "care." The word seemed somehow to fit our need, and I said, "Maybe someone in there speaks English. But if not, we can always try out our rusty Spanish."

Crossing the street, we opened the door and found a half dozen young people milling about. After asking a few of them, "Speak English? *Habla Espanol*?" one friendly young lady responded. She motioned for us to follow her, then led the way down a hall and into an office.

The attractive, well-dressed gentleman sitting behind the desk introduced himself as Graham from South Carolina and he seemed genuinely eager to help us.

Sitting down, we explained our situation. When we told him about our mail problems, he called in a worker, and in Creole, dispatched the man to the post office. While we waited, we learned about his organization: a hunger relief program funded by the United Nations. We also learned the do's and don'ts of sightseeing in Port au Prince, instructions on how to boil the water and what to eat and not to eat, and at the end of fifteen minutes we had some good advice, an invitation to dinner with his family, *and our mail*!

Best of all, Graham restored our faith in our fellow Americans.

The kids were on the deck of the boat waiting for us, as excited about receiving mail as we were. Tommy opened a letter from his cousin, Mike, that made him laugh, then run to hide it under his pillow. Janice received pen-pal letters full of games, puzzles, pictures, and Ron heard from a special friend he'd left behind in Miami. We opened Christmas cards, letters from family, and even some junk mail that Mother had sent along for good measure. Sears was running a sale on winter coats and a travel agency wanted to send us to Florida for the winter.

We were all feeling the pangs of homesickness when I reached the bottom of the stack and found an envelope with handwriting that looked wrenchingly familiar. Postmarks covered most of the front, a few more appeared on the back, and they clearly told of our path over the previous two years— the Keys, New Orleans, Miami, the Bahamas.

I started to read, but it was difficult as tears kept getting in the way. The letter was from Roger's mother Ruth, and the date at the top revealed it had been written six weeks before her death. "Where are you now?" she'd asked. "I know you are having a good time. Please write and send some pictures, especially of the kids."

As I put the letter in Roger's hands, I could see the dawn of recognition on his face, and the pain that followed. Abruptly he stood, stuffed the letter into his pocket, and disappeared into the forward cabin, closing the door behind him. For Roger, that letter was a reminder that he had not been there when she died. On our last visit with her she had outwardly accepted Roger's decision to cruise on a boat though she surely must have feared for our safety. What mother wouldn't? But she'd been supportive, and now, leaning back in the deck chair and looking out at the alien city before me, I could feel her presence still. Our Guardian Angel, watching over us. I could even hear her Norwegian epithet as she witnessed some of the ridiculous predicaments we kept getting ourselves into and out of.

"OOFTA!" she would say.

She was there and for the first time in two years, I was sure, we were going to be all right. But at the time I was gaining the faith, Roger was in the process of losing his.

Port au Prince was a larger edition of Cap Haitien, the narrow streets, the pastel stucco buildings, the wrought iron balconies—and if one didn't look too closely, or breathe too deeply, it was a pretty city. Dramatic mountains rose rapidly from the Bay, and between the water and the peaks lay a city, that in appearance belied the fact that it housed a population of close to a million people.

Situated at the base of the city was the filthiest harbor we'd seen anywhere. Rivers of raw sewage rushed through the open gutters beside the streets, flowed into the bay, and covered the water with a gray sudsy foam. The stench from it made us gag. Few fish survived in the airless septic environment, and if we'd bothered to catch anything, we never would have dared to eat it.

Swimming was the only means of bathing for many of the people, though it was strictly off-limits to our own kids and if any water splashed on them, they were sent immediately to the clubhouse shower to wash it off. The most serious problem from the bay water bathtub was typhoid, and it was a constant threat to the population. Grant had warned us of the dangers. Using his instructions, we purchased trucked-in water (at fees far too exorbitant for the average Haitian to afford), boiled it, doctored it, and still I worried.

Overpopulation, lack of rainwater, inadequate sewage treatment facilities, and abject poverty were all reasons for the pollution and diseases suffered by the city, and nowhere was it more evident than along the waterfront, where most of the population conducted their business. Painters, wood carvers, fruit and vegetable vendors, and basket weavers displayed their wares on the sides of the streets, and thousands of them came from the surrounding mountains, walking for days, to carry their merchandise to the market. And there they lived on the streets, until everything was sold.

It took us a while to get used to so much closeness, but once we adjusted, we found the people to be surprisingly cheerful, friendly, and honest. And it was a relief to experience no hostility or anti-American feelings. Often, the reverse was the case. Our difference in skin color was regarded as a novelty worthy of notice and sometimes gentle teasing. Because of his fair skin and blond hair, Tommy soon became as well known in Port au Prince as he had been in Cap Haitian. Ron and Janice had the advantage over us by being so suntanned they were able to move freely through the crowds without creating a stir. And Roger was called "Cap" by everyone we passed on the street, a title that stemmed from the natural camaraderie between the cruising sail boaters and the islanders.

But to me, the friendliness was sometimes disconcerting. One day, I went for a walk, alone, along the seawall, and as was usual, a young boy about thirteen came up to me and began his hustle.

"Hi, Missy. You need a guide?"

"No, thank you," I dismissed him.

"Are you from the big ship?" he said as he pointed to one of the cruise ships at the dock.

"No." I kept on walking.

But he was persistent. "Are you from hotel? Ah, I know. You live on hill with rich people, right?"

Though I was thinking I should ignore him, I answered anyway. "No."

Confused, he stopped for a second, then took a few skips to catch up and stand directly in front of me with his hands on his hips and his head tilted back to look into my eyes. "Okay, I give up. Where you stay?"

"On that sailboat over there." and I pointed at *Halcyon*.

He looked at the boat, back at me, then back to the boat, before he understood. Slowly the corners of his mouth turned upward, and his eyes twinkled as he said, "Well, Hello, Baby!"

Laughing at his reaction, I shooed him away, but before he rounded the corner he waved and called, "See you, Missy."

It was not only the open friendliness that seemed incongruous to the city, but also the sense of humor in the people was a delightful surprise. On one shopping expedition, we tired of walking and had stopped an English-speaking street urchin to ask him the whereabouts of the bus stop.

"Bus?" he asked with a puzzled look, then he grinned broadly, patted his rump, and exclaimed, "Tap, Tap! You want Tap, Tap!"

Later, I asked Angela how the name came about, and she explained, "Tap Tap is what you're behind does to the seat as you bounce along the street. It is a very good name for those buses, don't you agree?"

She was right. The bus system of Port au Prince was the most colorful and most efficient transportation system of any we'd ever seen. Minibuses, station wagons, and pickup trucks with cabins built on the back serviced ninety percent of the population at the cost of pennies per person.

We never had to wait for more than five minutes on any corner, anywhere for a bus, even though they followed no set route or schedule. Speed limits were to spit at, and if the weather was bad or particularly hot, the wildly smiling, suicidal drivers would obligingly take the passengers right to their doors or boat.

The market was a nightmare to me. I could not get inside the door that mobs of women did not descend, each one trying to convince me that their cabbages were the best or the cheapest. Sometimes it took hours for me to complete the shopping and I always came away feeling exhausted.

For a while I let Ron do the marketing. His suntan disguised the fact that he was a "rich, white, American," and he moved in and out of the stalls without creating even a ripple in the crowd. Because he didn't speak French, we hired a young boy named Charles to be his guide. The two of them made an unbeatable team and became good friends in the process. Together they never failed to get everything on my list, and at bargain prices—but most of all Ron received an education he would never forget.

At the end of his expeditions, Ron took center stage as he told of meeting a Voodoo priestess and another time, a lady selling cockroaches, the BIG ones!

When we asked Charles why cockroaches were sold, he replied, "Some people eat them. They are good!"

Janice went into such spasms of revulsion, Ron couldn't resist one further tidbit, "They eat CATS, too!" he said.

"Ron!" Janice clutched her throat. "You're just trying to make me sick."

"Nope." Ron was obviously pleased at being the conveyor of gross details. "I saw a lady sell a cat to someone, and Charles said people eat them on special holidays."

Charles smiled and nodded, but Janice looked pale as she mumbled, "I'm glad Sea Coral is in Biloxi."

The market may have been an education to Ron, but to Roger it was the best part of Haiti. One day he decided to explore further and put the motorbike on the dock.

The bike had not been off the boat since Key West, and it showed. Roger stood beside it looking at the mass of rust and salt deposits that had accumulated over the previous months, then he walked around it and kicked off great clumps of corrosion. I had my doubts about whether it would run, but I was not the only one. A small crowd of onlookers had gathered to watch, and one bystander spoke his mind: "Cap, Dot bike no damn good!"

Roger looked at him, grinned, climbed onto the seat, whacked the starter down once, and to everyone's amazement, the motor roared into action. "Doubting Thomas" just shook his head in stunned disbelief.

Roger's trips included a stop at the post office, another at the wire office to see if George had responded to our message, then a run by the market for fresh groceries. Soon this became a daily ritual.

Each morning, he got up early, donned his faded cut-offs, holey tennis shoes, a raggedy shirt, and topped it all with the Captain's hat that had turned a little frayed around the edges.

Once, when I complained about his appearance, he answered with "If I look better than this, I get charged double. It takes extreme measures to get any pity in Haiti." Then he went outside, climbed aboard the bike, kicked it into action, and wheeled away down the crowded street. Doubting Thomas always seemed to be present for the send-off, as though waiting for the chance to say, "I told you so." Roger never gave him the opportunity.

Along the way, the street vendors would call, "Bon Jour, Capitan," and occasionally, "Sacre Bleu," or "Mon Dieu," for emphasis. I never dared guess what they meant by it.

Roger was born with a sweet tooth, and a no-fail sensing device. After stopping at the post office and the wire office, he headed for the French bakery next door to the market. His radar seemed to know exactly what time of the morning a fresh batch of honey raisin muffins came out of the oven, and the proprietress of the store must have taken pity on him because she faithfully tossed in a few extra muffins on top of the baker's dozen she'd already provided. With bag in hand, Roger would lock up the bike and enter the market to find another of his girlfriends, the Egg Lady.

Egg Lady was ancient (probably my age), near toothless, and she had a stall that sold only eggs. The first time Roger met her, he actually gave her one of his precious muffins. From then on, whenever he appeared, she insisted that he sit beside her on a three-legged stool and flirted openly with him as she showed him how to separate the good eggs from the bad.

Then to show he was her favorite customer, she would call over to the other vendors and proceed to fill my grocery list by selecting the best of the fruits and vegetables as they were paraded before her stall. Roger and Egg Lady could spend a full hour together, bargaining for groceries, sharing jokes, and eating all the muffins though neither of them spoke a word of the other's language. But I got the best bargains—and all my groceries.

Roger gained five pounds before word came from George that the *Bewitched* would be on the south coast of Haiti in ten days. That seemed like plenty of time for us to get there, and even be waiting when they arrived.

Before we could leave, Roger had to do a minor engine checkup, and in the process, he noticed an unusual amount of exhaust in the engine room. Hoping to get rid of whatever was causing it, he changed the oil, replaced some old odds and ends, and pronounced the problem cured.

Next came the formality of clearing the country, a process that ended up taking four days, and was the perfect example of a bureaucratic merry-go-round. Roger took the passports and boat's papers to the same office that had stamped us in, but that wasn't enough. The official informed Roger he needed a picture of the family for the government record.

Roger rushed to the boat, dug out a family photo that looked presentable, and returned with it to the Immigration office. The photo wasn't good enough. The government wanted individual photos, in triplicate.

Back at the boat, Roger rounded us up and whisked us off to the photographer, unbathed, unchanged, and uncombed. Several hours later he returned with photos in hand.

Another trip to the official's office where stamps were applied, and one set of photos was handed over. "Where do the other pictures go?" Roger asked. He should have kept his mouth shut. He was given addresses of more offices, half of which turned out to be closed for someone's funeral.

Two days later Roger was still trying to find someone to take the other photos when he walked into an office filled with one desk, one chair, and three employees. He put the papers on the desk, then one girl sat down, took out the proper purple seal, and stamped away in four places. She stood and a second sat down, selected another seal, and repeated the stampings. The third employee took the pictures. The papers were finally completed!

That night after dinner, Roger and I took out the passports and looked at the mess of blue, black, and purple ink blobs.

"Very impressive, indeed," he said, and he picked up one of the booklets. "Like this one right here," and he pointed at a large purple seal.

"What do you suppose it says?"

"Don't open 'til Christmas."

Haiti is shaped like a giant horseshoe, and the Bay of Gonave makes up the water between the north and south arms of the "shoe." Port au Prince sits at the very center of the curve, and the Windward Passage crosses the open end. Situated in the middle of the bay is a very large island called Gonave, and though surrounded by reefs, shoals, and treacherous water, it also supplies a lee shore for anchoring.

Angela, Gilbert, and Zack stood on the dock and saw us off as we motored away on the twenty- mile trip to Gonave Island and the first leg of our trip to meet *Bewitched*. We didn't have even a breath of wind and knew we'd have a motorboat ride all day, but Roger was sure we'd be safely at anchor before dark. Ten miles out of Port au Prince, *Halcyon* began to lose power, and Roger went below to check it out. The engine room was full of smoke! He shut down the motor, but after two hours of trying to sail with no wind, he started it up again, and we limped slowly toward Gonave Island.

The fathometer was still not registering bottom when the sun dipped below the mountains on the island, and all the lights went out. "Damn this country!" Roger muttered from the wheel. "They could at least run one navigation light."

"I'd better get the grapple ready," I said. "It's the best anchor in this coral." And I dashed forward to dig in the deck box for it. The box was a mess. Anchor, line, and chain were turned upside down, and hadn't been straightened since our arrival in Port au Prince. The best shackles were on the wrong anchors, the shackle on the grapple was frozen with salt, I couldn't find the pliers, and I stubbed my toe. My anger was evident when I yelled back, "Roger!" Far be it for me to complain, but this mess...."

He ignored me. "You better toss out the lead line. I think we're getting close to the reef."

Nursing my toe, I looked around, but it was too dark to see beyond the deck. Ron came up with the spotlight to scan the water, and I went back to looking for the lead line. It wasn't where it should have been. "I can't find it," I wailed.

"Try the tackle box!" Le Capitan ordered.

And there it was, all tangled up with the fishing line, hooks, and seining net.

"Hurry up, Toni!" Roger shouted, then told Ron, "See if you can spot anything, I'm not getting a reading on the fathometer, but the chart says it comes up fast."

"I think I see something," Ron answered.

In near panic, I abandoned the lead line and ran back to the anchor. "Can't you shut this thing down?" I hollered.

"We're barely moving as it is. Do you want us to go backwards?" Roger smarted off. "What does the lead line say?"

"Who the heck knows?" I shrieked. "I'm trying to connect the anchor!"

Tommy and Janice popped their heads up from the hatches then flipped them back and forth as though watching a ping-pong match. Their crazy parents were at it again.

Though trying to control my anger, I couldn't resist asking, "Have you ever heard of the phrase, 'ship-shape'?"

"Ship-shape is the crew's responsibility," Roger answered imperialistically.

"Well, this crew member will not take responsibility for that mess!" And I pointed at the tangle of lines in the deck box.

It was a gentle impact of steel against coral, but it effectively ended the argument. Roger and I rushed to the side and gasped as Ron panned the light around at the jagged pieces of coral protruding above the water.

We were only resting the bow on the reef, and it took less than five minutes to kedge *Halcyon* off. However, I did wonder why we had to hit it to begin with—and said as much.

"Maybe you'd like to take over as Captain," he snarled. "And while you're at it, figure out what's wrong with the damn motor!"

Roger and Ron straightened out the deck gear while Janice and I fixed dinner, and by bedtime a truce had been declared. But I got in one last lick when the sun rose the next morning. Sitting up in my bunk, I peeked out the porthole, and for a moment couldn't figure out where we were. Blinking, I looked again, then began to giggle.

"What's the matter with you?" Roger asked as he sat up in his bunk.

"In two years, we've hit two docks, been rammed by a tanker, run aground more times than I care to count, but last night we very nearly topped them all. We almost hit *that house!*"

Roger was on deck in a flash, and I joined him to see less than a hundred yards off our port side a flat shelf of the reef, no bigger than the deck of the *Halcyon*. On that piece of rock sat a one-room, thatched-roof hut and it covered every square inch of the surface. If we had been a mere hundred yards to our left, we would have plowed the bowsprit right into some poor fisherman's front door.

We both agreed, with the engine still smoking, that the only sensible choice was to turn *Halcyon* back to Port au Prince for repairs. By the time we reached the Yacht Club we had no engine at all, and for the first time we sailed right up to a dock. It was a truly professional performance, but I added the experience to the list of things I have done once, and don't plan to do again.

Roger spent two days with the best diesel mechanic in town as they took the engine apart, put it together again, cleaned it, replaced filters, and repaired a variety of bolts and washers. The bill came to exactly two hundred and fifty dollars, the amount we had set aside for the next leg of the trip.

Since it would have taken a week to have more money wired from the States, we sold the dinghy engine to Zack and Gilbert for a hundred dollars, and kept our fingers crossed that it would be enough.

While Roger worked on the motor, I went up to the Yacht Club bar and asked the bartender if he knew how to get a message to Port Salud on the south coast of the island. He wasn't any help, but a drunk at the end of the bar was more than willing to come to my aid.

He turned out to be an American working on a construction crew and was due to fly by private plane to Port Salud the next day. As he mumbled about how lonely he was, I reached into my pocket, pulled out the letter to George, and handed it to the bleary-eyed man.

"Just give this to the Port Salud police, or to the Catholic priest if you can find one," I said.

"Sure, Shweety!" my messenger promised. I was skeptical about the chances that the letter would get through, but it was the best we could do on short notice.

Angela prepared a farewell dinner of Hungarian goulash, and Gilbert serenaded us on his guitar. They were all on the dock at daybreak to wave goodbye.

The wind was right. We had the sails up in no time and were enjoying the spectacular scenery as *Halcyon* sailed across the bay. There seemed no reason to stop, but as we neared the end of Gonave Island, the weather turned nasty, clouds rolled in from the north, and the waves whipped up viciously. Since we still had enough daylight to get close to shore and anchor, Roger decided to try for it. But the moment he started the engine, the boat looked like it was on fire! Turning around, we sailed back to Port au Prince.

Gilbert met us at the dock with only one question, "What do you Americans call that toy that goes up and down on a string? A yo-yo, I think."

Roger gave him a dirty look.

We hired a second mechanic, replaced the fuel-injector pump and some more filters, hoses, and belts. Bought enough spare parts to build two new engines and sold the motorbike to Doubting Thomas for enough money to cover the expenses. When we were through, we had about $20, and only one more day to meet George.

As we untied the dock lines for the third time, Gilbert stuck his head out of the hatchway of his boat, and called, "We will have dinner ready at six o'clock."

We sailed nonstop for forty-eight hours, then put in at a little port called Jeramie for fuel and a night's rest. While I fixed dinner and Roger tied down and covered the sails, Ron tried to reach George by radio, but he couldn't even pick up a passing ship. After dinner, Roger started the engine to test it; the smoke came back as thick as before.

It was an unhappy crew that went to bed that night, and it didn't get better when the next morning, our five-man raft was gone from its spot across the stern of the boat. Had it been stolen? Were the lines poorly tied? Did the wind blow it away? Only *Halcyon* knew, and she wasn't telling. But one thing for sure, when disaster strikes DUCK!

We left Jeramie with our last few dollars in our pocket, no life raft (except George's), no dinghy motor, no sewing machine, no motorbike, no wind, no word from the *Bewitched*, and almost no motor.

When I suggested we return to Port au Prince for another try at repairs, Roger roared, "If the whole damn boat burns to waterline, I am not going back into that miserable port!"

Crossing my fingers, I wondered if women and children still went first in the lifeboat. Since all we had left was the two-man raft and an inner tube, I figured that was a rather pertinent question.

Halcyon sailed into the Windward Passage, rounded the southern peninsula, and headed toward Port Salud. When the wind died, we turned on the engine, and huge clouds of smoke billowed behind us. But Roger was driven. He refused to turn the motor off until the wind picked up again, and once it did, we raised sails and he crawled into the engine room to tinker, swear, bang, and curse.

Through it all, Ron continued to call *Bewitched*, but no one answered. Two days later we limped into Port Salud, dropped sails and anchor. Only then did Roger crawl out of the engine room, so covered with

Sailing Against the Wind – Toni Larson 297

soot the whites of his eyes looked like neon lights, and so crabby he could hardly speak without growling. But we'd made it, a week overdue—and *Bewitched* wasn't there!

Port Salud was slightly larger than the Mole, not as poor, and far prettier. The houses were one room huts with thatch-palm roofs, and decorated, with homemade furniture and pictures from travel poster on the walls. Flowers grew in beds around the doorways, and a picturesque mountain stream flowed into the center of town, providing clean water for drinking and bathing.

A large white Catholic church overlooked the village, and we climbed the hill to meet Port Salud's only English-speaking resident, Father John from Ohio.

Father John invited us into his office and promptly established a lasting friendship with the kids by offering them Cokes, COLD Cokes.

"Are you the ones that sent that American here with the letter?" the priest asked.

"I hope he didn't give you any trouble," I apologized. "He was the only one I could find coming this way, and I thought he might be more reliable to carry a message than the Haitian Post Office."

"Oh, he was interesting," was the only comment Father John made about my drunken friend.

"How about the *Bewitched*?" Roger asked. "Did you meet George and Peg? Did you see the boat?"

"No, I haven't seen another sailboat in months, but that doesn't mean they were not anchored somewhere else along our coast. I would suggest you ask around the village, and perhaps someone else has seen them."

Father John returned our undelivered letter and gave each child a Coke for the road. We promised to visit him again before we left. With only the two-man raft, our mobility was definitely curtailed.

That afternoon we used the case of fishhooks to hire a native and his small skiff to taxi us back and forth from the boat to the town. As we walked the streets looking for anyone who had seen another sailboat, we discovered that most of the inhabitants were Cuban refugees and for the first time since arriving in Haiti we felt we could talk to the locals. But we couldn't find even a trace of George.

Roger even took a day to hitchhike into a neighboring town, only to return with no news. He had been thinking all along that having that "buddy boat" would make this entire leg of the trip safer and more enjoyable. "Someone to commiserate with," he said. It was finally dawning on him that we might never catch up to the *Bewitched*.

We were discouraged when we strolled up to the church again to visit with the kind priest, and enjoy for a while, the rare treat of conversing in English. Father John's office was comfortable with massive, overstuffed chairs and sofa, a large mahogany desk, and walls lined with bookshelves. Father John seemed intrigued with our adventure and soon we were describing the places we'd been and the things we'd seen.

When he heard about our motor trouble, running out of money, and being low on food, he laughed and said, "I guess sailing is not all sunsets and fair winds, as most people believe. But then, nothing in life is, I suppose."

We asked if there was any bank on the south coast where we might have our monthly allotment wired from the States.

"No, you would have to go back to Jeramie, and even then, you might have trouble getting money wired. The only sure place would be Port au Prince." I had only to look at Roger's face to see he had no intention of going back there.

While we chatted, a small red hen sashayed in through the outside door of the office, sauntered across the room, and jumped into the bookcase exactly as though she belonged there. The kids were charmed, and they wanted to know if they could have a pet chicken. I pretended not to hear. Since the loss of Sea Coral, they had been continuously asking for a pet of one kind or another, and every time I began to weaken, I forced myself to remember what life had been like with eight kittens.

But Roger didn't think the idea was so absurd. "A chicken sounds great! Then we could have fresh eggs every morning!"

I gave him a look that should have singed his hair and started to say something, when the chicken cackled, jumped down from the shelf, and waddled back out the door.

Janice dashed to the bookcase and picked up a very freshly laid egg. "Wow!" was her response as she held it up for us to see. "It's still warm!"

The priest smiled at her enthusiasm over the discovery. "Please keep the egg. Charlotte will never miss it. She has a terrible habit of leaving her eggs all over the rectory. See, here is one from yesterday." And he moved *Webster's Unabridged Dictionary* to reveal a second egg.

When it came time to go, we thanked Father John for the eggs and for his information. He offered one more piece of advice: "There is a European resort on the beach about three miles from here. They might cash a check for you and maybe they have seen your friends."

The next morning, we put on our hiking shoes, blew the horn for our taxi, and made the three-mile trek to find a sprawling beachside resort run by an Austrian woman named Dina.

"Oh, of course I met George and Peg!" the petite, gamin-faced woman said. "They anchored their lovely boat right there for a week." And she pointed out at a much protected, clear water cove. "But they have been gone for several days now. Are you the Larsons?"

We nodded and she went on in her nonstop chatter. "They left you a letter. I'll go up to the house and get it, and while you wait for me, please sit here by the pool. You can go swimming if you like. The kids would enjoy that, I'm sure. Or they might prefer to go horseback riding; just send them over there to see Danny. He works at the stable, and he'll pick out some gentle horses. I'll be right back." And she was gone.

Ron asked if they could go riding, Roger gave his permission, and the kids went bounding away to look for Danny.

We sat down under a Martini Rossi umbrella and looked around at the beautiful setting of Spanish-style bungalows situated between the snowy white beach to the south, and the rolling green meadows to the north. Horses grazed on the hillside, and we saw several guests riding along the surf. Beyond the pool was a shuffleboard court, a tennis court, an outdoor band stage, dance floor, and a bar with a hand lettered sign hanging from a bamboo pole, "Bartender off duty, mix your own, put money in the till and CLEAN UP YOUR MESS!"

The cordiality and serenity of the surroundings was so overwhelming that I sat there like one of the kids with mouth open, and eyes big as saucers. We could hear the waves lapping on the beach, a horse neighing in the distance, and Dina's voice as she called a greeting to a guest on the tennis court.

The atmosphere was such a contrast to the Port au Prince harbor that I could not help but make the comparison, and knew Roger was thinking much the same thing when he said, "George and Peg spent a WEEK here?"

I chuckled. "Can you imagine? Riding horses and playing tennis all day, swimming in a pool, eating European cuisine at night, dancing by starlight, then sleeping on a sailboat off that gorgeous beach? My, how they must have suffered while they waited for us."

Leaning back in the lawn chair, Roger stretched out his legs, and sighed. "Somehow I don't think it's the same as spending a week in a three-by-four-foot soot-filled engine room."

Dina returned with the letter, then excused herself while we read." Dear Larsons: We waited for you for a week, then decided you'd changed your minds. We are on our way to Panama, then back to California. Catch us if you can. Bon Voyage. George, Peg, and Kids. P.S. Dina is a Doll!"

Tucking the letter in my pocket, I said, "Well, what do we do now? Panama is a week away over open sea. Do we go after them?"

Roger looked thoughtful. "I don't see how we can chance it. There is something seriously wrong with the motor, and I still can't figure out what it is. It might not matter if the trade winds are steady enough for us to sail all the way, but what if someone fell overboard? That's frightening to think about without the option of a motor."

It was surprising to hear Roger even suggest the possibility of such a disaster. We had learned the rescue drills and practiced them often, but I had always thought Roger did them to appease me, not because he took the possibility of such an event seriously. Obviously, he did. And he did not seem disappointed that George had gone on without us.

Wondering about other alternatives, I said, "We could always go back to the Bahamas. We have all those charts, and there are about three hundred islands we haven't seen yet." Surprisingly, the idea interested me. "Besides, one of those islands may have a good diesel mechanic."

Roger frowned. "I agree on one thing, we have to get the motor repaired as soon as possible. Then we need to find someplace to stop sailing. Don't you think it's time to get off that boat?"

My mouth flopped open for the second time that morning, and I stared at him in stunned silence. Had he really said it? Did he mean it?

Before I could find out, Dina arrived leading a large swarthy, middle-aged man by the hand. "I want you two lovely people to meet my nice friend from Jamaica. Burke, these are the Larsons."

We shook hands and invited our new acquaintance to join us under the umbrella. "You must get to know each other," Dina went on. "Burke is here on vacation, he arrived this morning.

"Now I have to go see if the chef has lunch ready. You must stay for lunch; we are having lobster salad and mango torte for dessert. The kids will love the torte. Where are they now? Oh, I see them up there on the riding trail. Well, see you later." And she was gone in a flurry.

Burke was indeed a nice man. We talked for an hour, then had lunch by the pool. The kids loved the mango torte. Roger quizzed Burke endlessly about Jamaica, and its very unsettled politics, and when he asked, "Where is the best town on the Jamaican coast to live?" I knew he had something in mind.

Burke did not even hesitate. "Negril. It is a popular resort town and there is always work there, even when the rest of the island is suffering from unemployment and political turmoil. It is also the most beautiful spot in all of Jamaica."

When Danny came over to tell us he was driving into Port Salud and would be happy to give us a ride, we collected the kids, thanked Dina for her kindnesses, and left. As we bounced over the rutty road to Port Salud in the back of the hotel pickup truck, Roger remarked, "On our next trip around the world, I want to stay only in hotels like Dina's."

The handwriting was on the wall, in letters large enough for me to read. The cruise was almost over!

Engines repel me. They smell, they vibrate, they belch, they guzzle fuel, and they always break down when they are needed the most. *Halcyon's* motor was no exception. Roger spent another day playing mechanic before he gave up altogether. Whatever was wrong was going to take an expert to repair and cost an arm and a leg in the process.

So where were we going to find an expert? On our seventh day in Port Salud, Roger drug out all the charts, cruising books, a National Geographic map of the Caribbean, and we looked at the alternatives. Port au Prince was out! We both agreed on that. The other towns in Haiti were too small to rely on them having mechanics and/or banks. The same was true of the Bahamas except for Nassau, and that was over four hundred miles away. Florida was more than five hundred. The Dominican Republic was to the east which meant sailing upwind against the trades, but Jamaica was to the west and downhill all the way.

"We don't have any charts on Jamaica," I protested. That seemed riskier than not having an engine.

"But the National Geographic map shows a blow-up of Kingston Harbor, including the water depths. If we enter it at high noon, we should be able to navigate by sight, and Kingston is a large city.
There would be no problem getting the engine repaired."

But I knew there was another reason that Roger wanted to go to Jamaica, and I thought about our conversation with Burke. "Roger, are you thinking of staying in Jamaica?"

"Well, I've been considering it. The Island is English speaking, and there are no work restrictions on foreigners. With my restaurant background it might be possible for me to get a manager's job in one of the resort hotels.

"But what about the politics? The Island is on the verge of an uneasy election. And what about the kids?"

"I think the kids would enjoy going to school on an island. They were even ready to enroll in the one on Farmer's Cay. And as for the politics, Burke says the coming election will change all that. And if we've learned anything in Haiti, it is that the people of the area are not necessarily the same as the government." When he saw the doubt on my face he quickly added, "But we can decide those things when we get to Jamaica."

(If we had been reading any newspapers over the previous six months, we probably would not have chosen to go. What we knew about Jamaica's troubles wasn't much, and typical of all cruising sailors, we truly believed we could stay out of the way of politics.)

On our last visit to see Father John, he expressed his concern over our lack of funds and motor. We assured him we would be fine, but I had the feeling he didn't believe it. As we started to leave, he gave me a small package and said, "I will pray for your safe voyage."

We stopped in the market and I bought some bananas, mangoes, and a pumpkin. Looking around after making my purchases, I noticed Roger and the kids talking to an old man with a crate full of chickens. "Oh no!" I squealed and went flying over to demand what they were up to. "You can't turn us into a poultry farm!"

"Wouldn't you like to have fried chicken one night?" Roger asked innocently. "It's been months since we've had any."

The kids agreed it was a splendid idea. "We can keep the chicken on the deck and fatten it up," Ron beamed.

"And maybe it would lay eggs for us." Janice took up the cause.

"Sure," said Roger. "Fresh eggs every morning would be nice. Don't you agree, Toni?" He was as much a kid as they were.

I answered with a growl. "Oh yes, we could have fresh eggs, and fresh fertilizer to go on the fresh plants we can grow in the fresh air on the deck. And you are fresh out of good sense!"

But I lost the vote, and Roger paid one dollar for a scrawny bedraggled-looking bird that obviously hadn't had a square meal in its whole life. The chicken was dumped unceremoniously into a gunny sack, and Roger slung it over his shoulder as we headed back to the boat.

On board *Halcyon*, Ron tethered the chicken to the binnacle, and I forgot all about it as we made ready to leave Haiti. Roger started the smoky motor, we raised anchor, and *Halcyon*'s bow turned toward the open ocean. When the church bells began to ring, we looked to see Father John waving from the side of the church. We waved back.

It was then I remembered the package he had given us and went below to retrieve it from our market purchases. Removing the wrapping, I found a five-pound bag of something that looked like flour, but the English label read, "Hi Protein Mix a Gift from the American People-Not to be Resold." Somehow it seemed like a perfect farewell gift from Haiti.

First the food disappeared. Some leftover biscuits I had made at breakfast and saved for lunch were not where I'd left them, and when I looked around the galley, I found that someone had been in the oatmeal, the raisins, and the protein mix Father John had given us. Obviously, the noises I'd heard when I'd been resting in my bunk were more than just mice. Going up on deck, I found Roger napping on a cushion, Ron at the wheel, and Tommy and Janice trying to force-feed a biscuit into the chicken's beak.

"What is going on here?" I demanded with my hands on my hips.

Janice was quick to explain, "He didn't like the oatmeal or that stuff from Father John."

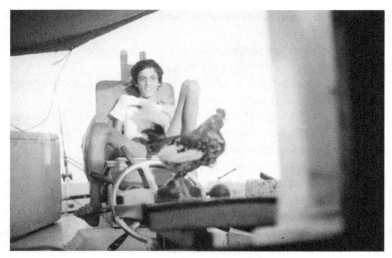

Ron at the wheel with rooster.

Tommy added, "Sea Coral likes raisins though."

"Sea Coral?" I sat down on the cushion next to Roger and tried to calm my anger as I insisted, "We are not going to keep a pet chicken on this boat!"

"Can't we just name him, Mom?" Tommy looked at me with pleading eyes. "Don't you think 'Sea Coral the Second' is a good name?"

I could feel Roger shaking as he tried to stifle a laugh, and it only made me more annoyed. "Roger, this is not funny. You could at least watch these kids when I'm not up here. They are going to empty the larder into that chicken." Then I spied my best towels in a pile on the deck. "What are those doing here?" I shrieked.

"Sea Coral's nest." The tone of Janice's voice suggested I should have known without asking. "She has to have someplace to lay her eggs."

As if to stress the point, Sea Coral II hopped up onto the binnacle, dropped a little pile of wet goo over west by southwest, and crowed!

Roger was convulsed with laughter as I poked him in the side. "Didn't someone say we were going to get eggs from that chicken?"

"I Um Hmm," was his muffled reply.

"Can't you tell a rooster from a hen?" My resolve cracked and I began to laugh with him.

Roger raised his head and tried to compose his face into a serious expression. "Well, next time I'll check under the tail feathers."

"Oh no! There won't be a next time!" I was determined. "That rooster is going in a pot as soon as the weather is calm enough to cook him!"

The kids protested, but I meant it.

Our first day out of Port Salud was the best. A twenty-knot wind moved us steadily along, and the kids had no trouble holding the wheel during the day. They also were entertained by the rooster trying to balance himself on the binnacle with the boat heeled twenty degrees to starboard.

Following the Haitian coast all afternoon, we stayed far enough off shore to avoid any shoaling water. After an easy dinner of fruit and sandwiches, Tommy and Janice went to bed, and Roger and I had coffee on the deck and watched the stars come out.

About nine o'clock, with Roger at the wheel and Ron keeping him company, I went to bed. It felt so good to be sleeping again with the natural rhythms of the boat moving through the water. *Halcyon* rode smoothly, and only the slight swish of the water rushing along the hull broke the silence. The feel of the boat as she lifted over the tops of the waves and settled back into the troughs was as soothing a motion as sitting in a rocking chair on a lazy afternoon. Once more I was reminded that Halcyon means peaceful.

After a sound sleep, (which seemed like only seconds,) Ron was waking me to take my turn at the wheel.

I dressed, switched on the galley light, poured a cup of coffee, then made my way up onto the dark deck. The stars were brilliant, and even the silhouette of Haiti's mountains could be seen in the north. "How much longer before we clear the island?" I asked Roger as I hooked the lifeline to my vest, then slipped into the Captain's seat. "We'll be in the Windward Passage by morning," he answered. As he started below to make a fresh pot of coffee, he turned and made a suggestion. "You might check the compass heading. We haven't had to readjust the sails in over twelve hours, but it's been a while since we've checked our course."

Putting down the coffee cup, I turned on the deck light, and was assaulted by the most horrifying noise on earth—Sea Coral crowed! My scream startled that rooster almost as much as he startled me, and we both came very close to jumping over opposite sides of the boat.

I let loose with a stream of colorful language, and Roger called from the galley, "Do you always have to scream?"

"Can you blame me? A *cock-a-doodle-do* twenty miles from land is enough to scare anyone to death! And why can't that dumb bird tell the sun from a twelve-volt light bulb?"

I was a little calmer when Roger came up on deck with the fresh coffee. He was amused but I was determined that his good humor would not affect my decision. "We are having rooster and dumplings for dinner tomorrow night. I don't care if it's blowing a gale!"

"Shall we draw straws to see who wrings his neck?" Roger teased.

"Nope. It's your bird!"

Sailing Against the Wind – Toni Larson   305

The rooster survived thirty-six more hours, then Roger beheaded it. The kids objected, Janice cried and called us cannibals, but I relished every mouthful of that chicken stew. As I tossed the bones into the foaming wake of the boat, Roger came to stand beside me, and he had a thoughtful look. "You know, we could build a chicken coup out over the stern of the boat, and the droppings would fall in the water. Then there wouldn't be a mess, and we could still have fresh eggs every morning for breakfast."

I studied him carefully. There had been a time when I would have called him conservative, predictable, and even saner than most, but that was a very long time ago. Raising kids on a boat might be crazy, but chickens? "Roger, sometimes I feel like I'm reliving Alice in Wonderland, and you are the Mad Hatter."

"Well, hens don't crow," he said in all seriousness.

"Off with your head!"

It was only appropriate that, as we entered the Windward Passage, the wind died, the water turned glassy calm, and we drifted. Roger tried the motor, but the smoke continued to choke it, and finally he shut it down for good. Swift currents carried us north, and by my calculations, we were going to miss Jamaica entirely if a breeze didn't arrive, and soon. With our luck, when we hit Cuba, it would not be Guantanamo Bay.

By late afternoon, we sighted Navassa Island, a mere pimple of a rock island in the center of the Windward Passage. Navassa is owned by the United States, and our Caribbean chart showed that the U.S. maintained a navigation beacon on the island. Otherwise, the only residents were wild goats.

Floating into the lee we dropped anchor and looked over the rocky cliff rising straight up from the water. A rope ladder hung down the sheer face, probably left there by whoever changed the lightbulbs in the beacon.

When Roger came up from the engine room with my father's gun in his hand, I flinched. "What are you going to do with that?"

"I thought I'd go ashore and shoot us a goat for dinner," he said matter-of-factly.

"NOOOOOOO!"

The boys were ecstatic with the idea of being big-game hunters. Ron quickly lowered the two-man raft over the side, and Janice and I watched as our three brave men climbed in. I couldn't resist a warning as I watched the overloaded raft pull away from *Halcyon*. "You'd better pick out a small one or someone's going to have to swim back to the boat!" Then another thought occurred to me and I shouted again, "You also better kill it because there is no way I am going to scrub up goat droppings!"

Janice and I made ourselves comfortable on the deck and watched the boys play Tarzan. One by one they swung precariously up the ladder to stand triumphantly atop the cliff.

"How do you cook a goat?" Janice wondered aloud.

"I don't know," I sighed. "Better than that, I don't even know how to clean one."

But we were lucky—the hunters returned empty-handed.

The wind freshened, so we pulled anchor and headed the boat southwest, the direction of Jamaica. Roger and Ron spent the day poring over the diesel repair manual to track down the source of the smoke problem while the kids and I spelled each other at the helm.

As I sat my turn, with feet propped on the spokes of the wheel to hold it steady and hands resting like pillows behind my head, I looked around the horizon. Navassa had faded away to nothing, and there was no land to be seen anywhere—only a vast expanse of living, breathing ocean heaving us up, then letting us down in a gentle pulsing rhythm.

I could hear Ron and Roger talking away about gaskets, seals, filters, and pumps, and thought to myself, it truly would be nicer to never have to use the engine at all. When the only sound on Earth is the wind, and the only smell is the sea, then man and boat and nature are truly one.

But I had to agree it was dangerous not to have that engine. The 12-volt lights used batteries, and batteries needed charging. Without the motor, docking and anchoring had to be done under sail, a risky business that was not worth the trauma. There were shoaling waters, and days with no wind, and scariest of all, someone could fall overboard.

The sails fluttered and I tilted the wheel a few degrees to starboard. When had we first seen signs of smoke? My mind traveled back through Haiti, then even further back into the Bahamas. Weren't there some heavy fumes from the engine when we were on our way to Great Inagua? Could it have started then? What kind of repair work had Roger done on the engine when he bought that can of marine glue? Wasn't it something about the exhaust pipe?

Ron came up out of the cabin to relieve me at the wheel, and Roger followed him looking bleary eyed and troubled. "We just can't figure it out," he said. "As far as I can tell, there is no reason for that smoke to continue to accumulate."

"Don't exhaust pipes carry smoke?" I asked.

He gave me an indulgent look. My mechanical knowledge bordered on the illiterate, and he knew it. But something told me my idea was not dumb. "Do you remember when you patched a hole with that horridly expensive glue? Could the patch have come off?"

The indulgent look was replaced by a little white balloon over his head, and a lightbulb that flashed BOING. Roger bounded down the companionway, grabbed the flashlight, and disappeared into *Halcyon*'s bowels. I turned the wheel over to Ron and followed Roger to the engine room doors. He worked his way far astern and after a few bangs, his voice echoed out from the grimy black machinery, "Here it is! I FOUND IT"

As he crawled out of the tiny space to get some more of the metal glue, I put a hand on his arm to stop him. Puffing out my chest, I looked him in the eye and said, "Oh no, my friend. I found it."

My reward was a grubby hug, a sooty kiss, and a rare compliment: "Have you ever thought of becoming a mechanic?"

"Only as a sideline to selling sewing machines and raising chickens."

It took another hour to clear the air filter, wipe down the motor and surrounding area, and purge the lines of carbon. When the engine roared into action, great billows of smoke poured out the back, then slowly subsided to nothing. The motor was truly fixed for no more than the cost of a small can of glue. But we had a super new tune up, new fuel injector (and a good old one), new washers, bolts, screws, belts, rubber bands, and I don't know what all. Roger also had a lot more experience in repairing diesel motors, and we all had a lot more room on the boat without that bike and dinghy motor.

By late afternoon the Windward Passage began to live up to its name. The wind had risen steadily all afternoon and was topping forty knots when I stuck my fingers into the air to gauge the remaining daylight. Forty-five minutes! Where was Jamaica?

Roger went to the top of the ratlines to try and spot land but all he could see was water. Climbing down, he inched his way back to the cockpit and said, "The waves are cresting at fifteen feet. We could have a rough night if they get any higher."

They were already way too high for me. I felt better when he came to sit beside me at the wheel and together, we stared at the western horizon. If Jamaica was as bad as Haiti, then there might not be any navigation lights along the coast. How close were we, and were there shoals or reefs that did not show on our "magazine map"? Should we reef the sails? Heave to? Run with it? We were both edgy and very tired, and I would have given anything to stop for a night's rest.

The sun was a fiery red ball as it sank rapidly into the ocean. Twilight descended, and still no sight of land. "What now?" I asked.

Roger stood and gazed intently into the darkening sky, then he said quietly, "Do you see that?"

I looked and saw nothing, then a flash of light as dim as a firefly. "Count!" Roger ordered.

"One thousand one, one thousand two," I ticked off the seconds. At thirty seconds, the light flashed again.

"It's a beacon!" We cheered.

Hearing our shouts, the kids came barreling up the stairs. "What do you see?" Ron asked.

"Land!" and Roger pointed to the light. "We see Jamaica!"

Going below and pulling the hatch over my head to close out the wash of spray from the deck, I turned to survey the cabin in the dim light from the galley. Preparing dinner in such rough seas had been difficult but everything had finally been cleared away and the children were safely in bed. They were such trusting creatures, believing without question, that their parents would never lead them into harm.

Ron slept soundly on the top bunk on the starboard side, his head resting on the life jacket he hated to wear. Life jackets were a requirement on deck for everyone, but once below it was a fight to keep Ron in his.

Halcyon lurched crazily, then did a sharp drop as though she'd sailed off a cliff and was falling into space. Tommy sounded agitated as he mumbled from his place in the lower bunk, "Catch the dog, Ron! Here comes Janice!" Even in his sleep Janice was his adversary. I noticed his bedpan was lying at the foot of the bunk and realized he hadn't needed it since the Bahamas. He'd finally gained his sealegs.

Hanging tightly to the table divider I worked my way forward to check on Janice, where she slept peacefully in her dad's bunk. She was wearing her life jacket and had pillows wedged completely around her, so the rolling of the boat did not bother her in the least.

It was time to relieve Roger at the wheel. Back in the galley, I lit the gimballed stove and tried to make a pot of coffee, but each time I let go of my handhold I went careening across the galley to slam against the opposite bulkhead. After the second crash, I connected the galley strap to my waist and wondered why I was as stubborn about that strap as Ron was about the life jacket.

With the thermos full of strong coffee, I inched my way back to the companionway, eased up the ladder, and opened the hatch a bare inch. "Tell me when," I called to Roger, then closing the hatch, I waited.

Five seconds passed before I felt the stern of the boat rise into the air, and the long sharp descent as *Halcyon* rode down the face of the wave at breathtaking speed.

"Okay," came Roger's muffled voice, and opening the hatch, I stepped quickly onto the darkened deck.

After connecting the lifeline from the mizzen mast to a halter under my vest, I sat down at the wheel. "Why don't you go down and dry off?" I urged. He was clearly tired and soaking wet from the sea spray.

"I should," he agreed. "But that would mean stripping to the skin. This foul-weather gear really doesn't keep me dry."

"You need to do what I did," I told him. "After changing wet clothes for the third time, I just didn't put any back on."

He looked at my rain suit. "You mean you don't have anything under that?"

I grinned and shook my head. "These things are a lot more comfortable without clothes underneath." They were also more convenient. The pants to the suit were held up by suspenders, and with a jacket on top, and several layers of clothes under that, it had been a major production every time I had to go to the bathroom. And though the suit did not keep me dry, the one-humungous-size-fits-all did keep me warm.

The beacon we had spotted at sundown on the western horizon had moved to well off our stern quarter, and we were searching for the Kingston channel marker. If we were on course, it would be showing up sometime just before dawn.

My arms strained against the wheel trying to hold *Halcyon* at an angle to the waves, but it was tough. Even though it was impossible to see anything in the pitch-dark night, I could tell by the motion of the boat and the pressure against the wheel, that the waves were much higher than they had been that afternoon, easily topping twenty feet. I had to admit I was in the grip of near panic each time one lifted our puny little scrap of a boat and tossed her down into the black hole. But there was no longer any way for me to give into my fears—Ron and Roger had pulled most of the heavy shifts, and now both were far too tired to be manning the wheel. Anyway, I was toughening. Hours earlier my hands had formed blisters, the blisters had broken, and even the sting from the open sores had numbed to a throb that I no longer noticed.

Roger scanned the night with the binoculars, then cursed as a wave tossed him onto his fanny. "I'm going up the ratlines," he said. "These waves are too high for me to see anything."

"Good Lord, Roger! Not in this sea! If you fell over, I wouldn't even be able to turn the boat around much less see you."

"I'll keep the harness and lifeline on, and I've got the distress light pinned to the life jacket, the police whistle around my neck, and we're trailing a two-hundred-foot line behind the boat. You can call to me every few seconds, and if I don't answer then throw over that string of plastic milk jugs, the diving flag, and anything else that might float." When he stopped for breath, I realized he was worried too.

He inched his way forward and was out of sight before he was halfway to the ratlines. Every few seconds I called his name, and he answered with, "I'm still here."

As I waited, I thought to myself that this was the longest night of my life. The waves seemed to grow higher as each one overtook us, and the previous few had sounded like runaway locomotives bearing down on us.

Halcyon's rear began to climb, and I glanced back over my shoulder. The wall of water reflected by the stern lights was terrifying. Gasping, I snapped back around, clutched tightly to the wheel and closed my eyes.

"ROGER!" I yelled as my stomach rose then plummeted with the roller coaster ride of the boat.

"I'm still here."

My fingers relaxed slightly, but I was careful not to let go of the wheel, and I knew I couldn't look back again. When I'd seen the size of that wave, my instinct had been to cover my head and duck. And if *Halcyon* should turn sideways to the waves, a twenty-foot wall of water against her side would have rolled us over as easily as if we'd been a little ball.

"Do you see anything?" I called again.

His answer sounded like, "I glmph thlo."

"What did you say?" The roar that rose behind me sounded like ten trains.

"Watch out!" I heard Roger yell. "This one's breaking ..."

That was all I heard as water came down on me with a force so strong it drove my head all the way to my waist. The wheel bucked against my hands, and I felt the entire boat shudder under the weight of thousands of gallons of ocean water. Then *Halcyon* slid upward into the air, and the mammoth breaking wave rolled out from under her.

The water on deck was as deep as my armpits, and I found myself floating a full foot above the Captain's seat. But my hands never let go of the wheel! As the residue of the wave surged forward in its race to wash back into the sea, I settled down into the seat, spit out a mouthful of salty water, and shouted, "Roger, are you there?" Nothing. "ROGER!"

Fear flooded in, even stronger than the wave. With one hand still holding the wheel, I reached for the milk jugs, and just as I touched them, I heard Roger's voice. "I'm here!" It was then that something hit me! My screams came again and this time they didn't stop. Whatever had me was climbing right up my pants leg, stabbing, and pricking, and biting the bare flesh as it went! Jumping to my feet, I began thrashing my leg in the air like a berserk windmill, and all the time I screamed, "Roger! Something's got me! Help! Where are you?"

He was at my side and taking the wheel before I even knew he was there. At that moment, a very unhappy flying fish flopped out of my pants leg and onto the deck of the boat.

Roger was grinning as he said, "Do you know, you are the noisiest sailor I have ever met."

At least he called me a sailor.

Communism seemed to be the direction Jamaican politics was headed at the time we appeared on the scene. Haiti's repressive dictatorship had taught us much about 'rule through fear,' but Jamaica's equally repressive communism showed us that life was not much better on the other side of the coin.

The Island's central problems apparently began at a time of prosperity in the late 1950s, when tourism had grown into the main industry of the land. The wealth from tourist dollars lured the rural Jamaicans from the farms and sugar plantations, into the cities. As a result of the migration, the people left behind most of the crafts and occupations of their forefathers. But no one noticed. Money was plentiful, and the middle class grew.

The arrival of the 70s saw more goods being imported from other countries than were being produced on the island, and as fast as the tourist dollars poured in, they poured out again. There were just too many wonderful things to buy. The farmer who had forgotten how to farm had learned how to dress in more expensive clothes and drive imported cars. The basket weaver, in discovering how to operate a microwave oven, had forgotten how to weave. And every teenager owned a stereo and the latest watch. And once Jamaicans were well hooked on all the wonderful consumer goods of the Western world the oil shortage hit.

Rising fuel prices rapidly changed the money drain from a serious situation to an all-out crisis. In 1972, Michael Manley won the position of Prime Minister, and brought into office the belief that the economic woes of Jamaica could be cured by shunning U.S. capitalism, and embracing instead, the ideologies of Cuba and the Soviet Union.

Manley began his economic reforms by stopping purchase of any "luxury" items from foreign countries. Fuel was rationed, processed foods disappeared from the supermarkets, and with no one farming, unprocessed foods became as scarce as everything else. Prices on even the most basic of foods became outrageous—and no politician is likely to be popular for long when his constituents are hungry.

Newspapers, radio, and TV stations were seized by the government in an effort to calm the masses and quiet the dissenting voices. It didn't work. Unemployment in the cities rose to more than fifty percent, and violence grew in relation to the hunger. When American tourists were attacked in the streets, they naturally began to look for more friendly places to spend their vacations, and their money.

The Jamaica we stumbled into was a mess!

It was 10 a.m. as we approached Kingston Harbor, and our navigation can only be described as commendable considering the inadequacies of our charts. Roger was at the wheel and I radioed the Kingston Harbor Master to ask which of the many small islands we should go between to enter the port.

"Describe your location, please," the voice on the radio requested.

"We don't have a chart, sir, but according to my map, we appear to be just southeast of Lime Cay.

"Map? Come again?" The voice sounded disbelieving.

"Yes sir. It is a National Geographic map of Kingston Harbor. You know, one of those fold-out, full-color ......

"Don't move! Stay where you are! Someone will be there shortly to escort you in."

Going up on deck, I relayed the news to Roger, then said, "He is probably worried that some fool sailor will sink in his channel and block traffic."

"Well, can you blame him?" Roger asked.

In less than fifteen minutes, we had an escort.

Clearing into Jamaica went easily enough. The Immigration officers boarded quickly, and our papers were found to be in order though slightly illegible with all the Haitian black ink.

As we sat at the table going through the formalities, one of the officials asked a question I'd never heard before: "How much money are you carrying?"

"Not much," Roger answered wryly. "But we expect to have some wired within a day or two."

The officer said, "I would like to count what you have anyway, and you must keep proof of all money transactions while you are here."

Thinking that was strange, I asked, "Why?"

"The Jamaican Government does not want you to leave with any more than you came with," he answered.

Roger and I laughed at the absurdity of it, and Roger remarked, "Until now, we've had the opposite problem. If we can reverse the flow of money, it would be a neat trick, but I don't think it's likely."

"Don't be too sure it can't happen," the official said cryptically. "Just remember, you will have to account for every penny before you leave the Island, and it is a criminal offense to carry any money that does not belong to you."

The man's warning was so stern, Janice leaped to the toy locker and pulled out her collection of foreign coins. "Do you want to count these?" she asked with a troubled voice.

He gave her a friendly smile, but he counted the coins anyway—all two dollars' worth. Then he redirected his attention to Roger. "Where do you plan to go from here?"

"Negril," Roger answered. "I'd like to check out the possibility of working in one of the hotels there."

The expression on the man's face changed noticeably, and he stared at us a long moment before saying, "You will have to get that permission from the Immigration officer in the town of Black River."

When Roger pressed for more information, the man merely repeated his previous statement, and though we wondered what was wrong, we decided not to ask any more questions. It seemed best just to do as instructed and stay out of trouble.

The most important errand was to search out a bank, and we located one a few blocks from the wharf. As we stepped into the plush interior of the marble-fronted building, we were a little surprised to find the interior hotter than the street. Air conditioning was undoubtedly a "luxury" Prime Minister Manley had banned.

A pleasant young man ushered us into one of the inner offices. We sat and then explained to him our need to have money wired from California.

"We can have it here in an hour if you would like to wait," he said.

It was such a rarity to have funds in less than several days that we elected to wait. The kids retired to the lobby to read magazines while the banker asked us about our travels. Being a banker, his questions were directed primarily toward our money situation, and he was curious about how we managed when we were out of range of any town. Roger explained that the payments from the sale of our business were doled out to us in monthly installments via our bank in the States. Then he related our troubles of money going to one island while we were on another. Mr. Jamison's interest increased when he heard about our running out of funds altogether whenever we had a cross-up or a delay in wires.

"Do you find it difficult to cash checks?" he asked.

"Well, we don't always look like rich tourists," I snickered as I looked down at our rather rumpled clothes.

Roger backed up my statement. "Banks, restaurants, and hotels hesitate to cash checks signed by transients, especially those dressed in cut offs and tennis shoes."

Mr. Jamison nodded with amusement, then asked, "Do you carry cards?"

"Yes, we have the usual assortment of plastic," Roger said. "But that doesn't help much when we run out of checks to pay their bills, and the checks are harder to get than money. As a matter of fact, we have several orders of new checks floating around somewhere in the Caribbean right now. It has also been six months since we've seen a statement from any credit card company. I think we are current, but who knows? A check mailed from the islands is as likely to get lost as a letter."

Mr. Jamison studied the situation a moment. "Let's see. The wires cost you money, and telephone calls to California cost even more. Credit cards are all right except for the invoices and keeping them current. I suppose you have no choice, but to take your income payments a month at a time, for tax purposes?"

We nodded.

"I have a suggestion," he said and proceeded to solve our problem in the most obvious way. I couldn't help but wonder why we were always learning things that we could just as easily have thought of ourselves. "Use your credit card account as though it were a checking account. Notify your banker that you want your income payments deposited directly into the card account. Cards are probably more acceptable than a check anywhere in the world..." He smiled slightly, then continued, "Even when you are wearing cut offs and tennis shoes. And unless you are in a very remote situation, any bank affiliate, and most large hotels, should be able to advance you money on your card. It will mean your card account will have a surplus of money in it, but that shouldn't be any more of a problem than having surplus money in your checking account." (He turned out to be right. After following his advice, our money problems seemed to vanish.)

When it was time to leave, the banker handed us our allotment along with verification that it had come from the States. We were curious, and Roger asked, "What is all of this about keeping track of our money?"

There was sadness in his voice as he said, "It is the problem of our economy. Jamaica is losing so many of her skilled and educated population. Lawyers, writers, doctors, and businessmen are selling their homes and businesses for a fraction of the value and in American dollars, not Jamaican. Then the people are fleeing the country with those valuable dollars. Since the government will not allow more than fifty dollars to leave the island with any one person, the money is being smuggled out by every possible means. And anyone on a sailboat is a prime suspect for smuggling."

I gave Roger a look that said, "Here we go again," then he asked one more question. "Is there any reason we should not go to Negril?"

The banker looked pensive before shaking his head defiantly. "Absolutely not! Negril is the jewel of our island, and you will love it." But he added as an afterthought, "Please be cautious."

Kingston wasn't pleasant. Everywhere were signs: anti-American, anti-CIA, and political party slogans. There was an aura of hostility and anger in the people we passed, and with the 50 percent unemployment rate and runaway inflation, it was easy to see why emotions were out of control. Kingston was the top of a volcano and that volcano was rumbling.

After stopping in two grocery stores, we gave up. There was nothing to buy. However, we came upon a marine store and were relieved to find charts on Jamaica and the Cayman Islands. At last we would be able to see where we were going! The window of a travel office beckoned, and we stopped in to pick up a half dozen brochures on Negril. The pictures of palm trees, white beaches, and tanned smiling people were a glaring contrast to the atmosphere all around us, and even more inviting because of it.

By then we had become aware that the Jamaica of the calypso songs no longer existed, and our plans to live and work on the island were already being scrapped. But Negril was why we had come, and we were going to see it—come hell or high water!

The cruising sailor considers stories of pirates only slightly less exciting than those of sunken treasure. We were no exception.

The history of Jamaica offers more pirate lore than any other island in the Caribbean, and for that reason we chose to visit Port Royal, the small town on the south side of Kingston harbor. Anchoring off Port Royal's seawall, we went ashore to explore.

As we walked along the beach, the kids proceeded to pick up shells and bits of colored glass to stuff in their pockets while I told them what I knew of the history of the town.

During the 1600s Port Royal was considered the unofficial capital of all the islands. The Governor of the town was an unscrupulous rogue, who for a small fee provided a protected haven to all the great pirates of the day. There were many, but the most notorious, Captain Morgan, Jack Rackham (known as "Calico Jack" because of his colorful underwear), Ann Bonney, and Mary Reade were regular visitors. They added their presence to a population that was the most boisterous, sinful, dangerous, and wealthy of any in the Western Hemisphere.

The high living came to an abrupt halt in 1692 when an earthquake, followed by an enormous tidal wave, hit the city. More than half of Port Royal disappeared into the sea. Thousands of people died in the disaster, and supposedly, millions of pounds of gold and treasure disappeared at the same time. The more notorious of the pirates escaped unharmed. Port Royal never regained its unbridled decadence but grew instead into a quiet peaceful little town in its rebirth.

Leaving the beach, we walked along the neatly laid-out tree-shaded streets and passed small white board houses with only huge wooden shutters for adornment, a protection of sorts against the onslaught of weather.

We found the museum that commemorated the destruction of Port Royal and entered to view the treasures recovered from the sea; artifacts from a city that had existed three hundred years before. As we gazed at the cases of coral encrusted guns, broken furniture, and pieces of pottery, Tommy suddenly exclaimed, "Look at that plate!"

It was clear what was so special about the cream-colored plate with the blue pattern when we saw what Tommy held in his hand; a pottery shard with the identical colors and markings, his treasure from the beach. Somehow history feels closer when a piece of it is personally found and riding in your own pocket.

Our plan was to stay in Black River only long enough to obtain clearance to Negril, but the atmosphere of the town and the friendliness of the people kept us a day longer.

We found the Customs and Immigration offices at the end of the dock, and Roger and I left the kids playing along the shore as we walked over with our papers. The officer behaved much like the one in Kingston, refusing to grant us the permission we needed. When we asked why, he suggested we see someone in a town further west called Savanna La Mar. Feeling slightly confused, we agreed to do as he instructed, then left the office.

"Roger, this is sounding more mysterious all the time. Are you sure we shouldn't get out of here?"

"I don't think we need to worry—they are just behaving like bureaucrats," he said. "It's their way to make their jobs feel more important." I hoped he was right.

Halcyon was tied to the dock at the mouth of the Savanna River, which bore the same name as the town. As we neared *Halcyon,* we could see the kids. They were admiring a shiny new fiberglass-and-chrome cabin cruiser that was tied up right behind us.

A broad-shouldered, broad-bellied Jamaican with a friendly face and a raucous laugh was standing at the rail talking to the kids. As we walked up, he introduced himself as Buddy. We learned he owned a furniture factory, was on vacation, and that times were tough. "I may as well fish, the furniture business is no good," he said.

After exchanging tours of our respective boats, Buddy presented us with a bag of mangoes, some cold drinks, and a bottle of his homemade pimento wine. And as if that weren't enough, he invited us to go on his boat the next morning for a tour of the river. "This river is famous for its alligators," he said with a wink at the kids. To them it sounded too good to miss.

Our new friend was a masterful guide as he skimmed us along over five miles of river reminiscent of a Louisiana bayou, complete with tree-shaded banks and purple water hyacinths. But unlike a bayou, the water was

Sailing Against the Wind – Toni Larson   317

crystal clear, clean, and very cold. Roger, Buddy, and the kids braved the elements to swim, but Janice and I watched for alligators. She saw fifty or sixty, but I didn't see any.

Buddy seemed to sincerely enjoy the company of the children. On our return trip he made a stop along the bank of the river, cut sugar cane for them to chew, and was thoroughly delighted at their reactions to the sweet, rummy taste. As he gently teased the kids, then laughed in great rolling booms, I couldn't resist asking, "Buddy, do you have a family?"

"Oh yes," he beamed. "I have a big, fluffy wife, and three, big fluffy daughters."

The mental image of his words made me giggle, but I would have throttled Roger if he ever described us that way.

That night we were invited to have dinner with Buddy and several of his friends. It gave us the opportunity to learn a little more about the plight of the Jamaican. One couple had closed their drugstore, a business that had operated nonstop for three generations. The only stock they had left were some comic books, and those they gave to the kids. When we asked what they were going to do for work, they merely shook their heads.

Another out-of-work couple kept a small garden and fished. As meager as their wealth was, they insisted on sharing their home-grown vegetables and shrimp they'd caught that morning, with us. From each of them we heard the tone of helplessness, fear of the future, and remorse over a political situation that seemed headed for disaster. Buddy's explanation of how he acquired his boat was indicative of the way many people there solved the problem. "One day my neighbor came to my door and handed me the keys. He said he could not find a buyer for the boat, so he gave it to me to keep until he comes back. The next day he was gone to Houston, I hear. He didn't want to go, but there was nothing he could do."

All of them were optimistic when they talked of the coming election. "Mr. Edward Seaga is challenging Prime Minister Manley. If someone does not assassinate him or steal the election, Mr. Seaga will win. And that is what most Jamaicans want."

"We'll keep our fingers crossed," I promised.

Neither Buddy nor the others asked us to smuggle any money for them or anything else. But I did sense they were looking for help.

We made one significant purchase in Black River—a small aluminum dinghy and it was wonderful to have adequate transportation again.

The Savanna La Mar official stroked his long curling mustache pridefully as he asked us the same question for the third time, "WHY do you want to go to Negril?"

Roger's temper was firmly under control, but I was getting testy. "Because we were told it was the most beautiful spot along the coast of your island, and because we read your travel brochures and they actually urge the tourists to visit!" My voice had reached an angry pitch.

Roger stepped in and spoke more calmly. "We are looking for a small town with a protected harbor to spend a quiet week or two. Our children like to snorkel and swim, and the harbors we've visited lately have not been very good for swimming."

Stroking his mustache, the official studied us closely. "Who told you about Negril?"

Roger explained about meeting a Jamaican in Haiti, then about the recommendations given by the people we'd met in Jamaica. I showed him the brochures we'd picked up at the agency, and I asked, "Is Negril off-limits to boaters?"

"No," he said slowly. "There are no regulations that say you cannot go there. But are you aware of the smuggling of money that occurs from our island?"

Roger answered, "Yes, we've heard about the problems of controlling the flow of money and we've already guessed that Negril is one of the more active places for those activities. But I'm really not interested in jeopardizing our boat, or the safety of my family."

The official seemed to be thinking over the situation, then he asked, "Do you understand that I can't let you leave the country from Negril? You will have to return here or continue on to Montego Bay for clearance."

I jumped at the opening. "We can do that! We understand why you're worried, and we're perfectly willing to cooperate."

"So why do you want to go to Negril?" he asked yet again. What language did these officials speak? Whatever it was, we weren't getting through. More confusing still was that no one had yet said we *couldn't* go.

Roger started the whole explanation from the beginning, and I ended it with the question, "Are you going to forbid us clearance to Negril?"

"Oh no! As far as I am concerned you can stop there, but if you give us any reason at all, we will board your boat!" I was startled to hear his vehement anger and thought we'd best get out while we still had our heads.

"Will you stamp our passports so we can go?"

When he handed them back, the visas read, "Montego Bay." Roger raised an eyebrow, and the officer smiled a cold, unpleasant smile. "You may stop in Negril for a few days, and it is not necessary for the papers to show that. But after two days, I want you out of there."

We left the offices with our papers, and more questions than answers. Why the extreme reaction to the mere mention of the town? Why the runaround? If the Government really didn't want us there, then why not just come out and say so? And why couldn't they see that if we were going to smuggle, then we could do it just as easily from any other port on the island?

A mile out of Savanna La Mar, we looked back to see the police boat following us. Thinking they were out for a spin, we gave a friendly wave, then turned *Halcyon* toward the western tip of the island.

The trip took most of the afternoon, and with the trade winds, we made excellent time. But by the time we rounded the point we were truly tired and ready for a rest, and Negril was going to provide it for us.

The moment we saw the town, we knew why we had come. Negril was beautiful. Cliffs riddled with caves rose from the water's edge on either end of the bay, tropical green forests and rolling hills filled in the middle. Great expanses of sugar-white beaches, castle-like coral islands, sparkling clean, aqua-blue water. It was paradise, and it was protected from the wind and the waves in every direction.

The boys began talking about the "neat" snorkeling, and Janice wanted to picnic on the beach for dinner—something we hadn't done in months.

Looking toward the beach, I had no trouble picturing the pirates of centuries ago as they cavorted in the sand. I told the kids, "This is the very spot that Calico Jack anchored. It was on that beach that he, and his sweetheart Anne Bonney, went picnicking.

"They were swimming in the nude right over there when an English Navy ship sailed up, and an ambitious young officer arrested them."

Janice snickered and I revised her impression of the crime committed: "For piracy, not indecent exposure."

"What happened to them?" Ron asked, his eyes focusing on the past.

"Jack Rackham was taken to Kingston and hanged. Anne Bonney claimed she was pregnant, and her life was spared, though she died in prison."

While the kids were mulling over the days of buccaneers and wenches, the police boat we'd seen earlier roared alongside, and the captain of the boat leaned over to yell loudly, "You cannot stay here! Raise your anchor and leave immediately!"

Roger muttered, "Here we go again," then answered the officer in a calm voice, "We have permission from the head of the Immigration Office in Savanna La Mar to anchor here for two days."

The Captain/policeman was not impressed. "You do not have permission to go anywhere but Montego Bay!"

Poking Roger in the ribs, I whispered, "How does he know that?"

Roger tried again. "We have verbal permission to stay, and I would be glad to go with you to a telephone. We can call Savanna La Mar and you can talk to the officer yourself."

The man sneered slightly, then said, "You can call anyone you like from Montego Bay! You are not staying here—even one day! Now will you please pull that anchor and be on your way before we board your boat!"

Roger was not intimidated. "It's almost dark. You can't expect us to sail a strange coast after dark."

"The waters aren't dangerous if you stay far enough offshore.

"We are nearly out of fuel."

"You are a sailboat—sail!"

"But the wind is from the east, and Montego Bay is to the east."

"The wind will change before morning."

I could see Roger was getting nowhere, and suddenly I'd had enough. "We came to Jamaica to see Negril! No one has said we cannot come here, but now you say we can't stay. I think you owe us an explanation. We haven't done anything wrong, and I want to know why you want us to leave!" My voice had reached a volume that probably carried as far as the town.

The policeman's explanation sounded like a broken record: "Because your papers read Montego Bay!"

Obviously, we'd lost the war, but Roger was not ready to lose the battle. He set his jaw, and spoke firmly, saying, "Okay, we won't stay in Negril. But I refuse to jeopardize my family's safety by moving this boat before morning!"

The Captain started to protest, but I interrupted him to express my opinion of the Manley regime. Turning quickly, Roger pushed me hard toward the companionway, then rudely down the stairs. As I sat on the bottom rung of the ladder, I fumed to myself about the idiocies and incompetencies of government officials while Roger stayed on deck and soothed the ruffled feathers of the Captain.

The arguing continued in lower tones, but Roger won a concession when the policeman said, "You are not to leave the boat, talk to anyone who might come near, or even go swimming in the water! You will leave here by first daylight and we are going to stay here all night to make sure you do. If you violate even one of my rules, you will be arrested."

As the police boat pulled away, I heard one last remark, "Mon, your wife sure has a mean tongue."

There was murder in my eyes as I came flying up the companionway, but Roger caught me and firmly turned me around. Later I wondered how much more trouble we might have been in if he hadn't stopped me when he did.

The outcome was a disappointment to all of us. The kids had not had a chance to truly swim since the Bahamas, and Roger was literally aching to go spearing in some water that wasn't polluted, or full of dead coral. I simply wanted to sit still for a while. After dinner, we sat on deck and gazed longingly at the lights from the deceivingly peaceful town as they reflected in the water along the beach. The police boat at anchor a few hundred yards away reminded us that we were being watched. Suddenly I remembered an old Jamaican saying, "Never curse de alligator's long mouth till you done crost de river." It was a lesson well learned.

Pulling anchor at sunup we motored away from the picture-postcard setting and as we passed the police boat, I couldn't resist tooting the horn and waving pleasantly. Roger looked startled, then shook his head in resignation. It must be difficult to have a wife with a "mean tongue."

Halcyon bucked a northeast wind for ten hours, and still we were less than halfway to Montego Bay. The policeman was wrong about one thing, the wind never changed. When we were down to our last few gallons of fuel, Roger chose to head for the protected harbor of Lucea and spend the night, but not before radioing the Harbor Patrol in Montego Bay for permission.

"Right now, a hurricane couldn't make me drop anchor without an okay from the Government!" he grumbled.

The beach was deserted as we left the dinghy and walked the mile into Lucea to find the first Government employee to say "Welcome" on the entire coast of Jamaica and we felt he meant it. He'd hardly spoken the word when a second uniformed officer came roaring in, to demand, "Is that your dinghy on the beach at the end of the street?" Roger gave a puzzled nod. "Well, it is on my property!" the man snapped at us. "And I want it off immediately!"

Roger flashed me a look that I translated as "Keep your mouth shut!" then we hastily retreated to the beach to move the trespassing dinghy to a less-offensive spot. The angry man came with us to let us know where his property line was, but after he left some of his neighbors approached and apologized for the man's rudeness.

"He don't have nothin' better to do than to order people around," one man said with a sorrowful expression. As a gesture of goodwill, the others brought us coconuts by the dozens until there was barely any room left in the dinghy for our feet. At that moment we were convinced the Government was the bad guy, and everyone else wore a white hat.

It was a hammering ride to Montego Bay as we beat hard against the trade winds and the heavy seas, but the long trip gave me lots of time for soul searching. "I know it's my fault," I told Roger. "We probably could have stayed a year in Negril if I hadn't been so sassy."

Roger didn't agree and it made sense when he said, "The Captain on the police boat knew what our papers said without even reading them. The only way he could have known was if the official in Savanna La Mar told him. I think they never intended to let us stay there, and I even believe the Kingston officers knew we wouldn't get permission. For whatever reason, we've been led around by a carrot on a stick, and you didn't make things any worse..." Then he smiled, "But you sure came close."

"You might be right, but I'm going to change my attitude anyway. I'm going to smother the next official with so much kindness, it will be impossible for him to be rude."

Before reaching Montego Bay, I opened a tin of cookies, made a pot of tea, combed my hair, and even put on makeup (the first in a year). When we were boarded, I was ready. Roger led the uniformed man down the steps, and the kids followed close behind. Putting the refreshments on the table, and displaying my best syrupy sweet smile, I offered him cookies and tea.

The man wasn't moved. He didn't smile, didn't say welcome, he didn't even say hello! What he did say was, "What are you doing in Jamaica?"

The poor guy never knew what hit him. I railed on for minutes about him, his inhospitable government, Communists in general, Manley in particular, and finished it all with "If you ever visit the United States, I hope you get a foul-tempered Customs officer who thinks all Jamaicans are smugglers and junkies."

Stopping for breath, I looked around. The kids were staring, bug-eyed from their perches on the upper bunks. Roger was sitting with his arms crossed, and a slightly amused grin on his face.

When the man began to ruffle the papers in front of him, I realized he was uncomfortable, and suddenly felt very contrite for my outburst. Reaching for the pot, I poured him a cup of tea, forced a cookie on him, and sat down. As the customary paperwork began, the tensions eased.

"How long do you want to stay in Montego Bay?" the man asked.

"About a week," Roger answered.

"And where are you going from here?" He sat poised with his pen ready to fill in the appropriate space on the form, but his body stiffened noticeably when Roger casually asked, "How about Negril?"

Fidgeting in his seat, the man said, "I can give you written clearance to Savanna La Mar."

"Can we stop in Negril?" I leaned forward to hear the answer.

"Well, if you want to." He wouldn't look me in the eye.

"Why can't you write 'Negril' on the clearance papers?" I really wanted to know.

All he would answer was "It's not necessary."

Roger and I exchanged glances as we imagined a repeat of the whole process going in the opposite direction. Again, I wondered what was so secretive about Negril, but even more than that, I wondered what Negril was really like.

We asked for clearance to the Cayman Islands, and got it. When the officer stepped onto the dock, he turned to me and gave me a timid and very apologetic smile. "Mrs. Larson, I really do hope you enjoy your visit to our island. And I would like you to know the Jamaican people are the friendliest you will find anywhere in the world."

There was nothing he could have said to make me feel any guiltier.

Black Rooster was the perfect name for the young man living on the old sailboat tied next to ours. His complexion was a deep cocoa brown, and his hair was an elaborate array of matted curls that he kept puffed out and groomed with a long-handled brass pick comb. Black Rooster was one of the many unemployed and he was penniless to boot, but he was as cocksure of his worth as any rooster could be.

The Immigration officer had been gone a mere thirty seconds when Black Rooster made his first of many neighborly calls. "Mon, Whayoobefom?" he asked with a jaunty smile as he leaned casually against our backstay.

"Huh?" Roger asked.

"I think he wants to know where we are from," I translated.

In a few short minutes our new friend was comfortably lounging on the deck of the *Halcyon* and for the next week we did a lot of translating as he cheerfully, and continuously, chattered away about his island, its history, its customs, and all in that peculiar Jamaican lingo that is almost, but not quite, English.

There seemed to be no ulterior motives connected with Black Rooster's desire to show us and to tell us about the city he loved so much. And it was purely friendship that motivated him to drag us from dawn to dusk, over every corner of Montego Bay.

Shopping trips to the market were much more fun, and productive, with Black Rooster along. Once he watched me buy oranges, then demonstrated how to get bigger ones at half the price. The trick seemed to be connected to the shouting. The loudest voice was the one that named the price. To the kids, his strange dress and peculiar words were fascinating, and they followed in his shadow everywhere, absorbing all he had to teach them. We learned that papayas were Paw paws, a turnip was a Cho-Cho. And the kids giggled with delight when they heard that a big, bumpy orange like fruit had a name befitting its appearance, Ugli fruit.

Jamaican words and expressions seemed to come from a childlike imagination, and are built around pictures and sounds, rather than the staid old Latin words that the English language draws from. Thieves are called squeezers, a swamp is known as The Great Morass, fireflies are Peenie-Waulies. And good day, or "goodbye" becomes a near blessing when translated into the Jamaican expression "Walk good".

On the way back to the boat, Ron spied a sign that puzzled him, and pointing it out to Black Rooster, he asked, "Why does that say "Sleeping Policeman?"

"You know, Mon," Black Rooster tried to explain. "It be one of dose bumps in da road. Da kind of bump dot make da car go slow."

I had seen hundreds of them in supermarket parking lots and thought of them as nuisances. Somehow, I would always hit them too hard, and inevitably would dump the groceries on the floor of the car. Never again would I be able to curse one after discovering the things were really sleeping policemen.

The quaint language even extended into the naming of towns and states with Barbecue Bottom, Fairy Hill, A Walk, and Put Together all shown on our map. The most curious to me was the State of Look Behind. Whatever the origin, the mental picture the name created was certainly more interesting than Kansas.

Evenings were spent with Black Rooster teaching me how to cook curried goat, aki-aki, and pepper pot soup, and at the same time instructing the kids on the history of the island. His stories were colorful and gory enough to capture the kid's full attention. I thought how much more they could have learned if Black Rooster had been teaching them their schoolwork instead of me.

Roger however, soon tired of Black Rooster's cooking classes, history lessons, and strange-sounding, indecipherable dialect, and begged for a respite. Since the kids were suffering from hamburger deprivation, we left Black Rooster behind to watch the boat and caught a bus to the world-famous hotel strip of Montego Bay.

Stepping off the bus in front of one of the biggest of the American-owned hotels, we walked up the palm-shaded curved drive, pushed open the plate-glass door, and stepped into that "other world" of overeating, overdrinking, overspending tourists trying to have fun before their money ran out. At a table by the pool, we gave our order to a waiter, then sat back to watch a very handsome bronze-toned entertainment director instruct a large herd of semi-sober vacationers on the complexities of the Limbo.

"Bend your knees!" he shouted at one particularly portly, huffing gentleman. "You can make it! Bend your knees!"

The man bent his knees, fell flat on his butt and the crowd cheered.

"Black Rooster would make a better entertainment director," Roger said with a chuckle.

Our hamburgers arrived and we gobbled them down then left to the sounds of the group leader encouraging the first man to try again. "Come on," he urged. "Are you going to let your wife out do you?"

The bus bumped along the winding road on its way into town. The kids sat, scattered about, Ron talking to the driver, and Janice and Tommy each monopolizing their own window. Roger and I shared a seat and reflected on the contrast between our experiences and those of the people in the hotel.

"I can't help but feel sad that so few of our fellow Americans get a chance to meet the real Jamaicans," I said as I looked out the window at the flashes of beach that separated one hotel from the next.

"If you mean Black Rooster, he would probably scare most of those people to death." Then Roger spoke quietly, saying, "It's really too bad that we can't stay around and meet a few more like him, but I suspect that finding a job would be hard if all those closed-up hotels out there are any indication."

Following his gaze, I could see the reason for his observation. Only the very largest of the hotels were operating, and here it was the peak of the season. "Do you think Cayman will be any better than Jamaica?" I wondered.

"I don't know, but whatever we find I'd like to give it a try."

"Well, I hope the government is friendlier than what we've found lately." Then I giggled. "And just to make sure we do have an easier time of it, I promise to keep my 'mean tongue' under control."

Montego Bay held the reputation for being one of the most romantic cities in the world, and we weren't going to leave without experiencing some of that romance for ourselves. It was on our last night in Jamaica that Roger and I put the kids to bed, then stepped next door to the rickety old sailboat to alert Black Rooster that we would be gone for a while. Looking slightly disappointed that we weren't going to invite him to come along, Black Rooster grudgingly promised to keep an eye on the boat and the kids until we returned.

There was a full moon over the water, the sand glistened in the silvery light, and there were no tourists anywhere as Roger and I held hands and walked along the shore. When we tired of walking, we sat under a coconut palm, leaned our backs against the trunk, listened to the soft slapping of gentle waves along the shore, and watched the twinkling lights of a passing ship on the dark horizon.

"If I don't remember another thing twenty years from now, I hope I never forget this moment," I sighed.

Roger stretched his arm across my shoulder and teased lightly, "Have you actually converted to a believer of sunset-and-margarita sailing after all the proof we've had to the contrary?"

"No, not entirely. I think I have finally started to look at cruising through a more accurate prism. The dark colors are still there, but now I know they must be. You see, without them all the other colors would not be as bright."

"I'll be damned!" Roger laughed. "I do believe you have become a 'born again' sailor."

I scooped a handful of sand and let it thread slowly through my fingers. "You may be right, and maybe that's why I feel so sad when I think about it all ending."

"There's no reason to feel it's over. We can always sail again."

He started to say more when a voice broke in with, "We play a song for you?"

Turning around, we found three gaudily dressed, broadly smiling, young boys standing behind us, each carrying a musical instrument.

"Sorry," Roger said to send them away. "We can't afford strolling musicians."

"That's okay, Mon," one of them told us. "We play free for lovers. Anyway, tourist business be so bad that we need the practice, or we forget all the songs."

"What you wanna hear?" another one asked.

Thinking a minute, I asked, "How about a calypso song? We have been here for a month now, and all we've heard is reggae. Doesn't anyone play calypso anymore?"

They followed us along the street playing and singing, as Roger and I strolled arm in arm back to the boat. Harry Belafonte would have been aghast, but we loved every off-key note of "The Banana Boat Song."

We thanked them, and Roger paid them some money. "Just com bock and see our island again someday," one said. As the trio walked away from us and down the street, the sound of their music floated back over a harbor, washed in the ethereally unreal Montego moon. It was 'Jamaica Farewell,'

"I took a trip on a sailing ship, and when I reached Jamaica, I made a stop..."

We awoke the next morning to find a box of food on the afterdeck: cho-chos, greens, a bunch of bananas, and a bag of ugli fruit. It could only have come from Black Rooster, but when we went to thank him and tell him goodbye, he was not on his boat.

Our sailing time had been decided the day before and Black Rooster had been told, so we could only assume he did not plan to see us off. There was still no sign of him when an hour later, we untied the dock lines and began to make our way out of the harbor.

As we neared the final marker in the harbor, the shouts reached us. "Wait! Come back!" Turning, we saw Black Rooster waving something over his head. Roger swung the boat in a large arc and steered it back to the end of the dock. When we neared the pilings, Black Rooster leaned out and tossed a small package onto the deck of the boat, then called, "When you com bock to Montego, I be here. Goo bye and Walk Good!" And he pushed hard against the sprit to give *Halcyon* the momentum to complete the circle.

Sailing Against the Wind – Toni Larson

At the mouth of the channel, we were still waving until Black Rooster was no more than a tiny spot in the distance, then I opened the brown paper bag and took out a book—"The White Witch of Rose Hall."

In Jamaica there is a purely nonsense expression that sounds like, "boonoo, noo, noo." It means "something nice."

Postscript: In October of 1980, Michael Manley's Socialist Party was defeated in an election that put a much more moderate Edward Seaga of the Jamaican Labor Party in his place.

When I read the results in the newspaper, I thought of Negril, Buddy and his friends, our strolling musicians, and of course, Black Rooster. Hopefully, Mr. Seaga will be an improvement over Mr. Manley. The people of Jamaica deserve better than what they'd been getting.

CHAPTER 18: FROM PEACEFUL TO PLEASANT

Jamaica faded away, the trade winds strengthened, the waves pushed us higher and higher. Beneath *Halcyon*'s hull lay the Cayman Trench, 24,700 feet deep; ahead of her bow stretched 160 miles of open ocean. The first landfall of the Cayman Islands (If we were lucky, and our navigation was on target) was not much to aim for. Three puny little islands, unmarked by mountains or long-range beacons and if *Halcyon* missed them, the next stop was Honduras, 700 miles beyond.

Even though I trusted *Halcyon* completely, I was prepared for the worst. Stashed in the galley were jars of homemade soup, pickled fish, fresh bread, hard-boiled eggs, cookies, pudding, popcorn, and cheese. There was a thermos full of hot coffee, and another filled with hot water for making bouillon, tea, chocolate, and instant oatmeal. We weren't going to be hungry even if we didn't see land for a week.

The extra preparations proved unnecessary, as twenty-four hours after leaving Montego Bay, we spotted Little Cayman, the smallest and least populated of the three islands. Though we'd planned to go right to Grand Cayman, our bodies resisted. We ducked around the western end of the island and dropped anchor in a quiet cove. Leaving the boys to fish and Janice to read, Roger and I stretched out on our bunks for a much-needed nap after our sleepless night.

"Dad! Wake up! Someone's coming!"

"Umph, go away," Roger plainly refused to disturb his sleep for any crisis, but I wondered who could be out here. Little Cayman boasted no more than twelve residents, and they all lived on the opposite end of the ten-mile-long island. Maybe one of them was a fisherman who had seen us anchor.

As I started up the companionway, I looked to the head of the stairs and saw three men staring down at me! My God! After all we'd been through, we were about to be hijacked!

With heart thumping I backed slowly toward the galley and began talking as loudly as possible to alert Roger, who naturally was snoring his life away in the forward cabin. "What do you want? You can't come on board this boat!" That was smart—they were already on board. I looked, but didn't see a gun, and they weren't wearing uniforms. "Who are you?"

The probable leader (the only one wearing shoes) stepped down the ladder and informed me he was the Custom's Officer as well as a policeman, guide, and storekeeper.

A groggy Roger appeared at my side as the second man, wearing a straw hat, T-shirt, and blue jeans, introduced himself as the Immigration Officer and barber.

Roger yawned and I gave a relieved giggle as the third one, a young man dressed in nothing but a swim trunks, said, "I'm a fisherman, and I just came along for the ride."

Inviting them to sit down, I told myself they probably did not meet many sailors in the course of a year and as a result they knew little of the etiquette of boarding a boat.

That was not all they didn't know. Roger had to instruct them on what information they needed from us: passport numbers, crew list, nationalities, vessel documentation, etc., and I had to lend them a pencil and paper to write it all down. It was certainly a switch from our experiences with the officials of Jamaica and Haiti.

With the paperwork done, we had coffee and got acquainted. They urged us to visit their homes, but when we heard that the closest house was five miles away over a coral footpath we declined. An hour later they sped away in their fishing launch and left us totally alone for the first time since the Bahamas.

It was a Halcyonic, lazy, wonderful three days that we spent swimming, snorkeling, and doing nothing. When Roger and the boys tired of spearing fish and I tired of pickling and cooking them, I packed several pounds of peanut butter sandwiches, hung the whistle around Ron's neck, and sent the three rowdy kids to the beach to build sandcastles.

Roger and I lay scrunched together on my bunk, the cool breezes blowing down on us from the overhead hatch as we listened to the kids squealing and playing on the beach a few hundred yards away. The only other noise was the slap of an occasional wave against the hull and the groan of the anchor line as it stretched tight around the stanchion.

"Roger, do you really want to give this up?" I asked as I snuggled against him. "I could spend a month right here with no trouble at all."

"We'd run out of food before a month is up."

"Then we'd just have to live on snapper, lobster, and grouper."

"What would we do when the peanut butter runs out? The kids don't like snapper sandwiches."

"Now you sound like me. When did you start worrying about all those petty little details like food? The next thing you are going to ask is, what if someone gets sick? or What if we run out of money? Okay, I agree. We can't live for very long in this little cove, but why do we have to give up sailing? What would be wrong with another year at sea?" I couldn't believe I'd said that.

Roger was quiet for a minute then he shifted slightly so he could look me in the eye. "We could do it, I suppose, except I've begun to think of cruising as work, HARD work."

A slow wry smile crossed his face as he added, "I think I now can understand your feelings about the boat when we first started out. The constant mishaps were a challenge to me, but for you they were always monumental disasters."

"It was only because we were learning. But we survived and it can only get easier from here."

He put his hand up to hush me. "It seems our roles are reversing. You sound so confident, and I feel so unsure."

When I gave him a disbelieving look he hastily added, "Don't get me wrong. Sailing is still as much fun and as challenging as ever, maybe more so, but I think I'd better stop while I'm ahead."

I was on the verge of arguing further when the whistle blew. We dressed in forty seconds flat and were up on deck to catch the dinghy painter as Ron rowed alongside. When the kids deposited five pounds of sand on the deck, it crossed my mind that Roger might be right, a change would be nice.

While in that cove, we saw only one other boat. A fifty-foot-long trader dropped anchor for the afternoon about a half mile down the beach. We saw no one on deck, no one left the trader to go ashore, and it was gone before dark. A week later we would have cause to remember it.

Halcyon rode us up on the crest, plunged us down into the blue hole, gave us ten seconds to catch our breath, and then did it again and again as the following sea surfed us along the coast of Grand Cayman. Roger clearly loved every minute of the trip. He sat at the wheel and rode *Halcyon* like a cowboy on a bucking bronco, and I would not have been surprised had he taken off the Captain's hat, waved it in the air, and shouted, "Yippee!"

The three kids were crowded around the table in the cabin playing Monopoly! And if the motion of the boat was unusual, they hadn't noticed. They were more concerned about who was winning—Janice!

We had adjusted to the madcap existence, but I didn't feel we were jaded. The thrill was still there even more than in the beginning. The thrill of discovering a new country, meeting new people, wondering what adventure was coming. I put the last stitches in the Cayman courtesy flag and set it aside to raise with the yellow quarantine flag.

As we entered the Georgetown harbor, coral-heads loomed all around us just below the surface. Feeling certain we would soon be sitting on top of one of the monster corals, I threw the lead-line repeatedly, but never even touched the top of one. The water was so clear the depths of sixty and seventy feet seemed to rise right to our hull and those ominous-looking lumps of coral were over forty feet deep!

We were awestruck by the scenery of brain, antler, and staghorn corals, and angelfish fully eighteen inches across. Leopard rays, barracuda, and schools of clownfish swam around the sides of the boat and we were in the very heart of the harbor!

Clearing customs in Georgetown was as informal as in Little Cayman. No search, no restrictions on where we could go, just a pleasant smile and a welcome. With paperwork done, we rented a car and set out to discover what Grand Cayman was like, and everywhere we looked, everyone we met, and everything we experienced told us Cayman was far different than the Bahamas, the opposite of Haiti, and much less threatening than Jamaica.

The island was twenty miles long by seven miles wide. The population of Georgetown was ten thousand, the entire island was no more than eighteen thousand. Tropical flowers and trees grew from the sandy soil, and a beautiful stand of pine trees sheltered the southern side of the island. There were no mountains to protect the land from storms, and nothing to break up the trade winds. Grand Cayman was air conditioned by nature.

We heard it was called the "Little Switzerland" of the Western Hemisphere, and the name made sense. Georgetown boasted more than a hundred banks in the few square blocks of its downtown. Otherwise, the town was not particularly remarkable. The white clapboard houses along the waterfront were reminiscent of the fishing villages of New England, but the heart of downtown had its share of shopping centers and cinder-block buildings like any small community in the States. I was sorry to see that the supermarkets had replaced the open-air markets so prevalent on the other islands, and the food in the stores was covered with the familiar labels of Campbell's, Del Monte, and Heinz.

At first glance, Georgetown seemed American in design and Puritan in custom. There were more churches than bars, the only crime was petty, and there was no T.V., no bowling alley, no golf course, and only one movie house. There was also no pollution, no traffic jams, no stoplights, little poverty, almost no illiteracy, and no racial problems (everyone was related, no matter the color).

The island also had no taxes, property, inheritance, income, personal, or otherwise. Revenues came from a flat import fee and a bed tax on hotel rooms. Yet, the Government operated continuously in the black and the public school system, the police, and the socialized healthcare were available to everyone, and efficiently well run.

The politics were no more complicated than that of Small-town USA with a governing board elected by the people, and a figurehead Governor appointed by the UK. The only political upheaval we heard about was when a young upstart decided to promote the Socialist Party. When he installed a soap box in the town square, the populace yawned broadly, and went to the beach to get out of range of his noisy loudspeaker.

We covered the entire island, every single road, in one afternoon in our rental car. I took up backseat driving by often reminding Roger of the Caymanian admonition to "Keep the bush on de left." The Islanders drove on the wrong side of the road.

The people we met were as friendly as any we'd encountered on the other islands, and their sing song dialect of English, Jamaican, and American slang was easy to understand. We listened to the only radio station and learned it kept infrequent hours but played good music. We found the only pizza parlor five miles from town at the end of a dead-end road and as we munched away on a giant size with everything except "anchovies," we decided to give Grand Cayman a chance. It took a week to catch up on laundry, clean the boat, and do a few maintenance chores. One morning Roger decided he couldn't put it off any longer. It was time to begin the necessary steps of finding a job. After breakfast, he went out to buy a newspaper to look at the want ads.

When he returned to the boat, he tossed the paper into my lap and said, "Look at the picture on the front page. Doesn't that look familiar?"

Scanning the front page, I saw immediately what he was talking about. It was a picture of the very cove we'd anchored in not a week before. The caption under the picture read, "Marijuana found on the beach of Little Cayman." Reading further, I learned that the police had discovered a dozen large plastic garbage sacks behind some bushes on the beach, and it was believed they were put there during the full moon. "Roger," I gasped, "that's when we were there!"

"And if you read further," he answered, "you will find out the police arrived just hours after we left. I think we came very close to being caught in the middle of a smuggling operation."

I was worried. Maybe it was paranoia after our experiences in Jamaica, but I convinced Roger that we should tell someone. Within the hour we found the Customs office and confessed to a very confused-looking officer that we had anchored off that beach. He smiled with amusement when we explained that we hadn't unloaded the marijuana, weren't there to pick it up, and hadn't seen anyone else do it either. But he took the description of the trader we had seen and commented that it might have been there to pick up the bags. Our presence just may have scared them off. When he told us we weren't under suspicion and really didn't look like the smuggling type, I said, "If only the Jamaican Government had seen us that way, we might still be in Negril."

The man smiled. "I think you are lucky for two reasons. First of all, the smugglers did not see fit to 'deal with you,' and secondly, Cayman is a much better place to live than Jamaica."

The job offering in the want ads looked promising, Food and Beverage Manager of one of the largest hotels. Roger dug out his only suit and took it to the cleaners, then I gave him a haircut and trimmed his mustache and goatee. Before our eyes, our suntanned pirate was transformed into a debonair businessman.

The hotel was a mile away and he was gone for an hour before returning with a bottle of wine, and a smile. He had the job!

"Mr. Liston is the manager's name, and he would like to meet you," Roger said as we sipped our wine and talked excitedly about the new steps that were going to change our lives.

"Great, when?"

"He's coming down to the wharf tomorrow, and I told him we'd join him for coffee at that restaurant that overlooks the harbor."

The next morning Ron rowed us to shore and left us while he returned to the boat.

Earlier in the day, we had anchored *Halcyon* close to shore, and Ron had instructions to run the cruising flag up the mast if there were any problems. The harbor was small, there were a number of ships at the dock, and five or six sailboats were squeezed into the anchorage. We wanted to keep an eye out should anyone need room to get out.

Leaving the beach, we entered the small restaurant, climbed the stairs to the dining area, and found Mr. Liston waiting for us at a table next to the window. He was a red-headed Scotsman and he spoke with a *burr* as he greeted us.

Sitting down, we ordered coffee, and had chatted only a few minutes when Mr. Liston asked, "Are those your children?"

Glancing out the window, I saw Ron tying up the dinghy on the stern of *Halcyon*, Tommy sitting at the rail with his fishing rod, and Janice hanging up a dishtowel. It had been her day to do the breakfast dishes. I nodded.

"How have they handled living on a boat," Mr. Liston was interested.

"They are great!" Roger spoke with pride. "Ron is our thirteen-year-old and he's the best mate anyone could ask for. I would trust him to sail that boat all by himself."

"Really?" Mr. Liston seemed surprised.

"Well, only if he had to," Roger amended.

"That's him there," I said and pointed to where Ron was standing and talking to someone in a small boat that had pulled alongside *Halcyon*. Small letters on the side of the craft read. "Cayman Harbor Patrol."

"The two younger kids are helpful, too," Roger said. "They know most of the basics of sailing, and they follow orders well."

The patrol boat moved away as Tommy walked toward the bowsprit and picked up the anchor line. "That's our nine-year-old," I bragged. "He's checking the anchor to make sure it's secure."

Janice went to stand behind Tommy, and I hadn't noticed what she doing until Mr. Liston said, "I see your daughter is coiling that line?"

Roger's voice sounded puzzled as he asked, "Is the boat moving?"

I jumped out of my chair so fast it hit the floor with an explosive bang. "Tommy's not checking the anchor, HE'S PULLING IT!"

Leaping to his feet beside me, Roger shouted, "What in the hell are those crazy kids doing? People had turned to stare at us, but we were unaware of them. All we could see was Tommy raising the forty-pound anchor up onto the deck, and Ron at the wheel, deftly turning the boat out to sea.

"I think the young laddies have just run away," Mr. Liston spoke drolly.

Grabbing my arm, Roger led me out of the restaurant on a dead run! One fisherman sitting on the dock looked startled when Roger collared him, pointed at the departing *Halcyon*, and ordered, "Follow that boat!"

It took the little wooden skiff five minutes to catch up to *Halcyon*, and when Ron dropped the ladder over the side and we climbed on board, Roger was livid. "What is going on here?" he demanded.

Ron stammered, "The patrol boat ordered us to move. The man said we were blocking the ship tied at the dock. I tried to tell him you would be back as soon as I could raise the flag, but he said we had to move, right then! Besides, Dad, I knew what I was doing."

The kids were so obviously proud of themselves that Roger found it impossible to scold any further. We dropped the anchor at a safe distance from the ships, and I looked around to see the captains of all the other sailboats, standing on their decks and watching us, presumably in preparation to getting out of the way if necessary.

All was truly forgiven when one of the sailors rowed over in his dinghy to tell Roger, "You sure have some smart kids there."

Roger and I both had to agree.

It took two months to get a work permit. The island Government may have been uncomplicated, but it was also slow. However, the two months gave us time to explore the island, get to know the people and customs, do schoolwork, look for a house, and enjoy what we knew were our last Halcyonic days.

When Easter arrived, we entered the Easter Day Regatta and Fishing Derby. Roger was certain we'd win the race. After all, *Halcyon* was built for heavy weather sailing and the wind was blowing fiercely. And with all our experience, he was sure we were the best crew in the race. The moment we crossed the starting line Roger was madly barking orders and the kids were running back and forth wildly to complete one order before the next one fell on their heads. Sheets were tightened, then loosened, then tightened again.

Sails went up, sails came down; nobody furled, and it took mere seconds for every sail we owned to be piled in a heap on the deck.

Manning the helm, I tried hard to follow his demands—fall off, close the angle, read the compass, watch the wind direction, and naturally all at the same time. I was aghast at Roger's fervor and total disregard for our carefully learned safety precautions. He had gone crazy again; all he wanted to do was win.

"Watch where you're going!" he yelled.

"I *am* watching! Why don't you take the wheel and let me play Captain?"

He chose not to hear me. "I'm going to raise the Genny. Be ready to come about as soon as that big tree bears ninety degrees. You're losing speed! Fall off! You're not watching the wind direction!"

"Oh, go to blazes!"

During that regatta I discovered one absolute fact: racing was madness and bore no relationship whatsoever to cruising.

We crossed the finish line in forty minutes and took first in our class and third overall. Not too good considering there were only three boats in the race, and we were the only one in our class.

After two aspirins and a nap, my headache went away.

The fishing derby wasn't any better. Again, Roger felt confident. After all we had fished commercially in the Florida Keys. Inviting a friend (he had to show off), we went out looking for the perfect reef, found it, dropped anchor and then it rained nonstop until the derby ended. Our total catch was three bad colds.

To the very end, shouting at each other was an affliction we couldn't shake.

Obviously, boats are not the best places to cultivate lasting friendships, or to strengthen marriages. A great many of the cruisers we'd met, including ourselves, were testimony to the fact that if you don't have it when you start, you sure won't find it on a boat. We knew couples who had broken up, marriages that had collapsed, and lifetime friendships that had been reduced to drawn swords at thirty paces. There were even two women who separately stole their boats from their husbands, and were going home "Without the old farts!"

The startling facts about those women were that neither had been sailors when they started the cruise, and both had been happily married for ten years or more. How does it happen? Well, there is something unsettling about trusting one's life completely in the hands of someone else. Sometimes it's tougher, and even more unsettling when the hands belong to the "weaker' sex." There are endless conflicts that come from sharing decisions, to hell with who's captain; sharing the cooking, sharing the head, sleeping in shifts, and living for days at a level of discomfort that would surely have discouraged the pioneers.

Tensions grow when there is no private place to fight, or cry, or make love. Romances fade rapidly when lovers are daily confronted by the loved one's bad habits, black moods, or the "crazies".

It was with a smug feeling that I realized our marriage had made it and as a result was even stronger. But the shouting had to stop!

The radio told of the coming of a strong north wind, and in preparation, all the boats in the harbor sought safer anchorage on the south side of the island. We joined the rest and found the protected cove crowded with sailboats, fishing boats, and expensive powerboats, all anchored shoulder to shoulder as they waited for the storm to arrive. With the heavy-duty anchor in place, we went below to listen to the radio and wait for the norther and were battening down when the sound of angry voices, quite close to the boat, sent us scrambling back up on the deck.

An elegant power boat was just entering the cove and was equipped for deep sea fishing with a high "tuna tower" above the deck. The tower is a platform designed for spotting fish from a long distance, and the structure is built up over the deck with a separate set of controls for steering from either the platform or the deck.

A hefty, rather formidable woman was on the tower, and her anger was undeniable. Obscenities flowed at top volume as she raced from the wheel to the rail, and back to the wheel.

On the deck below was her adversary, a middle-aged man dressed in a rain jacket and wearing a straw hat. He was running a path opposite to hers: from the railing to the deck wheel, and back to the railing—and his trips were equally as vocal.

The boat jerked erratically into the cove, circled the other boats, backed up, shot forward, then turned in another circle. Clearly, they were both working the controls, but not at the same time, and not in agreement!

"I don't want to anchor in this goddamn cove!" she shouted over the edge of the tower. The boat jerked forward, kicking spray out behind it as it narrowly missed the anchor line of another boat.

"Shut your mouth, you stupid woman! You ain't got the sense you was born with!" the man shouted as he raised his head in her direction.

The boat turned and began to slow.

"You can't call me stupid! Only a jackass would anchor in the bloody little sound!" And as she spun the wheel, the boat whirled and barreled back toward the entrance to the cove.

Unfortunately, the man had been working his way toward the bow of the boat with a small grapple anchor in his hand, and the motion of the boat drove him to the deck. Abandoning the anchor, he picked himself up and raced for his set of controls. "You goldarn fool!" he bellowed. The boat slowed, backed up, and very nearly rammed a neighboring sailboat.

Roger and Janice set up the deck chairs, Ron brought up a jar of peanuts, and we settled in for the show. Looking around, I noticed all the other crews in the harbor were doing much the same. It was a wonderful performance. The obscenities flowed for a full twenty minutes, and our performers managed to narrowly miss every other boat in the cove before they finally inched their way back in the direction they had come. We were sorry to see the woman win the battle. It could have turned into a riotous two days if they had stayed.

Last we saw of the boat it was making funny little circles and squiggly zigzag lines as it danced around the bend and out of sight. On that very day, Roger and I made a promise. We would never shout at each other again—on the deck of a boat, in a crowded harbor.

The highest point on Grand Cayman is Mount Pleasant, twenty-two feet above sea level. It was there that we rented a house. There were three bedrooms and luxuries beyond belief: a modern kitchen, hot and cold running water, ice cubes, a refrigerator, electricity, a garden with fruit trees growing right outside the window, and carpet on the floor.

Roger's work permit arrived on the morning of our fifteenth wedding anniversary, and that afternoon we moved ashore.

Halcyon went into the boatyard soon afterward. Her hull was sandblasted and repainted, all the woodwork was varnished, and enough minor repairs were tackled to keep us working every evening for two months. When we were through, she looked beautiful, and we were broke. But that was the way it went with *Halcyon*; she was never happy until she had our last penny.

I didn't protest when, in October, we sold her.

CHAPTER 19: EVERY BOAT HAS AN EPILOGUE

The little green house on Grand Cayman Island was our home for over a year, and initially it was as exciting and as novel as moving onto the boat had been. Undoubtedly, we were ready for the change. The last few months on the boat had seen a total reversal in Roger's attitude toward motors, grease, maintenance chores, and even *Halcyon* herself, and he was willing to give it all up with no regrets.

In the first few weeks he left for work each morning at 8 a.m. sharp, driven to promptness by the flush of fresh money. It wasn't long before he learned how rapidly the money could be spent on clothes, rent, school supplies, food, a car, and eventually an alarm clock.

Though I regretted leaving the sea, I was more than eager to relegate the experiences of poverty, celibacy, and communal living to the past and had high hopes of never having to deal with them again.

There were so many things to rediscover, and I looked at them all with the eyes of a Rip Van Winkle who had been asleep for a hundred years. I marveled at the stove, the refrigerator, fresh hot water, the bathtub, enough room to walk around in, and the most wonderful of all: a bed with no sand. I was even amused when I found myself stacking dishes precariously in the cupboards with the realization that the shelves were not going to tilt and dump everything onto the floor. There was pleasure in being able to do the laundry in less than one day and not have to involve the entire family in the process. And the clothes dried just as quickly on horizontal lines as they had in the vertical rigging.

The kids relished the freedom the island afforded. They could escape from their parents' watchful eyes and they did so regularly. Over the long summer months, they hiked the many trails to the beaches, discovered the library, met all the neighbors for miles around, and learned the whereabouts of every wild fruit tree on Mount Pleasant.

But once the novelty of walking on land wore off, we each found ourselves to be somehow different—and it wasn't always in ways we had planned.

Halcyon lingered on in our lives for months as we spent the evenings, holidays, and days off dashing to the boatyard to work on varnishing her insides, painting her outsides, and scrubbing her top and bottom. When the nice young American couple bought her to use for chartering around the island, both Roger and I were relieved that the expenses and the work were finally over.

Sailing Against the Wind – Toni Larson

Captain Larson took on the role of the expert sailor as he showed the new owners, Gary and Jane, all of *Halcyon*'s talents and quirks. He would set aside every possible free moment to take the starry-eyed beginners out for short excursions. I went along for the ride, but only once. After spending a day with the hyper-exuberant couple, I turned down further trips.

"Why won't you come, Toni? It's a beautiful day for a sail," Roger coaxed me as he dressed for a day out around the island with the amateur sailors.

I put him off by saying, "Not now, I've got too much to do." I wasn't sure why I was reluctant. Perhaps it was Jane's incessant bragging about her latest purchases; new bedspreads, new porthole covers, matching new bath towels. When she had crowed, "The boat looks so much more charming when everything is color coordinated," I smiled weakly and thought of a carpet I once wanted so badly... it all seemed so long ago and so unimportant now.

After Roger left, I got busy making curtains for our little island house, then planted tomatoes in the garden, but couldn't seem to shake the vaguely depressed feeling.

Ron's first major accomplishment was to build a treehouse and nail a sign to the tree trunk that read, "NO GIRLS ALOUD!" His spelling hadn't improved while cruising. After enrolling in school though, he went right to the top of his class and stayed there. Never again did a teacher mention "learning problems."

Ron's eagerness to take advantage of all he had learned at sea was apparent when he quickly signed up for a SCUBA class and following that, he volunteered as crew on a sailboat. He spent a week on board the boat and by all reports, he expertly performed his duties. It was not easy for me to accept that Ron had become a fully adult young man in complete control of his own future.

Tommy continued to be Tommy and it took no time at all for him to become the talk of the island. It all began with Guineps.

Guineps are a small fruit that grows in clusters at the very top of Guinep trees. The fruit is the size of walnuts, has an inordinately large stone in the center, and a tart citrus flavor. The best way to get the flesh off the stone is to tuck the peeled fruit into one cheek and suck. Tommy wouldn't suck on just one, he had to fill both cheeks until they were puffed out like squirrel pouches.

Besides the wild Guinep trees, Cayman is blessed with a prolific plant known as "maiden plum." However, the name makes no sense at all. Maiden plum is neither a plum nor is it maiden. It is a poisonous vine akin to poison ivy, and when touched it leaves a fire-red rash on the skin and itches like fire. Maiden plum can be found growing everywhere, but mostly in the shade of Guinep trees. Naturally, Tommy found the vine.

To complete the scenario, Tommy's front teeth, that had grown in while cruising, were designed for someone twice his age and size, and he was doubly blessed with a mass of freckles that glowed continuously brighter in direct relation to the amount of time he spent in the sun scouting Guineps.

With Guineps in each cheek, maiden plum rash topped with freckles, a shock of sun-white hair, and two enormous front teeth that looked like prizes from a Cracker Jacks box, he had a face that everyone remembered.

It seemed to me that, with a face like that, he would have tried to keep a low profile. But not Tommy, and his fame came very close to notoriety on one occasion. It was during one of his forays in search of the wild Guineps that he came upon a pumpkin patch. While I was off visiting with a neighbor, Tommy carted the strange new fruit home one by one until there were six large pumpkins and one very irate farmer waiting for me at the back door.

A small crowd of curious Islanders gathered around as the farmer loudly informed me that he had grown those pumpkins to enter in the island fair, it had taken him years to cultivate that particular strain, and our son had ruined his chances of winning.

It took $32 ($1 per pound), and a promise to save him all the seeds before the angry man would agree not to call the police. Tommy got a lecture, then I spent the rest of the week learning how to make pumpkin bread, pumpkin cake, pumpkin soup, and pumpkin pickles. It was no surprise when Tommy became as well known, and as well recognized, on Grand Cayman as he had been in Haiti.

With hopes that Mount Pleasant would eventually live up to its name, I hung a hammock on the front porch and promised myself a routine that would daily include the hammock and a good book. But once the telephone was installed, I noticed a timing that bordered on the supernatural. I would climb into the hammock, count to ten, then get up and answer the phone. Within a week, I forgot the hammock was even there.

Janice also had great expectations for her new life. She started right in by getting a hairstyle that made her look like a girl and she remembered to wear her bathing suit top whether she needed it or not. Her most longed-for luxury was finally realized: a room of her own. She filled her room with doll houses made from cardboard boxes, then populated them with all the dolls she'd collected from the island markets. How rich could a little girl be? But somehow it was lonely in that room by herself. Especially when she could hear her brothers whisper secrets in the room next door, secrets she was no longer privy to. Somehow the new hairdo, the new girlish figure, and all the dolls and dollhouses did not help the feelings inside.

Of the three children, Janice had always been the most gregarious, the one to make friends before any of the rest of us even said more than "hello." For that reason alone, we were surprised to find that she was going to be our "special child." The one we'd been warned about by our friend back in Santa Barbara. The one who would be a "little different" from her peers.

Her year of school on the island went fairly well, but daily we saw signs of a new moodiness. And the moodiness grew when we returned to the States. Her new friends could not understand the thrill of catching a yellowtail on a handline, the accomplishment of learning to swim in the ocean instead of a pool, the excitement of riding a Tap-Tap, or the wonder of finding a freshly laid egg. Her new friendships were not as unconditional as those on Farmer's Cay, or as ageless as those with Sandy and Homer or Madeline.

When her new acquaintances talked about TV shows and rock bands, she remembered dancing with Dad in Bimini, catching a dolphin in the Exumas, sharing kittens with the Bionic Man. Why were clothes and makeup suddenly important when they had meant nothing at all before? Class distinctions, ethnic backgrounds, and the labels on the pockets of jeans were the yardsticks her classmates used to measure worth. How could she explain to them about her friendship with a barefoot, brown-skinned, little girl on Staniel Cay? For twelve-year-old Janice, the transition from sea to land was painful indeed.

"Come and see it, Toni. It's so pretty." Jane was on the other end of the phone.

"I can't today. I'm canning mango chutney. Maybe another time." I had not seen the boat in over a month, but I knew I couldn't keep putting her off.

"The wallpaper is beautiful," she gushed. "It really brightens up the boat after all that dark wood."

Wallpaper over all that mahogany! I felt ill. "I bet it does," I hedged. "Just remember to keep the portholes closed while you're sailing, or you are going to have some pretty wet and peeling wallpaper."

"I hadn't thought of that. Thanks, Toni." And after another flurry of remarks about tea towels and matching dishes, she hung up.

We had roast pork and mango chutney for dinner that night, and I noticed I'd gained five pounds. It was annoying to think I was going to have to start dieting again.

Christmas was traditional with a decorated tree and lots of presents and turkey. Friends and relatives visited, and life became a bustle of entertaining and sightseeing.

One night in January we were sitting in a restaurant with some old friends from California when the wife leaned toward the window and exclaimed, "Look at that gorgeous view!"

Turning, I saw the moon, shining full and silver on the calm waters of the harbor and it jolted me. It was as though I hadn't seen it in years. Had there really been a time when I could tell a full moon without looking at a calendar, when I could just feel it? What had happened to my "natural clock?"

It was a surprise to hear Tommy whine, "I sure would like to go sailing."

Roger and I exchanged glances and winks as we remembered the seasick little boy of times past. We agreed to let him stop at the beach each afternoon on his way home from school and soon he was a fixture around the rental shops. On the weekends he coaxed neighbors, or his dad into rides to the beach and once there he helped, or made a nuisance of himself, until one of the shopkeepers began to let him use a small day-sailer for an hour or two—without our knowledge.

I didn't know how serious Tommy was about the sport or how risky it had become until Easter rolled around. It was the annual regatta, and he had begged for days to go and watch. I relented.

He left for the beach immediately after breakfast and arrived back home at sundown, tired and sunburned to the point of being sick. I was furious. After scolding him soundly for not staying in the shade and protecting his face, I lathered him in creams and sent him to bed with the threat, "There will be no more trips to the beach until your skin has healed!"

The phone woke us the next morning. Roger answered it, and when he hung up, he was laughing. "Know what Tommy did yesterday?"

"I presume he watched the races," I answered sleepily.

"That was Edgar from the Race Committee. He called to tell us Tommy would be getting his name in the paper for taking second place in the regatta."

I sat up in bed with a start. "But he's not old enough. Where did he get the entrance fee? My God! Do you realize how far out those boats travel? He could have been caught by the trade winds and blown all the way to Honduras?"

"Come on, Toni. He's a better sailor than that."

Thinking about it, I calmed down a bit. "You're right, I suppose. He must be pretty good if he took second place."

Over breakfast we quizzed Tommy until we found out that he'd conned a tourist out of the money to enter the race with the promise to pay it back out of his allowance, conned the officials into forgetting his age, and had taken second place by less than a boat length.

Roger was as proud as a peacock, but I thought things were way out of hand. "Tommy, you had no business doing something like that without letting us know."

"But, Mom," he argued, "you wouldn't have let me go, and I really wanted to race. I'd have won too, if the wind had been a little stronger."

Sailing Against the Wind – Toni Larson   343

He was right. I wouldn't have allowed it. That ocean was too big, and too tricky.

"Well, your name is going to be in the paper," Roger told him.

Tommy wasn't impressed. "I'd rather have the trophy," he declared, "but next time I'll win."

Roger was still chuckling when he left for work that morning, and no wonder—he had discovered he had another "chip off the old block."

It was a balmy tropical morning when Jane called to tell me Gary was thinking of changing *Halcyon*'s name. "You can't do that!" I gasped.

"Why not?" she asked. "The *Cayman Belle* seems like a good name for the boat."

"But it's very bad luck," I insisted." You never change a boat's name once it's been christened!"

She agreed to talk to Gary about it and finished the conversation by telling me *Halcyon* was going in the boatyard again for another bottom painting. When I asked why, so soon after the last one, she sounded impatient with me. "Because we want to change the color, Toni. Surely it isn't bad luck to change the color."

I told her I didn't think so but felt great relief when the conversation ended.

I learned to cook breadfruit, planted another garden (the first one fizzled), and began packing our dinner every evening for picnics on the beach. Occasionally Roger could get away to join the kids and me, and it was on one such picnic that I caught him lost in thought while staring out at a boat on the horizon. I could sense his yearning and as I studied his face, I noticed that his tan had faded, and the sun lines at the corners of his eyes had been replaced by frown lines in his forehead. "A penny for your thoughts?" I asked.

He looked at me as though he hadn't heard, then he shook himself and growled, "Let's get home. The mosquitoes will be out in another few minutes."

It was a breezy April day when Roger called me from work. "Toni, how about coming to the hotel for lunch?"

Sure," I said. "But what's the occasion?"

"Nothing special. I thought we might eat out on the terrace and watch Gary and Jane bring *Halcyon* around to the beach. She's coming out of the boatyard today and she'll be anchored here. Wouldn't you like to see her?"

There was no easy excuse, so I dressed then drove to the hotel. I found Roger waiting for me in front of the palm shaded entrance. His eyes looked darker than usual as he said, "Let's walk down to the water before we eat; the boat is already anchored."

Strolling past the hotel and down to the beach, we plunked into the sand at the edge of the seawall and looked out at *Halcyon*. Though the water was calm and only a bare breeze disturbed the air, *Halcyon* moved restlessly against the anchor line like a wild animal held on a short tether.

"I don't like it," I moaned as the first shock of the new electric baby blue color struck me. She looked so gaudy, no longer a pirate's ship, but now simply a toy, not something to be taken seriously. "Do you think she likes the color?" I wondered out loud.

Roger's voice held a slight sneer as he said, "That was exactly my first thought. No, I don't think she does, and I bet she won't sail as well either. She's temperamental when she's unhappy."

It didn't surprise me anymore to hear Roger talk about her as though she were human. "You are right. There were so many difficult times, but she always came through for us. She taught us so much." My voice broke and my eyes were suddenly swimming with tears. "Oh, Roger, I'm almost sorry we ever did it—sail, that is. I feel like we've learned something so special, and now, on land, we can't seem to hold on to it. Do you know what I mean?"

"I think I do," he said softly, and reached out for me.

It was perfectly clear. I was feeling the loss over a way of life that I'd never truly appreciated when I'd had it. And mainly, I was crying over an old steel boat whose name really did mean "peaceful."

THE END

Dear Reader,

Thank you so much for reading this book. I do hope you enjoyed it. It would be truly appreciated if you chose to leave a review at the Amazon.com website for future readers.

And if you should wish to comment further, the author's email address is: larson_toni@hotmail.com.

Made in the USA
Las Vegas, NV
06 October 2023

78243263R00195